Sex Workers in the Maritimes Talk Back

Leslie Ann Jeffrey and Gayle MacDonald

Sex Workers in the Maritimes
Talk Back

UBCPress · Vancouver · Toronto

© UBC Press 2006

All rights reserved. No part of this publication may be reproduced, stored in a retrieval system, or transmitted, in any form or by any means, without prior written permission of the publisher, or, in Canada, in the case of photocopying or other reprographic copying, a licence from Access Copyright (Canadian Copyright Licensing Agency), www.accesscopyright.ca.

15 14 13 12 11 10 09 08 07 06   5 4 3 2 1

Printed in Canada on ancient-forest-free paper (100% post-consumer recycled) that is processed chlorine- and acid-free, with vegetable-based inks.

Library and Archives Canada Cataloguing in Publication

Jeffrey, Leslie Ann, 1967-
  Sex workers in the Maritimes talk back / Leslie Ann Jeffrey and Gayle MacDonald.

Includes bibliographical references and index.
ISBN-13: 978-0-7748-1331-0 (bound); 978-0-7748-1332-7 (pbk.)

  1. Prostitutes – New Brunswick. 2. Prostitutes – Nova Scotia. I. MacDonald, Gayle Michelle, 1957- II. Title.

HQ149.M37J43 2006   305.9'3067409715   C2006-904281-0

Canadä

UBC Press gratefully acknowledges the financial support for our publishing program of the Government of Canada through the Book Publishing Industry Development Program (BPIDP), and of the Canada Council for the Arts, and the British Columbia Arts Council.

This book has been published with the help of a grant from the Canadian Federation for the Humanities and Social Sciences, through the Aid to Scholarly Publications Programme, using funds provided by the Social Sciences and Humanities Research Council of Canada.

UBC Press
The University of British Columbia
2029 West Mall
Vancouver, BC V6T 1Z2
604-822-5959 / Fax: 604-822-6083
www.ubcpress.ca

*To Kim Grant, who wanted her name in this book,
and to all sex workers in the Maritimes who "talked back."
Thank you for sharing your stories.
Your words are not in vain.*

*And to Malcolm (Mackie) MacDonald (1932-2002),
who gave most of his life to social justice causes
and community work, and who supported this work
despite his conservative politics, rest in peace.*

Contents

Preface / ix

Acknowledgments / xi

Introduction / 1

1 It's the Money, Honey / 18

2 The Good, the Bad, and the Ugly / 62

3 Social Control, Policing, and Sex Work / 105

4 The Whore Stigma and the Media / 137

5 Whose Health? Whose Safety? / 174

6 Sex and Politics: Responding to Sex Workers / 203

Notes / 238

Bibliography / 256

Index / 265

Preface

This book began as a conversation in 1999. Or rather, the research that led to this book began as a conversation. This conversation took place after a lecture by Leslie Jeffrey to a class that Gayle MacDonald was teaching. Gayle was then an associate professor, Leslie a doctoral fellow at the same university. Leslie had spoken on sex work in Thailand, the topic of her dissertation and eventual book.[1] She was interested, however, in bringing the research home, and Gayle was interested in bringing together some of her work on socio-legal and sexuality issues. Very little research had been done on sex work in the Maritime provinces and the voices of sex workers from that region had rarely been heard in the Canadian literature. The conversation became a promise, a commitment to meet on the topic, which eventually led to a small Social Science and Humanities Research Council (SSHRC) Aid to Small Universities grant, which led to a pilot study and many, many talks with colleagues from academia and the community and, finally, to a Standard Research Grant entitled "Perceptions and Attitudes towards Prostitutes in the Maritimes," in April 2001. The study took three long years to complete, and writing the manuscript took another.

But this is the story of what has led to the writing of this book. The true story is what we found out in talking to sex workers and, indeed, what the reader will find in these pages: a story of the spirit, courage, tenacity, despair, and silencing of a group of women and men who make their living mostly in the sex trade in the Maritimes. These women and men, whom we feel privileged to have met and interviewed, have a critical analysis of society, life, and work that deserves to be heard. They resist the same economic marginalization and movements as do many other workers in the Maritimes, fight back against violence, and laugh at the hypocrisy they see around them. They are the true storytellers, the backbone of this book. As grateful as we are to all community groups, leaders, police, and health workers who talked to us during the research for this book, in the end, it is the sex worker her/himself who stands out. She or he speaks to us in a clear voice, "talking back" to all who would relegate her/him to the margins of the social world. It is to each and every sex worker in Fredericton, Saint John, Moncton, and Halifax that we dedicate this work.

Acknowledgments

The two or so names printed on the cover of a book do not reveal the many hands that were involved in that piece of writing. We'd like to name, acknowledge their contribution, and sincerely thank them here for their contributions: to the many research assistants who aided in both the research and the preparation for this book – Jason Doherty, Katie Daley, Erinor Jacobs, Meagan Cameron, Luanne Efford, Julie Leggett, Mike Fleming, and, most especially, Mary-Ellen Green – a heartfelt thanks for all of the meetings, emails, correspondence, and contact with community groups. A thank you, as well, to research assistant Patti Wheatley for assisting with editing in the final stages of the manuscript, and for finding all of the "last-minute" errors. To Anita Saunders and Anna Moran, secretaries extraordinaire, for all of the support and for aiding with the final editing of the manuscript, a sincere thanks. To Ann Macklem, UBC Press production editor, Judy Phillips, the meticulous copy editor, and, especially, the patient and determined senior editor at UBC Press, Emily Andrew: thank you. We'd also like to thank the many anonymous reviewers for their many suggestions and edits. Thanks also to Dr. JoAnn Majerovich for reading the health chapter in its infancy.

We'd also particularly like to thank the organizations and their staffs that hosted the interview process and were invaluable in carrying out the research for this book: Stepping Stone (Halifax), AIDS Nova Scotia, Coverdale (Saint John), and the Moncton Sexual Health Centre. And again, a thank you to all the people who took the time to be interviewed for this project.

We are indebted to the Research and Financial Offices of St. Thomas University, Fredericton, and the University of New Brunswick at Saint John for their support and management of this project.

We would like to acknowledge the contribution and support of the Social Sciences and Humanities Research Council of Canada (grant #410-2001-0330).

On a more personal level, Gayle MacDonald would like to acknowledge the support of some dear friends and colleagues, including Jeannette Gaudet,

Lori Beaman, and Rebecca Johnson, for their words of encouragement when the project looked too daunting. And to Jonathan Rahn, for great meals, for shared parenting of our children, and for supporting the work through some difficult years of illness, death, and separation, my gratitude. To Eris and Breagh MacDonald-Rahn, for celebrating the work when Mom needed it most, thanks, chickens. To Jo Lang, for bringing her lightness of being, her love of life and order, into the chaos that is the life of an academic, thanks will never be enough.

Leslie would like to thank Greg Cook for his continuing support (and many hours of editing and feedback).

Sex Workers in the Maritimes Talk Back

Introduction

> I mean, yourself, you're a professor. I got grade eight education. And you know what? I don't care. I'm happy, you're happy. It's not what you learn in school. My fiancé, I'm telling ya, he's got so much up here, and my sister, brains? But for someone so smart, they're so fucking stupid. When it comes to street smart and stuff, I'm like, holy God! (Dana, Halifax)

The object of this book is to feature sex workers in a marginalized region talking back to the powers that shape their lives and the world around them.[1] In particular, it focuses on sex workers' analysis of, and resistance to, common interpretations of their lives. Sex workers as subjects of study serve as the objects of a great deal of professional interpretation – by academics, policy makers, police, health professionals, and the media. Sex workers and sex work are the putative basis of some feminist theories, psychological frameworks, and criminological discourses, yet their own analyses of their lives are often missing. It is frequently assumed that sex workers cannot be knowers in the sense of being able to present a critical analysis of their lives. It is this silencing of their critical consciousness that lies at the base of their greatest oppression. This silencing has denied sex workers full citizenship and full humanity. In this book, we hope to at least begin to acknowledge and reveal sex workers, not only as agents but as critical analysts, who comment on their lives while laying bare the structures of power that affect all of us.

The book is based on research formulated from interviews with sixty sex workers (forty-eight women, ten men, two transgendered persons) ranging in age from eighteen to fifty-two years (the mean was thirty-two years) in three cities in the Canadian Maritime provinces of New Brunswick and Nova Scotia.[2] In a series of half-hour to hour-long interviews, we asked these workers about their issues, what was good and bad about the job, what their concerns were, and what they would like to say to society at large. We used their responses to structure the issue areas that would be addressed in each chapter, and as such, each chapter represents, in descending order, the most salient concerns of the sex workers. We draw on their analyses of the issue at hand and sometimes contrast their understandings with the dominant voices of society, such as journalists, police, health workers and policy makers, whom we also interviewed. Thus, we have tried to frame the issue in what we understood to be sex workers' perspectives, while providing an analysis of these dominant frameworks.

This privileging of the sex worker "voice" is not completely unique. While there has been some acceptance of sex workers as agents and as speakers, this acceptance is generally limited to a few sex workers who are pictured as more high class and more liberated; that is, those who are not constrained by poverty or otherwise marginalized. Alternatively, the voices of the most exploited sex workers are occasionally used to illustrate the evils of the trade, but not to present a fuller picture. As a relatively poor and marginalized part of Canada, the Maritimes – like other economically marginalized regions of the world – may be expected to house some of the more oppressive conditions of sex work – poverty, unemployment, addictions, as well as a conservative and judgmental culture. On the basis of this stereotypical picture of the Maritimes, sex workers here should be among the most oppressed and least liberated of those working in the trade.[3] Indeed, many assume that sex workers here should be seen on a different level from sex workers in the major centres of Toronto or Montreal, for instance, where they are considered to be more likely to have chosen their profession. The intimation of this particular reading of sex workers in the Maritimes is that they are unable to speak for themselves – or more appropriately, to understand for themselves – as other sex workers may be able to do. Someone else, a journalist, a policy maker, or police – it is assumed – must interpret for them the meaning of their lives. On the rare occasion that sex workers in the Maritimes are quoted or invited to speak, therefore, the most frequent focus is on the most negative aspects of their lives, as exemplars of the supposed reality of sex work in the region. That is, the framework is already determined by those asking the questions. However, this denies those who are more constrained by circumstance the ability to interpret their own lives. Such an approach also implies that "the rest of us" are both liberated and somehow more knowledgeable. Granted, many of the sex workers we interviewed were mostly working on the street (although this is a flexible concept); some had addictions and most struggled with the options of low-waged work or unemployment. Despite these potential difficulties in their lives and work, the men and women we spoke with were undoubtedly agents – in the sense that they were making choices and reflecting on those choices in a clear-eyed manner. They had much to tell us about the way the world works.

Knowledge about sex workers, particularly those who are marginalized by region, race, or economic circumstance, is often produced by so-called straight society, which seeks to reinforce its position of authority as both knower and (therefore) decision maker. We as authors of this book are not immune to this charge.[4] We are both academics, from outside the trade, who are trained to produce supposedly authoritative interpretations. As such, we have been trained to talk about sex work in theoretical terms and to think methodologically about how we ask questions, of whom, and how to interpret the answers we receive. It is just as difficult for us to step back and listen to sex workers as it is for any other professional hearing their words. We have no doubt influenced the framing of information in ways that make sense to us. Certainly, the questions that we asked determined the answers that we received. Our purpose was neither to find out why people became involved in the sex trade nor to determine an overall demographic picture. Rather, we asked questions designed to evoke a sex worker's own prioritization, and understanding, of issues. In particular, we wanted them to tell us what they thought about the society around them. To counterbalance our interpretation as much as possible, we have included some rather large portions of interviews so that readers may make their own interpretations, and so that the sex worker speaking can be more clearly heard in her/his own voice. And we have tried to include those voices that challenge or contradict our own line of reasoning. Overall, the selections of interviews that we present here try to show sex workers analyzing and evaluating: thinking through options and meanings and talking back – or resisting common interpretations and stereotypes. And, as much as possible, we try to follow their analyses. Of course, only books written by a wide variety of sex workers can fully accomplish this task, and we hope more of these books will be written.[5] In the end, we hope that, through this presentation of sex workers' voices, we at least open up the possibility of following Chandra Mohanty's charge: "It is time to move beyond the Marx who found it possible to say: they cannot represent themselves; they must be represented."[6] The resistance by sex workers that we document is a resistance to the dominant voices that represent them.

The methods in literature that correspond most closely to what we attempt to do here are Michel Foucault's understandings of knowledge and power, as well as critical qualitative analysis.[7] We hesitate to describe this work as ethnography, despite the ethnographic nature of sex workers' descriptions of their lives, as ethnography often includes a greater sense of physical space and context than we allow in this writing. Community action research techniques,[8] post-colonial theory,[9] and critical geography[10] have all informed this work. Last, but not least, we owe a debt to feminist analysis[11] in the reading of sex workers' lives, as most interviewees were women (although we did interview men and transgendered persons) living in less than ideal social circumstances – although we say this with caution. Not all feminists have always understood, empathized, or supported sex workers and sex work. As one of our interviewees eloquently put it:

> There are a lot of middle-class women that knows, when their husbands ain't home, where they're at. They're not at work, right? But they're not the ones that judge ya. But then there are women, if you ever talk to one face to face, she gonna have nothing bad to say about ya, right? Because she knows. But when they all get together, that's when it all comes out. Like a bullying thing. (Denise, Halifax)

Indeed, there are many divisions among feminist thinkers, all of whom would claim to have sex workers' best interests at the centre of their analyses. We document some of these theoretical struggles in later sections of this chapter. These struggles are premised on different understandings of sex work and, more specifically, on different understandings of who a sex worker is. We begin with this question in the next section.

Sex Worker, Prostitute, Whore?

Throughout this book, we use the term "sex worker" to refer to people who work in the sex trade or in commercial sex. We include in this skin work (strip or exotic dance) as well as erotic massage, escort, and street-based sex work. We have grouped the skin trade in with sex work (despite the differences and divisions between these types of work) mostly because we wanted to capture the broadest possible group of interviewees, and a few exotic dancers and strip workers did share their stories with us. For simplicity's sake, we have referred throughout this book to "sex work" as including exotic dance and strip.

Overall, we have chosen to use the term "sex work" rather than "prostitution" because we recognize what many of the women and men who spoke with us recognize: that this activity is, indeed, work. It is a way of making a living, sometimes a very good living, no matter how people judge it. The useful term "survival sex work" has been introduced by the sex-worker-run Prostitution Alternatives Counselling and Education (PACE) Society to distinguish those for whom there is less control over working conditions because, for example, of heavy addictions.[12] The term acknowledges that sex work is still work and that workers would all benefit from better conditions, but emphasizes that, for some, the job is more problematic than it is for others. Not all of our interviewees used the term "sex work"; in particular, those outside the larger centre of Halifax, where sex workers have their own outreach centre, did not use this term. In other cities, such as Saint John, terms such as "street girls" were still in use among the workers. But when researchers used the term "sex worker," there was a positive reception. As one young woman said, "'Sex worker': I like that."[13] However, we also want to make it clear that the men and women we spoke with are not only and not always sex workers. As another woman in the trade pointed out: "It's a job, not a person." More than almost any other group, sex workers seem to be understood only in that role. This is a gross simplification of their lives into one activity or one aspect of their lives. We use the term "sex worker" to refer to our interviewees who work or have worked in the trade, but we caution readers that this is merely shorthand. We sometimes use the terms "person who works in the trade" and "worker" and "wo/men" to remind readers of this.[14]

Above all, the usual terminology used to refer to sex work – for example, "prostitution" – is laden with meanings and overtones that reflect dominant society's agendas rather than any reality experienced by sex workers. Here, we need to distinguish between the concept of "the Prostitute" and the actual "prostitute." As Wendy Chapkis has made so plain in her work, "the Prostitute" is a social construction that reflects the meanings and understandings imposed by outside agents. "There is," she argues, "no such thing as 'the Prostitute'" – only the meanings attached to her/him by others.[15] The "reality" of sex work is flexible rather than fixed, and it depends on the meaning attached to it by those who experience it. Thus, one's experience of sex work can vary according to age, social location, gender, and even personality or mood. The term "prostitute," as used by others, however, carries with it an imposed meaning and an assumed knowledge about that lived reality. The concept of knowledge that the term "prostitute" is assumed to carry is precisely what we seek to challenge here. That is, the knowledge implicit in the term is an external reference. This means that the concept of understanding associated with "prostitute" comes not from the sex worker her/himself. It is an externalized, generalized understanding or social construction. We see this social construction in a series of portraits of sex workers emanating from a number of sources, including: the media, the police, neighbourhood associations, and health care workers. The sex workers we spoke with, though, show us other portraits of the sex worker: as sister, mother, wife, friend, and ally in time of need; and as people with great insight, humour, courage, and stamina.

In this study, as in any on sex workers, it is important to uncover what the dominant or prevalent concepts are that are used to describe sex work. Those are the concepts that people assume they know and understand implicitly – the concepts used most frequently in common language and in the media. Common perceptions are that the sex worker is a deviant who sells her/his body, who has no morals, who is a victim of abuse, who is probably poor, and who is most likely drug addicted. Even the most sympathetic portraits of sex workers portray them as victims. As a mode of explanation, this works quite well for most people, because it is only by understanding the sex worker as a victim that any "thinking, respectable" middle-class person believes s/he can make sense out of sex work. Another portrait of the sex worker depicts her as an agent in her own miserable demise, her pitiful life a result of poor choices, a legitimate target for abuse, ridicule, derision, and apathy. After all, the story goes, she made these bad choices, and now she has to live with them. An even more common theme is that she willingly participates in a risky life with drastic and violent consequences.

These strikingly different assumptions about the "prostitute" lie uncomfortably together. How can they be true? Is she at once a victim of exploitation and a person with very bad judgment? Is she a morally derisive character or an addict to be pitied? Is she to be rescued or further accused? Saved or left to reap the consequences of her behaviour? Is this lifestyle a choice or a habit?

It is important to recognize that these understandings are based less on knowledge than on presuppositions about proper sexual behaviour. These presuppositions are part of the gender structure that disciplines female behaviour in particular. The madonna/whore structure divides women into those who deserve respect and those who do not on the basis of their sexual behaviour. Men are not similarly judged (unless they engage in homosexual behaviour, in which case they lose their status as well). Those who recognize the unfairness of this double moral standard but do not wish to give up their madonna status tend to view the sex worker as a victim. Those who uphold the divide as correct see the sex worker as a whore and an agent in her own demise. This approach denies any responsibility on the part of the public. And it does not involve accountability on the part of the political process. It holds the "prostitute" in a particular kind of cocoon or vacuum, as if s/he is isolated in the social atmosphere, without clients, without interaction with others, and without identity beyond the label.

Perhaps even more important to the discussion is not the correctness of these portraits but an examination of the power these stereotypes hold.[16] Because these images of the sex worker are repeatedly reinforced to the public, for example, through the media, it is difficult to counter them with other portraits. As either a hyperbolized victim or an exaggerated provocateur, the Prostitute serves as an othered category, a deviantized symbol of all that is wrong, distasteful, or repugnant to the social world about human sexuality. S/he serves, as Chapkis outlines, as a symbolic mirror of what society generally knows about itself, but of which it really does not want to be reminded. As such a mirror, the Prostitute reflects all that is contradictory, counterintuitive, and rule-defying about our lived sexualities. The existence of prostitution services demands explanation – it forces us to realize that we would rather think we are served well enough through marriages, relationships, and love. Our overly romantic and sentimentalized view of love, always laced with its erotic, darker opposite, sexuality, prevents us from seeing that neither view (the romantic or the erotic) completely meets all sexual needs. The sex worker is a reminder of that irony. S/he stands as a testament to all that has gone wrong, according to the moral right. She is the whore that all women will become if they fail to be madonnas. S/he is godless, unattached, and available to all. S/he marks her days in the servicing of others and she is little more than a slave, by most accounts. Even when she is constructed alternatively, not as slave but as agent, she stands in the same spot: vilified for daring to do what social structure has failed to do, by servicing the social and sexual demands of a significant portion of men who are willing to pay for the service. For this, she stands as moral outrage, a damned spot to be cleansed from the public psyche, a non-woman who is, at the same time, Everywoman. She is unmarriageable, incapable of mothering, and not the least bit responsible for her actions.

At least that is what these portraits would like us to believe. However, it is important to remember what these images do *not* do. They do not present the sex worker as an agent *within* social structures. That is, they both see agency in black and white terms: either one has it or one does not. One is either completely free or completely exploited. Both deny any resistance on the part of the sex worker to the powerful structures that shape all our lives. The sex workers speaking in this book reject such a simplified view. They recognize the constraints, barriers, and power structures of society and they fight against them. Thus, in this work, we examine the nature and definition of these portraits in order to cast them in a different light, an illumination that comes from the very words of the wo/men themselves. Sex workers "talk back" to the dominant discourses and understandings of their lives by resisting the weight of stereotype and stigma with their words and in their actions.

Power and Knowledge

In this section, we explore discourse as a concept that includes the everyday talk, or use of language, that is dominant in the social world. The reason for this examination is twofold: to expose the language of dominance that surrounds the sex worker and to determine how this language is used to oppress her/him. Discourse, as Foucault tells us, is the site of the production of power. Discourse creates the world around us in ways that serve power and enable dominance and oppression. To call sex workers whores, victims, or criminals does little to help understand the lives or words of sex workers. If anything, the portraits of sex workers as victims, or as blameworthy, may in fact help perpetuate violence and stigma against sex workers. To understand the type of language used to describe the sex worker is to understand the power of words (discourse) and that power's relationship to sexuality generally.

The principal features of the relationship between power and sexuality, as Foucault tells us, may be summarized as: 1. The negative relation: Where sex and pleasure are concerned, power can *do* nothing but say no to them. What this produces, if anything, is absences and gaps; it overlooks elements, introduces discontinuities, separates what is joined, and marks off boundaries. Its effects take the general form of limit and lack. 2. The insistence of the rule: Power is essentially what dictates its law to sex. Sex is placed by power in a binary system: licit and illicit, permitted and forbidden. 3. The cycle of prohibition: Thou shalt not go near, thou shalt not touch, thou shalt not consume, thou shalt not experience pleasure, thou shalt not speak, thou shalt not show thyself; ultimately, thou shalt not exist, except in darkness and secrecy. To deal with sex, power employs nothing more than a power of prohibition. 4. The logic of censorship: This interdiction is thought to take three forms: affirming that such a thing is not permitted, preventing the thing from being said, and denying that the thing exists. 5. The uniformity of the apparatus: Power over sex is exercised through a legislative power on the one side and an obedient subject on the other.[17]

All of these interdictions can be applied to the existence of the sex worker. For example, we find the negative relation of sex and pleasure as "limit and lack" in the legal proscriptions against sex work. All serve to limit sexual contact of this nature, regardless of whether or not those engaged in the act are consenting adults. The second interdiction, the insistence of the rule, is apparent in the social regulation of sexuality, in the determination of which types of sex are permitted (within heterosexual marriage) and which are forbidden (all other types of sex). The third relationship of power and sexuality, the cycle of prohibition, represents the uneasy relationship most of the public has with sex: it is omnipresent yet secret. Sex is all over the media, yet not to be publicly experienced in any way(s). The fourth interdiction, the logic of censorship, helps us understand most public policy on sex work. Denying the sex worker voice in the media representation of the sex trade is yet another example of this censorship.

Finally, as Foucault understands it, power over sex is exercised the same way as are other forms of power: with the law on the one hand and the obedient subject on the other. The sex worker is, at the end of the day, a licit subject with illicit agency. In other words, in Canadian law, she is a legal entity that cannot act, because to do anything that invites, solicits, arranges, or communicates for the purposes of prostitution is to be subject to legal charge. However, she is subject to language that affirms her work as her identity and that locates her as an addict or as a criminal. The label "prostitute," for all it connotes, denies her the right to voice her own ideas or analysis or to talk to the very institutions that oppress her. This denial is part of what it is to have little power in the social world.

Yet, as Foucault also indicates, discourses are not only a site of power but also a point of resistance: "Discourses are not once and for all subservient to power or raised up against it, any more than silences are. We must make allowance for the complex and unstable process whereby discourse can be both an instrument and an effect of power, but also a hindrance, a stumbling-block, a point of resistance and a starting point for an opposing strategy. Discourse transmits and produces power; it reinforces it, but also undermines and exposes it, renders it fragile and makes it possible to thwart it."[18] We agree with Foucault's assertion that discourse "transmits and produces power" yet "undermines it and exposes it" at the same time. Dominant scripts, or stories, of the Prostitute are everywhere we look in this research: in the literature, in the words of professionals, sometimes in the words of sex workers themselves. The scripts we uncovered in interviews with social control agents, such as police and probation officers, vary little from the vacillating discourse between victim and criminal that we see elsewhere. But to buy into the commonplace narrative of the Prostitute is to misunderstand how resistance to narrative is just as easily present. Sex workers talk back to the storying of their lives in a poignant, angry, and declarative fashion. They resist stereotyping, violence, definition, and assimilation, and do so every day and night of their working lives. To do otherwise is to submit to dominant discourse, and to submit may cost them their lives. This is more than a game of words, and sex workers know it.

Agency, Resistance, and Feminist Theorizing

Despite all this denial and repression, there remains the possibility, indeed the necessity, of agency and resistance. Feminist theorists should be at the forefront of defending sex workers' agency and championing their resistance because feminists recognize that the relationship between power and sexuality is powerfully gendered. Nevertheless, many feminists have a great deal of difficulty with sex worker agency.

Much feminist theorizing of sex work has focused on the sex worker as victim. Radical feminists, such as Catharine MacKinnon, Sheila Jeffreys, and Kathleen Barry, insist on a feminism that renders sex workers passive victims. This type of feminism locates the sex worker body in a totalizing patriarchy, one that blames men for exploiting women's sexuality. Sex workers are victims and, therefore, unable to act or negotiate sex acts for themselves. Such perceptions of sex workers have increased criminalization in Sweden, for example.[19] In that country, claims that prostitution is simply exploitation have led directly to policies that further criminalize sex work. This strategy, it should be noted, has been tried in many countries and has yet to be proved effective. As Noah Zatz notes, "legal regimes ... play an important role in suppressing sex workers' attempts to articulate their practices as a form of work and promote its interpretation as fundamentally a sexual act."[20] That is, feminist theorizing and politics of this type may actually contribute to the power structure that can indeed oppress sex workers, a power structure of which middle-class academic feminists are a part. As one analyst of migrant sex work has put it, "There is a growing tendency to victimise poor people, weak people, uneducated people and migrant people. The trend, which began as a way of drawing attention to specific forms of violence committed against women, has now become a way of describing everyone on the lower rungs of power. Routinely, supporters position them as victims in order to claim rights for them, but this move also turns them into victims, and victims need help, need saving – which gives a primary role to supporters."[21] When sex workers refuse to play the victim role, they are quickly accused of selling out and giving in to the patriarchy. As Linda LeMoncheck points out, "Sex workers complain that they are doubly stigmatized; as morally incorrect by conservatives for their sexual license and permissiveness, and as politically incorrect by feminists for making sexual transactions with sexists and for taking advantage of a capitalist enterprise that profits from women's sexuality."[22]

A second feminist position, pro-rights feminism, views the sex worker as a worker first and foremost. Sex work is viewed as a choice made by women and men within more or less constraining circumstances. That is, pro-rights feminism is concerned with the individual's right to make her/his own choices, not having choices made for her/him (which radical feminism tends to do).[23] However, this position is not easily reduced to a liberal or libertarian form of feminism, where the only problematic barrier is in the state's interference with individual freedom. Pro-rights feminism recognizes that sex workers, like most individuals, are making choices within the constraining power structures of race, class, sexuality, and gender but, for pro-rights feminists, these structures are neither inevitable nor unchanging. Rather, they can be challenged and resisted through political organizing (among both non-sex workers and sex workers) and changed through political action. That is, breaking down the structures that constrain individuals requires recognizing the agency and individual freedom of sex workers. For pro-rights feminists, while sex work in its current form may be oppressive and exploitative for some, these conditions can be changed if sex workers' political agency is recognized and supported, for example, through the creation of rights-based movements or unions that lobby for and uphold good working conditions. Sex work, therefore, can be made at least safer and less exploitative for all and, ultimately, a freer choice.

A third feminist position on sex work, sex radicalism, builds on the second but it emphasizes the identity politics of sex work and the role of discursive power. This third position draws on postmodernist feminism and queer theory.[24] It views the sex worker as a resistant identity that exposes the suppression of women's sexuality and the exploitation of her labour. That is, sex radicalism emphasizes the radical potential of sex work in exploding and expanding the boundaries of sexuality and gender. According to Corina McKay, queer theory, for example, enables us to view the sex worker as a performer who challenges dominant arrangements of power. In this view, the sex worker "inverts the 'male gaze' by creating what the male gaze desires but on the sex worker's own terms."[25] Further, sex workers' negotiation over what sex acts will be performed for how much makes visible the absence of such overt negotiation in so-called hetero-normative relationships – despite the actual exchange of, for example, buying dinner for sex. Without being overtly negotiated, such relationships may, in fact, grant much more access to women's bodies than sex work.[26] Critics often accuse sex radicals of being overly "celebratory" in their focus on the empowered "outlaw whore" and their potential neglect of the structures that can make sex work a daily grind rather than a liberating experience. As Wendy Chapkis argues, however, not all sex radicals are of the libertarian perspective where sex is free from the constraints of power, rather, many view sex as a "terrain of struggle."[27] Sex radicals seek to recognize the potential in sex work for resistance to and subversion of the current sexual order even as they acknowledge the potential for oppression and exploitation. Sex radicalism allows us to see the importance of discursive power, the power to determine meaning, as one of the key arenas of political struggle over sex work.

In this book we emphasize sex workers' resistance not only to the material forces of work, law, and violence but, importantly, their discursive resistance to the social constructions that make such conditions of work, acts of law, and acts of violence possible. Acknowledging the discursive challenges made by sex workers to these interpretations of sex work as well as sexuality and gender, for example, is key to empowering sex workers and liberating sex work from oppressive conditions. That is, acknowledging and challenging discursive power does not disable progressive political change, rather, *it makes such change possible*. For example, viewing sex work as work rather than sexual exploitation or moral debauchery enables political approaches that recognize and support sex workers as rights-bearing political and social agents rather than objects of intervention and control. It also allows policy responses that are more likely to address sex workers' concerns and a politics based on solidarity rather than saving. Thus, in this book, we draw on these combined insights of sex radicalism and pro-rights feminism to enable us to hear sex workers' resistance to the discursive and material power relations that surround them.

Dangerous People: Sex Workers and Resistance
Resistance is a concept that enables us to think about agency within structure, about how people fight back and attempt to establish or retain control

even within difficult circumstances. Sex workers resist both economic and sexual power structures in their everyday lives by negotiating with clients and bosses, by shifting job locations, or by fighting against restrictive rules and unfair treatment. Sex workers also resist discursive power structures – the way they are constructed by experts and policy makers and feminists and the very real effects those constructions have. Sex workers recognize this discursive power – this refusal by others to hear and accept sex workers' own interpretations of their lives as valid and trustworthy – and they, in turn, refuse to internalize the dominant discourse. They continue to insist on their ability to describe their own reality in the face of this expert interpretation. We call this process of discursive resistance "talking back."

Resistance is generally conceptualized, following James C. Scott, as a "weapon of the weak" – it is often individualized and easily ignored or misinterpreted as submission, and there are often heavy costs associated with its practice (although less heavy than with outright rebellion).[28] It is not seen as the kind of political agency that achieves major changes, rather, it slows down and complicates the processes of power or provides temporary relief from exploitation. Resistance affirms the agency of less powerful political actors and it also lays bare the difficulty for marginalized groups to achieve political change. Discursive resistance, however – talking back and telling one's own stories – has the potential for collective political empowerment. Much as consciousness-raising worked in the early days of feminism, telling one's own story has been the starting point of many sex worker organizations fighting for political change. Chris Bruckert points to this process of collective resistance among exotic dancers in informally constructing a "shared meaning" that becomes "an ideological and personal resource that legitimates collective action and shapes the strategies employed."[29] That is, they themselves become the basis of political action. However, we also take heed of Sherry Ortner's warning that resistance should not be romanticized and that the politics among marginalized actors should be recognized.[30] And indeed, not all sex workers agree or share interpretations of their experience and we try to make this visible in our selection of interview material. However, most share a common will to resist the way they are perceived.

It is not just the elite of the sex trade who push these boundaries and challenge hetero-normative codes. Studies of migrant sex work or sex work in the developing world, for example, have also begun to recognize this resistant identity.[31] It was plain during our interviews that the women and men we were talking to – *even those who were also poor or addicted* – were intelligent, witty, articulate, independent, and willing to push the boundaries of "normal" or "acceptable" behaviour on many fronts. Indeed, the more marginalized people seemed to be, the more they seemed willing to articulate their resistance. For example, while only a handful of the workers we spoke with were racialized women, outsiders to not only the sexual and class order but to the racial order, they were often the most outspoken in their critiques of mainstream society. Thus, the resistance of the sex worker to societal norms and her/his challenge to mainstream readings of sex work are very audible in our conversations with sex workers in the Maritimes. They have what one analyst of sex work in Thailand has called the "spirit of a fighter" – always willing to challenge the strictures on them.

> Personally, I very much valued the spirit of struggle and the relatively independent and defying attitudes of the prostitutes I know which I rarely found in women who are not of their kind. They are women who have the spirit of a fighter – in sexual relations and others. While their middle-class sisters are being repressed by conservative values and the sexual double standards, they seem to have more autonomy in their personal and sexual lives ... Having marked themselves as whores, they have come out of their place – having broken so many repressive rules of good women, and developed the spirit of a fighter for survival and better living.[32]

Sex workers not only break the rules of "proper" sexual and gender behaviour, they break *all* the rules. The sex workers we spoke with displayed their agency and resistance in terms of not only challenging sexual codes but also resisting the constraints of neo-liberalism and global capitalism – by refusing demeaning minimum-wage work. They also refused and resisted the disciplinary mechanisms of the welfare state and critiqued its restructuring. And they challenged the interventionism of health experts and the heavy hand of punishment meted out by the law that criminalizes sex work and sex workers. Resistance is literally a way of life for sex workers.

Above all, the sex workers we spoke with resist the discourses that circumscribe their lives. They recognize the power of discourse, of the whore stigma, of being represented rather than being allowed to represent themselves. They "talk back" to these discourses and representations, and they refused to "hear" the stigmatizing and disrespectful talk of so-called experts, police, and agents of the state. Resistance, as a strategy of survival and of opposition to a dominant order that erases, ignores, vilifies, and marginalizes the existence of sex workers, is perhaps the most useful strategy of all in the arsenal of street sex workers. And, as this brief discussion outlines, sex workers have greater agency than might be assumed. Such agency is twisted by police officers as manipulative ploys for arrest, is misunderstood by feminists as subsuming to patriarchal order, and is controlled by capitalism through the appropriation of labour or of public space. Despite all of these incursions into her day or night of work, the sex worker lives on. We must be prepared, in the end, to listen to these voices that challenge the very self-perceptions of the dominant class. It is those who practise "forbidden sex" who point out the hypocrisies of us all. As Anne McClintock has observed:

> It is, therefore, not surprising that prostitutes are traditionally associated with challenges to rule, with figures of rebellion, revolt, insurrection and the criminal appropriation of property. The scandal of the whoerarchy amounts to flagrant female interference in male contests over property and power. Not for nothing did Parisian public health official Parent-Duchatelet call prostitutes "the most dangerous people in society."[33]

A Note on Method

As mentioned above, our research is based on a series of qualitative, open-ended interviews with sixty people working in the sex trade in Halifax, Moncton, and Saint John – as well as many others who work in outreach, policing, politics, law, and health. People working in the sex trade were contacted through local community agencies in Halifax, Moncton, and Saint John. We asked the community agencies, with which sex workers interact, to partner with us. These partner agencies examined our research proposal and questioned us, asking us what we would do with the results. They advertised our research to the sex workers, explained a bit of its purpose, and allowed us to use their premises for interviews. The agencies are Stepping Stone in Halifax, the only outreach agency for sex workers in the Atlantic provinces; AIDS Nova Scotia in Halifax; Coverdale Services for Women in Saint John, New Brunswick, an outreach centre for low income and criminalized women; and Moncton Sexual Health Centre, also in New Brunswick. The agencies established interview schedules, and the co-authors of this book travelled to all three centres to interview study participants. From the research grant, we paid the sex workers a flat rate for their interviews. The agencies' staff provided debriefing if participants were upset or needed to talk about the interview process. This service was provided to the interviewers as well. The purpose of the interviews and the guidelines on ethics were explained to the participants by the researchers.[34] Participants were also given the purpose and the ethics claims in writing. The interviews were taped and transcribed by trained transcribers, which included one departmental assistant and three research assistants. All research assistants were instructed in the confidentiality and professional ethics in obtaining, storing, citing, and keeping confidential the words of the participants.

Other interviews were conducted with three groups of participants, all loosely categorized as agents of social control, social advocacy, or sociopolitics. This group included police officers (regional and RCMP forces); probation officers; staff of community outreach agencies, AIDS organizations, and needle exchanges; health care providers, staff of health care clinics, and municipal and provincial politicians. Most of these interviews were obtained through either cold calls or by word of mouth. An interesting feature of the Maritime provinces is that the urban areas are so small, by city standards, that most of the professionals in various agencies knew each other, and we garnered many interview possibilities from a single source. With few exceptions, all those contacted granted interviews, for which we are grateful.

The interviews were transcribed and the texts were analyzed using a critical political analysis. The loosely structured, open-ended interview process allowed some patterns to emerge while giving plenty of room for sex workers simply to tell us what was on their minds and what they wanted to say to the world. We did ask, for example, what was best and worst about sex work; what sex workers thought of the groups with which they came into contact, such as police, health services, and government agencies, as well as society at large (that is, public attitudes toward sex workers) and the media. We also asked what sex workers would like to see change about their lives and work, and what services, groups, or programs were most helpful to them. Such a method of inquiry and analysis requires reading and rereading of interview text many times over to ascertain subversive and resistant strategies. In doing so, we followed the advice of Wendy Chapkis in interpreting the story or stories being told:

> There is no one overriding narrative spoken by prostitutes on prostitution. There are instead competing and sometimes conflicting stories, each with its own integrity. Accounts of sex work ... are often contradictory, without one being "true" and the other "false." Discussions of sex – commercial and otherwise – necessarily reveal both victimization and agency, exploitation and engaged complicity; in short, both the violence and wild defiance of sex ... We need to develop the capacity to listen to these stories without reducing them to competitors for the status of Truth. We need to listen for meaning rather than just "fact," to ask why a story is told in this way, how the location of speaker shapes the tale, how the position of the audience affects what is heard, and to carefully consider what is at stake politically, personally, and strategically in invoking this particular version at this moment in this context.[35]

In this book we present as many voices as we can so that the readers may read and analyze these various stories for themselves.

The Book's Structure

As mentioned above, the chapters are arranged in order of the responses, issues, and concerns raised by the sex workers we spoke with. That is, we have tried to follow their ordering of issues of importance in terms of what is good about the trade and what they would like to see redressed or responded to in some way.

We begin, therefore, in Chapter 1, with money – the nearly universal answer to what was good or what the people we spoke with liked about working in the trade. In following their analysis of money, Chapter 1 argues that sex work is not simply a response to poverty. It is also a resistant mode of work, in that many sex workers are actively refusing the disciplinary and frequently humiliating conditions of minimum-wage work and social assistance. Sex work is a fairly independent mode of work that allows for some individual control not only over money but over one's time. The sex worker is her/his own boss to a large degree. What we examine here, therefore, is how the sex workers we spoke with weighed their choices between different forms of work and different forms of sex work in response to the constrictions of a neo-liberal economic age. And we document how they critique the economic system in which we live.

In Chapter 2, we bring together sex workers' understandings of what is positive about sex work with the issue that sex workers felt – again nearly universally – was the most pressing: violence. A number of sex workers whom we interviewed mentioned things about the work that they enjoyed or liked or appreciated beyond the money that could be made. They talked about good clients as well as about the independence and freedom from society's rules and restrictions that sex work could give them. Thus, they resisted the easy classification of sex work as simply violent by presenting a careful analysis of violence and interaction with clients more generally. They pointed to specific sources of violence – particular clients rather than the trade itself – and the social context of that violence, particularly the general stigmatization and dehumanization of the sex worker by society at large. Further, sex workers gave us many examples of how they fought back against this violence and resisted these processes of dehumanization.

In Chapter 3, we address another issue that our interviewees raised as problematic – the potential conflict with the law that so many sex workers face daily. In this chapter, we look at sex workers' experience and analysis of their interactions with the personal face of the law that criminalizes sex work in Canada – police. And we deconstruct the discourse of police officers whom we have interviewed on their understanding of sex work and sex workers.

Chapter 4 explores sex workers' complaints about the burden of stigma – particularly given the difficulty of anonymity in the relatively small centres of the Maritimes. Importantly, rather than accepting the general reading of sex workers as suffering from low self-esteem, the women and men we spoke with frequently reversed the gaze of mainstream society by pointing to stigma and not some personality flaw of sex workers as the source of low self-esteem. Further, they identify the media as an important (re)producer of stigmatized images of sex work and sex workers. Taking their lead, we explore the images of sex work produced in the Maritimes' largest newspaper, the Halifax *Chronicle Herald,* since the mid-1980s.

In Chapter 5, we look at what outside experts often put heavy emphasis on, but which we found sex workers saw in a very different way: issues of health. For sex workers, health needs to be understood within the much broader context of working conditions, safety from violence, and socio-economic determinants of health. Sex workers also challenged health experts' understandings of the risk of sexually transmitted disease and the problem of addictions. Sex workers positioned themselves as sexual health experts and called attention to the much wider problems of addictions in the general society, challenging their supposed deviantization on this score. They critique and resist attempts to download blame onto individual sex workers for their "failure" to maintain their health and, instead, point the finger back at the wider system that determines their health.

Finally, Chapter 6 examines the politics of and policies on sex work in the Maritimes, and in Canada more broadly. Here, we see sex workers as willing participants in policy debates and negotiations on how to make sex work safe for everyone. We also hear from residents and policy makers and try to figure out what the barriers are to making more sensible policy on sex work in Canada. Most of the sex workers we spoke with were seeking some form of decriminalization of the trade – or "a safe, dry place to work" – and yet Canadian society as a whole has remained resistant to such a change. Here we explore the suggestions for change put forward by sex workers and their advocates.

In the end, however, we cannot cover all the important issues related to sex work in this book. Certainly, we tried to remain true to those issues that the sex workers we spoke with raised as most important to them. However, the study did focus on a small group of workers and, like many studies, overrepresents those who work mainly on the street and, therefore, the findings should not be too quickly assumed to be more widely applicable, particularly among the much larger but less researched group of indoor workers. Further, for reasons of time and resources, we were not able to include clients among our interviewees, which means that this large and critical gap in the research remains unaddressed. Finally, while we did try in some way to redress the researcher/researched power imbalance through the use of open-ended interviewing techniques, we recognize that such techniques only provide a small measure of balance. Overall, we view this study as a "first project," as Jacqueline Lewis and Eleanor Maticka-Tyndale describe it, one that helps build the rapport needed between sex workers and researchers for more inclusive and collaborative research in the future.[36] As a step in this direction, this book presents the voices of sex workers in the Maritimes "talking back" on economics, work, law, health, media, and politics and challenging those who would interpret their lives for them.

1
It's the Money, Honey

One of the first questions we asked when interviewing people working in the sex trade was: "What is the best part of the job?" What we were trying to invoke was sex workers' perceptions of their lives in the trade, without assuming that everything about the trade was necessarily problematic. As Wendy Rickard maintains, "Life history interpretation and analysis is governed by the questions that researchers ask."[1] And as sex work activist Carol Queen has said, "If a researcher or therapist only encourages someone to look at the down and difficult side of sex work, without asking any questions about what feels healthy and vibrant and alive about it to you, they're going to get a very partial story."[2] The nearly universal answer to the question of what was the best part of working in the sex trade was, understandably, money. For many of our interviewees, sex work's most important attribute was its potential for generating fairly large amounts of money in a relatively short period. It may not always have lived up to this potential, but the potential was always there. Sex work made sense to many of our interviewees as an income-generating strategy first and foremost; however, "money," understood simply as income, is not the whole picture. Sex work was for many a way to preserve a sense of self-respect and independence in the face of more limiting and oppressive choices, such as minimum-wage work and social assistance. That is, while "money" may have been the quick answer to what was good about sex work among our interviewees, this answer did not imply that these women and men were simply pushed into the trade by economic forces. Rather, as we shall see, they often made careful decisions about the economic choices available to them – such as minimum-wage work and welfare, and indoor and street-based sex work – decisions based not just on money but also on the amount of independence each option offered. Thus, our interviewees were no different than most Maritimers who, in an economy marked by un- and underemployment, cobble together a living among the options available but do not accept attempts to marginalize them.

Money also plays a symbolic role: its generation is part of the construction of social identity in modern society, an identity that gives people social and political, rather than simply economic, power.[3] Thus, the tag line "honey" carries this symbolic message of social wisdom or empowerment. It is meant to indicate that the speaker will not be talked down to as though s/he is a child or an innocent. Indeed, as the next chapter outlines, most of our interviewees did not talk about sex work as unrelentingly degrading or uniformly unpleasant, even though the majority of our interviewees worked mainly in the street trade rather than the more comfortable indoor trade. Some indicated that money is not the only benefit to be had from work in the sex trade. Respondents talked about the pleasures of good clients, of learning about oneself and becoming more self-confident, of travel and adventure – upsides outsiders rarely think about as part of the sex trade. While some may interpret this as denial or putting on a brave face, it is precisely the politics of representation that is at issue here. What some sex workers find degrading about the trade are the attitudes and perceptions of others toward the trade and those who work within it, as we will see in a later chapter. Emphasizing the positive aspects of the work is not denial; it is resistance to the disempowering discourse of mainstream society. Indeed, all of our respondents were able to quickly point out the various downsides of the trade, particularly under criminalized conditions, but they resisted a simple reading of the trade itself as necessarily and completely negative. Rather, they were often at pains to express the wide variety of possible experiences and the complexities of their lives more generally. What we want to emphasize here is that even if sex work comes about as a response to poverty or addiction, the women and men we spoke with showed great strength of character and a will to resist what life had served up to them both economically and socially. Like most people, they have indeed been constrained by life circumstances, in some instances more than most, but they were also – again, some more than most – in no way willing to accept those constraints.

There is a common tendency, however, to read sex work simply as a product of poverty and to then interpret this to mean that sex workers lack any real choice – otherwise they would not go into this line of work. While this interpretation appears to make sense at an abstract level – of course, for those who are not independently wealthy, there are various degrees of limitation on our economic choices – the problem of this quick read of sex work is that it denies agency both to the poor and to sex workers, and it encourages patronizing and disempowering responses. That is, simply reading sex workers as "victims of poverty" fails to investigate the precise role that material and economic factors have in shaping sex work experiences and how these larger forces are resisted (and, therefore, how they can be changed). Indeed, as Noah Zatz has argued, sex work itself, by explicitly requiring payment for the "sex/affective" or emotional labour that has traditionally been used to justify women's cheap labour, challenges "some of the structural conditions that narrow women's options in the first place." It is the criminalization of that labour that "helps patrol the boundary between the sex/affective labor routinely assigned to and expected of women and practices deserving of the financial status and rewards of 'work.'"[4] That is, sex work can itself be read as a resistant mode of female labour, a form of resistance that is constrained by the laws and social meanings that shape it, not by the work itself. Indeed, the analyses that sex workers put forward in this chapter make it plain that, for them, sex work offers a way of resisting the limitations of minimum wage, service-sector work, and social assistance. For these workers, sex work potentially provides both substantial income and independence in one's work. By understanding sex work as a resistant form of labour, rather than simply as a survival mechanism, we both see the lives of sex workers more clearly from their perspective and make room for a politics that includes them as agents of change rather than objects of intervention.

Feminist Theory, Economic Determinism, and Sex Work
The above discussion provides some insight into the problem of much feminist theorizing about the sex trade that emphasizes the role of structural constraints, such as women's poverty, in explaining women's, or youth's, entry into the trade. Certainly, because sex work is primarily an income-generating strategy for most workers, background economic conditions are central to analyzing sex work. This is even more the case in economically depressed regions such as the Maritimes. The Maritimes are most frequently referred to, in economic terms, as have-not provinces. The Maritimes as a whole are characterized by higher rates of unemployment and lower rates of economic growth than is the rest of Canada, resulting in higher transfer, or equalization, payments from the federal government – as well as higher rates of out-migration as Maritimers go "down the road" to seek economic opportunities elsewhere. The economy is also gendered in the Maritimes, where the gender/income gap is greater than that in other regions, and the median income of women is lower.[5] Not to account for the economic conditions under which sex work takes place in the Maritimes, therefore, would be to ignore an important reality of life in the Maritimes. But it is important to remember that these conditions affect many more people than sex workers in the Maritimes, that not all sex workers face these conditions to an equal degree, and that a context of relative poverty does not mean that all these people are simply victims without a sense of agency. What it does tell us is that conditions of work and rates of pay in most areas in the Maritimes – whether they are in call centres, fish plants, or the sex trade – are generally poor and need to be addressed.

Much mainstream Canadian feminist, as well as bureaucratic, discussion of the sex trade, however, has fallen into the structuralist trap; indeed, the emphasis on socioeconomic conditions (as opposed to male sexual power) is perhaps what distinguishes Canadian feminist readings from their American counterparts.[6] In one example of (admittedly strong) structural determinism, Kari Fedec argues that

> a more critical theoretical understanding of the sex trade would fall in line with various incarnations of feminist theory, including socialist feminism and Marxist feminism. These critical feminist orientations hold that power exists on the basis of race, class, gender and age, and that the sex trade industry is built on the framework of power distinctions ... For example, since women and children, in general occupy subordinate economic positions in patriarchal, capitalist societies, the hierarchical structure of society defines and creates a certain type of criminality for women and children, often based on imputed sexual morality. For most prostitutes, then, selling sex is a survival mechanism. The seller's decision to engage in prostitution-related activities is not usually a choice made by the sex trade worker based on free will. Deciding to do sex work is more often a way of getting necessary food and shelter.[7]

Such an approach, first, suffers from the problem of abstraction, which has been so hotly debated in feminist political economy circles.[8] That is, it abstractly designates a role for "race, class, gender and age" in shaping the industry and from that deduces the experience of women rather than investigating precisely how that role is played out in concrete historical circumstances. The importance of careful, grounded historical analysis is obvious when the results of field studies are compared to official data or common assumptions. Frances Shaver, for example, has frequently referred to the way in which traditional views, as well as official data, distort the extent of women's involvement in the trade and the conditions of work, and exaggerate the socioeconomic background of sex workers (which is more likely to be comfortable than impoverished).[9] Indeed, there is a tendency to universalize a wide variety of experiences. Even though the sex workers speaking here tend to represent a marginalized segment of workers (i.e., they were contacted through outreach groups that work with those experiencing some form of difficulty rather than with the larger number of mostly indoor workers who have no need for such supports), their economic background and experiences varied widely, from those who were indeed struggling to find food and shelter to those who found sex work an agreeable economic choice among a number of options.

Second, Fedec's approach also suffers from the essentialism referred to by post-colonial critics of socialist feminism.[10] Socialist feminist analyses tend to assume an already constituted group, such as "women" or "sex workers," that is (within the theoretical framework) by definition impoverished and victimized by capitalism and patriarchy rather than investigating the ways in which people are constituted as "women" or "sex workers" so that their labour is "*made* cheap," for example.[11] That is, it grants what capitalist patriarchy is trying to make true, that women or sex workers are victims, rather than seeing the ways in which this process is contested. Such approaches also frequently determine the meaning of the experience for the subjects rather than investigating it. Such approaches render feminists "expert" readers who are the only ones capable of understanding the problem and the only ones capable of creating change. It is no surprise then that the state should also find such a reading a useful tool for reinscribing its power; indeed, readings of sex workers as victims of poverty or, more recently, victims of addictions, are common in government literature.[12] If sex workers are simply victims of economic circumstances, then only the state or other experts can possibly know and prescribe what is good for them and what needs to be changed. (It is no coincidence that Fedec consistently uses the phrase "women and children" as if they can be simply lumped together, effectively giving women the political status of children.) By contrast, it is important that the sex workers speaking here interpret their experience not as victimization but as a process of resistance, as a way of refusing the dull compulsion of poverty or minimum-wage work and maximizing both one's income and one's independence. Indeed, it is precisely the dominant mode of representation of sex workers – as victims requiring aid rather than as workers and citizens demanding rights – that these workers resist. That is, what the sex workers speaking here identified as problematic was not some abstract notion of poverty but the way they were treated both in the workplace and by government assistance programs that limited their independence and options – these are the ways their labour was made "cheap" and exploitable.

The problems of structurally determinist readings of the sex trade also lead to a misreading of the problems at hand. At an abstract level, one could argue that almost all work in today's world is a product of, or shaped by, capitalist and, often, patriarchal and racist structures. But to argue for the elimination of work because of these structures is to confuse labour per se with the particular conditions of labour, particularly the exploitation of labour. As many feminist theorists have noted, both work and sex can be liberating or exploitative, depending on the conditions under which they are carried out. This is no less true when the two activities are combined. As Frances Shaver has remarked, "It is not prostitution which is unsavory or undesirable. It is the broader socio-economic conditions that support and maintain it *in its present form.*"[13] Indeed, research conducted with and by sex workers is careful to focus on the ways in which poverty among some women in the trade can make them more vulnerable to economic exploitation *within the trade* and therefore points us to the need to address these conditions, rather than eliminating the trade altogether.[14] Paying attention to workers' analyses of their experiences shows us that what can make sex work problematic are the conditions of illegality and disdain under which many sex workers operate (see the discussion in Chapters 3 and 6 regarding the legal status of prostitution in Canada, wherein prostitution itself is not illegal but all activities around it [communicating for the purposes of, and living on the avails of] *are*.) The sex workers speaking here were sometimes boxed in within the trade because they could not rely on legal protections against violence on the street, for example, nor on legal guarantees of working conditions off the street. Addressing these conditions would address many of the concerns expressed by sex workers.

Analyses that avoid structurally determinist readings of sex work and instead investigate the social constructions of women as workers or sex workers and the concrete consequences of these constructions in particular historical locations can engender a much greater understanding of the potential sites of political change. Women and sex workers are no longer assumed to be victims of the economic order. Rather, the ways in which the economic and social order in a particular historical location tries to render them cheap labour, for example, are investigated, as are the ways in which this process is resisted. In this study, we see that sex workers unequivocally identify the ways in which social discourses and socioeconomic processes attempt to render them cheap labour or exploitable labour – both within and outside sex work – and the ways in which they resist these attempts. Understanding sex work as resistance to economic exploitation allows us to engage in a politics that supports workers' efforts at maximizing their independence and control, a goal that lies at the heart of feminism itself.

Fast Cash and Easy Money: Sex Work as an Income-Generating Strategy

> I don't need money every day; I just prefer to have it. (Megan, Halifax)

> Yeah, all my money goes to them [my two kids] and if I have anything left over I'll buy myself a nice outfit, buy myself a lobster or something. But I mean, you walk into my kids' rooms and people look and say, "How many kids do you have?" Only two. I have enough toys for five kids, they've got toys, like toys, and there's four beds in the bedroom. They've got two sets of bunk beds for when they have friends over and they've got their little vanity. I've got two of everything 'cause they fight if you don't. (Patricia, Saint John)

> It's easy money. The only time I ever do it is when I absolutely need it. So that's the only reason I ever do it.
> *Interviewer: Is there anything else that is useful about the job?*
> Um, no. Because, anything I need, like food or cigarettes, if I need it I just go out and get it, or a place to sleep. A lot of times I would do it for a place to sleep. (Marc, Moncton)

The problem of simply viewing sex workers as victims of poverty was obvious from our respondents' explanations of their work. Our interviewees were in no way uniform in their economic circumstances. For some, sex work was a matter of survival; for others, it was a means of generating a regular, or supplemental, income. While it is true that a number of sex workers share backgrounds of low educational attainment and low incomes, one must consider that many Canadian women share these characteristics (along with histories of sexual abuse), that many sex workers do not share all or any of these characteristics, and that studies of sex work tend to over-represent those workers who are more likely to have these backgrounds (i.e., those in the more visible street-level trade.) Many recent studies, however, point to the heterogeneous socioeconomic background of sex workers and the heterogeneous reasons (beyond food and shelter) for entering the trade – including acquisition of consumer goods and explorations of sexual identity.[15] More concrete studies, therefore, render the reading of "prostitution as a product of poverty" problematic. Sex work may generally be about money, but what that means precisely needs to be investigated rather than assumed. In our discussions with sex workers, it was clear that sex work was a means of generating sometimes quite a bit of income while being able to maintain a fair amount of control over one's work.[16] Indeed, more sensitive socialist feminist analyses of sex work, such as Eileen McLeod's much earlier work in Britain in co-operation with the Programme for the Reform of the Law on Solicitation (PROS), the sex workers' rights organization, indicated similar findings of sex work as part of feminized labour under capitalist conditions. As McLeod argues, sex work "can bring comparatively substantial financial returns. There are also the attractions of its compatibility with the demands of childcare and domestic labour – still seen primarily as women's work. An enjoyable degree of 'workers' control' can also exist."[17]

Indeed, sex industry work is a fairly reliable income-generating strategy in that sex work – both indoor and on the street – and exotic dancing hold out the possibility of making a fair amount of money in a comparatively short period. Sex workers working the street in New Brunswick can expect between $20 and $50 per client. Incomes, of course, depend on how many clients a worker can get in any given week and how well each pays. Workers in Saint John reported nightly incomes of $30 (on a bad night) to $300 on a particularly good night. All reported also receiving some kind of income assistance, ranging from $264 to $558 per month. In Halifax, where most of our respondents worked on the street, incomes range from $40 to $300 per night. The highest weekly income reported was $5,000 to $6,000 in a very good week. The same respondent admitted, though, that, in low weeks, it is closer to $50 to $100. The general perception among workers was that not a lot of money could be made on the street and that incomes from street-level work are declining. Furthermore, the amount that can be generated varies widely, resulting in regular shifting between various types of sex work and exotic dancing in an effort to find the formula that maximizes income. However, a number told of instances of having hit the jackpot with certain clients. And, given that over 60 percent of women in Atlantic Canada had annual incomes under $13,786 and that the median income for women in the Atlantic provinces is $11,235, a sex worker would only have to bring in approximately $200 a week if she were receiving some assistance, or $300 if she were not, to be above that average.[18] As an income-generating strategy, therefore, sex work is not a bad option.

Escort work, while not without its drawbacks, is where some of the big money is made:

> I remember one time when I was a prostitute for one of the escort services, I made $2,000 in one night. Two thousand dollars in one night! And almost the whole time I was at this guy's house, all we did, it was like I was shooting the shit with one of my girlfriends. We watched movies, we drank, we smoked some dope, we just talked, and he had a wife, and he had problems of course, you gotta pretend like you really give a crap, and listen, you just kind of suck it up, and think, "Oh well, whatever," and you drink his drink and you smoke his dope, whatever, it's all free, so you figure what the hell, and you're there, getting paid a hundred bucks an hour, just to be there, to watch these movies. So yeah, I'll listen to your wife's problems, and he had me there all night. (Colleen, Moncton)

Incomes for indoor workers (escort and massage work) range from $50 to $80 an hour plus tips. One receptionist at a massage parlour explained:

> They say that usually on a ten-day stint they make somewhere between $2,000 and $5,000 ... in ten days ... For a half hour it's $80, of which the girl receives $35. For an hour it's $115, $50 for the woman. For a Turkish bath, which is those Jacuzzi, man jumps in, she jumps in with him [and] gives him a sponge bath – still the same hour: it's $150; she gets $75 ... For outcall it's $100 plus cab fare, for an hour. (Ashley, Fredericton)

These charges remained fairly standard across Nova Scotia and New Brunswick, perhaps because of the domination of the industry by two major owners. One escort worker, however, said that she made much better money in Moncton than in Saint John but, even so, in Saint John she prefers escort to street work for its safety:

> In Moncton the money was really good. Moncton you could make five, six, seven, eight, nine hundred dollars a night. Down here [in Saint John] you're lucky if you make $200 a week. It's a big difference unless you go on the streets; and I've got children, so I try to do the careful thing. I have a ... my daughter, her father is my ex-pimp. He killed himself, so I stay away from those people [pimps]. (Patricia, Saint John)

While the formalized indoor trade is common in the Maritimes, there are also more informal arrangements that do not correspond to either working on the street or organized escort or massage work and that can generate a fairly good income. Several of our respondents, particularly those who had worked in the trade for some time, had regulars who came to their homes, or to whom they made calls; some put advertisements in the local paper for in-call/out-call services; and a number combine these activities along with street work. These workers operate independently and have control over their working conditions and rates, which are often competitive with escort-service rates. One explained: "I found out that on the street I used to have to charge less at times. And I was desperate, too." Now she works out of her home with regulars or those who respond to an advertisement:

> I have a set rate and generally it's $50 to $150, depending. A sleep, or intercourse, is generally up to $150. And that's good money because a lot of the times, they don't last more than twenty minutes. (Angela, Halifax)

For one woman, the money that could be generated by an occasional job arranged by a friend was enough to overcome her initial apprehensions:

> A friend of mine called me one night and asked me if I wanted to make $200. I'm thinking, Yeah! But it was to go with these two guys that were in from out of town at this motel room. I'm just thinking, "I can't do this," not that I think I'm any better than those girls, but I thought to myself, "Don't do this." That's as low as it goes, you know what I mean. But anyways, she said, it was the sex thing. I didn't want to have sex with anybody, to me that's ... but anyway, give them a blow job or whatever. I didn't seem like it was as bad, so I said, "Okay, I'll go with ya." So that's all that we did or whatever, and we each made $200 and we drank and whatever ... So I'm thinking, "Jeez, this isn't too bad" ... So I guess that's

what got me started. And she's called a couple of times after that and these same two guys and whatever ... So we've kinda gotten to know them and it's kinda gotten to be this [regular thing]. (Kendra, Saint John)

On another occasion she made $250 when the client turned out to be an old friend who then just gave her the money after sitting around eating and telling stories.

Exotic dancing is another area in which fairly large incomes can be generated, and into which some of our respondents had moved from escort or street work. Incomes in strip clubs in Nova Scotia and New Brunswick range from $50 to $700 per night. The low end was reported by one woman who danced only on amateur night and another who indicated that "new girls" were limited in what they could earn ($100 to $300). A dancer with more experience reported being able to make up to $700 per night on a particularly good night.[19] Private dances were the most lucrative, at $12 a dance, with $2 of that going to the house. As Chris Bruckert's research demonstrates, how much a dancer can make is determined by a series of income maximization strategies – refusing free stage shows or keeping a private dance client as long as possible – that often take time to learn and perfect.[20] As one woman who switched out of sex work and into exotic dancing after having a condom break remarked, often money could be made by means of little physical (although quite a bit of emotional) labour:

After I had that condom break, that's when I really, I was like, I'm gonna have to do something else, and I mean, I still wanted to be a part of easy money, so I decided to dance instead.

There was a few times you know, you'd walk out with six, or seven hundred dollars in one night. And you just give them [management] a dollar per dance, that's not including your tips, or your drinks, or you know, some customer hands you a little piece of pot, "Here you go" ... And you never had to do anything. Like I had a lot of really nice customers, where, there was this one man, he is a very professional man. He works actually downtown in one of the bigger high-class buildings. And he was kind of a little scrawny old man, really kind of loser-looking type, but he always wore like these golf clothes, like the stupid-looking sweaters, and shorts and stuff, and the colourful bright shirts. But the guy was so made out of money. He would show up to the bar, and he was a regular customer of mine. He would come by at least once or twice every week, and if he didn't come by once or twice every week, he made sure he came on rent week. The week rent was due, he'd show up, and how it [worked] was, even though the dances were ten bucks a dance, he'd give me twenty. What you'd do is sit there. And I remember, it was an every week thing, we'd sit there for about three or four hours, and we'd just sit there and drink. This was the deal with him. He said, "I realize you could make money, mingling, and stuff, with the other customers, but I want you to myself, and if I can have you to myself, then it will be more than worth your while." So by the end of the night I had about $700 from him, including the dances and the tips. Because every dance was $10, he'd give me $20, plus he'd fork me over about an extra $25 every half an hour or so, just for talking to him. And then he'd buy you your drinks all night. (Colleen, Moncton)

Money was not the only factor involved in our respondents' decisions to work in the sex industry. Occasionally, our interviewees referred to sex work as "easy" money or "fast" money. While the reference to sex work as easy money by pundits is generally a put-down that suggests that no real work is involved, in this case the ease has to do with the speed with which relatively large amounts of cash can be generated. This is so much the case in sex work that some found it almost addictive:

I'm not addicted [to substances]. I'm used to the money and you know ... the lifestyle. You know, you're used to having so much money for the day to use or whatever, and now you don't have it no more and you're drawn back out ... And the men know too, like I mean a lot of times I haven't been working, just walking down the street and they haul in and they see you and they kind of connect, they know about you just as well as I know you're a trick, they know that I'm a working girl, even when you're not working, like going to get your groceries. It's hard to pass up the money sometimes when someone is offering you $100 and you're really broke, I guess that's why I grab it. (Valerie, Halifax)

The need for fast cash is generally shared among those without substantial savings or credit. Recently, in fact, there has been a rapid growth of rent-to-own furniture stores, telephone renewal services, cheque-cashing services, and other forms of fringe banking in the Maritimes, which speaks to the problems of survival on minimum or less than minimum wages or welfare.[21] While some of those we spoke with did indicate that the need for fast cash was linked to the need for drugs or alcohol, this was certainly not always the case. Those with dependants were quick to point to the expenses of raising children – prescription glasses, clothes, and so on. Others pointed to the costs of rent and utilities, and security payments on these.[22] All of this must be considered against the background of un- or underemployment and the generally low levels of social assistance provided in the Maritimes. When people have no savings to fall back on, sudden large expenses require fast cash. Since sex work, even on the street, can generate up to $300 for a few hours' work, it is an obvious way to meet this need. At the same time, sex work as fast cash can also be read not as the response to an immediate need but as resistance to the long and demanding hours of straight work, as we shall see below. That is, sex work can give workers control over the pace of their work – something usually reserved only for those in the professions.

Income and Resistance within the Sex Industry

While the sex industry is viewed by many of our respondents as a place where they can generate income while avoiding the debilitating limitations of service-sector work and the patronizing positioning of social assistance, the industry itself can be problematic. Income can vary widely, based on a whole series of factors, including region, gender, age, and racial distinctions. As well, the lack of safety on the streets can drive workers indoors, where they face disciplinary work structures without the protection of unions or workplace standards. However, sex industry workers continue to resist the restrictions on their income and independence by shifting work locations and talking back to clients and managers, among other modes of resistance.

How much money is made is, of course, highly variable, and depends on the type of work (indoor or street), what kind of day it is (in terms of clients, their demands, and their willingness to pay), and a sex worker's ability to hustle a client:

> There's some nights you don't make nothing. Then there's some nights, some times the guys try to rip you off. Like, excuse me, like you say a certain price, "Yeah, no problem, no problem," like, "I'll give you that." Then they try to beat you down lower ... 'Cause normally I wouldn't go any lower than twenty-five, thirty, forty dollars, you know. (Alison, Halifax)

Another explained that rates can go down over time, because of age and because of the relationships between clients and workers:

> I'll tell you what I find. When I first started, and I met a lot of men, it was like, and I don't know if it's 'cause we allow it or not, they're good to ya. And after a while, it sort of gets so that it's like they expect it and they, it's like one day you meet them and it's $20 and the next day, "Well, I only have $10." Then sometimes it's, can you do it for me tonight and I'll pay ya [later], and you get a lot of that after a while because they figure ... I think they figure you owe them. I get a lot of that now. (Brianna, Saint John)

One sex worker in Saint John confirmed that clients are constantly trying to lower the rates:

> Sometimes now, on cheque day or what do you call it, disability day or whatever, some guys only want to give you $10 or $5. (Deanna, Saint John)

In these instances, income is highly dependent on sex workers' willingness and ability to negotiate with clients. This ability is a product of both skill and structural factors. Indeed, the men and women we spoke with have a wide variety of techniques of resistance – hustling, negotiation, and arguing with clients; refusing clients; or voting with their feet by changing venues – for example, from street to escort or vice versa – that makes viewing them as victims of poverty an oversimplification.

When clients do not pay properly, remedial action sometimes has to be taken:

> I've been in the car before, too, when their pants are down around their ankles [and I've] reached for their wallet and stuff like that because, like, "Hey, I'm giving a blow job. You're giving me more than twenty bucks." (Robert, Moncton)

The partner of the sex worker quoted above confirmed that sometimes things have to be taken into the sex workers' own hands:

> The one time – actually, I did it twice – but the one time, the first time I ever did that though [take a client's wallet], the guy was an asshole to me. And he also lied to me and said that he had no money. I opened up his wallet and there was $140 in his wallet ... I felt bad for doing it. (Eric, Moncton)

On the streets, a few may opt to get around complicated negotiations with clients by combining petty crime with sex work. One respondent reported that she had shifted to escort work because "you can't make no kind of money on the streets unless you're into robbing people" (Tamara, Halifax). For a few sex workers, petty crime – taking clients' wallets or bank cards and PINs – has become an important source of supplemental income: "I'd – they'd be drunk – take them to the bank, whatever. Take the PIN number, take the card and do my thing" (Kisha, Halifax). Like many other techniques of resistance, this one had its drawbacks, not in the potential for arrest, since clients are often too embarrassed to report such incidents to police, but in the possibility of clients' seeking revenge. Several violent incidents of clients going after sex workers in revenge for being stiffed were reported during our field work in Saint John. Nonetheless, workers' willingness to take what they viewed as rightfully theirs if it was not forthcoming speaks to their resistance to being victimized.

Indeed, it is often assumed that, of all sex workers, those on the streets have the least negotiating power and are the most exploited and victimized by economic circumstance. Street-based workers are viewed as being forced onto the street and into remaining on the street by their poverty. However, we found that sex workers often make unmistakable choices between street and indoor work, and many move between types of sex industry work as another mechanism of resistance when conditions or income in one type of work prove inadequate.[23] In moving back and forth between different types of sex trade work, workers make choices based not only on income but on the conditions of work and the independence granted to workers in determining these conditions and incomes. Street-level work, contrary to general belief, is sometimes considered the best in terms of independence of work and ability to generate income.[24] Indoor work – in escort services or massage parlours – can mean higher incomes and greater safety to sex workers, but it also means entering into an employee-employer relationship that can be unduly constraining and can actually limit or fix potential incomes. It is the constraints of workplace discipline – the attempt to render the worker a passive bearer of the rules and regulations of the workplace – and, most importantly, the ability of management to constrain sex workers' income and determine the amount of work that will be done for what price that some workers feel is too high a cost in exchange for the relative safety of indoor work. Some of the sex workers we spoke with choose to work on the street because of these limitations in indoor work:

> Working the street is better money than working in an escort service ... Because who in their right mind is going to have sex for a half hour for thirty bucks? (Megan, Halifax)

Another confirmed:

> I mean, inside you're a little bit safe, and so I would prefer that, the safety aspect. But the streets: you have more control over everything and it's more money ... Now with the services, there are so many things set in place where this one cost is for this, and you have to give this service, and you can't ask extra. On the street it's like ya can get forty bucks and [then say], "Well, oh no; that's another twenty." "Well, that's another twenty." And you just keep getting up there and up there. Well, you can't do that in the services. There's not as much money to be made. (Katie, Halifax)

Indoor work, therefore, can limit the potential of these income-maximizing strategies since prices are set by management and income is more dependent on the number of clients than it is on the street. As a receptionist at a massage parlour commented,

> I've seen them make anywhere from – jeez, one day a girl, the last day she worked she didn't make anything. She had no trick whatsoever. There were only four calls in the entire day, and the other girl did them. And other days I've seen them make $600. (Ashley, Fredericton)

Generating extra tips for indoor work depends on the clients and the workers' willingness to risk being disciplined by management if they are caught – for they would have made the sex for exchange overt, which management desperately wants to avoid in order to ensure that it cannot be charged with "keeping a common bawdy house."[25] As another indoor worker explained:

> You can manipulate some of them, but if they're regulars and they know – you know what I mean? [If] they tip you, that's bad ... We're not supposed to ask for tips but ... well, we do ask 'cause how else are you really going to get your money, right? Of course you're going to hustle the men to get your money, right? But we had to sign a piece of paper stating that we know we're not allowed because therefore it's on the big boss man's head. So, as long as that's clear, if the police ever did happen – they don't 'cause most of them go there [as clients] – so if it happens it wouldn't be on their [the owners'] heads. It would be our own responsibility. (Bonnie, Moncton)[26]

Sex workers, therefore, have to trade off income maximization and independence for decreased risk of arrest and, as we shall see in the next chapter, of violence.

There is money to be made in the sex trade and exotic dancing, money that can be generated relatively quickly and as needed. At one level, we can see that, in relative terms, it is better money than many people, particularly women, in the Maritimes can make. There are, however, limitations on this money, and it is by no means guaranteed. As we saw above, these incomes are highly variable and subject to the whims of clients (although sex workers' negotiation skills mediate this). There are other potential limitations. Indoor workers, in particular, face a series of managerial constraints on their money-making ability, and a number of the workers we spoke with struggled with addictions that sometimes shifted their relationship to the work and their ability to keep or control their money. The variability in income within the trade can generate a great deal of stress, but it is balanced against the hope that larger rather than smaller amounts can be generated, and against the flexibility of the work itself.[27] Indeed, security of income is directly traded for independence, as women switch to work in strip clubs or escort services, where there is at least a perception of higher possible income and a reality of stronger workplace discipline.

Various elements of the indoor trade can eat into a worker's earnings. Strippers pay fees at some clubs, and escorts face fines at some agencies. An escort worker can be charged $25 for refusing a client or for failing to punch her time card. There are also fines for lateness, and a deposit (sometimes as much as $500) has to be made with the service when a worker starts her ten-day shift. The work days at massage parlours are very long. Workers need to be on the premises from 11 or 11:30 AM to 5 AM. However, most workers don't return to duty for another four to six weeks. Workers also face the problems of any of those serving in an informal and largely illegal trade. For example, they can be taken advantage of by employers or other staff:

> The new girl, the one who just arrived the day before I did, she – I was positive – she gave the manager $1,900 to put in the safe deposit box. That's the number that was in my head after watching her count the money ... but I was off all week, until my next shift. And as the shift ended on Sunday, they had to give her her deposit and money and stuff. So [the manager] gave it to her, and then the manager left. And she pulled out her money and she was counting it, and she had $1,060. She didn't say anything and I turned to her and said, "Didn't you have $1,900?" And she's like, "Oh my God, is that the number you thought too?" I said, "I was sure of it actually, that's the only number that jumps in my head, plus your deposit, plus this, plus that – $1,900." And she had no record of it, so she couldn't prove it. So it was like she was sucking and fucking for free. Nasty, nasty circumstance. What can you do? (Ashley, Fredericton)

One interviewee quit an escort agency for similar reasons:

> Yes, I have worked escort. It was three years ago I worked escort for as long as eight months and then I got out of it ... because the girl I was working for was crooked and started ripping people off and I just didn't want any part of that. (Brianna, Saint John)

This kind of exploitation is not unique to the sex trade, although the illegality of the trade contributes to the non- or minimal regulation of employment so that workers have little chance of taking employers to court or launching complaints with unions. Stories of companies that fold in the night and leave workers unpaid are legion. One interviewee who had tried to leave the streets through a job in construction related:

> In Calgary I gave up doing the streets for two weeks and I was insulating condominiums. And I was getting paid ten bucks an hour ... and I wasn't

using, wasn't on the street. I said, "I'm gonna get out [of the sex trade]. I'll start off with a room. I'll get the things, the material things I need and that, then I'll get an apartment and this is the end of 'er, right here." Yeah, and it went by ... the first week [I] didn't get paid, okay. The second week [I] don't get paid. So anyway, I'm there, pacing, pacing, and waiting for my pay; and the man didn't even show up. Nobody ever, ever seen him since. Then I said, "I'm back on the streets." (Juliana, Saint John)

Costs can also be high while the workers are indoors:

I know that one girl that had been there for ten days spent over $700 just on takeout; and one girl spent probably about $200. [She] spent at least $50 in delivery one day alone, just looking for this, looking for that, looking for this, looking for that. 'Cause once you get in there, and you're in that environment, like, there is no concept of reality, there really isn't. (Ashley, Fredericton)

These problems are not seen as inherent to indoor work so much as a function of bad management or a failure to understand the reality of women's lives when setting up the conditions of work. One escort worker, for example, laid out practical steps she would take, if she were manager, to rectify some of these issues:

I would supply the food for the girls because if you're in a booking for ten days most of your money is going to go towards food, you know, and stuff like that – shampoo, conditioner, soap, you know, makeup, condoms ... Yeah, I would supply that, therefore, they have no worries about ... they don't have enough money. 'Cause most girls have children to feed, that's why they do most of what they do, because of their children. So you have to take into consideration for that. And I wouldn't [charge a deposit], because if you're on a booking you have to pay up to $500 in deposit. (Bonnie, Moncton)

However, several workers were clear that bosses in the sex trade, even in the potentially restrictive escort and massage industry, face a certain labour resistance – that the workers can and do negotiate conditions to a certain degree. As one escort worker described one of the owners, whom she did not particularly care for:

Like, he is lenient to a certain extent because if he disrespects the girls – you know what I mean – if he's not lenient to a certain extent, they're not going to work for him and he'll lose all his good girls. (Bonnie, Moncton)

Another stated that she is careful in choosing which escort services she works for, to ensure that she has maximum control. In particular, she avoids those that penalize workers for, for example, refusing clients:

> I go with the services that's not going to get mad at me for nothing, 'cause I'm the woman, I'm the person who's out there making my money and you're not taking it for any other reason. If I want to work, I'm going to work; if I don't want to work, I'm not going to work, and no one's going to control that. (Patricia, Saint John)

Even within the more constraining field of indoor work, sex workers maintain a sense of their ability to negotiate and resist working conditions.

Indeed, the ability to be one's own boss in the sex trade is a major bonus of the job for some of our respondents, which speaks to their often independent and capable character. One identified working in the Maritimes as better than working in central Canada because it offers more independence:

> You're your own boss, you set your own hours, your own rates. You don't have someone telling ya, "You get out there and make this amount, or you're gonna get your legs broken," stuff like that. 'Cause I know that's what they do in Ontario. They didn't get me, but I knew some girls that were working for some guys, and they wanted me to, and I wouldn't. I wouldn't do that. (Violet, Saint John)

Pimping was not viewed as a major issue by our interviewees, as we shall see in the next chapter.[28]

Further, the income in the sex trade in the Atlantic provinces does not compare to the kind of money that can be made in the larger centres such as Toronto, Montreal, Vancouver, and even Ottawa. A number of our respondents had taken part in the Maritime tradition of "going down the road" or making their way to central or western Canada to make money and to seek the bright lights of the big city. Indeed, while the appearance of young Nova Scotian women in Toronto in the mid-1990s sparked a panic among the general public over trafficking between Toronto and the Maritimes, in fact, many of the women and young men we spoke with referred to this movement as simply part of a traditional migration pattern. Some travelled more frequently and widely – partly to work and partly simply to travel. It was understood by those who had worked outside the Maritimes that it was harder to make money in the Maritimes. This seemed to be particularly true for the male respondents. One male worker reported being able to bring in $10,000 a month in Montreal, while his highest income in Halifax was $2,000 a week.[29] Another explained that the better income was in part a product of the larger client base in the bigger cities:

> In Ottawa, you're done one client and you're right out to another one. You're done one, you go home for like ten minutes, fifteen minutes, you clean up and whatever, and you're out again. Sometimes you come back with one thousand, two thousand dollars a night. (Jason, Moncton)

His income in escort in Ottawa was

> $250 an hour and then $30 for the guy that I'm working for, and $20 for the driver. So I walk out with $200 in my pocket ... Like, here in Moncton I have tried ... and all they were going to give me is $50. Fifty dollars an hour ... Fuck that. I could stay home and make more money than that. (Jason, Moncton)

Yet another compared his street income in Toronto to that in Moncton (where he had returned after being mugged on the job in Toronto):

> Moncton is very small and there is really not much of anything out there. You would get maybe twenty bucks now, and in Toronto, anything goes for eighty. A client in Toronto would be starting out at $80 and moving up. And in Toronto, it's a lot bigger. (Marc, Moncton)

Women also reported lower earnings in the Maritimes than elsewhere. One worker who had worked in Alberta reported:

> Like here, $20 is the most that johns will pay for any type of deal. Out there [Calgary], sometimes, he'd set up dates [and] it'd be $500 between the two of us that we'd split, me and the other girl, $250 [each]. (Jill, Saint John)

According to one exotic dancer, the working arrangements in the clubs are more exploitative in the Maritimes:

> Working in the strip clubs down in Dallas and in New York and Saint Louis, all them, like it's a lot better because when you're dancing on stage they can throw money on the stage, they can stick it in your bra, stick it in your panties. You keep it. But when you're on stage up here in Moncton, no, you don't get paid. You don't get paid anything for being on the stage. And you have to dance for everybody, you dance for one person but everybody else is seeing it you know? (Alexis, Moncton)

These free stage shows minimize a worker's opportunity for the lucrative private dances. But the Maritimes is home for many of our respondents and, as for many Maritimers in other forms of work, stints of work elsewhere are seen as temporary; life in the Maritimes is preferable because of the support of family and friends. A number of the women were mothers who wanted to stay close to their children. Others had elderly parents in the region and so had decided to work in the Maritimes despite the loss of income. Some racialized women also complained that young white women had an advantage in attracting clients and, therefore, in generating income. However, white privilege is not unique to the sex industry.[30]

Where workers do see a problem unique to the sex industry is in the stigma attached to the trade, which contributes to violence and mistreatment, most importantly (as we shall see in the next chapter), but also to difficulty leaving the trade should the worker so desire. For example, there is the difficulty of moving into straight jobs when there is a gap in a worker's resumé because s/he was working only in the sex trade.[31] In the small cities of the Maritimes, a reputation that follows former sex workers is often an impediment:

> My life is kinda still hard, my name is still out there, and everywhere that I've went to apply for ... I've went to apply for two jobs, as soon as I said my name, they said, "You're an addict aren't you? You're a prostitute." I went for apartments not too long ago, which really frustrates me sometimes, 'cause I feel like giving up and just going back to that life. At least I felt I belonged with the other girls. Now it's like, I'm an outcast and I went to get an apartment and I told her my name and she gave me the apartment and everything else and I left, and she gave a call to my friend that I gave her the number and said, "She's a prostitute isn't she? She's into drugs." And he said, "Not anymore, she's been clean eighteen months." And she said, "We can't take the chance of her wrecking this place or stealing or taking stuff out of here." So it took me a long time to get the apartment that I have. (Beth, Saint John)

The continuing stigma of the trade is considered to be a barrier to moving into other work and the straight social world:

> Yeah, it's just, you know, all that, you start to lose your self-esteem after a while, you really do. You start to lose your self-esteem like that's all you deserve and that's all you're good enough to do. That's all, and then when you do try to get a regular job and they check out your history, once they see something like that on your record [prostitution charges], your chances are very slim of getting into any kind of job anyway. (Valerie, Halifax)

Another interviewee, on the other hand, pointed to the stigma attached to transsexualism as a barrier to straight jobs, a barrier she could transcend in sex work:

> To be very honest with you, I'm very proud of being a hooker and I mean I've had some amazing jobs in my life. I've been very lucky and, ah, I love this job. See, when I became "Susy," then with all my papers and certificates and everything that I had, it didn't mean anything. It was my face that meant ... I was a transsexual. So I totally gave up trying to get a job because, you know, after a while, getting your, ah, resumés thrown in your face and stuff like this you say what the hell ... so that's basically what I did. (April, Halifax)

But for a few who had left the trade, particularly youth, straight work was more appealing. As one young man stated:

> When I look back on it now, even if we [my partner and I] were to ever break up and I was to be in [financial trouble], I don't think I would ever do it again. I don't think I would ever step back on the street. (Robert, Moncton)

His partner, who had also worked in the trade, concurred:

> I'd rather work for twelve hours a day than go out stand for an hour in the cold. It's degrading. (Eric, Moncton)

Others recognized that full-time legitimate work could offer the advantage of benefits and union protections. But even for those who found the work degrading, there was grim humour about the reality of most service jobs available for women, especially the domestic work that has become the lot of a number of Afro-Canadian women in Halifax:

> *Interviewer: Okay, so what I should ask you first is, how long have you been working in the trade?*
> **Yeah, too many years. Twenty some years.**
> *Interviewer: Okay, so you've got a good long view of what's been going on.*
> **Oh yeah, real good long view. Front row centre.**
> *Interviewer: So over those twenty years, what have been the best things about the job?*
> **The money. That's it. There's no other upsides to it. I don't see them. The worst part is dealing with them people, them jerks, them dicks. Nasty people. I don't know. Some of them are okay but it's just, I don't know, I just don't like the job itself. To me it's a job. It's like going out and cleaning somebody's toilet. You know, seriously. It's a job. It's a dirty job and somebody has to do it, but that's the way I look at it, it's a job. I don't know too many people that like their cleaning job.** (Heidi, Halifax)

Thus, for many sex industry workers, the drawbacks and barriers experienced in the industry are similar to those experienced in other types of work, though the advantages of the work in terms of pay and independence can outweigh those potential problems. Addressing these problems means addressing the conditions of work within the trade, rather than simply pushing women out of the work itself. Sex workers' own words in analyzing their situations shows us how they resist the constraints on them and talk back to those who would treat them as undeserving.

Addictions, Money, and Sex Work
In recent years, addictions rather than poverty have become the most commonly understood reason people enter the trade. But discussions of the role of addictions often fall into the same traps as discussions of the role of poverty. Indeed, there is an increasingly problematic conflation of addictions and sex work that indicates a need for more careful analysis of the relationship between the two. The meaning and role of addictions, like those of poverty, have often been assumed rather than investigated, and yet, careful analysis once again warns us that these assumptions might be problematic. Certainly, studies differ as to the extent of addictions among sex workers, reflecting differential sources of data (e.g., police versus self-reporting, street-focus versus indoor).[32] Shaver observes that substance use varies by region, with workers in the Maritimes reporting higher usage than do workers elsewhere in Canada.[33] And, certainly, the relationship between addictions and sex work cannot be deduced from the mere presence of addictions among some sex workers. A number of our interviewees talked about having addictions or struggling with them in the past, but, again, our sample is likely over-representative in this regard. At the same time, these interviewees made it clear that the relationship between sex work and addictions is often less one of cause than of overlap, and sometimes less problematic than it might first appear. Indeed, addictions are not viewed as necessarily meaning a loss of control or income; rather, addictions are frequently managed in such a way as to ensure that control is maintained, and only the loss of that control – not the addiction itself – is seen as problematic, which, as several pointed out, is a condition they share with many other Canadians, including professionals and the wealthy. Overall, sex workers resist the too easy conflation of addictions, sex work, and lack of control.

Certainly, addictions can mean that, despite the relatively large sums being earned, workers have little to show in terms of savings. And for some of those who are heavily addicted to a substance before entering the trade, the issue is perhaps best understood as sex for exchange (i.e., drugs or drug money), not sex work per se:

> When I first started, my head was ... you get very numb from that stuff, from crack. I never ever thought of, that you weren't allowed to do it. It never ever crossed my mind that I could be picked up for prostitution. To me, I wasn't doing anything wrong. And I've seen me in the run of a night, get $800, and every penny of it went to the crack. (Beth, Saint John)

For this respondent, as for others, addictions and sex work were fused and only by exiting both was she able to regain a sense of control.

For others still, the relationship between sex work and addictions was much less determined. Importantly, in line with sex workers' general sense of independence, it is the loss of control over one's work and money, and not the addiction itself, that is seen as the problem – when a worker becomes, in the eyes of others, "a crack whore." As one woman said:

> Like I do crack, but I ain't no crack whore. Some guy said to me, "You give me some pussy and I'll fucking smoke a fucking half a gram with ya." I said, "Excuse me, you give me a gram and I'll fucking do it for ya. Because I ain't doing it for half a gram." (Megan, Halifax)

Her continued ability to negotiate the terms of her work was what she considered most important. Addictions per se are not the problem, but the potential loss of control is. Others explained that their use of some of their money from their trade for drugs does not mean they exchange sex for drug money only:

> Just because we are working the street, right ... some girls, yeah, they all are about the crack, and the alcohol, and whatever, right? Yeah, I work and, yeah, I buy fucking about fifty dollars' worth of crack a day or maybe about thirty dollars' worth of Dilaudids. That ain't nothing. That's one day. With the rest I just really sit down eat, have fun, just ... I just have fun. (Megan, Halifax)

Indeed, many manage their substance use so that it does not interfere with their work (for example, by using only when they are not working).

There certainly seemed to be self-esteem issues for those who found that they could not control their money because of addictions. When this happened, workers felt much less in control of their lives, had much less self-respect, and were much unhappier with being involved in the trade. But they also pointed out that they were similarly unhappy when, for example, bureaucratic strictures made them unable to control their income:

> See, I don't like giving nobody my money; it's bad enough I gotta give dope dealers my money. If I could take my money and go buy groceries,

instead of waiting for my welfare cheque, my disability cheque, no problem. I don't want to give nobody my money. That's my money. I'm out there blowin' or suckin' or whatever. That's my money. (Tara, Halifax)

For this sex worker, waiting for the cheque is as bad as having drug dealers take her money; that is, it is her lack of control over her money, whether because of drugs or red tape, that is the source of frustration.

Waking up to the reality of the costs of drug addiction can be a motivator for change. One worker explained how she kicked a crack addiction:

I knew I had an income tax cheque coming for $1,700 and I knew I had a choice. I could either sign the cheque and give it to the dope dealer, or I can go buy stuff for my house. 'Cause there's no point pretending I'm only gonna spend a hundred there. So, I know the money's coming but it's not here yet. There's a four-day wait to decide what am I gonna do. I made that decision [and] I went and bought myself some weed, and beer. And I had some groceries, and I locked myself in my house for four days. I wouldn't do a job or nothing, 'cause if I had the cash I'd go and buy the dope. After four days I had my cheque come, and I said to my girlfriend, "I want you to come with me, 'cause if I go myself, and I've even got $20 change, I'm gonna buy another stone." I spent every penny on my house, right down to toilet paper. And I never had 50¢ to buy a 50¢ ticket. That's the only thing I knew. I wasn't giving that $1,700 cash all in one lump. 'Cause when it come a hundred here and a hundred there, it doesn't look so bad. But a lump of seventeen $100 bills and I know it's gonna be gone in one day. I'm gonna have nothing to show for it. I couldn't do it to myself. And I haven't smoked since. (Belinda, Halifax)

Some argued that the easier access to, and different kinds of, drugs on the streets has undercut prices and professionalism in the sex trade, but they also indicated that the problem is in part a lack of management that coincided with the end of the pimping era:

It's got better and worse on two levels. Now, when there was a lot of pimps out there – now there's not any out there – it was kind of rough. But now it's worse, because most of them that don't have pimps they might ... They did better with the pimps, 'cause at least they [were] handed out $20 a day. Now all they're doing is running crack ... [There's] a lot of drug dealers today. It's more about drugs now. It's not about buying a car or doing this job. It's about getting high now ... The whole concept has changed. You know, twenty years ago, when we went out, you could never find a hooker after twelve o'clock. Really. And that's, you know, I think that's the part that really got you hooked. 'Cause you could go in at seven o'clock and be gone by eleven o'clock with five or six hundred dollars every night if you didn't lollygag and fool around fighting the cops. But now it's three and four o'clock in the morning and you're still trying to get a hundred bucks. Like what is that bullshit? ... But the industry, as far as money goes, has dropped substantially; because there're a lot of them out there that don't care. Twenty bucks and they don't care. Ten bucks ... I don't know. That causes a lot of problems, right? But that's life, you know. (Heidi, Halifax)

One escort worker used this technique to manage her money from an escort agency while she was addicted:

Well, I'll tell you, for me what I used to do and being addicted, you know, I didn't use for that full two weeks [at the escort service] because I'll tell ya, there are only a couple [of customers] that you can get away with using. The other ones are pretty particular, you know, and the customer's everything. Okay, now I have two weeks of money stored up. So I'd call ahead and make a reservation at a hotel, okay, for my own safety. I had an account that my mom was on one end and I was on the other. My mom had the bank card and I just made a deposit. Because, I mean, that way my mom, who knows I'm an addict – you know, I've been an addict since I was thirteen – so my mom would kind of regulate. So, you know, she'd be my daily limit. 'Cause there's ways to get around that ... So I kind a set up my little safety net there. (Dana, Halifax)

Alcohol abuse can be a problem for exotic dancers, since workers are sometimes encouraged to drink with clients.[34] One former exotic dancer explained that to make money in dance requires careful management with or without addictions:

Well, the main reason why I quit dancing [was addiction] ... I mean, mind you, I'd probably go back now if it weren't for my husband. Except this time I would really use my head. This time I would put the money in the bank account. I would leave the damn stuff in the bank account. Not touch it. I would actually not drink, just pretend I was – tell the bartender right out. (Colleen, Moncton)

Addictions may cost indoor sex workers and exotic dancers their jobs when management cracks down on drug or alcohol use. On the other hand, some sex workers on the street reported that those with addictions may actually make more money than do those without.

> I made more money when I was smoking cocaine then I can now, and it don't make sense. They should do a study on that. Watch one girl that's all dirty and you can tell they haven't been clean in days. And put someone else out there that looks nice and cleaned up. [The former will] make double her money. Don't ask me why, I don't know. When I was on cocaine I could get a date, go buy a twenty stone, go smoke it back there. I'd come out, get another date, and go down, get another stone, smoke it, come out, get another date. Now if I needed money to go pay the rent I'd stand there all night long, lucky to get a date or two. I don't know why. Ask any girl that you know [who] doesn't smoke and they'll tell you the same thing. The ones that smoke, just like that. And you can stand there and watch them go and it just sickens ya 'cause you know what they're gonna do with that money. They're just ... I have no idea why, I can't fathom it myself ... You just watch the young girls. They could be old, a hundred years old with a cane. If they do a hit of crack they can go make money. I don't know if it's the look of desperation or whatever it is, but believe me you are very enthused to get more money 'cause you want that high ... I can't explain it. (Belinda, Halifax)

The very availability of large amounts of money in sex work can be part of the problem:

> The money's crazy, but then the money gets to ya. Once you have so much money, you don't know what to do with it ... And my problem was – why I got out of it when I was out there – because I was smoking too much and I was smoking too much crack. The money got to me, because I'd go to a client and I'd get the money, and I'd go right to my dealer. I'd spend all the money and I'd just be waiting, you know, edging to go again. That was my problem. (Jason, Moncton)

But, as the same respondent commented, the "waste" of the money may also reflect the illegality of the trade and not the tendency of the trade to generate drug addiction:

> [Revenue Canada is] ... coming back saying where are you getting your money? And you can't tell them you're a sex worker 'cause that's all under the table. Then they're going to take it all from you. They're going to seize it, 'cause they're going to think it's the profit of narcotics. Seriously, it comes right down to it. So what else are you going to spend your money on? What else? If you're going to buy that stuff, you're going to get busted for it. What's the sense of doing it? Why not spend your money on drugs? Is that a good point? Is this not a good point? When you're listening to

that tape, you can add that in there, because that's a good point. (Jason, Moncton)

Again it must be noted that addictions can be a problem in other professions and walks of life. As one respondent pointed out:

> I mean, there's doctors and lawyers that do drugs and they make the money to do it, you know what I mean? And if they were to lose their jobs, what would they be doing for it? It's true. I know a lawyer in X that probably spends his whole friggin' week's wealth on it. (Kendra, Saint John)

Clearly, the relationship between addictions and sex work is much more complicated than cause and effect, but it is also true that addictions can mean that the money disappears quickly. Again, not only is this not unique to sex work, but a number of sex workers we spoke with had found ways to overcome this potential barrier. One of the main concerns addicted sex workers have is for the loss of control over their work. That is, many sex workers do not view addictions and sex work as necessarily intertwined; rather, they see addiction as a factor that can affect conditions of work by making it more difficult for a worker to control her income and pace of work.

Minimum Wage and Service-Sector Work

> You work your butt off for minimum wage, $6 an hour, you know what I mean? That's crazy. (Kendra, Saint John)

Certainly, there are caveats to the good money that can be made in sex work. However, many of these caveats apply to other forms of work as well. Most of our interviewees had weighed sex work and its advantages and disadvantages against other forms of work and found that sex work, overall, was an optimal work choice. Maybe it was not what they had originally intended to do or what they would ultimately like to be doing (although it certainly was for some), but, upon careful consideration and experience of other options, it was the best choice in the circumstances. What most of the workers we talked to faced, as an alternative means of generating income, was work in the growing service-oriented, minimum-wage sector, which carries many of the costs and few of the benefits of sex work. In particular, what many sex workers disliked about minimum-wage work was, along with the low pay, the workplace discipline and control that limited their independence and attempted to force them into the straitjacket of cheap labour. Many explained how, given that the downsides of sex work were likely to be experienced in other service-sector and minimum-wage jobs, their most likely other route, sex work, was the more lucrative option. Even more importantly, many of those who had worked in the service-sector and minimum-wage economy found the way they were treated in these jobs and the constraints placed on them unacceptable. Sex work, on the other hand, provided relative independence. That is, what the women and men whom we spoke with were resisting were the attempts to render them passive labourers and, therefore, impoverished labourers, in the capitalist system.

Many of the interviewees reported working in other jobs either in the past or currently, simultaneously with sex work, and many were familiar with the possible incomes that could be generated through straight jobs in the Maritimes economy, including service-sector and personal-service jobs, manual labour, and clerical work. As this sex worker states:

> Oh, Christ. I worked at a bakery once and let me tell ya, three and a half months ... and I'm not anyone special, but I'd never want a straight job again. I worked for minimum wage to be bossed around and in the end I said to her [the boss], "You know how much money I'm fuckin' missing sitting here with you. You're paying me five something an hour to sit here and listen to your fucking ignorance." Those were my exact words, I know I'm quitting anyway. "You can't fire me 'cause I'm quitting." And then they didn't want you to leave on the lunch break, I figured you get a fifteen-minute break in the morning, a half-hour lunch, and a fifteen-minute break in the afternoon. I'm thinking, okay, I can set my dates up during lunch, that gives me an hour. Oh, no, no, no, no. You have to take a fifteen here, and a fifteen and half hour, and you can't leave the place.
>
> Three and a half months, that's all I could handle it. I missed three hundred and some dollars every two weeks. When they gave out the paycheque I thought they were missing a one on the front. I didn't realize how much it was, I said, "Oh, fuck. Oh, no, no, no, no." Three and a half months, I couldn't do it no more, I tried, I tried. I can't do it. If it was children or something like that, and they paid me good, I'd love it. I love kids or animals or elderly people, that I could handle, if the pay was good – but not for five something an hour. I couldn't live on that. Well, by the time I pay my rent and do everything else, I'd rather sit on welfare 'cause at least with that I get $251 to spend after my rent's paid. Oh, no, no, no. I don't want no job, I don't want no job. (Belinda, Halifax)

Several of our interviewees had worked in service-sector jobs such as fast-food counter and kitchen help, waiting on tables, sales, homecare, and elder care. That sex work is a rational income-generating strategy becomes apparent when these other options are examined. Half of the women working in Nova Scotia, for example, are employed in the clerical/sales/service sector, the lowest paying of all categories.³⁵ The average income of women in sales or service is $17,261 (or $330 a week) and, in clerical, $23,763 (or $457 a week) before taxes.³⁶ Take-home pay would of course be lower. Once again, sex workers, under the right conditions, could potentially make this kind of money much more quickly.

Many of the jobs available to women and youth in the Maritimes are minimum- or just above minimum-wage jobs. It is these jobs to which most of those in the Maritimes without post-secondary education (and even some of those with such education) can aspire. While many of the sex workers we interviewed had not completed high school, this does not make them an unusual group in the Maritimes.³⁷ Rates of non-completion of high school are high in the Maritimes. In the 1990s, about one-third of Saint Johners and Haligonians had less than a grade twelve education, according to the Canadian Council on Social Development (CCSD).³⁸ One response to the growing rate of unemployment and the decline of the primary sector, on which the Maritimes has traditionally depended, is the move toward a knowledge-based economy, championed most significantly by the McKenna government in New Brunswick. Government grants and tax relief to private investors has resulted in the mushrooming of call centres and service sector industries that have become primary employers even for university graduates. These are, however, among the lowest paid industries, most likely to be non-unionized, part-time, and low or minimum wage. As one ex-stripper/sex worker related:

> There's one woman at my work [a call centre], she's a psychology major, she has her Master's. And she's working at a call centre for $8.00 an hour. I think she's making a little bit more now 'cause she's been there for a long time. I think she's making $8.40 an hour. Like, still, you spent $50,000 on university, to make $8.40 an hour? (Colleen, Moncton)

Or, as the university-graduate receptionist in a massage parlour, who makes $7.50 an hour, put it:

> What's weird for me personally is that every time that I'm in that environment, I can't help but to think, why not? You know, it's ten days, $3,000 to $5,000. It's such a plausible way to make money. Then I go home that night, and I'll be like, "I sat there for the same amount of time as they did, I made $60; and they made $500." I can't help but to consider it. (Ashley, Fredericton)

Given the low level of wages in the Maritimes, sex work is a comparably good work choice. In New Brunswick, according to Ken Battle's study, the minimum wage hovers just under $6.00 an hour (in 2002 dollars), the fourth lowest rate in Canada. Nova Scotia pays its minimum-wage workers even less at $5.85 an hour.[39] However, minimum-wage workers are overrepresented in New Brunswick, which has the second highest incidence of minimum-wage workers (6 percent) in Canada, most of whom (61 percent) are women.[40] Further, as Thom Workman's study shows, not only are minimum wages low in Atlantic Canada, they are declining in real terms, that is, once inflation is accounted for.[41] The income of single persons living on minimum wage is sufficient to meet only about three-quarters of their living expenses.[42] And, as Thom Workman points out, this is the "best case scenario," where a worker is supporting only her/himself and not a child or children (and, we might add, is working full time).[43] Women, who are most likely to be caring for children, are also most likely to remain in jobs that are minimum wage or close to minimum wage longer than do their male counterparts.[44] As Workman details:

> A disproportionate number of women work at rates close to the minimum wage in all four Atlantic provinces. Moreover, the median hourly wage for women in each province was never more than $5.40 above the minimum wage ... It is not merely the case that the average wages of women are lower than those of their male counterparts, but rather that so many female workers throughout the region are working in the low end, low wage jobs ... The conclusion that women disproportionately bear the burden of low wage work in Atlantic Canada is inescapable.[45]

Workers' resistance to this neo-liberal age of unlivable minimum wages is often to refuse the work altogether. As Workman observes, there are indeed minimum-wage jobs that go unfilled in Atlantic Canada, but "working people know that low wages often do not go far enough. And when one factors in the bad hours, the child care problems, the workplace harassment and so forth, it just isn't worth it."[46] Many of the sex workers we spoke with had recognized this reality and opted for a more entrepreneurial method of survival.

Sex work also provides that other key ingredient: flexibility. It is important to remember that, for women in particular, it is the combination of time constraints and minimum wages that makes for particular economic hardship. According to one recent study, "For a single mother with one child in the workforce, it takes 73 hours of work per week at the minimum wage to reach the LICO [low income cut-off]."[47] Women throughout Canada have often turned to, or been forced into, part-time work – with its low pay and lack of benefits – in order to cope with the demands of family. In New Brunswick, women make up the majority of part-time workers at over 72 percent.[48] Similarly, self-employment (or "self-account" work) has increasingly become a strategy of Canadian women faced with double days, the burden of which only increases as the welfare state shrinks.[49] According to Karen Hadley's research, women in the Atlantic provinces in non-standard – that is, not full-time/full-year – work were more likely than anyone else in Canada to have income below the LICO.[50]

Sex work, on the other hand, provides both the required flexibility and potentially higher incomes. Many of our respondents have children (although they are not necessarily living with them), and a number took care of sick or elderly parents. One woman explained how she was the primary caregiver for her ailing mother:

> *Interviewer: Is she dependent on you?*
> **Yeah, she is. She really is. It's like I'm the mother, she's the daughter. She didn't raise me, she put me in a foster home because of her MS and none of her family don't do nothing for her, so it's like, it's all on me. And that's another thing, if she doesn't have something in the house, and she needs it, I'll go and work and get it for her. So really, you might say she's my pimp, really, when you really break it down.** (Katrina, Halifax)

Another (Valerie, Halifax) drove back and forth between Montreal and Halifax to care for her aging mother. Sex work, which can allow women to make relatively large amounts of money in relatively short periods of time and which can also be made to fit their schedules, provides a way around the constraints of minimum-wage work.

While incomes in sex work are unpredictable, so are incomes in minimum-wage shift-based service work. One sex worker who had done several jobs in the service industry complained: "I was supposed to be hired under full time, and I was only getting part-time hours" (Bonnie, Moncton). The prerogative of managers in, for example, assigning hours is a major source of complaint for many of those – particularly youth – who work in the service sector and who find that their hours and incomes can fluctuate wildly, depending, in part, on how well they can get in with managers.[51] As a CCSD report has noted, "A growing number of young, involuntary part time workers face jobs that are organized into split shifts, for example, in fast food establishments where employees are called in for a few hours only around mealtimes. Such jobs typically have no benefits, no training beyond an initial orientation, and no means of advancing to better jobs. Even in more skilled sectors, the trend towards using contract and temporary staff grew over the 1990s."[52]

The demands of minimum-wage work, in terms of its physical and emotional tolls, are also weighed against the possible benefits and costs of work in the sex industry. One young mother called moving from waitressing in a strip club to dancing as the "easy, lazy way out of waitressing" (Audrey, Fredericton). Another woman reported:

I've worked at McDonald's, I've worked at call centres, I've like, you know ... mowed lawns, shovelled driveways, type thing, you know what I mean.
Interviewer: You've done those minimum-wage McDonald's jobs, and if you had to weigh them one against the other, how do they compare?
Well, really, working at McDonald's is the perfect example. You still got all the [backbiting]. It's all younger people who know each other; it's even more immature because they're so much younger, so it's worse. Even the managers themselves – you know first-hand, 'cause she works with you, right, at McDonald's – some of them will talk behind your back, you know like ... You got to put up with customers' bullshit, and you only get paid minimum wage. Your feet are tired, your back. We [at the escort service] get to kick back in our lazy boy and watch soaps or something.
(Bonnie, Moncton)

While such backbiting can also be experienced in the escort setting, this respondent felt that the situation was easier to avoid in sex work (by hanging out with the receptionist or watching television). Arlie Hochschild's work on the emotional labour of service-sector workers, such as airline staff, is now a common reference point in the sex work literature. Her work shows that the presumed emotional burden of sex workers is shared across service industries, where workers are expected to appear to enjoy their work and their customers, despite what they might actually feel.[53] Thus, in terms of emotional or psychological stress, sex work and service work can be quite similar.

The physical burdens of sex work can also be similar to those of other industries. Frances Shaver has drawn out the similarities in the physical complaints of sex workers with those of other workers.[54] Some observers claim that the importance of youthfulness and good looks in the sex industry is problematic. Indeed, this is the case for some, particularly in the male trade and strip work. A thirty-four-year-old male sex worker reported that, while he could still make between $50 and $60 a night, his income had declined with age. As Chris Bruckert points out, work in exotic dancing (and, we could add, the sex trade) is parallel to that of many working-class jobs in that it demands physical labour that relies on youthfulness and has high health costs.[55] Hustling for tips as wait staff also becomes more difficult as workers get older. But attractiveness can be compensated for with skill in both the sex and service trades. And, certainly, it appears that, given the mean age (32) of our respondents, the amount of money one could make appeared to them to rely more on one's skills in managing clients so that they pay as much as possible, rather than on passive characteristics such as beauty or youthfulness. The tendency to dismiss sex workers as declining with age reflects society's general unwillingness to recognize the amount of labour and skill that goes into the work. Thus, the physical and emotional burdens of sex work do not necessarily make it a less attractive form of work, given that physical and emotional stressors are common in other forms of work as well.

The authority structure of bosses and managers is also a source of dissatisfaction with straight jobs. Indeed, it is this frustration with the control exercised by management – particularly the more social disciplinary mechanisms, or having to "listen to [her] fucking ignorance," as the former bakery worker put it – that epitomizes many sex workers' frustration with straight work in general. A young male escort worker was unambiguous about his impatience with workplace authority:

> I won't even work for anything under $10 an hour, I won't. 'Cause what's the sense of busting my balls for that? And listen to somebody yelling at you, telling you what to do. 'Cause I can't take authority from nobody, I can't let nobody tell me what to do. This job [sex work], that's how it turned me. I'm kinda my own boss, and I get so much good money off it. No, it [a straight job] just won't work. (Jason, Moncton)

What sex workers are refusing in refusing straight work is not just the conditions of work but the disciplinary structures that attempt to control their work and render them passive and cheap labour.

Comparative Incomes: Social Assistance

The other source of income to which some of our interviewees – among whom poor women and youth were over-represented – could turn was social assistance. However, it too was seen as having many drawbacks, being insufficient to meet survival needs and demeaning at the same time. Once again, what many of our interviewees expressed was a resistance to being positioned as a vulnerable person, as someone who needs the guidance of policy experts and bureaucrats because of their inability to make or manage money and as someone who should be grateful for the help s/he receives. Most importantly, they resisted the way in which social assistance is designed to force them back into the labour market by keeping rates as low as possible – in the Maritimes, lower than the actual costs of living. They resisted this positioning most often by "talking back" to social workers and policy makers.

Most respondents reported receiving social assistance income that ranged from $200 a month to $535. This, however, reflects the bias of our sample, which was reached mostly through outreach services, so the respondents were most often women and youth who were already in contact with the system in various ways. For example, several of our respondents were receiving disability benefits for addictions. It should also be kept in mind that women are the majority of social assistance recipients in Nova Scotia, and, in New Brunswick, female single parents are more likely to be receiving assistance. Given the work options outlined above, plus the likely burden of child care, it is obvious why this is the case.[56] However, among our respondents, older, more independent workers and some escort and strip workers, like the majority of indoor workers, maintained a living income without assistance.

Some respondents combined social assistance with sex work, even though social assistance levels in Atlantic Canada are very low. This should not be surprising because, for example, New Brunswick has the lowest social assistance rates in Canada. Single employables receive the lowest amount at $264 a month.[57] Assistance rates throughout Atlantic Canada provide incomes that are well below the poverty line.[58] The gap between levels of income assistance and the poverty line is greatest for single persons, but there is also a gap of 30 to 40 percent for single parents, who are most likely to be women.[59] Workman argues that such low levels of income assistance are an attempt to drive Atlantic Canadians into accepting low-wage work that appears to provide an income that is at least higher than social assistance, but, as we have seen, in fact does not provide a living wage and adds further complications – such as child or elder care.[60]

Social assistance rarely provides people, particularly women with dependants, with sufficient income to cover even basic necessities. One young mother began strip work in Saint John to cover the extra costs of having a child:

> **It's cash in my pocket. Welfare doesn't know. It gives my son better clothes, better food ... I spend all my money on him.** (Jacqueline, Saint John)

One ex-sex worker in recovery from addiction reported:

> **I'm just on a disability. I get $485 a month, which is really hard, because I have a one-bedroom apartment, [to be] close to my kids. It's walking distance for them, and I pay $395, and I got $65 left, and it's whether, do I buy food with it, or do I pay bills with it?** (Beth, Saint John)

For youth, poverty and social assistance are major problems. According to the Canadian Council on Social Development, "The wage gap between young men and women is narrowing, mainly because young men's earnings have been falling ... Young men in their mid-20s earned approximately 20% less in the 1990s than those with equivalent education in the 1960s."[61] Youth unemployment fell to only 15 percent, compared to 7 percent for adults, in the 1990s, and remains highest among the fifteen- to nineteen-year-old group at 20 percent.[62] For the younger sex workers, those who started in sex work between the ages of sixteen and nineteen, the unavailability of social assistance was a major barrier. When youth do receive assistance, it is likely to be at the lowest possible rates, since they are viewed as potential workers. One seventeen-year-old former dancer refused income assistance:

> I have no income support at all. Welfare is a bitch ... They want to give me – because I'm seventeen years old – they want to give me $300 a month to stay in school, and I'm allowed to make $115 on the side. So altogether I'm only allowed to have $415 a month – and that is not even my rent, not even my rent, period. And that doesn't include lights, heat, groceries, like hygiene stuff, nothing ... I was accepted for it [assistance] and everything and he was like, "Bring in your last pay stub from the last time that you worked and then we'll start sending you the cheques and you let us know if anything changes." I never called them back. It was $415 a month. Who's gonna live off that? My cat wouldn't live off that. (Alexis, Moncton)

It is widely acknowledged that social assistance incomes are insufficient to provide even minimal survival. As two young male former sex workers in Moncton commented, after the rent is paid, there is very little left for food or other necessities:

> *Robert:* In Toronto at least I know the cost of living is higher but I mean you can still rent a room in Toronto for $300 a month. But they give you $675 if you're one person. And they break it down on your cheque: this month is January, you're going to need more money for this. So they give you more money in January. But here in Moncton, you get $300 a month and that's it ... really, $264. If you go in a rooming house you pay $250, which gives you $14 a month.
> *Eric:* You're lucky to find one for $200. The lowest rooming house I ever found was $190 and the room was like ...
> *Robert:* The size of this chair. (Robert and Eric, Moncton)

The Catch-22 of finding accommodation before Social Assistance will issue a cheque is often a problem. A young male sex worker who works in the trade for money to buy food and shelter commented:

> And like, social assistance is retarded here because you have to have an address in order to get a cheque and if you don't have an address, you can't get a cheque. But you can't get an address unless you get money, and you can't get money unless you have an address. And it's retarded because if you have no place to stay, you're stuck, unless someone wants to let you move in without paying the money. It just doesn't happen very often, it's thirty years [out-of-date]. It's bullshit. It's horrible.

> I had it before when I lived in Toronto. Like you get $195 just living on the street and if you give that to a landlord they'll let you move in, and they'll sign ya the statement and they'll give you the full cheque, plus $800 and plus you're entitled to a hundred bucks' transportation. It's so good, you can survive.
>
> And here, once you get on social assistance, all you get is $264 for a single person. You can afford a room maybe, a room is like $250. You may have fourteen bucks left for the month to eat. There's two soup kitchens that open once a day at the same time and they are both really horrible. And the soup bus is horrible, like I'll go there sometimes, but I haven't all month. I'd rather not eat. (Marc, Moncton)

Another sex worker prefers earning her own money in the sex trade over enduring the public disgrace of food banks and social assistance:

> I ate at soup kitchens, I went to food banks, I've done the whole, fight, fight, fight for whichever church gives the best stuff. And yeah, you could budget your money, you really could, but do you want to degrade yourself? I mean, personally, me: to go to soup kitchens and food banks? Yes, for some people that might be their cup of tea. To me, I'd rather go sell my ass in private, and have it discreet, and be able to buy my own stuff, than to go and ask for charity from a church all the time. Because nobody knows about you selling your ass on the side, sure you're degrading yourself a lot more than asking for a hand-out, but nobody knows about it. It's all private. It's confidential ... And you earned the money, even though you degraded yourself, you still earned that money. You're not asking for a friggin' hand-out. So yeah, you could budget your money, you really could, but do you really want to live like that? Going to soup kitchens every day, going to food banks every week, going to soup kitchens all the time, like do you really want to go cash that welfare cheque every month? (Colleen, Moncton)

Yet another respondent related how difficult it was to stay out of the trade when she had so little money to live on, despite her best budgeting efforts:

> And I'm cheap when it comes to money. I don't like to spend money. I don't. Now if I get some things, like when I go grocery shopping for some things ... it has to be name brand, like ketchup ... Anything else I don't care if it's second name brand. Certain things I want the money for. But I want to save it for something else. Like toilet paper, no name brand. Ketchup, it's gotta be Heinz. I will splurge the 40¢ for Heinz or the extra 60¢ for Miracle Whip but other than that ... pop, Big 8. I'm not buying Pepsi. Like, you gotta save the money 'cause if not, when you're broke,

what are you gonna do? Right back up [to the stroll]. And I've only got another month for my probation. So, there's no way ... I hope to never have to go back up there, but when you only get $251 per month, and you gotta pay your cable, and you gotta pay your lights, you've gotta pay your phone, and you've gotta eat. Like I said to the woman, "I gotta go to the gas station to get toilet paper to wipe my ass. I can't afford to buy it. Where am I gonna buy everything?"

When your money runs out, what option do I have? For a single person going to the food bank, they'll give you a bag the size of them little brown candy bags. "Here, take that." They gave me a bag with one can of tomato soup. You know what I said to her? "Dear, you keep that for someone else 'cause they're gonna need it. I don't need one can of tomato soup from whatever you got, no thank you." I'll take my chances on fish and chips, fuck that. Lord. (Belinda, Halifax)

Many of our interviewees who are struggling with poverty resist the sometimes patronizing charity of the system and the daily humiliations that receiving assistance can entail. Even those in the most straitened circumstances find charity difficult to take. One spoke of a Christian couple who buys her coffee and a doughnut every morning: "And lots of times I'll accept the coffee but I try not to accept the doughnut or anything like that, 'cause I guess it's pride, I don't know" (Juliana, Saint John). The spirit of a fighter that marks so many of those who work in the sex industry is also apparent in how they deal with poverty. That is, they refuse to internalize the image of themselves as undeserving that is key to turning them into obedient workers and subjects of the state.

Talking Back to the System: "My Opinion Is Going to Be Heard"

Our interviewees resist the patronizing attitudes of social assistance providers they often encounter, the bureaucratic runaround of the welfare system, and the expectation that they should simply be grateful for what little they receive. They are unafraid to talk back to those social assistance providers and others who do not treat the poor with respect. One respondent told the story of how she coped with a landlord who was demanding too much money:

I paid $425 for a room downtown but I got there [and] the room looked like a pigpen. This room here [her new one], I didn't mind living in there. But a pigpen? No windows in it, no lock on my door; and buddy expects $425? I told him, before I go in and sit down, "I'll bring CTV cameras down here and show them the way that you got people livin' here in slums." Jeez, no wonder people turn to drugs and everything, you know. (Dawne, Halifax)

Another interviewee, a mother who brooks no nonsense and who brought her son to the outreach centre while she did the interview, explained:

> When I pay my rent, you know, what I get to live off, me and my kids, $379. That's got to buy my groceries, that's got to feed him [my son], [pay for] cable, phone, lights, plus any other thing he needs. I don't understand how anybody can live from month to month on a welfare cheque ... People get excited: "It's cheque day!" What? Where is the money? What are you excited about? ... Like that's crazy, with a kid. My girlfriend has four kids. You know what she gets after she pays her rent? – $380. Yes. That's just retarded. So if her, if the father of her children were to come back and say, "Okay, I got a good job and I'm going to give you $400 a month," then she'll owe them [Social Assistance] probably a dollar. Yeah, like and they wonder why [we work in the sex trade] ... $400 a month. (Heidi, Halifax)

Her resistance to disrespectful and misinformed attitudes is marked in her reversal of the power relationship, by refusing to "hear" or internalize these attitudes, much as those in power fail to hear her interpretations. For example, when her social worker suggested that her work in the trade is detrimental to her kids, she responded quickly:

> I said, number one, that doesn't make me an unfit parent. And if that's the reason why you think that you should take my child, I think you need to go rent a couple of U-Hauls ... 'cause there's a lot of mothers out there doing it. Whether it's inside or outside, they're doing it, because it's called survival. So I ain't hearing that. (Heidi, Halifax)

The inability of middle-class professionals to understand the ridiculous constraints placed on those receiving assistance and the reality of trying to live on social assistance infuriated her:

> Everything has a catch to it. It's like, you're never going to get ahead. So they wonder why people do what they do. This is why they do what they do. This is why people sell dope ... Because the economy, everything, is so high. And what we have to live on, like, it's like one time I asked them ... the woman told me to [get a line of credit] ... I said, "Excuse me, they don't give people a line of credit." She was telling me, "Well, you're over the budget." Over the budget? Well, how many thousands am I under the budget? Seriously. How many thousands am I under the poverty line? So you're telling me to go get some credit ...
>
> It's like they are always on this budget, budget, budget. This budget thing. My boy needed glasses, you know I had to fight tooth and nail to

get them glasses. No, but he really needs his glasses, 'cause his eyes are bad. So these glasses are $275. This jerk down here is telling me, he's going to give me ninety bucks. "Excuse me? You're going to give me ninety bucks? Where am I getting the other hundred and eighty some dollars? Where is that going to come from?" I told [the supervisor], I said, "Listen, he's trying to give me a $90 voucher, so I tell you what, if you two together, 'cause you're the supervisor, can go in there and pull out my file and show me where $275 fits in my budget, I'll pay it. So there. I'm not hearing you people. No, it's not in my budget. You find it in my budget."

They ended up paying for them, but it's just that I had to go through all this bullshit, you know. And then, he was so headstrong that he still ended up [sending] the $90 voucher. So there I got to go all the way back up there and say, "Get your supervisor out here." I said, "You need to straighten this out because I'm not making another trip back here. 'Cause I'm going to end up in jail." Seriously. You know, like I told [the supervisor], as far as he goes she needs to keep him in check. 'Cause like I told her, "You look here, don't you stand here talking down talk to me and think that you can talk to me any way you want because I'm on the system. Because it's people like you that keep me part of the system. So don't." "Well," she said, "well, I'll talk to him about that." "You better. 'Cause don't you come out here and think you can talk down to me because I'm on the system ... you wouldn't have paycheques." Seriously. But this is like all the bullshit they give you. Seriously. They're just retarded like that. Everybody seems to have the double fucking standards and nobody understands. (Heidi, Halifax)

Some of the most frustrating things for her are the inability of assistance workers and government to understand how poverty works, particularly the need for fast cash:

It's like this stupid dental plan they're putting in progress. Welfare, they said, okay. Then they set up a program. Any dental work you need, Health Canada will cover it. Oh, they'll cover it? But here's the catch, if I go to my dentist, and I need $400 worth of work, I need to pay him $400. He does my work, send his, the bill, to Health Canada, and they send me back a cheque. Where am I getting the $400 to start? So what was the sense of that program? What was the sense of that? What did they put that in effect for? It's not doing a damn thing. It's like, it's a Catch-22. [Provincial] Welfare puts a cheque out, the big boys [the federal government] put the cheque out, [then] Welfare wants it down [i.e., claws it back]. So you're not winning, women – one government is giving and the other government is taking it away. (Heidi, Halifax)

The problem of upfront costs is particularly burdensome for women who want their children back (from foster homes, Family Services, or other family members). One interviewee wanted her son to come and live with her but, at $264 a month from Social Assistance, she could not afford the apartment and equipment (fridge, stove, furniture) that was required before her son would be allowed to live with her. Nor would Social Assistance increase her cheque to cover the costs of her son until her son was actually living with her – a classic Catch-22. Recently, after a stint in jail, she had been avoiding work in the trade; however,

> [it's] rough at times, thinking about it. It's rough, 'cause like I said, income assistance won't help me out, and I think and say, okay, I feel like going out and doing it. And [I'm] thinking, it's not worth it if I get caught, know what I mean? I don't know. It's rough. (Candace, Saint John)

Another worker spoke about the problem of moving out of the trade when Social Assistance rules make it difficult to get ahead, and straight jobs make her unable to care for her daughter:

> And my daughter, she's fourteen, I've been having a lot of trouble with her. Like, last year she got put out on home school and the type of job I just found was back shifts from one in the morning 'til seven in the morning. It wasn't working with my daughter – me not being home, being out at those hours for her ... Bringing boys in the house, smoking weed, things like that. So, I had to call in and let them know that I couldn't come in and things like that, due to my daughter's situation and stuff. So, I was let go from that job.
>
> So here I am today, and I'm doing this interview and after this interview, I need to go downstairs, 'cause my worker from Community Services, she then sends me a letter telling me she's not going to help me for the next two months. And I'm like, "Hello, what do you mean? At least give me rent money." They don't want to give me nothing now? I don't understand. Because I was out there in the workforce, and working, and was let go from the job. There's a new policy, I guess, with Community Services that they don't have to help you for the next six-week sequence to that date you were let go. So that's not very good and it sort of now, because, due to being a prostitute for so many years, I feel like I'm being backed into a corner. Where's my rent money coming from for two more months? You know, this is the only trade I really know. I did go to school last year. I mean, I just don't know, I don't ... They're sort of backing me into a corner, like I said, leaving me with [only] that option ...

Despite all these setbacks, she still kept on fighting:

> I've made some contacts. She sent me an appeal thing, I have that in my purse, I filled it out. I'm gonna talk, like I said, after I'm done my interview. We're gonna see what can be done ... So, if I have to go there, I just feel, though, that it's not fair. Because I feel like they're gonna make me go out there and have to humiliate myself because I got to do what I got to do. And I am out there working, you know, trying to find some work now. Working on this place and that place and dropping résumés off but there's nothing yet. Hopefully, you know, I don't think I'll be left in any situation that I'll have to turn back to the streets right now.

She, too, was willing to talk back to Social Assistance:

> Well, I called the worker and I said to the worker, "Listen, I'm a pretty reasonable person. Like, you don't have to pay me for my food this month, I don't care. I don't need your money for that. I need rent money though, I have children." "Oh well, I suggest maybe you move to your mother's." Move to my mother's? My mother and father live in the Towers there, in a one-bedroom apartment. There's no way. I have a three-bedroom townhouse that is fully furnished. Where is my furniture going? Like I don't think they look at them things. So, I don't know. I think it's going to come to a hearing. So I will get to voice my opinion with them, because I have to go through the appeal process ... So, it'll be probably the end of next month before ... but I think it is definitely going to come to that. My opinion is going to be heard. (Kisha, Halifax)

Not all of our interviewees had hard feelings for their welfare workers. One kidded:

> I was over to see her [the welfare worker] yesterday. She went and broke her ankle or something. Poor sod. "Why'd ya go and do that?" I told her, "I'll break them off if you want them broke off." (laughter) I'm just teasing her though; she's a sweet thing. (Dawne, Halifax)

Economics 101: Sex Workers Do the Math

Women's socioeconomic circumstances – the burdens of motherhood, the general unreliability of men and marriage as a support system, and the minimal pay associated with service sector jobs – is summed up most effectively by one of our interviewees who had worked in sex work and was currently working in exotic dance. Her analysis lays bare the structural constraints that women face and makes it clear that barriers such as lack of education are not, in fact, the issue at all:

And it's like when you're a single mother, and now you're stuck with pampers, formula, cribs, strollers, rent, bills, bills, bills, and more bills. And you go to work for six bucks an hour; you work a fifty-hour week; so you never see your kid. So for example, eight bucks an hour: you work forty hours a week. That's $320 a week, before taxes. So you come home with about $265, $270 a week. Times that by four, that brings you to maybe $900 a month, after the taxes. And since you're working full time, [you need] a daycare. The cheapest one I've found so far was $20 a day, five days a week, that's $100. So there's $400 a month, you take your $900 you've made clear, you minus $400, so now you're left with $500. And you've now got rent, formula, pampers, stroller, cribs, food, and more bills, but you've got $500 to pay your rent and everything else you need.

So, when you're a single mother, yeah. No wonder why women become prostitutes. You're making $2,000 in a night. Hello! You can hire a sitter for one night, and pay all your bills, and spend the rest of the month with your kid. To me, that's logical to me, and if it was all legal, and all screened, then you wouldn't have to worry as much, about catching something. And you buy heavy-duty condoms, and you make sure you use them. If you got to double them up, then double them up. That way you don't bring nothing home to your kids. But to me it makes perfect sense.

Like, I've debated it in my head forever, that if my husband were ever to leave me, what would I ever do? I have no high school diploma, I have lots of experience in shit jobs, Tim Hortons, whatever. I've done waitressing, which paid all right with the tips, but still you put up with a lot of shit for the tips – drunks and all. But I thought to myself, okay, [with] no education. Even if I did have an education, that doesn't go very far nowadays anyhow. I mean, there's college graduates who have master's degrees who are working at my work for eight bucks an hour right now ...

So I always thought to myself, that would be like the perfect thing for a single mother to do. Even though, yes, I'll admit, it's dangerous. It's kind of nasty. It is. But I mean, so is flipping burgers. It's still nasty, [you] get no friggin' pay ... and not only that: you don't spend no time with your kids – no time at all. And you're paid these shit wages that you can't even live off of. So it would just make perfect sense to me, to be a class citizen, have a real job from nine to five, and once your kid goes to bed, you maybe do two calls a night, two hours at the most, and you at least make, anywheres from one hundred to two hundred if not more – depending on what you're willing to do for what tips ... Say buddy wanted a, I don't know, he wanted his hour, which is a hundred bucks. Right there you gotta give half that away to the service owner. So you get fifty bucks right there, to walk in the door and do their hour. Well, that only includes sexual intercourse. So there's lots of other favours to be done, or to have done. Like lots of men love to eat women out, so the women charge that, and you can get anywheres from eighty to a hundred bucks to let a man go down on you. So ... you could leave there – buddy could have wanted different little things – you could leave there in one hour, with like five hundred bucks, and you're only away from your kid for an hour.

I've thought a lot about that, because, I mean, love, yeah, sure it lasts forever, white picket fence ... Maybe some people last fifty years, some people last two minutes. Nothing in this life is guaranteed. I love my man with all my heart and soul, and I would die for him ... [But], I mean, we could fall out of love. We could be so in debt that we're just too stressed and we start hating each other. It could be just various things. Maybe I find somebody closer to my own age, or maybe he finds someone younger. Anything could happen. I could have a second kid and be a fat pig, and he could just not be attracted to me no more, and go cheat on me, and then I'd have to kick him out. You know, anything. As well as, you know ... nothing in this life is a guarantee. Everything happens for a reason. There's no guarantees. So if I were ever to be a single mother, there's no way I'm gonna be flipping no burgers for $6 an hour, and trying to support a kid. And then once they get older, they want that Tommy Hilfiger, and they want that Fubu and they want ...

Interviewer: And they want to know why you're never around.
Oh, I'm never around 'cause I gotta ask people if they want to upsize their fries. So, even with a college degree ... (Colleen, Moncton)

Conclusion

While the fact that sex workers are "doing it for the money" is generally (although not completely) accepted, few understand the true meaning of these words. The women and men we spoke with went into sex work not because they were forced into it by economic circumstances or addictions (although these sometimes played important roles) but because they were resisting the other options available to them in their given circumstances. What is striking about so many of the people we spoke with is their spirit of resistance: their refusal to accept the economic options that force them to accept being treated as cheap labour or as "the poor." Sex workers had looked at, and often experienced, other forms of survival – minimum wage or service-sector work and social assistance – and found them wanting. Sex work was seen as a logical way to piece together a living that offers both financial rewards and independence and flexibility of work. One could also argue that sex workers are resisting the age of neo-liberalism and its tendency, as Thom Workman has explained, to view social problems as individual problems and to attempt "to change the behaviour of the poor forcibly through a system of punishment and rewards."[63] What the sex workers speaking here make clear is that it is the system, rather than them, that is not working. They refuse to accept this system and they refuse to be treated as if they do not deserve better. That is, they refuse to internalize the discourses that attempt to render them "cheap labour" and they fight back against the economic system that tries to exploit them by trying to maximize their control over their own labour.

2
The Good, the Bad, and the Ugly

> I don't know, I don't know what it is, I don't think I can stop 'cause I tried. And I wish I could, but I like the money and I like going out there. I guess I'm a risk-taker. (Kristin, Halifax)

In relying on the sex worker as the narrator of her own story, we find that sex workers, like all workers, have a complex relationship to their work. They reflect on and articulate these complexities in explaining their work in this study. Many of our informants had a wide variety of negative experiences in the trade – stigma, fear of arrest, health concerns; and, most importantly, violence or the threat of violence. At the same time, they made it plain that there is often more that is good about the job than just the money. Several of these sex workers experienced positive interactions with clients in their work, felt a sense of empowerment, and gained or maintained their independence. These negative and positive experiences are not mutually exclusive. While some workers may be less able to refuse dangerous or poor working conditions and, therefore, are more likely to have negative experiences, they too may have some good clients or experience a sense of camaraderie with other workers.[1] Listening to sex workers' stories, as Wendy Rickard has pointed out, "reminds feminists that while gender and economics are central, the politics of pleasure might also be a useful reference in deepening feminist understanding of key sex worker questions."[2]

Paying attention to pleasure, however, runs counter to much feminist theorizing of sex work. In particular, radical feminist readings tend to view sex work itself as a form of violence against women.[3] While radical feminist approaches have been thoroughly critiqued in much sex work literature for their essentialization of women as victims and men as all powerful, and their elision of sex with rape, such approaches have gained new ground in recent years with the growing concern about issues such as trafficking and youth prostitution. All entry into prostitution is read as a product of force (as in pimping), or susceptibility to violence because of previous childhood victimization, for example. The sex trade is seen simply as a continuation of this violence and abuse. This approach, like the prostitution as poverty reading, suffers from the same problems of abstraction and overdetermination. Close examinations of the actual relationship between, for example, childhood sexual exploitation and entry into sex work reveal a much less clear link between the two.[4] As Frances Shaver writes, "A history of violence and abuse may not be peculiar to those entering prostitution," given the relatively commonality of experiences of unwanted sexual acts.[5] The literature on pimping is similarly indeterminate. Both John Lowman and Shaver argue that the problem of pimping has been exaggerated in the literature.[6] And, as we shall see below, there is a problem of interpretation when any man in a relationship with a sex worker is viewed through the framework of pimping.

Indeed, we could also point out how, since radical feminists view sex work as inherently violent, they have contributed little to the investigation of how, when, and where it is violent and how violence by clients or others can be minimized. The sex workers speaking here identify important factors contributing to a client's propensity for violence, factors such as age. Contrary to those who see sex work as violence, our interviewees distinguished between sex work, which could sometimes be the source of pleasure and pride, and violence within sex work, which was seen as a product not of the trade but of social attitudes toward sex work. These findings parallel the study of indoor workers in which Chris Bruckert, Colette Parent, and Pascale Robitaille found that, "contrary to common beliefs about work in the industry, it is neither duress nor despair that led these women to make this choice, but rather reasons very much like those motivating the choice to enter other professions. The main reasons provided relate to the need to meet people, to be able to provide basic necessities, to experience an enjoyable social life and/or explore sexuality."[7] The sex workers speaking here identify similar good things in sex work, even as they recount the bad and the ugly.

Sex Work and Resistant Meanings
The debate over the interpretation of prostitution as the ultimate violence against women or as an expression of sexual freedom has been of long standing, particularly between radical feminists and sex radicals. Radical feminists have been critiqued as presenting an essentialist view of women as victims and men as predators, while sex radicals are accused of celebrating sexual liberation without taking into account the constraints of gender, race, and class that structure our sexuality and life choices. The debate has often been understood as occurring between two distinct groups – sexually conservative feminists and libertarian sex workers – but has always been much more complex, with debates over choice, freedom, violence, and resistance occurring as much among sex workers themselves as within the

feminist movement (which includes sex workers). Certainly, the sex workers speaking here do not present a one-sided analysis of sex work as either inherently good or bad, but carefully distinguish between what works and what does not, which clients are good and which ones pose a threat, under what conditions having someone act as a protector is problematic and when it is not. Further, they refuse the simplistic assumption that past bad experiences lead inevitably to future bad experiences. A number of workers were able to build on previous negative experiences, either inside or outside the trade, as sources of strength. These more complex analyses challenge the oversimplifications inherent in much theorizing and point to more productive responses to the need to improve working conditions within the trade. Further, it becomes clear that addressing these conditions requires first and foremost an end to the silencing of sex workers' voices. The violence experienced in the trade is not seen so much as a product of the trade but a product of the attitudes that dehumanize sex workers – that, for example, deny them the right to speak for themselves.

Recent academic critiques have tried to move beyond the essentialism of both radical feminist and sex radical approaches by emphasizing the historical contingency of the sex work experience. But sex worker perspectives sometimes find the continued reluctance to accept positive readings of the trade frustrating. Jane Scoular, in a recent review of studies of the sex trade, provides an excellent critique of both radical feminist and sex radical approaches and commends postmodern approaches, such as Shannon Bell's, that challenge the dualisms (good/bad, victim/subject) inherent in both radical feminist and sex radical positions by viewing sex work as neither inherently subversive nor inherently oppressive.[8] Bell's work emphasizes the resistant discourses in sex work performances that refuse and challenge such simplistic notions. That is, she points to sex workers' resistant production of meaning.[9] Even here, however, feminist scholars can become uncomfortable with the possibility that sex worker agency is being overestimated. Scoular, while praising Bell's work, again raises the problem of "celebratory" accounts of sex work and questions how much ability a sex worker may have "to mount discursive challenges." She discusses the studies by, for example, Julia O'Connell Davidson as ones that more clearly outline the possibilities both for agency and for structural forces to limit that agency.[10]

But even these more balanced readings may fall into the traps laid out by Jill Nagle in her review of several books on sex work, in particular, the continued denial of the importance of the resistant meanings of sex work articulated by sex workers themselves as sources of social and political change. As Nagle notes, there is a tendency to view "nonacademician sex workers as inherently unique among other laborers, as objects of study and objects of outside forces rather than as producers of knowledge and producers of counter-cultural meanings."[11] Again, it is precisely this silencing that many sex workers experience as oppressive. That oppression is produced by "knowledge-makers" such as academics and the media, and yet non-sex-worker academics tend not to examine their own position as powerful producers of knowledge. Nagle finds that, even in sensitive studies such as O'Connell Davidson's, there is a tendency to impose negative readings of the sex worker-client encounter – as "social death" for the sex worker, for example – rather than admitting the "possibility of multiple meanings of paid sex, specifically, those created by whores themselves?"[12]

Similarly, Nagle criticizes the tendency by academics to too quickly dismiss sex radicals' claims without fully understanding the political importance of positive readings of the sex industry, which are possible when a reader recognizes the discursive construction of oppressive structures. Nagle notes the importance of this "whore counter culture ... to fashion new meanings within oppressive circumstances."[13] The importance of the production of alternative meanings becomes even more evident in Noah Zatz's discussion of sex work as a "bifurcated moment" in which the meaning of the act can differ according to the participants – for example, while the client may interpret the moment as having his sexual demands met by a compliant partner, the sex worker may not feel subservient at all. While it is true that discursive resistance can be constrained by structures – his fist may be, at an immediate level, more powerful than is her interpretation of what is going on – this is not absolute or a given. Indeed, the voices speaking here show us how sex workers' discursive refusal to internalize blame for violence (much as the feminist movement taught women not to internalize blame for rape) is an important step toward fighting back against – or possibly preventing – that violence.

Further, if one understands that the meaning of the encounter is not predetermined, how the moment is experienced can change or be changed. Sex workers (and clients) can learn to understand themselves differently and, therefore, experience the work differently or insist on a better experience if, for example, they are part of a community that reads the experience differently. Carol Queen has similarly identified how important sex-positive thought, that is, sex radicalism, is to ensuring that sex workers do not experience a loss of self-esteem or find sex work damaging.[14] Legal regimes such as criminalization, on the other hand, may suppress particular understandings or discourses (sex work as work, for example) as well as supportive communities, thereby contributing to more negative experiences of the work.[15] Radical feminism, therefore, might itself contribute to the oppression of sex workers by supporting legal regimes that marginalize and stigmatize sex workers in the name of freeing them from violent pimps and johns.[16]

At the same time, analysts such as Zatz make the important point that sex radical readings of sex work as a positive sexual *identity* and *sexual* experience may fail to fully account for the majority of sex workers' viewing sex in this context as work, not identity.[17] Again, however, sex worker analysts such as Queen and Nagle do not argue for a singular understanding of sex work, only for openness to the possibility of positive experiences. Further, as Queen observes, the creation of sex-positive readings of sex work are an important part of making that work a positive rather than a negative experience. Queen suggests that if feminists truly wanted to ensure good conditions for sex workers, they would work against the legal and social stigmatization that makes violence and mistreatment possible and they would work for a more sex-positive message:

> If these activists truly wanted to improve the lot of sex workers ... they would insist upon thorough and nonjudgemental sex information for clients as well as whores. One basic piece of information would be that women – and whores – do not exist to be sexually used by men, but that any sexually interaction, including a paid one, benefits from *negotiation*. This would facilitate the climate of respect that anti-sex-work demagogues claim is absent in a paid act of sexual entertainment or gratification. The paucity of sex-positive discussion about what is possible in a commodified context often negatively affects sex workers themselves.[18]

Barbara Sullivan has maintained that "utilizing discursive resources to contest dominant understandings of prostitution ... should be a necessary part of a feminist strategy in relation to prostitution" – a strategy that expands sex workers' capacity to resist relations of power, including violence.[19]

Similarly, sex workers' analyses here show us that violence and victimization are not necessary or unchanging conditions. Even those workers who were involved with pimps or abusive partners were able to leave, others refused to become involved with them, and still others fought back against violent clients and took their cases to court. Understanding and supporting that process will lead to much more positive change in the working conditions of marginalized sex workers than will simple condemnation of the trade as violent. Seeing the variety of meanings that are possible in any given encounter between sex worker and client, and taking sex workers' words seriously, shows us how good working conditions are possible and how poor ones can be changed. For example, sex worker organizations can help workers build up the strength to resist maltreatment and disrespect. Sex workers' own analyses also show us how changing clients' as well as the public, police, and policy makers' views of sex workers is vital to ending violence against sex workers.

Challenging Victimization: Pride and Pleasure in Sex Work

Many of our interviewees talked about the upsides of the trade, including those rewards beyond the money – various benefits such as good clients, adventure, friendships, acceptance, sexual experimentation, and finding oneself and one's own strength. These upsides were expressed not only by highly paid, well-protected escorts. It is important to note, therefore, that sex workers are challenging not only the disciplinary norms of capitalist society but also its social and sexual norms. This resistance is perhaps most audible in some sex workers' presentations of the client. While the client is nearly universally reviled by outside observers, and, certainly, many of our interviewees complained about clients, particularly in regard to the propensity of some for violence, a number also said that clients, or "dates," can be a source of pleasure and pride in the job.

There is an easy tendency to dismiss sex workers' positive assessments of clients as simply their putting on a brave face. However, as we have seen, our respondents were in no way defensively painting clients as nothing but good. Rather, the sex workers we spoke with presented a textured analysis of clients. There were some who were good and kind, some who were threatening, some who were "jerks," and still others who were viewed as bizarre. The relationships between sex workers and clients, like many relationships, can range from friendly to abusive. Indeed, the small but growing academic literature on the client confirms that a wide variety of men seek the services of sex workers for a wide variety of reasons.[20] Luke Xantidis and Marita McCabe's research, for example, shows three main types of clients: the business-oriented client who is looking for quick, non-committal sexual exchange; the romantic/friendly type who is looking to establish some sort of bond; and the misogynist. The misogynist group, it was confirmed in other research, was most likely the smallest.[21] Indeed, even if men's purchase of sexual service is reflective of a larger social construct of male sex-right and male economic and social power, it is a gross generalization to translate these abstractions into the individual character of the men involved. As sex workers consistently point out to women who condemn sex work, "They are your husbands." While the payment for sex can be seen as part of a broader male sex-right, it is reductionist in the extreme to then paint all clients of sex workers as exploiters of women – much as it would be reductionist to view all men in positions of authority (which is also part of masculine privilege) as necessarily abusive toward women. It is not the payment for sex that is problematic but the abusive behaviour that some men believe is licensed by payment for sex. According to our respondents, there are both good and bad clients, and sorting the two out is a matter of vital importance to making sex work a positive experience.

The second most popular answer to our questions about the good part of the work was "meeting nice people." A number of interviewees spoke of how they appreciated "good" clients, the "nice" ones, as well as the opportunities for "romance" or friendship; or the simple attention and courtesy paid to the worker by a good date. Many also spoke about feeling good about their ability to relieve a client's loneliness or help other sex workers. As one respondent said:

> The best is having the nice ones come to you, right, and say, "I'm lonely, can you help me out? I'll pay you x number of dollars," you know, "Let's go out for a beer," or something like that or whatever. And the worst thing is, when they try to hurt ya ... [but] I've had nothing but nice ones. Really, they [were] so nice that they'd even take me back wherever I wanted to go to. Like, say if we're done the job and I wanted to go out for something to eat or something, they'd even take me to where I was going. Like that's how nice they were. (Alison, Halifax)

Another clarified that she was under no illusions, but she could still see the good in many clients:

> Most of them are extremely nice and give a shit about you. I mean there are actually guys who come in to see you that care more about you than they care about themselves. You know, they'd rather please you and make you feel good then ... You see that, you actually see that, you know. It's not like Hollywood but ... (April, Halifax)

Another of our interviewees told similar stories about the job. She described the best part of the job as:

> The people ... the money. It can be really interesting you know. I mean sometimes you get guys crying on your shoulders. I mean who knows about that? I have one guy who pays me $35 for a piece of pie, a piece of lemon meringue pie ... that keeps him happy ... every week. I had another guy, he wanted me to wear stilettos and walk on him. I mean I can't wear stilts! I mean I'd be falling over, falling down, I'd be staggering with them on for Chrissake, but he would still pay me to do that for him. I mean he still pays $100 to model these fucking shoes! So what is he? I mean what is that? Prostitution? I mean what does that have to do with sex? I mean I only have seven dates [out of a regular twenty-five] that I do sex with. (Hannah, Halifax)

As Zatz has argued, the experience of sex work may be quite different for client and sex worker; the "sex worker may not be providing what the client is receiving."[22] That is, what is a sexual experience for him may be downright silly for her. Certainly, the interactions between sex workers and clients are much less predetermined than radical feminist interpretations would have us believe. The emotional labour that sex workers provide can even lead to a blurring of the lines between friendship and sex worker-client relationship. Indeed, while sex workers' claims to empowerment through sex work have sometimes been dismissed by feminist and others, or at least considered to be limited to those who work exclusively in high-class locations or come from privileged backgrounds, several of our interviewees who do not share these characteristics also expressed some sense of empowerment through sex work.

Most of our respondents were careful to note that the majority of their clients are "regular guys." One massage parlour worker spoke to the frequent failure to understand clients in a humane way:

> These people don't even realize, the men that come in there [the massage parlour], it's not about sex. It's not even about sex. It's ... they're missing something, and that's what you're there for. And the young girls that are just starting in the business don't realize that either. They think it's all about sex, and it's not. It's ... they're missing something, whether it's they don't have a wife at home that's giving them enough attention, or they have no one in their lives. You know, some of them just need to be close to someone, or they just need somebody to love them even if it's just a half hour or hour at a time ... They refer to them as "tricks," and you know, demean them really, when all they want is just what everyone else wants too. They just want to be loved. (Felicity, Halifax)

An independent worker spoke quite fondly of her regulars and provided much insight into the roles that a sex worker plays with her clients:

> *Interviewer: Are you treated well by your clients?*
> Oh gosh yeah.
> *Interviewer: Do you have regulars?*
> All of them. I've gone from a size seven and up to a twenty-two and down again and back up, and all of my clients have stayed with me the whole time.
> *Interviewer: That's interesting.*
> Well, it's your stuffing. It's your stuff on the inside that makes you – not what you look like on the outside.
> *Interviewer: What is the kind of occupation [and] age of your clients?*
> Um, I don't feel comfortable seeing young guys.

Interviewer: I've heard that more than once. What's that about?
Well, now for me, it's my age – the fact that I have a fourteen-year-old son (laughs). There are the occasional young guys that want to be with someone who's older, but my clientele basically are suits, forty-plus – suits, professionals, politicians, those types. And there's only so much you can listen to when it comes to New Brunswick politics.

Interviewer: Oh really, [you] get a lot of New Brunswick people? Isn't that interesting.
You know the rule, don't play in your own backyard.

Interviewer: What percentage would you say come from New Brunswick, you know, half, a third, a quarter?
Of the political side, I would say a quarter of my clients.

Interviewer: That kills me.
I mean during the [election] race, I thought I was going to go crazy before [Premier] Bernard Lord went in, I was like, Oh my God, please!

Interviewer: This is rich (laughs).
Every day I was hearing it and I was like, "No, I'm not a political person in any way, shape, or form."

Interviewer: Apparently, they thought you were, or were interested.
Well, I'm an ear.

Interviewer: And they maybe think they are paying for the ear.
Well they are. Well, [for] half an hour, an hour, you know. Fifteen more minutes listening to this can't be that bad, right? I have a – I have a lot of disabled clients as well, so ...

Interviewer: Disabled in what way? Physically you mean?
Physically disabled clients, people with MS. Their minds are still there; it's their bodies that won't agree to go along with them for some reason. I had one of my clients die on me a couple of years ago, and, my God, I was heartbroken. I was heartbroken. I think I cried for two weeks.

Interviewer: It must have been someone you knew well.
Oh, I used to see him twice a week. And when he died, I just, it broke my heart. It really did, because he was so sweet. You couldn't ask for a better person ...

You have to be a strong character to do it, and you have to learn how to separate one from the other. Now me, I've never been able to do that. Me, I go home worrying about some of my clients. I had a client call me two years ago, and he was in tears and he had to see me. So I went, I walked through the door and his wife had passed away. She had been in a nursing home. I sat down and planned her funeral.

Interviewer: Oh my God! That's amazing!
No, well you do what you gotta do for people. Sometimes they can't cope on their own, and they need ...

Interviewer: You're the other closest person to him, that would, you know.
And the thing is, he had children, and he called me. Probably he just felt more comfortable with me.

Interviewer: Yeah, I imagine that was a first.
Yeah, for that.

Interviewer: Do you get those kinds of calls often?
Odd and weird and wonderful things all of the time. My mother always used to tell me that I wear the weight of the world on my shoulders; I hear too much, she used to say. Both my parents have passed on. I think it really pays to show empathy, but sometimes people will misconstrue that as weakness. (Felicity, Halifax)

The emotional toll of sex work, then, can be quite different from how it is often construed by outsiders. Annie Sprinkle, the sex work diva, has provided tools for relieving the "sex worker burnout" that comes with the emotional burdens sex workers often take on.[23] One Los Angeles-based study showed that, while indoor workers are considered more likely to offer "emotional services" to clients, street-based workers also devote "a surprising amount of time and personal service" to their clients, particularly regulars.[24] Clearly, the "personal service" being rendered challenges narrow definitions of sex work.

Sex Work, Sex Therapy, and Personal Growth

Several of our interviewees talked about sex work as a therapeutic process, for the clients and for themselves. Others saw it as an opportunity to explore their identity and exercise their freedom. One interviewee had read up on sex work and was in touch with the pro-sex work movements in Canada and the United States. She pointed to academic and sex worker Carol Queen's writing on clients as reflective of her viewpoint.[25] When asked how she would respond to society's view of clients, she stated:

> I would mention things like, okay, you've seen nine out of ten buddies out there who never get any, they're too shy or something and they think they're ugly or whatever ... And like, please, you know. (Joan, Halifax)

She also pointed to the tradition of the "holy whore" as a source of pride in her work and herself:

> And I would be the kind of person to talk about the ancient tradition, 'cause I've been reading. And I have a couple of books – one that was published in '54 or '57, that talked about China, Africa, Greece – and it's really good. So I would definitely be talking [about that] and ... people would not be expecting to hear [such] originality. (Joan, Halifax)

She then went on to explain that sex work gave her a sense of control around men and a sense of nobility:

> The other upside I was going to mention – 'cause it's kind of unusual maybe – is just, I got to be around a lot of men whereas I was avoiding and pretty afraid of men [before] ... Through [sex work] I got to be around a lot of men and got to be a lot less scared. I was in a situation where I was in control. I also got to give pleasure and there was almost a spiritual side. I realized that, wow, these guys are lonely. They can't ask anyone for a date [and] stuff like that. So I felt that there really can be some nobility in this. (Joan, Halifax)

Another interviewee also sees the work in a therapeutic way:

> *Interviewer: So the general question is kind of, what's the best part of the work and what's the worst part of the work?*
> Money, of course, you know ... and, um, I enjoy ... I was always the person that likes making people happy and helping people. And, ah, see I don't work the streets very often. I'm a call girl. They call me and they come over. I get a lot of enjoyment out of seeing a smile on their face and making them happy when they leave. I basically call myself a hookapist. 'Cause it's like they book an hour. There's half an hour of sex and there's half an hour of complaining about something or other. And, you know, I just kind of deal with that, because I used to do therapy work for [palliative care]. So I used to do that. So I just kind of combined it. (April, Halifax)

Indeed, sex work is a therapeutic step for her as well:

> I guess I should explain that ... ten years ago I was raped by two cops and I was totally afraid of men, period. And believe it or not, a therapist said to me, "You ever tried hooking?" And, if I would have been made correctly from day one, I probably would have been a hooker at sixteen. Because it's something that I've always wanted to do. (April, Halifax)

It also helped her regain a sense of control over men:

> After I did it for a little bit of time, I regained my control over men, which is – it sounds funny. It's not that I want control over men, but I want to be in control. (April, Halifax)

Further, sex work helped her through a gender transition:

> When I became a transsexual, I mean, nobody would come near me with a ten-foot pole. The minute I started charging – well, I'll give you an

> example: the first week I put an ad in the paper, I had 186 calls. (April, Halifax)

For some of the male sex workers we spoke with, sex work provides an opportunity to explore queer identity and their sexuality:

> Some people just like the danger and the excitement – as I did in the beginning, of getting away with something; something that is taboo, something that we're not supposed to be doing with our bodies, something that we were told to use our bodies as our temples and not let any stranger in ... It's sexy at times. It's intriguing. It's dangerous. Which makes it all that more intriguing and sexy in some people's eyes. Like I said, in some people's eyes, it's like creating the biggest taboo. It's something like, I'm getting away with this; or maybe I won't get away with this – the fear of getting caught [and] the fear of meeting new people. There are times that I met some really nice people in my dates, some genuine, honest-to-God hardworking, just like everybody. A taxpayer, ya know, not hurting anybody. All they want is a little company. Sometimes it's not sex. Sometimes it's just talking to someone who is like you, or someone who likes the same gender. For me, I mean the money was nice, but the socialization was better. Because I didn't have that with my family. (Charles, Halifax)

A few others mentioned a sense of family and the ability to feel good about oneself by "helping others out" – meaning other people in the trade – as a good aspect of working in the trade. One man who had occasionally worked on the male stroll as a teenager said:

> There was somewhat of a social group. Each hustler took care of themselves and each other, watched out over each other. It was kind of a family. One that I never had during those years, because of my parents' attitudes of my being gay and how that developed. (Charles, Halifax)

One woman explained how she enjoyed being part of a community and being a helper within that community, even though she had since left that behind. One of the best parts of working in the trade, for her, was "getting to know girls and helping them to get them off the streets, and trying to get them to learn how to control the crack and that." She was eventually able to turn this helpfulness toward others into help for herself:

> But, I was helping people out there before I was helping myself. So I was doing more for others than I was myself. But now I'm starting my self-esteem up. I love myself. I got a better outlook on life. I mean, my

eyes are wide open and I see what's going on. Nobody's going to play me and nobody's going to flare up my head anymore. I'm not a sucker for punishment. (Kasey, Saint John)

Of course, there were certainly a few people, mostly in Saint John, who felt debased by the work, no matter how nice the clients. One said:

It's degrading, it's like when you go to jail and they tell you to bend and cough, that's degrading, that's just the same: degrading. (Deanna, Saint John)

Another respondent who worked the streets because of an addiction, and who had lost a home and a business because of that addiction, had a similar feeling:

Interviewer: What's the best part about the job?
There isn't one. There isn't one. I don't know how anyone can enjoy it ...
Interviewer: What do you think are major risks on the streets?
Disease, well your safety and then disease – that would be the two risks. I mean other than you lose a lot of self-respect. You lose a lot of who you are when you're out there. Because I don't know about the other ones but I know me. When I'm out there, that's not me, that's not me. I totally disassociate, you know, totally disassociate. (Tabitha, Saint John)

Six others, again most of them in Saint John, identified servicing clients as the worst part of the job. One Saint John respondent – who also appreciated the ability to make money, be her own boss, and set her own hours – admitted that she disliked

doing that for them. Doing what they want ya to do. I just kind of like detach myself from it. Like it's a job. And then I just try to put myself some place else while that's going on. It bothers me, but I do it. (Violet, Saint John)

This pattern of feeling degraded, in Saint John particularly, may be related to the attitudes and behaviours of the public and clients in that city, where harassment seemed particularly common, and to the lack of a sex worker support group.

However, even for those with violent experiences and addiction problems, there is still the possibility of positive experiences in the trade:

Interviewer: What do you think the best part of the work is?
Meeting new people. Associating with, you know, some of them are nice and they're just lonely and want to talk. (Kasey, Saint John)

> I hate to think of myself that I'm even down there doing that. I just started a few weeks ago, doing it on the street ... But I was working escort service for a while. And [working the street] is almost the same thing, just cheaper. All the guys I've met, they've been pretty nice. A lot of older men, I think they're lonely ... Yeah, one guy paid me $150 last week just to sit there with him. I said, "Okay, no problem." (Krista, Saint John)

While few of our respondents spoke of clients as uniformly bad, most much prefer older men and try to avoid the younger ones, not only because younger men can be more dangerous, as we shall see below, but because older men are easier to handle, in that they are less demanding in terms of the physical work:

> *Interviewer: Do you find some clients better than others?*
> I like the older men. Fifty and older 'cause they can't do nothing with it. And they're nicer. And if you get the right one you can get some money out of them. I told one guy I have six kids and that my boyfriend beat me up. And I got like $1,000 out of him that was mine. And I've seen him, I still see him once in a while, every so often ... You'll get your money, if they got their money. They're willing to pay for anything. And the older men are more sweethearts about everything. "Oh dear, I can't get it up, we're going to have to sit here and talk or cuddle." (Patricia, Saint John)

Another, however, finds older clients too tedious because they sometimes overstep the boundaries between paid labour and friendship, whereas younger clients are less emotionally demanding and more business-like:

> Younger guys are easier to deal with. They're quicker in and out. They've got things to do. Older men got nothing better to do. They want to sit around and talk, and go through this; and I don't want to hear about their grandkids. I don't want to know your grandkids, you know. If you want to pay me for conversation, no problem! I'll sit and listen to him, anything you want to tell me. (Belinda, Halifax)

In keeping with the independence of many of our respondents, too much caring by a client is seen as having the potential danger of shifting paid labour to an unpaid "caring" relationship. For example, one woman explained:

> I had one man, this one man that owned this really big house right on [a lake] and he was in love with me. He just wanted to take me away but I just don't want no kind of a man ... And he wanted to take care of me, and I don't want that, I'm an independent. (Megan, Halifax)

While many of the workers we spoke with talked about clients with sympathy, there was questioning of the particular demands of some clients. There was particular belittling of those who demand specialized services, and some newcomers expressed shock at what they saw as the bizarre nature of certain fetishes. As one worker said:

> I know this guy. I'll take all my clothes off. And he'll take my panties and put them on his head, [and] chew them in his mouth and give me $150. Sick. (Kasey, Saint John)

One woman who had worked in both the sex and exotic dance industries spoke of similar reservations about some clients:

> Well, I'll admit, some of them ... I've met a lot of really nice men over the periods of time of working in those two types of industry.
> *Interviewer: Right. The good clients and the not so good.*
> Then you got the really whackos too. Really, really strange individuals, that just – they're not even humanly, mentally capable of anything. You know, I think my cat has more of a brain than some of them do. Yeah, and I just don't understand what possesses people to think in those certain ways. There was men who used to call who wanted to be chained up and pissed on. What is with that? Or to be shit on. They want to give you an enema and lay them in the tub and shit all over them. (Colleen, Moncton)

Exotic dancers also sometimes have negative attitudes toward customers. One young former dancer referred to the customers as

> just a bunch of perverts, drunk perverts. Wedding rings on their fingers. Just got their paycheque and headed out to the club. (Alexis, Moncton)

However, as Chris Bruckert has explained, the belittling of customers in strip clubs is part of the process of resistance and subversion of the client-dancer relationship, which puts the dancer rather than the client in the position of agent by reversing the public script of male-dominated sexual relations.[26] A similar process can be seen in the way some of our respondents resisted the way they themselves are often portrayed as bizarre by pointing to the practices of certain clients as the source of true bizarreness.

Generally, though, negative experiences were not seen as inevitable. Even though younger workers, aged seventeen to twenty-one, usually had the most negative reactions to being in the trade, they also did not assume that working in the sex trade necessarily meant being victimized. One young woman working in escort, but making plans to go into social work, commented:

> The biggest thing is that they [other workers] feel sorry for themselves ... The majority sit there and feel sorry for themselves like, it's never too late to get an education, even a GED. You know what I mean, like really. 'Cause you make your life what you make it. You make your decisions, especially for grown women. Like, I'm only eighteen years old, and I very seldom feel sorry for myself. Like, I'm a human, I do feel sorry for myself, but very seldom. 'Cause I know the decisions I make before I make them. I think very thoroughly about it. So get off your ass and stop feeling so sorry for yourself. If you don't like what you're doing, don't do it ... 'Cause I've had a pretty rough life. Big deal. Get over it. (Bonnie, Moncton)

Another young, male ex-street worker also did not think that sex work was necessarily destructive; it depended on how people approach their work:

> Before you start to do it, sit ... If someone said this to me ... before you start to do it, sit back and think about your motives and about the reasons why you're doing it. Don't just do it for the money. If you're comfortable with doing it, and it's not going to affect your day-to-day life, you know what I mean? Then go ahead and go out and do it. But if you're doing it, and you also realize that, hey, I have no self-esteem, hey, I hate my life, oh my God I have an ugly body. And you're just doing it because you don't care ... But if you can actually go out and say I'm comfortable with myself and I'm going out to do it because I'm comfortable with the fact that this person is paying me to give them a blow job and that's all it is, then I can accept that, and I can handle that and, oh, I still have a great body. You know what I mean? And just because he's giving me a blow job, and I'm letting him pay me money for it, doesn't mean I'm ugly. I don't know, that was one of my things. At first it was like, "oh God, I'm ugly." Once I realized that I did care, I realized that I couldn't [work in the sex trade] anymore. (Robert, Moncton)

Whether one's experience in the trade is positive or negative depends on more than one's structural location. It depends also on attitude, or "where one's head is" when going into the trade. This is something that sex worker advocates have long argued: not that the work will be great for everyone but that people need to carefully analyze their motives for and attitudes toward the work. As Carol Queen has said, "It is the responsibility of the culture to work on its negative attitudes about sex and about us and our work; but it is whores' responsibility to work on our negative attitudes about ourselves."[27] Disgust with certain client fetishes, for example, may mean that a sex worker needs to examine her motives and boundaries in her work. Further, as most of our interviewees made clear, negative experiences, or being victimized in one aspect of life or work, does not mean that the experience of sex work itself will be uniformly exploitative and negative. One male worker, who had started in an abusive situation as a child, claimed the best part of the work was

> freedom, choice. I have choice. See, I have a belief that my ass is my ass, okay? If I wanna sell it, well, that's fine. Why can someone sell hot dogs and sunglasses on that corner, and I can't sell my ass on that corner? It's my ass, you know, that's always been here, it's always been ... People keep telling me that I can't sell my own ass. And it's my own body and they're telling me what I can and can't do with it. It's sort of, I can compare it to sort of the abortion issue in a way. I really do. You know, women should have the right to choose, that's my belief. (Scott, Halifax)

For this worker, the potentially negative aspects of the trade come from the restrictions on the work, not the work itself or his past.

A sense of personal growth and control was most eloquently expressed by a former sex worker in Halifax who does not see the work necessarily as sex therapy. Indeed, she had faced great personal tragedy and had a variety of violent experiences in the trade. Yet, she articulated her recognition of her own strength, her ability to survive and to see the world for what it really is, including the reality of women's lives and the hypocrisy of non-sex workers, as some of the good things that had come out of her time in the trade:

> I learned a lot. I learned a lot about myself: how strong I really could be. I met a lot of other people, like girls like myself. We were all normal, and then things happened. And I learned a lot about people in general: how they look at other people and [how] they focus on ya. The working women in the Halifax-Dartmouth area right now, we're like contaminated rats to the other cities ... [I learned] about my own strength. I can survive, and I have survived. I have become strong. You look into the face of death every day [and] you're either gonna make it or break it. You're gonna be found dead, or you're gonna survive. But with me, I survived – thank God – and I have a new life, a good life. But I never forget the times and I'm not embarrassed. I learned a lot about society, and the law. (Denise, Halifax)

Thus, even negative experiences within sex work do not make sex work an entirely negative experience for most sex workers. Rather, the trade is viewed as being potentially negative or positive depending on a wide variety of factors, including the workers' self-awareness and growth, and the availability of communities of support. Also important are the attitudes of clients and their respectful treatment of workers, and workers' ability to manage their relationships with clients to maximize workers' independence and job satisfaction. None of these things is seen as essential characteristics of the trade but as changeable conditions that can shape a worker's experience. One of the key conditions is a worker's sense of personal safety, as we shall see below.

Violence: The Worst Part

While the sex workers we spoke with identified a number of good things about sex work, almost all identified as the worst part of the trade one issue – violence:

> The worst parts of it are, you know, danger. I put myself into danger of being beaten, raped and, at times, being taken advantage of and not being paid right. Um, that's a disadvantage ... I can honestly say there was a time I was gang-raped by three people, three guys, three younger guys, right? Because they got me in that position and you can't fight three, you know? (Angela, Halifax)

> I've been raped. Busted cheek bones. Taken to a hotel and tied down to a bed and drugged. German shepherds watching me. Guns to my head. Jumping through windows, rolling out of cars, being threatened, you know, it made me cautious. (Katrina, Halifax)

> Major risks? Getting the shit kicked out of them and killed or ending up in a ditch somewhere. Or disappearing somewhere and they dope you up for whatever and take advantage of ya. That's happened to girls. They take you somewhere, like you know, and they get you all high or drunk or whatever. I don't know, but ... I mean, I've even, this happened to me one time. That some guys was making videotapes of what was going on. So in other words, I was on the Internet. They even got it on the Internet. (Alison, Halifax)

> I've had a few really scary experiences, I got through it. I've been raped, beat, you know, way out [in the] industrial park. I had to walk from there. (Alyssa, Saint John)

> Well, I got raped before. Had a knife pulled on me. You gotta know what you're getting into. You can't trust nobody. They may seem like the nicest person, and they'll change on ya in a minute. (Dawne, Halifax)

My girlfriend stood outside the truck after we were done. She was outside the truck, fixing her clothes and I was putting my shoes on. I had one shoe on with the money in it and I was putting the other shoe on. The guy took it and he was hitting me with the shoe, and then he took my other one, and he threw me out of the truck. And then, when he threw me out of the truck, he drove forward a little bit and then he backed up over my leg. (Katie, Halifax – about working in Moncton)

I'm the only one left of all my friends. They are all dead from prostitution, being killed. And I'm the only one left, and I was left for dead. The cops had to cut the belt off my neck, and the person was charged with attempted murder, with attempt to kill. The cops had pictures of my body, with my face and everything. They told my mother they didn't think I was going to live. I have a speech impediment now, I stutter sometimes. And my jaw, both of them were broke, since that attack, too. And they took pictures, and I was in the hospital four and a half days on life support. They didn't know if I was going to live. I have scars here from life-support and oxygen. There was not enough oxygen going to my brain, they put me in the round machine there, CAT scan it was, and I'm lucky to be alive now. And it's just like ... I'm jumping now ... I went from being left for dead, and all my other friends are dead, okay. And to me, I got to the point I didn't care if I died or not, but this person that did this to me got off because he ratted out another drug dealer. (Denise, Halifax)

Researchers and sex worker advocates have been pointing to an epidemic of violence against sex workers for several years.[28] Academic and government studies on the effects of the communicating law on violence against sex workers showed that large numbers of sex workers had been victims of violence, particularly by clients, and that the streets had become a more dangerous place to work in the wake of the law.[29] (The law is discussed in more detail in Chapter 3.) Indeed, John Lowman has argued that sex workers are many times more likely to be murdered than are other Canadian women, and the Canadian Centre for Justice Statistics has found that sex workers "face the highest occupational risk of homicide."[30] Lowman's research shows that sex workers are the victims of both situational violence (disputes over the transaction that become violent) and predatory (premeditated) violence, which is even more frightening – although both can result in death.[31] Predatory violence is particularly vicious. It is "very physical ... very intimate ... and designed to hurt."[32] Other reports note the frequency of all sorts of types of violence against sex workers, particularly those on the streets, from robbery to assault with a weapon to kidnapping and forcible confinement to attempted murder.³³ For male sex workers, while violence by clients is less of a concern (though still present), there is the continued threat of gay bashing. It must be said, however, that the level of violence reported by our interviewees is again a product of the bias of our community sample, in that many of our respondents are survival workers who worked mainly on the street. Indeed, some indoor workers distinguish themselves from street-based workers because they are more in control of their working conditions and do not necessarily view violence as "their issue." As one escort worker stated:

> **It's as safe as you want to make it ...**
> *Interviewer: I was thinking if I was on the street, I may not have control on who's drunk and who's not, who's trying to get me in the car ...*
> **Then you don't go in that car. It depends on how desperate you are for the money.** (Felicity, Halifax)

Although indoor work is generally viewed as safer than outdoor work – and certainly the incidence of murder appears to be lower – violence is also a continuing threat for escort workers (particularly those on out-call) and exotic dancers, who still do not have the full protection of labour codes.³⁴ The epidemic of violence against sex workers would be a national emergency if any other group were involved; but sex workers, particularly those who are working on the street and may have addictions or be racialized, have not been the object of any great concern.

It is, sadly, not surprising then that violence, particularly by clients, is the primary concern identified by the interviewees. A number specifically identified beatings, stabbings, rape, and murder; and many identified clients as the source of this violence. As one long-time worker, who had worked in both indoor and outdoor settings, observed, "It used to be pimps, then other sex workers; now it's johns" (Dana, Halifax). Violence and the fear of violence, along with the fear many of them harbour that the police are not willing to protect them, are overwhelming factors in these workers' lives. As one woman put it, "We put our life on the line as soon as we walk out the door" (Kisha, Halifax).

Both situational and predatory violence were reported by the women and men we spoke with. As one woman chillingly detailed,

> **For about four or five years, every summer we'd get some kind of fucking nut that would go off the whole summer, right? I think we got through this summer without one, but it seems like every summer we've got some kind of loser.** (Heidi, Halifax)

The size of Maritime towns makes it relatively easy for predatory clients to track down sex workers' homes:

> It's such a small place is part of the reason I quit too, because I could be very noticeable ... If somebody was actually in town, and they were a client, they might be able to find out where I lived; because it's a small area. (Celeste, Halifax)

And certainly, the fear of getting into a car with "some crazy psycho" was shared by nearly all those who worked the streets. Even situational violence might be worse in the Maritimes; according to some respondents:

> In Montreal, most of the men tend to be five foot six or five foot seven or shorter, so they can't really be that ... they're not very intimidating, so it's very easy to intimidate them, to feel that you have power over them. But here in the Maritimes, a lot of the men are like six foot two. (Celeste, Halifax)

Being murdered is the biggest fear and a very real risk for sex workers in Canada. Sex workers are keenly aware of the reality of this possibility, especially in the wake of the murder trial of Robert William Pickton, suspected of killing many of the sixty-plus sex workers missing in British Columbia. The British Columbian murders and the murder of sex workers in Halifax, particularly the murder of a pregnant sex worker, were all very present for the women we spoke with:

> You gotta put up with a lot of assholes like when they're drinkin'. They want their money back, or they're violent. So you have to figure out how to get out of that situation. Sometimes – personally, knock on wood, for me I got out of a lot of it – but for my friends that got murdered, they didn't get out of it, right? So ... I mean, don't get me wrong, it's easy money but it's dangerous money ... Yeah, and I gets scared out there. Like, I get really scared because what about I get an asshole that's gonna rape me and kill me? And then look at me, God only knows where he'd bury me or whatever. (Tara, Halifax)

> Yeah, even in escorts, there are some freaks. There are freaks everywhere. Even us women are freaks, 'cause the johns don't know what we're about, no more than we know what they're about. So ... vice versa, they don't know ... But we have to be more cautious than they do, 'cause they're choosing us, and we don't know what they've got in store for us when we're out there ... My best friend was murdered. She was eight months pregnant, had the baby slashed right out of her. (Katrina, Halifax)

> Like that man up in BC [Pickton], killin' all them girls up there, okay? Every night I think my friend's up there dead. I walk past the park, or even these streets, I look in the alleyways. One of my friends was seven months pregnant. They found her. They thought it was a mannequin. She was stabbed to death, and they found her dead, on X Street and I mean, I was just with her. This is scary. (Denise, Halifax)

Missing sex workers in Halifax also came up in casual conversations outside the interview room. There had been no police investigations into, or any concern on the part of anyone other than community outreach workers about, these cases at that point. A former sex worker, now working in outreach, reported:

> It's happening here, too. Well, one of our program users, she's been gone a year now and it's kind of sad because I've known her for years, and I worked with her. I used with her, and then I worked with her here, trying to help her out and she would be clean and she'd be off the streets ... So now, she's been missing for a year and it's kind of really sad. They just found a body, thirty-five years old or thirty-two, just recently – a week or two ago. I was hopeful it was her [for the sale of closure], but the age didn't match. She was my age. So they haven't found her yet, but there are a lot of women going missing. (Mandy, Halifax)

A few months later Halifax police admitted, in the aftermath of yet another murder of a sex worker, that at least eight women linked to the sex and/or drug trade had mysteriously gone missing or been murdered over the past twenty years.[35] It later turned out that, since 2002, police had been collecting hair from sex workers for DNA identification in case they were found dead.[36]

The belief that no one cares about the violence experienced by sex workers is deeply embedded among those we spoke with. As one worker poignantly put it:

> See, I get scared where I was raped. I get really paranoid, but I got to do something to eat, you know, smoke. So that's what I am doing tonight, trying to go out and make some money to get a room, and the public don't even feel bad. They'll know when I gets stabbed or beat up or whatever. (Deanna, Saint John)

Younger men are definitely seen as much more dangerous:

> I don't trust young guys. I was out, when I first started, I went with a young guy once out by the airport, and he wanted to have sex without a

condom. And I told him no. So, this mark right here, he stabbed me. And I had to walk from the airport back into here because I don't hitchhike. And after that, I never went out with a young guy again; I only like the older men. They're more, um, they talk to you better. They respect a little bit more ... even though what you're doing, your trade. And they're gentle with ya. And they take their time with ya and that's what I like. (Brianna, Saint John)

Avoiding younger men is a common method of self-protection:

I hate the younger ones, I usually refuse them. Under thirty for sure 'cause they're just there for the sex and they want their way and it's too dangerous. And I've got two kids and I've got a fiancé so, you know. (Patricia, Saint John)

While men are generally less susceptible to violence by clients, there is a continuing threat of gay bashing:[37]

Bashings. That's the worst, I guess, for the males, because we are in such a secluded area there is no escape. That's just the way it is, you know. You can either jump over the hills, [except] there is nowhere to go. You're trapped between the fence and the road. So if ten guys are comin' at you in their car and they stop, you're trapped.
Interviewer: Has that happened often?
Four or five times this summer, including a couple of stabbings. They won't pick on bigger guys usually. Like what happens if there are four or five of us out there, like one time these cars were driving around, and I was by myself, they started coming at me and I – you know – you sort of just had a big rock or, you know, [look for] where there's a stick or something. At that time I just got up there and I didn't have anything set up, but I managed to get down around the side where T was, a friend of mine, and there was other people there. So when they came around the four of us all had sticks and rocks. And if they wanted to get out of their car it was like, "[Go ahead,] get out of your car," you know. "There is eight of you in the car and there is four of us here ... so let's go." It's amazing how they change their mind when it's four people instead of one. You know they don't want to fight four people, but most of them are just mouth, you know, just yelling out of the car obscenity. And I yell at them right back (laughs).

I don't let them get away with shit unless they're bigger than me – one on one it's like, "Okay, you win," you know. That's just the way it is. I don't go out looking for people. I don't go up to straight people and say,

"Oh, you're straight, fuck off," you know. I don't see why they have the right to do the same. (Scott, Halifax)

Sex workers obviously do not accept this constant threat of violence and harassment. They do not see it as something that simply goes with the job. One interviewee felt that this violence is a product of public attitudes that position sex workers as disposable or as non-people. She argued that the media in particular have portrayed the sex worker as "a stereotypical low-life person and a disposable person and the more that the media continues do that, the more the tricks feel that they are allowed to be violent" (Dana, Halifax). John Lowman has similarly traced the increasing violence to the rise of a "discourse of disposal" in the media and in public discussion of the sex trade.[38] It is these prevalent public and government attitudes toward "getting rid" of sex workers and prostitution that have given "predatory misogynistic men a rationale for doing it in a situation where they don't think too many people will care."[39]

Certainly, street-based sex workers face a climate of harassment that indicates they are held in low regard and are, therefore, considered fair game for both situational and predatory violence. Harassing behaviour and uncaring attitudes on the part of both clients and the larger public were reported by several of the sex workers we spoke with. For example, clients sometimes drove workers far out of town and then left them there:

There's one guy in particular, he drove somewhere and I had to hitchhike back home 'cause he wouldn't take me back. (Alison, Halifax)

Another Halifax worker reported abusive behaviour by passers-by:

I've had a girlfriend go out, even in the winter time, [they'd] throw a snowball and hit her right in the face and stuff. You'd be surprised what young drunken people will do. And the worst part of it is, if they weren't with their little friends yelling and hollering, they'd probably be down there paying ya. It's a fact, you'd be surprised at the younger people. (Belinda, Halifax)

The harassment from clients does not end when workers are off the job:

I had the baby one day. I was straight for a couple of days. I went to get the baby, I was walking down Z Street with the baby in the stroller and this fella came up to me. But it enraged me. Then I thought that maybe, you know, maybe I had something to do with him at one time.
Interviewer: So wherever you go ...

> You're propositioned, yeah. And I mean if you're a drug addict, you're not gonna say no.
> *Interviewer: So what did you do that day?*
> I just said, "Look it, I've got my grandson here." I said, "You stay the fuck away from me and me grandchild." Period. I've never seen him again. I've never seen him again after that. But I mean, you see the same people, the same business men, lawyers, doctors. (Tanya, Saint John)

One woman reported being stalked after leaving the trade altogether:

> And these johns are so sick. I got a stalker. He's honest-to-God, he's a stalker and I kicked his car. He won't leave me alone, but he doesn't ... He follows me. He followed me last night and the night before that. [I say,] "Get! Go! Get! Go!" You know, "Like don't, like don't. You're going to get hurt. Just leave me alone!" He can't believe ... like I go up and ... I barely remembered him at first and then I found out who he was. But anyways, if they had any sense at all, these, these tricks, if they had any sense at all they wouldn't say nothing. I prefer older men. (Alyssa, Saint John)

Harassing behaviour by clients and the wider public was particularly noticeable in Saint John, where there were many reports of people taunting, taking advantage of, and harassing sex workers. One woman talked about the way people harassed her when she worked:

> We have a lot of young guys drive around hollering stuff out the window – "Five bucks, five bucks, fucky, fucky." You know, being smart and stuff like that. And girls driving around [calling out] "whore" and "bitch" and "slut." (Brianna, Saint John)

One young man who had worked in Saint John left because he found it particularly difficult:

> 'Cause in Saint John especially, quite a few times ... there was other people out on the block, and they were always telling you about people who would pick you up and try to rob you. They weren't actually out to pick you up, they were out to rob you. And there's also people, [like] a guy in Saint John who would take you somewhere and you'd think, okay, we're going to do this ... But he would take you and he would tie you up and leave you there. (Eric, Moncton)

His partner agreed that working in Saint John was problematic and that the police presence might increase the incidence of being driven out of town and forced to walk back:

Yeah, and there's always that fear of the police maybe coming around the corner when you're parked in a car somewhere. And I've had that happen once. And there's also like, one time actually when I was in Saint John, I had somebody drive me and they just drove and I was like, "Let me out of the car." And they just kept driving around and I was like ... I knew there was something fishy when I got in and they drove around and then they dropped me off way out by McAllister Place [the eastside shopping mall]. I had to come all the way to town. I had to walk and he just drove around. He was just driving around and he kept trying to touch me and I was like, "No, don't touch me." As soon as I got into the car I knew something was up. (Robert, Moncton)

Workers struggling with addictions spoke of johns driving by in cars, waving money out the window just as they were trying to get clean, and of clients beating down the price because they knew of the worker's addiction. It is perhaps not surprising then that Saint John workers were the most likely to complain of low self-esteem. There were also cases of low self-esteem issues in Halifax. One worker, who was not addicted and usually worked the high-track stroll, reported on her attempts at working the low-track stroll in Halifax:

Now downtown is considered a high track, that's where the girls are a little bit more ... They're supposed to be a little more, I guess more on a professional basis. They dress for the work, and they're not so much on drugs. And they pay a little more for these girls. I don't want to say that they're any better than the other ones, but a little bit more of a higher class of prostitution. And then you have the other strolls where [there] are mostly the girls that are on drugs and would probably take almost anything the man offers them. They're the ones I really feel sorry for, because they get the most abuse ... You know, I'm glad I can't put myself in that category, but I've been there too, I've been there too, and I've experienced it, I don't want to go that way no more. If I wanna do it, at least I am gonna go downtown and take the high track, 'cause I'll take the time and fix myself up and go down there and do what I gotta do.
Interviewer: And you make more money too.
Yeah, yeah, you make more money too. Well they know downtown's really more, more than those girls [can make], say, on X Street. I don't know because I don't work up there. I work downtown, but I heard that ... I tried it a couple of times up there and the men offered real low money and I got upset and left. You know, they play all kinds of games with your head. (Valerie, Halifax)

For street workers, the struggle to be properly paid for their work in the face of stigma and illegality is made more difficult by the climate of violence. A cycle of violence and mistreatment appeared to be growing on the streets of Saint John as some sex workers tried to settle the score with clients who failed to pay properly. Sex workers there reported concerns about angry johns who had been stolen from in the past. Some sex workers (sometimes in conjunction with their partners) coax johns – often drunk – into giving up their wallets or bank cards and PINs. Other times, a man is taken to a room by a woman, believing he has procured the services of a sex worker, and then her boyfriend appears, takes the money, and leaves with the woman. The johns who are taken advantage of are usually too ashamed to go to police and more likely to try to remedy the situation themselves by tracking down and threatening or beating up sex workers they believe have taken advantage of them. As one woman warned,

> It's going to get really rough because a bunch of the girls, 'cause they rip people off when they're uptown. It makes it look bad on other women. "You're going to find yourselves face up in the gutter." I always keep telling them that. (Deanna, Saint John)

There were similar stories in Halifax:

> The police know that too, because it's a high rate with the prostitutes with the drugs, and then there's crime involved. Because then the girls ain't making enough, and the guys know they're out there for dope, the dates, so they don't want to give them the money they're asking for. So they end up trying to get it cheaper. And then they know it's only for drugs, and then the crime comes in. 'Cause that's when some of the girls start robbing them and stuff. (Denise, Halifax)

Violence in the trade is not seen by sex workers as an inherent problem of the sex trade itself; rather, it is viewed as a product of stigma and public attitudes, as well as poor working conditions, which leaves them struggling with disrespectful clients, over being properly paid or using protection, clients who could easily turn violent. Sex workers have a nuanced reading of the trade and their clients. They recognize the violence but still maintain pride in their work. One woman who had worked many years in the trade before quitting both her addiction and the trade presented one such nuanced understanding:

> Oh, you get your odd ... You know something, I'll tell you right now, I've met some really, really good people and I've met some real winners too.

Scary, eh? See, when I talk about this I kinda disassociate myself from it, that's so I won't get all ... I've met some nice people, some nice men, but there's sick men too. They know these girls are sick, and they thrive on that, you see? They're getting twenty bucks, or ten bucks, or whatever. It's terrible. It just makes my heart break, eh. And like the johns, something should be happening with them too, eh. They're dirty, very dirty. You know you see them one day and they give you enough. And then they cut you down, and, "Here, here, $5." Hello! See ya! Five dollars, I don't think so! For a bag of chips and a bottle of pop. No. But see I started when I was seventeen, you see, and then I wasn't on the street, I was working for this gentleman. He was not a gentleman, but anyways. And that's where I started and then I ended up on the streets. I was the oldest out there and looking the finest. (Alyssa, Saint John)

Coping with Violence: "It's as Safe as You Want to Make It"
Many of our respondents do not feel altogether powerless against the violence and, indeed, have their own ways of coping with it. Some cope by turning to drugs or alcohol to shield them from harassment and fear. Or they turn inward, shielding themselves through silence and refusal to acknowledge the harassment. One Saint John woman responded to harassment by holding on to her pride as best she could:

That doesn't bother me. I just turn my head, whatever, you know. It doesn't bother me, 'cause I know what I am. I'm the one that chose to be that way, so ... (Brianna, Saint John)

Most workers have developed a series of safety measures. The need to screen clients – to pick the safe ones and weed out the potentially dangerous ones – has led sex workers to adopt certain measures. These range from moving into escort work to choosing older clients to arming themselves, all in an attempt to minimize the risks as much as possible. But given the alarming amount of violence directed against sex workers, none of these techniques provides full protection.

Indoor work, while limiting in terms of control over one's work, is generally viewed as safer. Many of the people we spoke with felt escort work was "much safer" because clients were screened to some extent (for in-call), or someone waits for the worker or knows where she is (with out-call). But escort work is not available to (or wanted by) everyone as an option, nor is it any guarantee of safety. The semi-legality of indoor work – it must operate under the fiction that sex for exchange is not taking place on its premises – means owners and managers can be leery of calling on police for protection. And because there is little outside pressure on owners to respect the rights of employees to workplace safety, they can ignore on-the-job safety issues. A former receptionist at a club in Fredericton (who worked there for only a few weeks) explained:

> There was two times that girls were attacked and nothing was done either time. Police weren't phoned. That kind of disturbed me, because one of the girls was the one that hates doing out-calls. This one that's been there for three, three and a half years. She went on that call, and he got very, very violent with her and she got black eyes, and she was all bruised up, fat lip and stuff and she got back around to the club, and they didn't do anything. They didn't even send the police around. And I asked them, like, "Well, why not?" You know, it's like, "This is a legitimate business, did we forget that? Did we forget how it is that we're managing a staff load here? We do have the right to phone the police." And the manager said, "Yeah, but we couldn't prove it." (Ashley, Fredericton)

Out-call work – while protecting workers from having to stand on the street – still means that a worker may end up alone in a secluded location with a client. An escort worker in Halifax doubted the relative safety of out-call escort work:

> The worst? I just find safety was. I used to think that escort was safe, 'cause people know where you are and whatever. But it's not. It's a big headache. You meet a lot of really crazy people. I don't do house calls no more. I won't go to a private home 'cause I had a really bad experience. So I stopped doing it. I just basically do hotel calls, and I will go to a home if it's a two-girl call, but not by myself. (Tamara, Halifax)

Others, though, pointed out that it is quite possible that "no one can hear you scream" in a hotel room and that clients are desperate to make sure they are not caught. One worker in Saint John reported that she received her most vicious beating in a hotel. Another Saint John worker had similar feelings about escort work:

> I was scared ... 'cause I didn't know them. You meet someone over the phone, and you run into them. You don't know what you're getting into. Same on the streets.
> *Interviewer: Yeah, which do you find more dangerous?*
> Both. But, see, a lot of the guys on the street I know now. It's not like I take anyone, 'cause I'm scared to. 'Cause I had friends in Halifax here that got killed. One, I don't know if you heard of her, she got killed and she had two kids. She was a prostitute and they found her out in North Preston. (Deanna, Saint John)

For those who operate more independently, maintaining regulars is another way of trying to reduce the risk, both on the street or when working out of their homes. A Halifax worker who worked independently out of her home explained how she had handled bad dates:

> I've only had problems with two people. And I've dealt with it, um, like I got pepper spray and everything around the house. But the way I dealt with it was, I just said to the guy ... His, his thing was, he refused to use a condom, you know. And I said, "There's no way, I told you that on the phone and everything." And he says, well, he says, "I'll just kick the shit out of you." And I said, "And I'll just yell very loud because," I said, "you don't know what's behind door number one, door number two, [or] door number three in this apartment." And, like he was gone like a flash. I had the money and he was gone. (April, Halifax)

Another, however, expressed concern that "even regulars" could become violent:

> You never know who you're gonna get to come in. And even if that person is a regular, one day he could turn on ya. You could be seeing this person for six months to a year, and him not do nothing to you ... then all of a sudden he turns on you.
> *Interviewer: Has that happened to you?*
> A few times. (Hope, Halifax)

While strip clubs are supposed to have better security, with bouncers and bartenders keeping an eye on the floor and the backrooms, customer aggression occurs there as well.[40] A Moncton-based dancer reported an experience in Newfoundland:

> But there was one time – I think I was in Newfoundland, at one of the bars in Newfoundland – and there was this one guy I was dancing for. And when I had turned my back towards him – to do my little dance – he had tried to stick his finger up my bum ... Oh yeah, drove it right up my ass ... Well, I remember, they wanted to bar me from the bar and never allow me to work there again, because what I had done was, I turned around, and I shoved my foot so far in his scrotum. So, with spiked heel and all. And I drove it and I drove it and I drove it and all of a sudden you see blood starting to just pour down buddy's legs and everything through his jeans.
> And anyways, buddy had gotten a hold of the owner of the bar and pretty much ratted me out. And I explained to the bar owner, what had happened, he had shoved his finger right up my ass, without me even

being aware that it was coming. I said, "So yeah, the first reflex was to turn around, and shove the foot, and the groin, I didn't purposely aim for the groin. I could have hit him in the head, in the chest, but just the way I turned around, the groin was right there." He said, "Well, are you aware that buddy is going to need some extensive surgery and that he wants to press criminal charges?" I said, "Well, great, then I want to press charges too." I said, "He wants to press charges for what? For self-defence?" I said, "The guy shoved his finger up my bum." I said, "Hello, my husband doesn't even do that. So, no, no, if he wants to press charges, great, go ahead, I'll sign up all the paperwork and let's get my paperwork started too."

Anyways, once buddy found out that I wanted to charge him as well, he dropped all the charges. And he had medical benefits at work, so they had paid for the surgery – whatever kind of surgery he had needed. And the bar was going to bar me from working there altogether. And then once he dropped the charges, I dropped the charges, everything was kind of smoothed over. It had been like six months, the bar called me, and said, "Well, you can come back to work if you'd like to." And I said, "Well, I'm telling you one thing right now, if that ever happens again, buddy will be lucky if it gets him in the scrotum 'cause the next time it may be in the head." (Colleen, Moncton)

Clearly, workers are willing to fight back if need be. On the streets, where sex workers are much more likely to be targeted for violence, a number reported carrying small weapons such as knives to protect themselves. They argued that weapons charges should not be laid against sex-trade workers who were only trying to protect themselves from sure and certain violence, from which the police are unwilling to protect them. Watching each others' backs, or having someone to watch one's own back, has become more and more important. Without police protection, workers turn to each other or to a wider circle of friend or boyfriends or other protectors. Teaming up is one method:

> See, that's why I would never go in a car with somebody. Like I would only be [working] if there's somebody else there with me. I would never go by myself. (Kendra, Saint John)

Other workers talked about watching out for each other and memorizing licence plates:

> But some nights when I don't want to walk down to work, and if N does, I go out and watch her back. If she gets in a car, I'll write down the number. You know what I mean, the licence plate number. And I time her. And if

she's not back, I freak. The girls pick on her uptown and I am not doing it. I think it's good for me to watch N's back. And there's a lot of other girls up there some nights, you know. I come out and watch them.

(Deanna, Saint John)

Other Sex Workers

While sex workers can be a source of support and protection for each other, the competition of the trade and the violent climate can turn workers against each other. On the streets, some of our interviewees fear other sex workers – being beaten or robbed by them – as much as their clients, since retributive violence can be part of the protector role some sex workers perform for other workers:

> I got kicked [shows interviewer a large bruise on her thigh].
> *Interviewer: That today?*
> No, last night, the night before.
> *Interviewer: So is it the johns who are the most dangerous?*
> Yeah, actually the girls too, they're both the same. I'm more scared of the girls than the guys. (Megan, Halifax)

One worker described how she went after one of the girls on the strip for robbing a friend and a member of her family:

> I'm a ... what do you call it? I'm a survivor. But when I get mad, and I would've went drinking, I probably would have killed somebody. That's why I don't drink no more. One girl ripped N off, and I went uptown and wrenched her right there ...
>
> She ripped my brother-in-law off, too, for sixty bucks. She said, "Well, if it had've been anybody else, you wouldn't have said nothing." I said, "Yeah, well, you don't rip people off like that, 'cause you make the other girls look bad." And I wasn't going to let her beat up N either, 'cause N has a problem. And if she goes off, look out, 'cause she'll kill ya. So I'd rather be with her. (Deanna, Saint John)

The tightening up of income on the street and the increase in drug use may be contributing to violence among sex workers as workers compete or attempt to rob one another. But, as Bruckert notes, the aggression between workers can be a reflection of the aggression that they face from clients: "They're taking the violence that they get from a customer out on another dancer. They're taking their frustrations out on her."[41] Inter-worker aggression is a survival instinct in a violent climate. A long-time worker referred to the era of pimping in Halifax as one that provoked inter-worker violence:

> In the early nineties they became very, very violent within the pimp situation to the point where they even had the women being violent with each other. They would say, "Okay, you're beating up your wife-in-law" – the wife-in-law is, if I have a pimp and he has more than one woman, the association of those women to me is wife-in-law, that's the name. So he would set, say, three girls to beat up a wife-in-law who was stashing money or something, right? He would say, "You guys take care of that."
>
> *Interviewer: They'd use one against the other.*
>
> Exactly. And they did that too in a sense where, "Well, of course I spend more time with her. She makes more money than you," right? Which again would make the women jealous of each other. It would also make the women more apt to do things they wouldn't ordinarily do, such as maybe anal sex, 'cause they knew that was maybe a five hundred dollar job or whatever. (Dana, Halifax)

Certainly, there are conflicts between sex workers. Indeed, a number of our interviewees who had worked elsewhere, such as in Montreal, found sex workers in the Maritimes much less co-operative and helpful than were those in other places. Again, this likely reflects the absence of sex worker organizations such as there are in larger centres. One woman who had worked in the United States remarked that the lack of support among workers is not a function of the job itself but a result of the lack of organization in the Maritimes:

> The downside is, I would say, the lack of support among the girls. I would say that's sorta internally in the job instead of the downside of this as opposed to other jobs. There are people obviously in San Francisco that know they're doing it right in San Francisco, the ladies out there. I would really like to go out there. (Joan, Halifax)

Another confirmed this perception by observing the difference in working in Montreal, where the sex-worker-run organization Stella provides support and advocacy for sex workers:

> I'm telling you, this [Halifax] is the worst place to work, if you've just come to this city and you don't know anybody. Even if you did, none of these girls will help ya. They won't. They'll try to rob a date from you before. You know what I mean: while he's robbin' you, they'll rob you. That's how pathetic it is. Like, as far as like licence plate numbers and stuff like that, they don't even take a glance. They don't help you out like that. Montreal, God, the girls out there are A-1. All the women stick together up there. Down here ... everybody's on crack down here ... Up

there, I mean the girls might be on drugs but they, they make their money first, before. Like the ones out here are wired ... They get it, they go do their thing. They come back out, [and] they do their thing. Montreal is totally different. (Samantha, Halifax)

Hired Guns

Without an organization of sex workers to provide support and protection, sex workers sometimes have to turn to others. But having someone to watch out for you can mean a protector who expects something in return, and who can themselves be a source of violence. This is a murky area, because of the common mythology of the pimp. The mythology, based as myths often are, in a small piece of reality, is that some men pressure women into the sex trade and/or run women in the trade, in order to make a profit for themselves. This mythology is based on a deep racial and sexual bias against black men: the pimp in North American culture is widely depicted as, and understood to be, a black man. Indeed, the racist undercurrent of the pimp mythology is most likely the root, and not a branch, of the myth. The fear of the black male, and black male sexuality, goes back to the days of slavery and imperialism. It became wrapped up in prostitution mythology with the birth of the white slave panic of the 1800s – a panic that was reproduced several times throughout the following century and is reproduced today in the anti-trafficking-in-women discourse.[42] In Halifax, as we shall see in Chapter 4, the pimping panic of the early 1990s played directly on this racialized discourse of sexual fear. The stereotyped image of the pimp, therefore, has become an easy way of understanding the trade – and an easy way to dismiss the violence against sex workers as a product of a subculture of violent black pimps rather than the product of negative social attitudes toward sex workers. Any male who associates with a female sex worker is widely understood as her pimp, who provides protection in exchange for money, but who is also the primary source of violence for the sex worker. But there are a wide variety of roles and relationships here that do not necessarily correspond with this singular portrayal. In part, this portrayal rests on a false depiction of sex workers as uniformly powerless or as exclusively sex workers without other kinds of relationships. And, as sex worker organizations note, there is frequent confusion of women's being forced to work for someone else with women's working in the trade and sharing their money with someone else or supporting someone else – a distinction that is not unclear in any other type of work. This confusion makes it difficult for the general public to understand that sex workers also have husbands and boyfriends, sometimes girlfriends, who provide support and protection but who are not exploiting them. It is also possible that sex workers may have abusive relationships which are simply that: abusive relationships, and which, as with the relationships of so many other women, are not necessarily or directly linked to their work in the sex trade. Even when workers talked about men who seemed to fit the fairly classic definition of a pimp, they emphasized the important role these men played as protectors from the violence of clients in the absence of police protection.

Some of the women we spoke with talked about having had "pimps" in the past (it is important to remember that this is not a permanent condition), whereas some talked about "boyfriends." Others talked about abusive relationships or about codependent, addiction-related relationships; some talked about husbands and boyfriends who look out for them but who are not running them; others about abusive boyfriends or husbands or ex's, some of whom also took their money. The failure to understand the wide variety of violence faced by sex workers and the wide variety of ways in which sex workers and their families and friends try to cope has led to the simple criminalization of anyone who tries to protect sex workers in any way. One respondent explained that protection and pimping are not necessarily one and the same thing, since husbands and boyfriends sometimes perform the role of spotter:[43]

> I don't understand that [having a pimp]; I never had one. My son's father, I knew him since I was sixteen and he used to watch me. Get the description of the car and the licence plate, just in case I didn't come back. But, I never gave him my money. I couldn't give my money to anybody else. Considering what I just did for my money, what's worse. (Jacqueline, Saint John)

Although there were respondents who talked about "pimps" per se, many saw the role of a pimp as that of a protector from the violence of clients. That is, they perform an important and useful function – even if they sometimes take advantage of this role. One young woman who, as an adolescent, had worked in the United States explained that a pimp could be viewed as protection but there was payback for this service:

> There's a few difficult customers, like I got a black eye from a customer before – but that's what you got your pimp for. That's the good side, they give you like the hook-ups, the protection, the security, the place to ... like they help you out, feed ya. But the downside is you just better work it. (Alexis, Moncton)

There were reports both of pimps who were violent and of those who were not. Some older sex workers in Halifax talked about the "old days," with men who were more like underground business managers, and the later days of violent pimps:

> The pimp era was quite a violent era, okay. Not the early ones, not the seventies and eighties, they were more the [regular] guys, and they weren't as violent. (Dana, Halifax)

Her timeframe points to something very important: the increase in violence by pimps may in part reflect the crossover of the drug trade in this later era and may also reflect the period of generally increased criminalization, disposal discourse, and the concomitant increase in violence.[44] That is, all men – clients, organizers, protectors, and so on – got the message that sex workers were disposable people.

However, when men are acting as pimps, they can become more of a threat than the clients from whom they are ostensibly protecting workers, which forces workers to choose their risks:

> *Interviewer: How long were you under a pimp?*
> Oh Lord, about seven and a half years.
> *Interviewer: How dangerous was that?*
> Believe it or not, I was more scared of him than I was the dates. Just imagine meeting a stranger, could be Charles Manson, you have no idea. But you're more willing to deal with this than the trouble at home. It's more like, we had a quota, if you don't have $100, don't come home. Don't matter what the weather is, if it's a snowstorm, and all you can get is drunk drivers plowing, you better get them to stop. Like that's, even Hallowe'en they'd want you to work. I'd take a beating before I'd work on Hallowe'en night. Some clown could pick you up and stab you ... They'd go up the street, there's fifty clowns. Oh, no, no, no, no. It's bad enough you're taking a chance on violence, but when you're going through a masquerade party ... It's like, to me, it's like you're looking for something bad to happen. (Belinda, Halifax)

One worker spoke of the problem of violent pimps in Montreal and Toronto:

> Oh, like in Toronto, I had a real bad experience, real bad experience – not only with the police but with other people wanting me to work for them. Guys wanting me to work for them and I refused.
> *Interviewer: Trying to pimp you?*
> Um, trying to pimp me and telling me that I couldn't work there unless I was with somebody. Like, I was giving my money to another man. And when I was refusing that and tried to work independently, I was beaten pretty severe. I mean, he broke both my jaws and I was in a coma for a couple of days in the hospital. They didn't even know who I was. I didn't

> have no I.D. on me. It was ... I couldn't even say who the person was, because the attacker came from behind, the attackers. I was in really bad shape for a while, really bad shape. (Valerie, Halifax)

Despite all the publicity on pimping in Halifax, she argued that it is Montreal and Toronto, not Halifax, where pimping is an issue:

> And if you don't have a pimp they don't want you down there [Montreal and Toronto] or they are trying to get into your business – [they] try to get you to choose – they all do, all of them. I don't know one girl that don't have a pimp. Now down here I find it different. Down here, I find the girls are more independent and they're just out there for, I don't know if for financial reasons or for a drug problem or something. But it's not mostly a man putting them there. Like in Montreal they've got to do it, like there are certain hours where they got to go and [bring] some home. And it usually is from eight to six in the morning, the girls I know.
> (Valerie, Halifax)

It was also noteworthy that being pimped is not viewed as a permanent or necessary condition. Rather, it is often a function of the age of the sex worker (those who reported being pimped were pimped at a young age) or location. Many of our respondents reported that the era of pimping was pretty much over in Halifax, although younger girls may be more likely to be taken advantage of.[45] Some of those who reported being pimped were referring to their pasts. About her former boyfriend-pimp, one young woman explained:

> Well, I was so young, right? And he was my boyfriend for a while, since I was eleven. He was a lot older than me, a lot bigger than me. And me and him would fight something terrible, you know. Especially if like, you know, if he needed a couple of bills for something and I didn't make quite enough to help out. Because pimps don't even mess around. They just take all your money. So, you know, he'd leave me some change to eat, or something but ... (Alexis, Moncton)

This relationship, however, should also be understood as sexual exploitation of a child – not simply pimping. Our respondent was able to fight back and get herself out of a bad situation:

> Yeah, see, like I mean my ex he would, we would fight something terrible. But the last time he ever hit me, I ripped half his face off a brick wall. So he never touched me again and then I moved out of town. (Alexis, Moncton)

Her male friend, Sean, who was currently working in the trade, interjected:

Sean: That's just like K and J. That's what K does, he takes all her money.
Alexis: Talks about "I ain't pimping her." Come on now. I feel for [J], I just want to take that girl and just fucking [take her] away from him.
Sean: She's the nicest thing.
Alexis: She's a sweetheart but she takes so much shit from him. (Alexis and Sean, Moncton)

Having lived through a similar experience herself, this worker respondent was able to recognize other exploitative relationships and wanted to help. Indeed, her experience and insight could be valuable to other workers if she were given the chance to share it through an outreach or support organization for sex workers.

The importance of sex workers' understandings and experiences as being front and centre in any solution to the issue of violence or pimping was made clear in Saint John, where sex-worker and outsider understandings of the situation diverged widely. In Saint John, what was commonly understood as pimping by police and the public was in fact more a case of addicted couples. At a follow-up workshop to these interviews with five current or former sex workers, the women explained that the men who were often seen on the strip with addicted sex workers were boyfriends who were also addicted. The women were working to get money for them both. There were reports of the women being beaten up by these boyfriends, but this is perhaps most helpfully understood within the framework of an abusive relationship rather than of pimping. Thus, there are complicated issues of love and mutual dependence that need to be taken into consideration.

There are other nuances in the role of men on the strip. Sometimes these men have a tenuous relationship to the women and may be there simply to rob them for drug money or take advantage of their having access to drugs. One worker explained:

The men now that are smoking drugs and that, they prey on the girls that work. You'll see a bunch of guys standing by Y Street now, 'cause when they see the girls working, they know the girls got money to go for the dope, so they beat them up, [and] take their money. Or follow behind them, and smoke dope with them. (Denise, Halifax)

Sometimes the relationship to the sex trade itself is tenuous – that is, a couple may engage in all sorts of schemes to support their addiction:

See, me and him were on the crack together – this was in '91, '92. Yeah, we got hooked into the crack together. And he got me, that's what kind of

> got me working, in a way. He'd get me to go up here, up on C Street and that, but the thing he had me doing, was getting the guys, and then take them to my place. And then he'd rush in, and I'd already have the money. And he'd just get rid of the guy. And then I was getting nervous of that, because these guys that he's rippin' off, are gonna get me when he's not around. So I stopped doing it for him. He got mad, but we worked through it. I didn't want to do that no more, 'cause, [I would] get killed or something. (Violet, Saint John)

And, in the case of addicted couples, the roles can be reversed, and the sex trade can be just one more method of providing income for both people:

> I been doing crack since 1990. Before [getting into the sex trade] I supported the habit with my boyfriend. He used to shoplift a lot. And then it was a welfare cheque at the end of the month. We'd split it on that. That's how I first started supportin' it. (Brianna, Saint John)

All of these examples problematize the simple understanding of pimping and reflect much more complex relationships and situations. Further, working for someone else or someone else's addiction is not seen as inescapable. One woman reported working to sustain her boyfriend's addiction, and then quitting after she'd had enough:

> But I don't understand. I'd like to understand myself – why I'm not hooked on the drugs, 'cause I'm not. Like, I never did any of those or nothing, nothing at all ... And I've been with men that does pills, that does needles. My first son's father, he was doing needles. My ex that I just split up with last year, he was a crackhead. And I seen it and seen it and seen it. And just at the end of it I got fed up with it and said, "No. See you. I ain't working the streets and giving you money and you buying crack. I quit." (Candace, Saint John)

Why and how some workers and not others become vulnerable to being taken advantage of in this way is a much more productive research question if the interest is in preventing such abuse from taking place, as is the question of how some are able to get out of bad situations. For example, one woman simply got fed up with having most of her money used up by her boyfriend:

> I just woke up one morning and knew that I had to [leave my boyfriend]. I'm either gonna die here today or I'm getting out. 'Cause I couldn't ... My allowance was $5 a day. No, I'm a liar, $20 a day. But I had to buy my

condoms. I had to buy whatever I'm gonna eat, and cigarettes ... Yeah, and that's *my* money. But I have to buy the condoms. I gotta buy the cigarettes and I gotta buy the food. And he's gonna smoke up the cigarettes and eat half the food, so ... And that's only hamburger and fries at McDonald's. He'll eat half of that. (Belinda, Halifax)

Leaving the trade and leaving an exploitative relationship are not always one and the same thing either: several of our respondents remained in the trade after leaving such a relationship. Others explained that their experiencing exploitation did not mean that the trade per se was degrading and exploitative:

Interviewer: Are you trying to exit at this point? You've made a decision that you ...
Yes. I'm not saying it's degrading and things. But for me, I guess, when I was thirteen I met a man and they were into the pimping scenes. I started to go with his best friend, and that's who my two kids are for. So, I didn't really get out and explore much. He was very controlling and it kept me in the trade for a lot of years. I quit school at age fifteen, you know, I just went back to school last year. I don't, like I said, I don't feel it's degrading and things, but it's just ... it's not me anymore. I don't want to abuse my body like that no more, and I shouldn't have to. (Kisha, Halifax)

Another interviewee was fighting her abusive boyfriend in court. K's story is an example of both the willpower and strength of many sex workers and the difficulties of pursuing exploiters because of the limiting language of pimping. K's boyfriend took most of her money, forced her to work when she did not want to, beat her when she refused, and stalked her when she tried to make a break. The relationship was a classic domestic abuse-stalking situation but, because of her work, it was understood legally within the framework of pimping.[46] The defence lawyer argued that because K was already working in the trade when she hooked up with her boyfriend, he could not be understood as a pimp. The defence lawyer claimed that "the woman's prior history coupled with [the accused's] drug addiction and his tendency toward violence 'would have resulted in things unfolding as they did ... [The accused] did not create a prostitute.'"[47] This shifted the blame back toward K and undermined her case. Further, the accused was later able to successfully make the argument that his conviction was "unfair" because K's testimony could not be trusted – the intimation being that, since she was a sex worker, she was not credible.[48] By framing the issue as one of pimping, the legal system muddied the issue rather than making it a clear case of partner abuse. K now faces returning to court to fight her abuser's appeal for a shorter sentence.

Understood from the perspective of sex workers, then, the issue of pimping is much less clear-cut than it may appear to be to outsiders. Sex workers who are in exploitative relationships are not simple victims of pimps or exploitative men. As always, they have their ways of fighting back. Programs and policies that seek to address the violence sex workers face must draw on this expertise if violence is to be effectively addressed. Meanwhile, sex workers have had to protect themselves, given that the illegality of the trade and the disregard with which sex workers are viewed has meant that the legal system rarely protects them from violence. However, many have been undeterred and are willing to take action.

"Next Time Just Pay the Forty Bucks": Sex Workers Fight Back

Sex workers use a variety of tactics to fight against violence and abuse. This is one woman's story:

> A lot of the women get beat up [but] they will not go to court. They don't report it because ... I had to report once and I can tell ya how I was treated and I was in my right mind. Like the thing is, if you are using, of course, they treat you like shit anyway. Okay? Plus they know that you are working, so that adds ... you know. Because the day that the guy pulled a knife on me ... I laughed because it was not the first time that someone has been violent with me. And I kind of have to laugh about it in a sense. But, anyway, he pulled the knife. And he grabbed me by the hair and he said to me, "You're gonna suck my cock and I'm gonna come down your throat." And I said, "The only way you're coming in my fucking throat is after I'm dead okay?"
>
> And I got freaked for a minute and I realized, I remembered, a light comes on. And, like I say, I was in my right mind that day. Good thing, because I don't know if I had been using and working how I would have reacted. [But] I hadn't been using yet, okay. But I did get panicky for a minute and I thought, okay, pull it together 'cause if you don't buddy is going to fuck you up. He is either going to force you to do something or he may even ... but I didn't ... you get a sense, you know if a guy is just trying to scare ya, or if he's a real lunatic. This guy was more trying to scare me. But when I felt that, I grabbed the blade of the knife with my hand and I said, "If you're crazy enough to cut my throat then you're crazy enough to cut my fingers off. Then do it. And if you're not that crazy then you picked the wrong bitch. 'Cause I am crazy." "Okay you proved your point, you're macho. Get out of my truck," [he said]. I said, "No, you get the fuck out, because if you think I'm getting out so you can stab me in the parking lot and have less evidence, it's not happening."
>
> So when he went to get out of his truck this way, I went the other way

through the window. And there was a hole in the fence because I scanned my area right away – and I learned that from being a child that was abused and never knowing when my dad was going to come home drunk and having to kind of scan my space so I know where a safe space is, you know. Then being married and being in an abusive relationship ... When you are the oldest child of all the children and there is a whole lot of violence within the home, you learn these things. They are natural things that seem to come to you and you feel that you are protecting the younger ones too. So I noticed that there was a hole in the fence that would be big enough to kind of weasel through, right? So I noticed that and I went through the fence. And this guy was taking out his garbage and he had a bag of garbage in each hand, and the door was open so he could set the garbage out ... And I ran right into their house, right? And his woman was in there and she was like, "Ahh!" And I said, "This guy is trying to kill me, could you call the cops?"

Now, luckily for me they were law students that were going to university. And things just fell in that particular day – the Creator was looking after me – because when the cops came [the students] were so appalled by the way the cops treated me. [The cop] said, "What do you want us to do about it?" That's what he said, when they came to the house: "Well, what do you want us to do about it?" "What do you mean what do I want you to do? I want you to do your fucking job, that's what I want, okay?" And he said, "But you girls want us to do all this and then you don't even show up to court." "First off, buddy, I haven't been a girl for a very long time, I'm a woman, okay? First off. I'm older than you, okay? Second off, here's the guy's licence plate number," which was the first thing I wanted to get, his licence plate number. "Here is a description, to the scar on his cheek to the buckles on his boots. You've got five days. If you do not find him in five days, I will have every gay and lesbian organization, every prostitution organization, every HIV/AIDS organization, every organization that I have ever had any association with, every women's organization on your ass. Now find buddy!" They called me here in three days. They had him. (Dana, Halifax)

The man, who turned out to be the owner of a local business, was not convicted of the charges. But he did have to hire an expensive lawyer:

So I said to buddy when I was leaving – 'cause his poor wife, I felt bad for her, because I could see just by that, she was a person that was abused, you can just tell, right? And I said on the way, I said, "Well, now there is a $10,000 blow job that you didn't get. Next time just pay the forty bucks, buddy." (Dana, Halifax)

Conclusion

Sex workers present a textured analysis of their lives and work that refuses the simplistic categorization of them as either victim or "happy hooker." While they sometimes face an inordinate amount of violence and potential violence, particularly by clients, sex workers are also able to relate positive experiences in their work, including good clients and personal growth. Violence by clients or pimps is not seen as inevitable by the sex workers we spoke with. They fight back against this violence in many ways and refuse to accept the notion that they are somehow asking for the violence they receive. They also emphasized that violence is not common among all clients. Rather, it is the possibility that any client could turn out to be a "bad date" – or even a rapist or murderer – that makes their lives so dangerous. For these workers, the trade, including the clients, are not inherently violent. Instead, it is a climate of uncaring and inaction over this violence that makes the trade dangerous.

The sex workers here spoke as expert observers and gained personal strength from that position – of being able to see the world for what it is, the messy reality of sexuality, loneliness, and violence, as well as the pleasures of life – but it is precisely this voice, this source of pride and strength, that the dominant discourses on sex work seek to silence. Although many analysts speak of sex work as inherently violent, it is the silencing of workers' voices in social and political life that is the underlying source of violence in sex workers' lives. If we listen closely to sex workers' voices, we find a resistant reading of sex work that provides the basis for fighting back against those conditions that can lead to violent or oppressive experiences. Valuing those voices can provide the basis for a collective political movement to improve conditions for workers in the trade.

3
Social Control, Policing, and Sex Work

> I think it was the first, no second, time I got arrested. The cop says to me, well the one that was taking me to the station says, "Listen, you're so young, so pretty. Why don't you get a real job, like work in Tim Hortons or something?" I turned to him and said, "Listen, you work in Tim Hortons." I said, "You know, the way I look at it, we're not hurting anybody." I said, "Why don't you guys go after the killers and shit like that and leave us girls alone?" Like, we're not hurting anybody but ourselves, really. (Alison, Halifax)

For many of the sex workers we spoke with, another of the daily burdens they named, beyond the fear of violence, was the potential conflict with police and the law. Sex workers spoke about the constant fear of arrest, potential harassment by police, the attitudes of judges, and the legal system as a source of constant frustration and anger in their lives. Their anger was heightened by the sense that they were an unfair target of these attitudes and practices – given the hypocrisy of law and society on sexual practices – and by the failure of the legal system to protect them from violence. What sex workers are naming here is the burden of social control – the social mechanisms designed to discipline members of society into prescribed modes of behaviour, mechanisms that target those groups deemed most problematic for particular intervention and control. The movements of sex workers, their activities, and their sheer existence are all subject to varying forms of social control. The next three chapters document sex workers' response to varying types of social control – to law and policing, to media depictions and public stigma, and to attempts to overdetermine specific definitions of health. However, the most pronounced, and most immediate, of all social control experiences, not surprisingly, occurs in encounters with police.

What we reveal in this chapter is the manner by which many of the assumptions that underlie social control practices can be critiqued as contradictory at best and damaging at worst. We also examine the manner by which a variety of social control mechanisms, including policing and sentencing patterns, are legitimated, become part of the hegemonic discourse on female sexuality, and serve to justify seemingly inconsistent practices and policies. But, above all, we document the voices of sex workers, their resistant strategies, their survival paradigms, and their incredible resilience in the face of opposition to their very existence.

In Conflict with the Law: Sex Workers and Police

Sex workers' encounters with police vary widely. While the sex workers we spoke with frequently distinguished between "nice" and "not so nice" officers, no matter what an officer's personal approach, s/he is charged with upholding a law that is widely viewed by sex workers as unjust – a law that has a daily negative impact on their lives:

> Oh, ya know, [police] can be very deceitful ... Busting you and you can't be in denial of it, because you don't have the proof. They have the proof so to speak.
> *Interviewer: So it was your word against the cops?*
> Yeah, your word against the cops, right? And I find that's once again really childish. I mean I'm not going out and raping somebody. I'm not going out and abusing somebody, you know. But they treat it as criminal.
> (Angela, Halifax)

Respondents complained of mistreatment by police officers who take advantage of their power to harass sex workers:

> I think it's just when they're bored. But basically, yeah, 'cause they never talk to you politely. They always, seems like they always have to have something smart to say. Seriously, they've always got to say something.
> (Heidi, Halifax)

> They harass me verbally every single night, like there has not been one night that they have not stopped me two or three times. You know, for instance, I was having a hard time about a week ago and these girls were threatening to beat me up and I flagged a car down and asked if they could drive me home, like just a drive home. And we got up on the road and the police stopped us and they asked the man where we was going. And he said, "Well, this lady asked me for a drive home," and they said, "Well, we think she better walk because she's not a lady." It made me sick, like it really did. (Valerie, Halifax)

Ultimately, sex workers are most angry at police (or, more exactly, society and the law of which police are a tool) not only because sex workers are treated as criminals but because the abuse of sex workers is not a priority for the law or police:

> But they don't like us. I mean, just say that I went out there and got murdered. "Oh yeah, [so-and-so] prostitute, crackhead, close the book. Don't hear nothin' about it no more." But if [it were] a woman – a different woman that didn't work the streets – they would try everything in their power to find their murderer. Why is that? (Tara, Halifax)

Sex workers challenge the prevailing presentation of the police role as those who "serve and protect" in that police have generally failed to protect sex workers from the inordinate amount of violence they face. One woman who worked in domination reported:

> I've had a lot of friends who have been beaten up in the business, not as a dominatrix, but doing other things when they have been beaten up. Almost everyone I know has been really terrified at some point, and a lot of it is because they feel they can't get any help. They feel as though they are completely on their own. It's just really unfair. I've heard stories here of women in hotel rooms who are being beaten by clients, who felt like they couldn't scream because they were afraid of revealing what was going on. (Celeste, Halifax)

Even in the domination business, she often feared for her safety, and

> I actually stopped running the dungeon because of the fear factor. I always had to make sure there was somebody else in the house with me. I was afraid I wouldn't be able to get help if I needed to get help ... Also I have problems with the Hell's Angels. I have the Hell's Angels snooping around. I felt that I couldn't really get protected by the police about that really anyways. Man that was scary. (Celeste, Halifax)

But, as she explained, there is a societal interest in her being able to go to the police since, as a dominatrix, she sees the "scary ones" that are a threat to everyone. In other words, she sees clients whom she knows could easily hurt other people. She would like to be able to report them to the police. Frustration with police inaction may actually contribute to an under-reporting of the amount of violence that is occurring:

> It's changed from when I first started working [in the mid-1980s], that's for sure. There was a lot [of violence] back then. It's still there, it's ... I think it's still there maybe. Maybe quite as much. Maybe it just doesn't get reported as much now. Or, you know, 'cause people kinda over the years,

they kinda get discouraged from seeing one of their friends go and report something and nothing gets done ... And they [the cops] have seen us down there plenty of times having problems with somebody. Like, not a trick, like just maybe a group of men walking by or something and us having to call the police, and you know, "They're drunk, can you please come remove them?" Hours upon hours later nobody's still, nobody comes. We end up having to flag a police car over, the first thing is, "Well, what did you say to them? What did you do to them?" Like we did something, right? Yeah, it kinda discouraged us. (Katie, Halifax)

Sex workers put this low prioritization down to police failure to see sex workers as people:

If a secretary gets murdered, she's a woman first not a secretary first, and until they get it that prostitution is the job and not the person. (Dana, Halifax)

Clients, though, are often viewed more humanely by police and are therefore able to get away with mistreatment of sex workers. One worker framed the pattern of ignoring sex workers' concerns as a lack of basic rights for sex workers:

I've seen girls on the corner one night and in the grave the next day, or a few days later. I've seen a lot of things in my time: violence, girls being hurt and stuff.

Interviewer: You think that's the major risk of the trade?
Yeah, I think that's the major risk. You don't know who you're with, that is the major risk. That's one of the most biggest. [The] major risk is your clients. Now, as far as the feds go, they're ignorant. They don't even really care about you. They don't care about most prostitutes anyways that I know. Like, there's no big investigation, [if] we found a hooker or a prostitute in an alleyway. They don't investigate like a big investigation like if, "Oh, we just found a college student on their way to Dalhousie somewhere dead in an alleyway," you know what I mean? You know what I'm trying to say? The difference. There's no big investigation for us because we are just like ... They tell you when you shouldn't be out there. "Get another job," that's their attitude. I went to the police a lot of times when I had been beaten up or robbed and things like that. They just told me, "Well, why don't you change your work?"

Interviewer: So you don't get the protection that other people do.
No, they don't protect us at all.

> *Interviewer: No? They don't see prostitutes as citizens?*
> That's what I mean, we're not citizens. In other words, we're just here, but we're not no pillar of society. We're just here. No, we don't have any rights when it comes to that as far as protecting. I've never seen no police officer yet go after the date. I've seen them go after the girl, but I've never seen them go after the customer. All the man gotta do is just start talking and say, "I gave her some money." The next thing she's automatically immoral. All you have to say is, "She was trying to steal something from me." And maybe she was; it happens. Some of the girls do steal from the men, but a lot of the times it's not true. But it's easier for [clients] to say and it makes everything all right for him to beat her head in. Maybe because she didn't want to do it the way he did. She didn't want to take the condom off or something. They get attitudes, call you names and stuff. (Valerie, Halifax)

When police increase their presence on the street, they do so not to protect sex workers but in response to community demands to decrease or move the trade. The results are often not helpful for sex workers:

> Constant arresting and patrolling an area has actually worked in the long run, but it just creates other problems ... I mean, there are rapes happening, you know. Girls are missing ... There's absolutely no sign of them [the cops] when you need them ... you know. You really don't know what you're dealing with, who you're getting in the car with ... I mean, I use my woman's intuition, if I can say that, to pick and choose. But you know, you're not always right.
> *Interviewer: Are the cops patrolling the area?*
> Jeez, yes. I ended up in the back alleys all the time you know, it's really bad. (Hannah, Halifax)

While policing is supposed to protect citizens from harm, sex workers report quite the opposite. From their point of view, not only does policing fail to protect them, it is harmful in its own right. How is it that citizens such as sex workers, whose activities cannot be easily constructed as immediately harmful to others, can be denied their right to protection? This is not simply the function of the dispositions of individual police officers or police forces. It is a function of the legal framework that positions sex workers as objects of social control rather than as citizens.

Law, Sex Work, and Social Control

Sex workers are not primarily treated as citizens under the law. Rather, they are positioned as objects of the law in two ways: as criminals who deserve punishment, and as victims who require rescue. Both these understandings are embedded in the law that police are mandated to uphold. Section 212 of the Criminal Code positions the sex worker as in need of protection from pimps and other exploiters. Section 213, however, which penalizes "communicating for the purposes of prostitution," punishes the sex worker as a threat to both communities and community decency. In neither case is the sex worker simply viewed as a citizen with rights. The purpose of the law is less about policing sex work per se than about policing female sexuality. (Male sex workers are much less frequently targeted by the law and police than are their female counterparts.) That is, the law is historically rooted in the gender system that denied women sexual independence and instead viewed her as the property of men. Women were viewed as passive sexual and social beings on the one hand, and evil influences on the other. If women were sexually active outside the marriage contract, there were only two explanations for her behaviour: either she was the victim of an evil man (who forced her to betray her naturally innocent ways) or she was indeed bad, or a whore. In neither case were the stifling strictures on female sexuality seen to be the problem. In Canadian law, therefore, two ways were developed to deal with female sexual "misbehaviour" in sex work. The bawdy house provisions (restricting anyone who allows a place to be used for acts of prostitution) were originally adopted from British law and functioned to protect "innocent" women from "evil" men (presumed not to be their husbands or fathers). And, until the 1960s, the Vagrancy Act, also adopted from British law, punished women for being found outside the home at night, unable to "account for themselves" and, therefore, not under the control of a husband or father. The law's function was not to protect women from violence, sexual or otherwise (marital rape and domestic violence were not considered crimes and charges of rape hinged on a woman's "sexual innocence"), but to discipline women into maintaining their chastity or fidelity.[1]

In the twentieth century, however, the law could not continue to function so obviously as a disciplinary mechanism against a particular group. Thus, the Vagrancy Act has been replaced with the communicating law, which technically targets both clients and sex workers (both male and female) for being a nuisance to the communities in which the trade is practised. The Vagrancy Act was deemed unacceptable in a modern liberal country because it criminalized a person's status rather than a person's act, and because it targeted only women. The communicating law is meant to overcome all these biases so that sex work and being a sex worker are not technically illegal under Canadian law. In practice, though, because the bawdy house provisions remain in place, it is next to impossible to practise sex work legally in Canada. And, at the same time, female sex workers remain the major target of the law, not clients (under section 213) or even pimps or "procurers" (under section 212).[2] Thus, in the end, the law continues to function as a way to police female sexual behaviour, to keep women from using their sexuality in any way other than the prescribed modes of motherhood and matrimony.

On top of this central function of controlling women's sexuality, the law today has a spatial function. The communicating law was in many ways a response to community complaints about the presence of sex workers and their clients.[3] It was ostensibly designed to remove sex work from the public sphere in order to protect "the community." Sex workers are seen as a threat to communities because they violate the public-private divide that women have always experienced. Uneasiness pervades all public perceptions of sex work. There are two very different reasons for this uneasiness. The first is the openly public nature of sex work. Sex work that occurs on the street, in public places, or that is advertised in public places, renders the work suspect simply because it makes sexuality public. The second reason for this unease is the drive to protect private property, which appears in the practices of upholding law, for all practical purposes, as the protection of community or business interest.

Despite the prevalence of sexual commodification in many venues of social life, the sex act itself is expected to be private and is expected to occur in private spaces (read "bedrooms"). Private spaces connote control over the practitioners and, presumably, the activities that take place. At the very least, members of the public are able to believe that they will not be exposed to unsanctioned acts if they take place in private. Paradoxically, sex and sex acts are still considered by the general public to be private, despite the proliferation of sexuality in film, popular culture, television, and the like. Sex solicitation occurs on television and through email at all hours of the day. Daytime soap operas are rife with sexual innuendo, and reality television shows feature bachelor (or bachelorette) A picking a bride (or groom) from a bevy of eager young women (or men) in a matter of three or four episodes. Sex solicitation by a woman or man standing on the street, however, is viewed as an unacceptable breach of privacy. The hypocrisy of this is not lost on the sex worker. As one sex worker put it: "Now they're talking about going online to chat rooms and stuff. And I'm there thinking holy Jesus and I'm a whore?" (Denise, Halifax).

Sex workers transcend all boundaries, real or perceived. Sex workers who solicit customers publicly, who have cell phones to reach clients or escort services, have transgressed the normative ways of eliciting sex work.[4] To a God-fearing public, the boundary-crossing behaviours of many groups – gays/lesbian/bi/transgendered communities as well as sex workers – are all indecipherable and, as such, can contribute to a culture of fear. As David Sibley argues, the public clings to the idea that there is a pure environment, which results in "a heightened consciousness of difference and, thus, a fear of mixing or the disintegration of boundaries."[5] This culture of fear often manifests itself as a desire to control space, a desire which can be seen in everything from gated communities, on a large scale, to a shop owner calling the police on a "working girl" standing outside his place of business. Control of space, then, can be equated with control of sex work.

Public sex work also poses a risk to another fundamental principle of middle-class life: the sanctity of private property. Often what drives both police policy and practice is the protection of this property. Business owners concerned with the appearance of their property call police for everything from a condom left on their doorstep to a woman standing on "their" sidewalk. Thus, private property is protected through public law. Business owners can feel quite free to call on the public law to "protect" heating grates (these are used for warmth by sex workers) near their premises, or to "protect" their customers from intercessions from inconvenient others, such as sex workers.[6] Many feel free to take the law into their own hands. One sex worker experienced this blurring of public and private space:

> I remember there was a kind of paint studio down there. The guy used to come out of his window, he used to throw hot water on us to get us to move. Oh yeah, he'd come out with a bucket of hot water and throw it down. (Katie, Halifax)

The owner of the paint studio identified the public sidewalk in front of his business as his own and thought that he could exercise his property rights by assaulting sex workers with bucketfuls of water, a strategy often used to remove dogs from properties in rural areas of the Maritimes. Here again, private and public space intercede, with private space expanding into the purview of the public; or at the very least, the lines are quite blurred.[7]

The law regarding sex work, therefore, has a variety of functions beyond policing female sexuality, including protecting the public from private sexuality, and protecting private property from public intervention. Sex workers are the object of all these functions. Police are structurally positioned (no matter what their personal views may be) to approach the sex worker as a problem for the community that police must address, rather than treating her as a citizen to whom they are responsible. The result of all these functions is that there are several potentially conflicting mandates for police within the law, including protecting communities from sex workers, punishing sex workers and clients for their behaviour (or at least encouraging them to change their ways), and protecting sex workers from pimps. None involves protecting the sex workers from violent clients, the one thing that sex workers would demand of police.

Policing and Sex Work

For sex workers it appears that the "serve and protect" motto of the police is geared toward only one community: middle- to upper-class consumers. Indeed, police in the Maritimes most often respond to community demands for protection from the nuisance of sex workers and their clients. No matter how small the perceived problem is, the middle-class community affected is often politically efficacious and able to communicate its demands to local governments, and therefore to police:

> *Officer:* It's so minute [the number of sex workers] that I doubt that even the people driving through the city would even know that they're there ... we're talking two, three, or maximum five that may be in a certain area of the city.
> *Interviewer: But it's amazing how those two, three, or five women can make the front pages.*
> *Sergeant:* As soon as somebody in a neighbourhood – if there's a business in that area that is not happy with this happening, they go to their [city] councillor and the councillor goes to council.
> *Interviewer: Do you think that there's kind of two groups of opposition, at least that's what I'm beginning to characterize in my own mind, the property owners and [the] religious right?*
> *Sergeant:* I think the two main groups are business and residential.
> (Fredericton RCMP, 4 February 2000)

This demand-driven policing is a fairly constant feature of policing of sex work. Neighbourhood and business complaints – often communicated through political leaders – lead to police sweeps of a particular area to arrest sex workers and clients under section 213 of the Criminal Code or more frequent patrolling of an area in order to at least encourage them to move on. The police, in this passage, speak to their response to community complaints:

> And there was one section, one residential area the girls worked ... The sergeant did the queries before he went to talk to this group – one street had more than six hundred files where patrol units were called in a period of time. So that's tying up much more resources from the guys going down there. There is no charge for being there; you're not going to communicate with the guy in uniform, so: "Move along, move along. They're complaining. Move down the street." When a neighbour calls, either you have to do something like you did here, or [you] have to [use] a police car with them. Just follow them up and down the street, so they don't get any business. That's just not feasible. (Halifax Regional Police, 26 March 2003)

Sex workers experience this policing as harassment:

> There's not much really good about prostitution, and my worst is the police (chuckles) ... They really harass me. Like they stop me two or three times a night just to degrade and use their power where they shouldn't be using it. Yeah, they give me more hard time than any of the johns that I've met in the twelve years. They are very insensitive, like a lot of them are very insensitive, very much so. (Tara, Halifax)

Although some officers may see policing sex workers as something the community forces them to do, despite their own reservations, others take their role of protecting the community quite personally:

> The one experience I had with the police, I was on M Street and they pulled up and they wanted to talk to me. And there was one cop from the neighbourhood, one wasn't. And the guy from the neighbourhood was really pissed off that I was dirtying up his street where his family's children live. He was personal about it, right? And he insisted to have my name and, "Okay, if you don't give me your name, I'm going to take you in" and all that stuff. And I stupidly gave him my real name. (Joan, Halifax)

While some officers can reinforce their personal power as citizens, sex workers are denied the right to belong to, or be in, a community. Indeed, changes to sentencing patterns have made this denial of citizenship even more obvious.

While the law is ostensibly designed to reduce the supposed nuisance of sex work to a community, as a criminal procedure it fails in this task because the law – in criminalizing both indoor and outdoor sex work – gives sex workers no legal place to go. Sex workers simply continue to be subjected to arrest, fines, or brief imprisonment. The ridiculousness of the law is obvious to sex workers, and they are not afraid to point this out to those who enforce it:

> *Interviewer: Have you been arrested before?*
> Oh yes. Quite a few times.
> *Interviewer: What's the charge mainly?*
> Communication for the purposes of prostitution ... Yeah, and what didn't make sense to me, I even asked the judge, if you're gonna give me a fine – the most I had to pay was $330 – where does he suspect I'm gonna get this money to pay him?
> *Interviewer: Exactly.*
> So, I wanted, I asked my lawyer to ask the judge, when I come to pay that clerk that $330, who's gonna [arrest] that clerk for living off my avails?

Because if I gave that to somebody else out there, they're gonna go to jail for it. They didn't have an answer. And I didn't like that my lawyer said, "Oh, I don't advise you to ask the judge." That's your advice, but I'm not taking your advice. I asked the judge. And he sat there and looked at me dumbfounded and asked me, is there anything else I'd like to know? In other words, he didn't have an answer either. No response. That doesn't make sense to me. (Belinda, Halifax)

Sex workers get no answer when they ask about the fundamental internal inconsistency of the law. But the legal system has responded to the complaints of communities and police about the ineffectiveness of the law. Police officers complain that the revolving door of arrest, punishment, and return to the same community means that the problem is never really solved and so neighbourhood complaints continue unabated. New arrest and release procedures banning sex workers from returning to certain communities as a condition of their release were therefore developed:

Officer: Before, it was just a matter of girls on the street: you charge her and release her and ten or fifteen minutes after you released her, she'd be back out on the street again.
Interviewer: A revolving door.
Officer: So what we came up with, was releasing them on conditions. So I pick you up tonight, on let's say G Street, and charge you. Then when I release you, part of your conditions for being released is that you can't be on G Street. If I drive down G Street fifteen minutes later and you're there on the street corner, then I can pick you up and arrest you again and hold you until morning for court. So with the fact that we've used boundaries as conditions has sort of made it more difficult for that girl for at least six months to be in that area again. Because if the next night, for example, she moves across the harbour to Dartmouth, and we pick her up, then we ban her from Dartmouth – from the streets in Dartmouth. (Halifax Regional Police, 26 March 2003)

When released on conditions, sex workers are advised to maintain certain boundaries, that is, to carry out daily life within certain parameters. These parameters are often maps of city blocks, which are far from randomly selected. They often put out of reach friends' houses and the services that some sex workers need for treatment, such as methadone programs and outreach centres. In two cities we researched, we discovered that sentencing conditions included staying out of areas in which the stroll was located, as well as probation offices. To violate these boundaries is to breach the conditions of release, often a far more serious charge than the initial communicating charges:

Officer: So when you have patrol members out there working that neighbourhood, and they see the girl walking and they know who she is, 'cause a lot of the time they become very well known, they run her name. It comes up on our computer system, as an undertaking, as conditions, and they read the conditions. She's not allowed to be here. Boom, they scoop her [and] put her in cells until the next day, depending on the time of day. Or they'll take her right down to court, and then she has to appear for violation of this undertaking.
Interviewer: And that's a more serious charge.
Officer: Yes, because they're saying, "Well, you're not abiding by the conditions of your release, so we're going to sentence you now. How do you plead on this? And of course the poor girl is guilty, right? I mean, she's going to be found guilty of the offence, the original offence of communication. And then she's sentenced on that plus with the undertaking charges, and it gets more severe each time. And it's a cycle that keeps occurring; [and it's one] that you can't seem to get away from.
Interviewer: And it's not addressing the issue.
Officer: **Not at all.** (Halifax Regional Police, 27 March 2003)

The fallacy of this practice is not lost on police officers:

Interviewer: They could breach a condition by going home.
Officer: Well, see that's where we get into a problem. Because they're still saying, "Put them on conditions." That's our typical protocol when we arrest a girl. So let's say they're on A Street but it [the order] encompasses all the way down to S Street, all the way up to X Street, way down to B Street, [and] all the way up to R Street, so that's a huge, huge area. And where these girls come from ... there are so many different agencies that they need to access, the methadone program, Stepping Stone, Avalon, all these places. And they'll say, "How am I supposed to get there? How am I supposed to see this family member or that friend?" Because this is their community. And now we're saying, "Okay, you can't be in this community anymore." (Halifax Regional Police, March 27, 2003)

As sex workers are well aware, this kind of treatment is a denial of their fundamental citizenship rights, a denial that they refuse to accept:

Now the police put us on boundaries ... We're Canadian women, and I mean, it's supposed to be a free country ... I have paper home to show ya. I'm not allowed from neither side of N Street to C Street and R Street to B ... I fought it. And I told them to go [to hell], I'm not. I said, "This is a free country. I'm Canadian. I don't think so." (Denise, Halifax)

Who Is the Pimp? Symbolism and Police Mandates

Pimps often symbolically represent, for police and others, the business and exploitation version of prostitution. Despite the denials by many of the sex workers that pimping was currently a major problem – and their more nuanced understanding of the role of protectors and husbands/boyfriends in sex work – police in the Maritimes frequently continue to claim that pimping is a major problem. In Halifax, heightened concern in the early 1990s led to the creation of an entire task force on prostitution mandated to address the pimping problem. Despite sex workers' claims that this era of pimping is long since over, the task force remains in place. Yet the focus on the pimp remains, most importantly because it justifies intervention in and control over sex workers' lives. It serves the purpose of social control, even in an age where some view the criminalization of sex work as outmoded or inappropriate.

The pimp is a convenient category into which all moral outrage surrounding the trade can be conveniently deposited. After all, the pimp can be held responsible for the capture of "innocent" young women, for the violence or torture that is always assumed to be part of the prostitute's life, and for the stark, unforgiving exploitation of women and women's sexuality. In Halifax in particular, there is a racialized image of the pimp as a black man, which is a trope common to the white-dominated Western world.[8] The pimp, figured as a black man, can also be read as a "non" person, as are many racialized categories of criminality. As a "non" person, the black man as pimp can serve as the repository of public outrage, of condemnation and of criminality. The pimp, not the woman, can be the battle cry of police forces, eager to find a *cause célèbre* to both capture the imagination of a naïve public and the support of politicians and feminists alike.

Pimp discourse renders sex workers agentless and makes their choices unimportant. Sex workers cannot be seen as architects of their own lives or solutions. Therefore, the discourse simultaneously reauthorizes the position of police, and the "straight society" that they protect, to intervene in and control the lives of sex workers. Police are, symbolically at least, the "good men" who can protect victimized women (sex workers) from "bad men" (pimps). As a specifically racialized discourse in Nova Scotia, the story of the pimp also further sets (predominantly white) police apart from other men.

Exploring the world of police officers whose mandate it is to arrest pimps reveals an interesting portrait of social control. Police mandates include, as everyone knows, arresting criminals. But how criminals get defined, who gets arrested, and how law is interpreted is illuminated when one talks directly to the officers involved. The definitions of who a pimp is, for example, seem to have some fluidity. When evidence for one form is not present, other scenarios are proposed that also justify constructing the issue as one of pimping. Three scenarios were put forward in interviews with Halifax police: the pimp as an individual opportunistic (black) man; the pimp as part of the escort or strip management; and the pimp not as a person at all but as a drug. There is clearly a slippage between different definitions of what constitutes a pimp, which indicates that the evidence of pimping is much less solid than most believe.

The following excerpt from a two-officer interview illustrates some of this slippage:

Officer 1: **The primary risk we deal with are the pimps. Very few of the girls we deal with have chosen this as a career, or type of work they've wanted to do. Their pimps treat them very badly. Another risk is that [of] clients on the street, of the clients in the escort service. Of course, there's the lifestyle. The chance of catching several diseases. A lot of girls we deal with have been infected with HIV, hepatitis, and lots of STDs. And just the lifestyle in general [means that] a lot of the girls become addicted to drugs, and that lifestyle is unhealthy as well. When they leave the streets they have a lower self-image of themselves; they find it difficult to get into legitimate jobs. We've had girls get into legitimate jobs. They're recognized by someone, and they're out of work all of a sudden. It's very difficult to get back into legitimate work.**

Interviewer: Do you think that police are more likely to see women that are pimped [rather] than women who are working independently?

Officer 2: **Around here, yes. From what I've read, it's not that way all across Canada, but the girls that we see on the street are addicted. If you want to call it being pimped, it's being pimped by crack now, the few we see on the street. The pimps are still recruiting young girls. When they can trust them enough they put them in the escort services. And the escort services here, most of make them toe the line until he [the pimp] comes back to pick them up or whatever. And some of the younger ones are taken to Montreal [or] Toronto until they're old enough to get in the services. And a lot of them are starting them off in the strip clubs.**

Interviewer: A lot of people that I've interviewed are not being pimped, so I'm wondering if the characterization of the women who you're seeing are maybe ... Are they younger or are they more likely to be on the street, more likely to be addicted ...? I'm wondering what the differences are.

Officer 2: **The thing is that we view it as two types of pimping. Either you're being pimped by a person, either a male or female, or you're out there because of drug addiction so that would be your pimp, [or] alcoholism. Something else is keeping you out there on the street. As my partner said earlier, that's not the type of lifestyle somebody just wakes up some** morning and says, "I want to be a prostitute." It's a result of a number of factors coming into play. (Halifax Regional Police Force, 26 March 2003)

Painfully obvious in this interview is how the officers defined pimps in various ways, as well as inaccurately, according to the procuring law. The definition of pimps shifted from people to drugs. This reasoning is not as convoluted as it might appear at first glance. There are sound conceptual reasons to define pimps in this way, as addictive substances require the addict to be far more tied to their habit than they are to any person, including themselves. This conceptual shift, however, has implications for policing practices. If the pimp is a person, the rationalization for the existence of the task force stands. If the pimp is an addictive substance, then it would follow that the role of the law would have to change. This definition hardly justifies the existence of a police task force on prostitution, though it may justify the existence of addiction services, or even increased resources for the drug squad. Further, all the other risks that sex workers face – such as violence by clients or addictions – are viewed as natural by-products of a particular lifestyle rather than as unacceptable threats to citizens. In this way, if, for example, sex workers are attacked by clients, it is their own fault, rather than any fault of the police.

The officers on the task force on prostitution who were interviewed readily admitted that their focus is on pimps. They give many stories of pimps plaguing the city and luring young women to a life in prostitution. When asked by the researcher for statistics to support this claim, they are both unwilling and, frankly, unable to provide them. Their unsubstantiated claim in this regard is given as a self-evident rationale for their continuing to posit pimps as the focus of their policing strategy. As we did not find evidence of the rampant pimping that the officers claimed existed, the researcher probed further, asking police who these pimps were and how they were characterized. A different officer from the same force, in a separate interview, categorized the pimps in particular ways:

Interviewer: So taking your three categories, as you just named them, the so-called business owner, the highly coercive [read "organized"] pimp, and the opportunist, how would you break down in the past four years on the task force, what percentage of each of these would you arrest? How many would fall into each of these categories? Are there more business ones than opportunist?
Officer: **We have arrested more opportunists and escort agencies than the organized ones. Most of the organized pimping goes on further parts west, in upper Canada and out west.** (Halifax Regional Police, 9 March 2000)

When asked to explain who is behind organized pimping, the officer referred back to the Maritimes, and back to an old racialized trope about pimps:

> Well, you get a group of guys who are, you know, for example, you go to North Preston ... The whole community is corrupt and what not, but what I mean really is an economically suppressed area. It's kind of isolated, semi-isolated, and they're all black and there's been all the other issues that go along with ... you know, you can't get a job, and you're not being treated fairly or equally; and I think that they just get tired of it. Get tired of being beaten down and treated like shit, and that's the way they grew up. You know these guys ... you don't become a pimp overnight. There's a lot going on in their home too. I mean, where do you learn to do somebody with a coat hanger? Where to you learn to dunk somebody under the water until they are almost drowned and then pull them back up, you know, you don't all of sudden wake up and go yeah, that's what I'll do. That's a learned thing. (Halifax Regional Police, 9 March 2000)

Although all three of these interviewees intimate an organized type of pimping, or rings that ship women from city to city, when questioned, the explanation falls apart ... or, rather, falls back to old racialized stereotypes of the black man as pimp.

Further, the existence of pimps in the stereotypical construction (scooping young women from their homes and schools and placing them on the street with threats and intimidation) has also been transplanted, or transplaced, in the two-officer interview. For these two officers, pimps have become the shadowy figures behind escort services – now the explanation of how women are shipped from province to province, or how the supposed transition from strip clubs to prostitution takes places. To place the pimp at the escort service level is also to remove him from view. The pimp is no longer on the street, so he becomes a secret operative who lures young women into the trade. The more secretive the pimp is seen to be, the more police claims that pimps are, indeed, a problem are rendered unassailable.

It is also important to note that escort services are notoriously difficult to police, especially with the onset of cell phone technology. Calls can be made from just about anywhere and to just about anyone. This means that a physical base is no longer necessary for operating out-calls. The geography-based form of policing is less relevant when this form of the trade predominates, and generally, few citizen complaints are levied against such operations. But portraying escort services as pimping operations gives police another rationale for intervening in the operation of the sex trade. For the sex workers we spoke with, however, the escort services are a potential site of safety and good pay. The exploitation they experienced there was described as labour exploitation and not as pimping. Sex workers did not wish to be "rescued" from these services, but to have more control over their work environment. These views are negated in this particular police discourse, while continued policing remains justified.[9]

In this same vein, another major theme that is apparent from interviews with police is the assumption that a young woman would never choose of her own volition sex work as a job: she must be lured by a pimp. The example of pimping cited by one officer was a case of a young woman who had been violently used and abused:

> [She was] prostituted from the time she was fifteen until she was twenty. She had been raped numerous times, stabbed, shot. And you know, she had been sexually abused by her uncle from the time that she was twelve until she was fifteen. Fifteen is when she told her mom, and her parents booted her out, and that's when she went to shelter. That's where these guys [pimps] know where to go; and they can tell. He says, "Okay, come on with me, here's some booze or here's some drugs, whatever you want. Let's go to a party. I'll give you a place to stay." So all of a sudden she's got all this love, what she thinks is love. He's telling her all the things that she wants to hear. So what he's doing is he's preparing her ... he's working on her ... So he's giving all of those and she thinks it's love, because he's saying, "I love you. You're beautiful." Whether she is or not, it's not relevant. It's exactly what she wants to hear. So then after a short period of time, then it's, "Now you owe me. You've got to pay [me] back." (Halifax Regional Police, 9 March 2000)

The interviewer was intrigued to know whether this was a true story or just an example. When asked what happened to the young woman, the officer answered that "she got tired of it. She just said, 'I got tired of it one day and I just left.'" He went on to explain that pimps "are not going to get a strong-willed person into prostitution." Yet, even this terribly victimized young woman had a strong will, since she got "tired of it" and left.

In an interesting turn, the officer then used the example of his daughter in an illustration of why police need to act aggressively against pimps:

> If somebody came to me and took my daughter ... Maybe I was having problems with my daughter, and all of a sudden she ran away. And this guy got a hold of her, and then he came back to my place and if I didn't make a stand ... I would probably have to threaten him: "If you don't get off my property, I will kill you." If you don't play by their rules then they will continue to try that. They've tried to intimidate families and they'll keep taking her. They don't want to put too much work into this, they're lazy. (Halifax Regional Police, 9 March 2000)

That the officer switched his point of reference from the victimized young sex worker to his own daughter is telling: it is how police officers, in general, make sense of the pimping story. The pimp, symbolically at least, is viewed as a threat to family. What the pimp promises the young woman in the first example is strangely similar to what courting men promise their belles, and once secured (that is, married), the woman often discovers there are hidden costs in the form of housework, sex, or children, all of which are expectations of the marriage contract. So the pimp, in order to be discursively othered from the marriage situation, needs to come after our daughters. Then the trope comes full circle. Any threat to the family apparently requires a great deal of protection, so the "if you don't get off my property, I will kill you" comment is anything but random. It is the heart of the matter. All women, not just sex workers, apparently cannot be the property of someone who just wants to make money from their sexuality; their sexuality needs to be the property of certain men, such as fathers and husbands, rather than pimps. In this scenario, the real issue is that the imaginary prostituted daughter is sleeping with too many men. The transaction required of the young woman with the pimp begins to resemble other not uncommon transactions in the social imaginary, such as marriage. The real posers here, then, are the police officers, not the pimps.

In other words, this is not just about law; it is about rampant surveillance of sex practices. This surveillance serves to perpetuate stigma and morality tropes about sexuality, particularly women's sexuality, in very real ways. The police exercise social control in various ways: by applying and interpreting the law, by reinforcing stigma, and by calling on moralistic rationales when others fail to resolve or justify contradictions in law and contradictions in policing practices. Further, it is *only* the police who mention pimping as a prevalent problem and continue to present it as a problem for the region. It is likely that the reason for continuing the story of pimping is closely related to the raison d'être for the Halifax police task force on prostitution. It is clearly not about protecting sex workers.

The Conflicting Goals of Policing

> The police? Actually the police are nice. I never had a lot of run-ins with them, and I'll tell you why. When I get drinking, I get violent. I just don't know why, I just get moody and I can see me out here sometimes and I'm walking and I guess you get stressed sometimes if you feel like you're not getting a date quick enough. And I get a little violent and a cop will go by, and it's just me and him, and he'll look at me and I get mad. You know, what the fuck are you looking at? You know? They'll say, "Patsy" – they all know me by Patsy – "Patsy, what's wrong?" "I don't want you to talk to me, leave me alone." And they say, "Patsy, you're drunk aren't you? Come on, we'll take you down to lock-up and let you sleep it off." And I know that's where I should go, but then, I'm the type if you put your

hands on me I got to fight back, right? But they're pretty good to me, they're really good to me. (Kasey, Saint John)

Just as there is confusion and conflict in the law that treats sex workers both as criminals and victims, so is there confusion and conflict in policing. Different police units and different police jurisdictions can have very different methods of policing sex work. Not only do police respond to public complaints but they also have their own goals, set by the force. In other words, both proactive policing (following a specific strategy or plan) and reactive policing (responding to public and business complaints) operate with sex work. The goals of police and their modes of operation, therefore, can vary from jurisdiction to jurisdiction. In Moncton and Saint John, for example, sex workers reported relatively non-conflictual relations with police. As one sex worker explained: "All they do is write you a fine and you're on your way. They don't throw you in jail, they just write you a fine. I think it's like a $60 fine" (Jason, Moncton). But policing patterns can also vary according to person-power available, time of the year, policies of municipal governments or mandates from the superior officer in the vice or criminal or prostitution unit; this means that goals of units may not always be certain and may certainly be contradictory.

In one jurisdiction in which we interviewed officers, we uncovered two units within the same police force operating with conflicting goals: one in which sex workers were arrested, the other in which they were not, sometimes on the same street in the same night. These purposes are not only highly contradictory but actually dysfunctional when placed together. One unit (the Task Force on Prostitution) performs a rescue mission of saving the sex workers both from their pimps and from themselves, the other unit (Vice) further criminalizes sex workers in attempts to curb the drug trade. The following interview excerpt illustrates the problem:

Officer 1: So if a pimp picks up a young girl, and typically if a young girl ends up on the street for some reason – for survival or whatever – she goes out and works for one or two nights before he spots her, and recruits her. Well, he can't be charged with procuring 'cause she's already been a prostitute. So there is no charge, but then he would be exercising control and living off the avails. She cannot be charged with living off her own avails. There is no charge there.

Interviewer: So how many charges then of living off the avails and control would you lay in the run of a year?

Officer 1: I don't know. It would vary from year to year.

Interviewer: So you don't charge for communicating for the purposes of ...

Officer 1: We don't charge the girls at all.

Officer 2: Now the Vice Section does charge for communicating.

Interviewer: How is a girl on the street going to know if you're task force or Vice?

Officer 2: If we see a girl on the street, we go up and tell who we are, give her our business cards, "If you're being pimped, call us, we'll try to help you." And we ask them if they want a coffee, whatever they're looking for, if it's a real cold night. We tell them who we are up front. And I've been approached by girls before. They give you their little spiel. [I say,] "I'm a police officer." I tell them right up front. Now the vice unit, if they're going to decoy somebody, obviously they'll just go up and start a conversation, and if she makes a deal, well, she's charged.

Officer 1: Now let me go a step further. In the course of that charge, when that girl is brought back to the police station, she is also asked if she's being pimped, and every effort is made to try to assist her. Because if she says yes she is pimped, then a call is made to the task force. And that person is introduced to them, and left to them, because we believe we see the girls on the street as being victims. And if they're being forced to be out there, then they're not of their own free will, and so every effort is made to try to assist those girls in getting off the street, and bringing charges to bear on whoever is forcing them to be on the streets.

Interviewer: Okay, let's, I'm just trying to work through this in my head. There's a scenario if you get some young woman who's been picked up and she says, "I'm not being pimped." What do you do then?

Officer 1: They're told not to talk to the police, and in a case if they say they're not being pimped, then the Vice Section could charge them, release them on conditions, and send them on their way.

Interviewer: So the Vice Section might charge them with communicating?

Officer 1: Yes, and the main condition is that they stay out of the area bounded by whatever streets the stroll is in.

Interviewer: So that might be court mandated.

Officer 1: No, that's on their release conditions.

Interviewer: Release from ...?

Officer 1: **From custody.** (Halifax Regional Police, 26 March 2003)

The contradictions in this interview are wide ranging and represent some of the contradictions that policing of sex work often exhibits. For example, the contrast between policing patterns is readily apparent in this particular exchange. One unit befriends the sex worker (with the explicit purpose of getting information on pimps), while the other arrests her. Three other current and former officers from the same unit either grudgingly or readily admitted the contradictions between unit focus and policing practices of two units that, for all logical purposes, should not be put together.

This interview shows the confusion of policing purposes in this jurisdiction. On the one hand, the task force is mandated with befriending the sex worker – encouraging her through coffees, and promises of a warm place to stay if it is a cold night – to get information on pimps. And the task force claims not to charge the women. However, they will not hesitate to hand them over to the vice section if pimping is not an issue. Even though the task force officers might perceive themselves as working for the best interests of the sex worker, because of the conflict between its mandate and that of Vice, its sister section within the unit, sex workers will in the end be arrested. Further, these units are now combined as one, with one commanding officer in charge. But it does not matter to a sex worker which unit is arresting her. The end result is the same: s/he is arrested. Both the purposes of each unit and the overall social control mandate of law are served well.

Another feature of policing that sex workers noted is the treatment by police. This refers, often, to the way in which individual police officers treat the workers, the language they use, how they approach the wo/men on the street, and how they are perceived by the sex workers. How police treat sex workers can be a function of two primary patterns: the first is non-engaging, repressive, and inflexible, and involves higher arrest rates, increased harassment, and inflexible negotiations at the time of arrest and custody. The manner in which sex workers are treated is rough, unfeeling, and callous. If it is determined that a sweep will take place, known sex workers are summarily rounded up, sometimes for insignificant charges, and brought to the police station. They are handcuffed and taken off the street in full view of others. Sex workers complain that their treatment while in custody is barely adequate; that they get no blankets or extra clothing in cold cells. This kind of policing can result in fairly regular harassment that targets people for who they are rather than what they are doing. As one worker put it: "They'll fine you for anything once they know you're a pro" (Monica, Halifax).

The second pattern can be described as more engaged, rehabilitative, and flexible. This is seen when police are more humane (although possibly also paternalistic) with the sex workers, actually knowing quite a bit about their lives, buying sex workers coffee. However, they do give talks to the sex workers about the errors of their ways. Police adopting this pattern are flexible about arrest – not even always arresting them – and humane in their treatment during custody.

The contradictions between these two patterns become visible at certain points, for example, when both appear within a single police force and are endorsed as differing mandates for different units. Individual officers within the same unit may exhibit both patterns when policing in the same jurisdiction, on the same night. The second, more engaged, pattern – although clearly the more desirable of the two – can always be vetoed by the first, more repressive, pattern. And it is the first pattern that has graver consequences, is more dangerous to the sex worker, and always involves arrest. The result for the sex worker is the constant threat of the first pattern of policing behaviour, despite the prevailing secondary-pattern focus of the police unit or force. The police always get their woman, so to speak, in the end. That is, the strategic goals of policing are always realized, as the following quotation illustrates:

> The cops all know me, so ... some of them let me go by a few times, some of them would warn me, and then after they warned me twice, they say, K, if I see you again I'm going to have to take you. So I go out, get high, forget all about what they said and I'd be taken to jail ... and another charge. (Katrina, Halifax)

Thus, the threat of arrest posed to sex workers, even by a police force practising the second pattern of policing, is always present.[10]

Despite all the contradictions between arresting and charging the sex workers or taking them "downtown for a talk," all the social control goals of not sanctioning prostitution, monitoring sex worker's sexuality, and addressing the business or residential neighbourhood complaint are ultimately satisfied. This is not to say that police behaviour is irrelevant to the sex worker; on the contrary, sex workers are more likely to be co-operative if police officers consistently treat them with humanity. This does not change the fact that sex workers are policed. Nor does it change the fact that policing does not operate according to any sense of what effectively reached policing goals might look like. Any police force can demonstrate that there has been a reduction of street prostitution for a time, or that arrest statistics have increased. But this is not the same as having solved the issue of sex work, which is constructed as both a legal and a social problem. Simply put, policing does not eradicate sex work. And, if past history in this country and others is any indication, it seems that policing never will work as a strategy for eradicating sex work. Where policing strategies do achieve some measure of success is in terms of political goals.

Neighbourhood associations that clamour for action to be taken by politicians can be mollified to some degree. Business owners can be reassured that police are doing everything in their power to deal with the "problem" of prostitution in business districts. The public can be placated in the press. But on the street, on the ground, the only result of more policing, whether or not it be repressive, is the movement of the trade even further underground. And with that move, sex workers are in ever increasing danger of encountering more violence by their johns, and by the public at large.

John and Jane School

The other convenient repository of social angst over public sexuality, or sex for sale, is the client. As the client, the john does garner some disgust as the dirty old man of stereotypic conjuring. By focusing on the clients – when public ire needs to be stoked or when police officers want to be seen as doing the right thing by the women – two things are accomplished: the trade continues to be policed, and police continue to have a role. Both actions fit into wider paradigms of social control. Widening the net away from the sex worker and toward the pimp and then the client serves the purpose of keeping the social control strategies of the state in place. It can also thwart any discussion that may arise regarding unfair treatment of the wo/men in the trade.

Given that many police and members of the public recognize that it is unfair and unhelpful to target only sex workers, another mode of policing has arisen that encourages the punishment of the client. The john school approach lies at the intersection of two approaches to sex work – that of the victim and that of the criminal. It shifts the blame away from the sex worker and toward the client. John school was first developed in San Francisco in the 1990s and the approach was quickly adopted by several Canadian municipalities, including Halifax in 1998. The program operates as a diversion program that offers arrested clients the option of paying a fine and undergoing the school program for a day, thereby avoiding a public trial. The john school program usually involves talks given by residents, police, former sex workers, and public health nurses on the legal, medical, and social implications of the trade in an effort to "cure" men of their sex-seeking behaviour.

One interview uncovered two explanations of how and why clients are arrested:

Interviewer: So you go out and do a sting to get customers for the john school?
Officer 2: **We certainly do!**
Officer 1: **I don't think filling up the john school is the reason you go out there. It's when you have a high volume of traffic, and for instance in a residential area, even some of the business areas, when they go out during the daytime hours, the businesses are calling.** (Halifax Regional Police, 26 March 2003)

When the interviewer asked about clients, police insisted that they should be charged, but then talked about how few of them they actually pick up. Police in Halifax had no numbers or statistics on how many women or how many pimps were arrested or how effective their strategies were. In other words, the police simply believed that their strategies and practices were effective.

There are a number of problems with the john school approach. To begin with, its very status in law is questionable. As Erin Gibbs van Brunschot notes, despite the fact that prostitution per se is not illegal in Canada – only communicating for the purposes of – the john school actually continues to treat participation in prostitution, and not communicating, as the crime. This makes the appropriateness of the schools under the law questionable in that the punishment is not commensurate with the crime. Further, the programs, which rely on sweeps to bring in the clients, typically bring in only those caught on the street. Therefore, they do not encompass the full spectrum of men involved as clients in the sex trade (making the police claim of addressing the sex trade rather than nuisance complaints doubtful). In particular, wealthier men, who can afford escort or massage services, are less likely to be caught. The men who are brought in, as van Brunschot explains, "tend to be those with the least financial and social power."[11] Lowman's research also shows that, in Vancouver, street sweeps regularly target those areas and venues in which lower-class men are more likely to make up the majority of the clients.[12]

Sex workers' rights groups typically view these programs as "a detriment to women's right to earn a living."[13] As van Brunschot notes, the john school approach is based on a view of "prostitution as 'disorder'" rather than as work.[14] In the case of Halifax, the monies collected from the john school program are used to fund a similar diversion-based jane school program for female sex workers:

> *Officer 2:* Coverdale [Halifax] runs a School 213, which is for prostitutes who have been charged for the first time. And the focus behind School 213 is to explain to the prostitute the dangers of prostitution, the types of diseases they could be in for, where prostitution is going to lead them, and to offer them an opportunity to be able to get off the street by encouraging them to take courses, to upgrade themselves. And [they are] even provided half of the funding for courses that they can take to upgrade themselves.
> *Interviewer:* What's their success rate?
> *Officer 2:* The success rate of School 213 has been tremendous. We've had girls who have been told that they are nothing, that they're pieces of shit, end up being first and second in their class, and we've had them going on as paralegals. (Halifax Regional Police, 26 March 2003)

While a few of the sex workers we spoke with in Halifax had taken advantage of the jane school program, which is run with some sensitivity by Coverdale, the outreach group for women in conflict with the law, they pointed out that at least technically the program requires sex workers to stop working in the trade in order to receive funding – a condition they found unacceptable and a indicator that the program's designers do not view sex work as work. Further, as mentioned in Chapter 1, it is not at all evident that training and education programs are that helpful given the often low pay and poor conditions of jobs even for the educated and trained.

Sex work advocacy and support groups have also argued that the campaign to target and shame johns only creates greater dangers for sex workers because they now have even more reason to negotiate quickly and move their transactions to out-of-the-way and potentially more dangerous spaces. There is some concern as well that the increasing threat of embarrassment campaigns and arrest for clients is most likely to impact older, married men who do not want their involvement known – precisely the clients that sex workers often prefer.

Sex workers are skeptical of the worth of john schools, particularly as a remedy ordered by judges and supported by lawyers and police. The irony of who the client is does not escape the sex worker, "especially when it's lawyers and judges that you're dating ... I mean, I've been with so many lawyers it isn't funny" (Valerie, Halifax). And, according to sex workers, members of the police force may also be clients:

> They're phoney. They don't like us doin' this; but they're doing it themselves. There's a lot of cops here that's tricks. I took a couple out, so they're phoney. You know, "I would never take a prostitute out" and "I think that's dirty." "Prostitutes are packed with AIDS," right? That's their attitude. "They're nothin' but crackheads and junkies." How do they know? They comes in plain clothes, taking the girls out, so, you know. And I used to tell them all the time to shut up, ya know, you guys do it ... But I won't mention the guy's name, because I don't want him to get fired. But if I really wanted to get dirty about it ... (Tara, Halifax)

More disturbingly, male police can use their power as officers of the law to enhance their sexual power and mistreatment of sex workers within personal relationships:

> I had one of them [who] wanted a blow job. And this is an officer, and I knew it was. And I'm giving him a blow job with a condom and he's yelling at me, telling me he didn't want the condom on. And I told him he might be a pig, but I'm still putting a condom on. And he was getting really mad at me then, and asking me questions while he was getting the blow job ... And finally I said, "Look, fuck off buddy, I want nothing to do with you" ... So after that, when he knew that I knew he was a cop, I had a lot of cops coming around where I was at – harassing me big time. I'd work on the street and they'd come up behind me, driving on the sidewalk, being smart, and make remarks about my breasts, my lifestyle. (Denise, Halifax)

Johns, therefore – whether police or not – may need to be schooled, but schooled in respect for sex workers.

Crime Prevention?

If sex workers were truly considered members of communities and full citizens, they – like residents and businesses – would be provided police protection through measures such as crime prevention. Crime prevention is a chief mandate of police forces. It is not uncommon for police forces to lobby municipalities for increased community policing programs, the rationale for which is to prevent crime. Although many of these programs are simply based on more traditional models of policing that connect police officers (rather than cruisers) with communities, it is nevertheless common in municipal politics across Canada to accept the model of community policing. The model is seen as new, relevant, and more importantly, one that will present those jurisdictions to their publics as forward-thinking, as not simply spending taxpayers' dollars on reactive policing. Crime prevention programs, which institutionally operationalize what community policing does on a more mundane level, are proliferating as well, with provinces eagerly spending money on ever increasing surveillance of the public.

Given the extent of violence experienced by sex workers, it is surprising that most crime prevention programs do not focus on the safety of sex workers.[15] Instead, policies that might (and should) protect sex workers are focused on reconstructing the sex worker as one from whom the public should be protected.[16] Sex workers, rather than being the beneficiaries of such a focus on preventing crime, are made the object of a new mode of social control. The "addicted" or "aggressive" sex worker is invoked quite easily in the public imagination as something against which communities should be protected, while little or no attention is paid to the daily violence faced by sex workers (often at the hands of so-called upstanding members of communities). Crime prevention programs, therefore, like the boundaries of sentencing and release plans, ignore the violence sex workers might face. These programs fail to protect sex workers and fail to respect even their basic rights to citizenship. Police end up enforcing prevention programs and community policing efforts that target sex workers as the problem, rather than creating strategies or dialogues that recognize them as worthy of protection from violence.

While the criminal law and community policing strategies position police as the protectors of society, sex workers challenge their claim to this role. Sex workers know that they will not get protection from police and that they need to protect themselves. Further, sex workers feel that they are blamed for the violence they experience (a pattern familiar in domestic violence and/or rape cases). As one Halifax worker stated: "When prostitutes are attacked by johns, the cops don't do anything. They treat [sex workers] like it's their fault" (Dana, Halifax). However, when sex workers take steps, concealing a knife, or carrying mace for example, to protect themselves, they may face weapons charges if arrested. As one sex worker argued:

> I'd just really like to see the day where ... certain conditions for these types of women wouldn't apply as harshly, if they're caught with weapons and stuff, that should just be a little misdemeanour thing, not criminal because of the type of work they are doing, they're in a dangerous field ... [it should] not be as harsh as somebody going around with a knife in their pocket and ready to stab somebody any minute, you know; they got it for a reason, just to protect themselves. (Valerie, Halifax)

Indeed, as another sex worker noted, police acknowledge through their own actions – by wearing weapons and by having recourse to back up support – that the street is a dangerous place.[17] Yet they deny protection to sex workers:

> You never see a cop out there without a gun and a billy [club] and driving in cars. Can you imagine them being in the street? I mean, where we are with nothing, I don't think they would have the nerve like that. So it does take a certain amount of courage. (Valerie, Halifax)

Thus, sex workers parody the construction of police as brave defenders of the community by pointing to the far greater courageousness of unprotected sex workers.

Sex Workers' Resistance

> I haven't been working for three years and these two officers ... I'm still a crackhead whore to them ... They can kiss my fuckin' ass. I don't mean to be ignorant. But that's what they can do. 'Cause I'm a taxpayer now. They can't even open my gate now. I'll tell them, they're a civil servant, they work for me. (Denise, Halifax)

> Well, first of all, it hasn't happened to me, but I've heard stories, of you know, cops calling them every name under the sun. And calling them that and then telling them you will refer to me as "sir." You know, and it's like fuck you, you know. The day I call you sir is like, you know. I mean, what a nerve. They think they're so perfect. Everyone knows they've got the best dope in town. Everybody knows they've got the best girls in town. Like, who the hell are they kidding? (April, Halifax)

Sex workers are well aware of the power imbalance between them and police, and they use whatever methods they have at hand to resist and refuse poor treatment meted out to them by the police and by the unfairness of the law. Some of the sex workers we spoke with also carefully distinguished between individual officers – between the nice ones and the not so nice ones. The nice ones – those who are friendly or who do not apply the law harshly – are appreciated; although this good treatment is not seen as something that should be particularly difficult for officers, given the inconsistency of the law. What sex workers also told us, however, is how they resist policing by *both* types of officers, using different strategies. One strategy might be obvious, a kind of in-your-face attitude toward police. The other may not appear immediately as resistance, as it might seem that the sex worker actually gets on with police officers. This second strategy can be read as resistance when, given certain circumstances, sex workers need police protection. To get on with police, then, can be a form of insurance. Whether or not a sex worker gets along with a police officer is not the point. The question is, can she ply her trade no matter how she treats him or her? Whether a sex worker foils a police officer's investigation deliberately, or ignores orders, or smiles politely and does what the officer wants – all can be construed as resistance strategies.

When police are humane in their approach, they are generally described by sex workers as "just doing their jobs." Here sex workers, being treated with some respect, recognize police as very much like themselves – doing what they have to do under circumstances not entirely under their control. According to one escort worker:

> **Only time in thirteen years [I was] busted, the police fined the owner but not the girls. Cops said they wouldn't have bothered, but a new neighbour moved in next door and called police to complain.** (Felicity, Halifax)

Sex workers can empathize with working-class beat police who are limited by the requirements of their job, but they recognize harassment when they experience it:

> **They don't care. They like to harass us: "Oh, hi T, what are you doin'?" "I'm walking. Do you see me standin' on one spot? No you don't, you see me walkin'."** (Tara, Halifax)

They also recognize that, while police are "just doing their job," that job is inherently unfair to sex workers:

> I understand they're just doing their job, but what I don't understand is why don't they leave us women alone and go after the real criminal, like the hard-core criminals. Like, fuck, always going up and down the stroll, trying to bust us, for what ... we ain't doing nothing. We're trying to make a living. How you gonna stop someone from trying to make a living? (Katrina, Halifax)

Others are adamant that the divisions between sex workers and police cannot be pasted over:

> [The police] wanted information on [drug dealers] and I wouldn't give it to them ... And, I like, I told them, they want the information, go get it. I'm not a rat. I love cheese, but I don't have a tail. And that's just myself. To me, bikers are bikers. Cops are cops. Hos are hos. My job is not to find out information about them to give to the police. That's what the police go to school for, and gets paid for. Find information out, right? So I mean, do your job. Never mind sittin' at Tim Hortons and bothering the prostitutes. Go get the real criminals. (Denise, Halifax)

Several are quick to lay out the potential hypocrisy and self-interest of police behaviour, particularly how police can make their careers through the fairly simple act of arresting sex workers (that is, "just doing their jobs" can potentially bring sizable benefits to police). In a letter to the editor, sex workers in Saint John challenged the dominant construction of themselves as the ones who perpetrate and benefit from the trade by bringing police into the same category and levelling the hierarchy between them, asking, "Are we the only ones to blame? What about the special crime unit that built its reputation off our shortcomings?"[18] In this case, the discursive act of presenting police as "doing their job, just like us" has a potentially subversive effect on the dominant discourse.

Sex workers have a sharp eye for hypocrisy, and one of the most frustrating issues that some interviewees reported was that not only are police sometimes clients but they can abuse their power or even be the source of violence:

> I never ever got busted, actually there was two cops, they knew what I was doing there and they were trying to – like having like sex with me – not to bust me and stuff like that. (Kristin, Halifax)

> I mean, I've got X-rays from my right ribs that were broken by police officers. It's not funny. (Denise, Halifax)

As one worker put it:

> You know what I mean, it's not fair. It's not fair 'cause they let the badge take over. And you know what, there's a lot of cops out there that is tricks. (Lydia, Halifax)

Sex workers resist mistreatment and harassment by the not so nice often by ignoring them or by talking back:

> Um, certain police officers are nice and other ones? Dear, I wouldn't talk to them if they had a warrant for my arrest. I still wouldn't respond to them. I would have nothing to say. I'd go with the flow, obviously, [but] to have conversation – no way. Just because of their attitudes. Some are like okay, they look the other way. It's not like I'm out in the middle of the street flagging down traffic. But the ones that know you're out there and they don't like ya, oh, they'll pull you over just for fun. It wouldn't matter if I was walking with an old lady: "What are you doing B? Come on over here. We're gonna check you out," and all this. "What's your date of birth?" All this and that stuff. And like I tell them, "I know my rights. Unless I'm under arrest, see you later." And I'll keep on walking. They don't like that because I know a little bit about my rights [in] that sense. So that's like, "Oh, she thinks she's all that." [I'll say,] "I have no warrant [out for me], so what are you gonna do? What are you gonna arrest me for? Walking down the street? You got a lovely case, let's go. I got nothing to do for the next five hours, take me downtown."
>
> Oh, but some police are really good. Oh, [officer's name,] I love him to death. He'll look the other way and just give you a look like, get going. You know better 'cause if he comes around again and you're there, he's gonna have to do his job. People like that you respect. The other guys that just want to be jerks, you'd like to give them a hard time just because the way they are. (Belinda, Halifax)

When policing is aggressive and inhumane, police become the objects of ridicule and scorn for picking on relatively powerless sex workers:

> They're a laugh and a half, they are, they're pathetic. There's a lot bigger crime going on in the city of Saint John than us girls walking down the street, you know. I have to go to court tomorrow actually for obstruction of justice, for saying, "Good evening, Officer." That's what I said. I blew his cover. (Tabitha, Saint John)

Rather than bowing to the power of police, sex workers dismiss them as "boys" driven by limited mentality and maturity and a masculine bravado, and lacking in human feeling and understanding: "Cops are arrogant; jails are cold" (Megan, Halifax). Or, as another worker put it: "They don't get it; they're just cowboys" (Hannah, Halifax). Such descriptions position the sex worker as the more mature, understanding, and sympathetic character – a portrayal which flies in the face of mainstream characterizations of police and sex workers.

Ridicule can become an effective resistance method by drawing attention to the potential hypocrisy of policing:

> (Laughter) The police. Well, some of them are pricks. Some of them I joke around with, some of them I can tell to fuck off, 'cause I ... that's just me. I carry on with the other people. I'm a joker, and so I'll say to the cops, "Get off my corner, you're blocking my traffic. Get off my corner, I'm trying to work. How can I work with you here?" I tell them. I'll say, "Go, go, go" ... "Well, if you're gonna pay me, drop here in front of me and, see what kind of man you are." So one day there's this officer, and I felt his privates through his uniform. And he said, "K, you're bad, my wife ain't gonna like that." I said, "Fuck your wife. Your wife don't have to know! What you driving on the stroll for, if you don't want no pussy?" That's what I tell them. And a lot of people don't understand how I can talk to them like that. And I tell them 'cause that's me. You have your way of dealing with it, and I have my way. You see, they don't like the way I deal with them 'cause I carry on with them. I don't give them a hard time, I just joke. That's just me, and it'll always be me. But a lot of them are pricks. A lot of them just drive by maybe, and slow down, and want to know if I'm this, or I'm that, and ask me if I'm on curfew or stuff. Well, "Fuck off, check on your computer, that's what you get paid to do! Don't just sit there and watch me." Know what I mean? They try to follow me, try to set me up with the task force. But I know all the task force. They can't do that. I'm on to them, so they have to come up with a new game for me. (Katrina, Halifax)

Sex workers are aware that the treatment they receive from police undermines their rights as citizens – that they are worthy of at least humane treatment and do not deserve the disrespect they encounter:

> We really have to do something to survive and they should not treat us so much like we aren't citizens. We are citizens too. You know, give us a little bit more respect and dignity, you know. That's what they should do. And when they stop us and intercept us they should be nice about it. They're rude. They're ignorant. They call you whores and everything. They're awful. They don't have no respect for anybody like us, they think that we should all be put in a garbage can. (Valerie, Halifax)

Conclusion

The law regarding sex work is driven by two very different and competing discourses that have little to do with sex work per se – certainly not with protecting sex workers – and more to do with the social control functions of policing female sexuality and protecting private or community space. The result of these laws, and the enactment of these laws, is to exclude the sex worker from the community and from citizenship and, at the same time, deny her/him fundamental protections and rights. No amount of attempts to make the law more effective through the use of sentencing conditions or john schools will make the law less contradictory or less harmful for sex workers.

The encounters between sex workers and police are highly determined by the social control structures that surround sex work. While officers and sex workers can try to resist them, ultimately, these structures determine how sex workers are treated by the law and its upholders. No matter which discourse on sex work or which pattern of interaction is adopted by police, the purpose of social control – of disciplining sex workers and denying them full citizenship – is served. Sex workers recognize and resist these strategies of social control. They are not fooled by sympathetic police or protective strategies. As long as sex work remains criminalized, sex workers will face unfair punishment and will, simultaneously, fail to be protected from harm. Sex workers see and name these processes for what they are – a denial of citizenship – and they resist this denial as best they can.

4
The Whore Stigma and the Media

Stigma is one of the central issues, and major burdens, for people working in the sex trade. Sex worker advocates have long maintained that it is the stigma attached to the sex trade, not the sex trade itself, that is the cause of suffering for sex workers.[1] The sex workers we spoke with identified stigma as one of the major problems they face. In doing so, sex workers resist the common discourse of low self-esteem that permeates government agencies, police, and some outreach organizations. While many commentators understand low self-esteem as a problem for sex workers and a cause of entry into the trade, sex workers frequently turn this discourse around to talk about stigma as a major cause of low self-esteem. That is, sex workers resist the individualizing and psychologizing discourse of self-esteem and re-politicize the issue by pointing to the attitudes of the public rather than the psychological makeup of the sex workers as the problem.

Stigmatizing attitudes that paint sex workers as backward, victims, uneducated, addicted, and whores are, according to sex workers, common among the wider public as well as among police, government, and the media, and they contribute to the climate of violence and marginalization that sex workers face. Sex workers frequently point to the media as a major purveyor of these attitudes, zeroing in on sex workers only as sex workers, not as fuller human beings. The media present simplified and stereotypical images of sex work and sex workers, make sex workers the objects of (negative) attention, and silence sex workers as speakers in their own right. The media also fail to draw attention to the role that the rest of society plays in the trade. We argue that what sex workers are naming here, in articulating their experience of stigma and their analysis of the media, is the process of surveillance and social control in which the media play a major role. In this chapter, we use these insights to explore the production of images of the sex worker in a major Maritime newspaper, the Halifax *Chronicle Herald*, over the past decade and a half.

Public Perceptions: "They Look at Ya like We're Nothing"

One of the central issues discussed during the interviews was public perceptions of people working in the sex trade. The answer was nearly universally negative. Interviewees overwhelmingly responded that they are seen as "whores," "dirty whores," or "nobodies." This sense of being looked down upon and excluded from the community echoed through their responses. Workers and former workers were frustrated by society's inability to see them as whole persons, as parts of families, as people struggling with issues such as addiction, or to understand the wide variation of life experiences among those in the trade.

Many complained about being judged and condemned by people who have no understanding of sex workers' lives:

> Whore, dirty skank, you've heard all them names; I don't need to tell ya. And it's not – it's like the majority of the girls I know in escort and everything ... you know why they're there: is so that they can feed their children, things like that. They're just going out and getting money. Just they're not going about it the way that you know Uncle Sam wants them to so ... oh wait, we're in Canada, I'm trying to think, Uncle Chrétien [former Prime Minister Jean Chrétien], I don't know. (Alexis, Moncton)

In Saint John, where the small street trade is closely linked to addictions, many complained about the intertwining stigmas of addictions and sex work:

> Many of the girls that are on the street don't want to be there. A lot of people run them down. They think they're just losers, crackhead prostitutes. That's all they are, but they don't want to be there. They got an addiction that's controlling their life, and everybody blocks you out ... your family, you don't have anybody. All you have is the street, and people that use. That's all you know, so you stay in it. (Beth, Saint John)

> When I was out there, I was thinking, well, they're probably looking at me and saying, "Look at that dirty prostitute" or something like that. Some people think different, and some people, they understand that there's a problem or something around. Some people just think piggish of us, but ... (Candace, Saint John)

Others said that people outside the sex trade have no right to judge sex workers and believe themselves somehow immune to "that kind of life":

> Some of them condemn it, but yet they realize a person has to do what a person has to do. So I'm just saying that you should put yourself in my

shoes. Do not talk to me about something you don't know nothing about. 'Cause if you had my life you'd be doing the same thing I'm doing. So how do you know your daughter's not out there? How do you know somebody in your family's not out there? How does anybody even know if you haven't done any? To me, I don't care. Well, I do, but I don't. As long as my family know what I do, I don't have no one else to think about. No one. I come in the world alone, I'm going out alone, and no one [lives] for free. Nobody. Screw them. (Katrina, Halifax)

Well, I think that Saint John, as great as it is, has a lot of old values, or whatever. I think a lot more people are [more] accept[ing] of it than they claim to be. But Saint John is just so old, everyone wants to think old ways ... But hey, 'til one of those people walks in my steps, don't tell me what to do. Don't judge me until you walk in my steps. You know, I come from a very affluent family, I have my grade twelve ... A lot of people say, well, how did this ever happen to you? Why, what makes me so special?

It's the drug, it's not, you know ... And a lot of people are shocked that that is what I do. But like I said, you tell me an easier way to, [make] anywhere from twenty to a hundred bucks within twenty minutes. You know what I am saying? I can be out doing crime, you know what I mean? This way I am not hurting anyone else but myself ...

Yeah, I think people should go outside their stereotypes and ... look at the reason why they're out there before they start shooting their mouths off and putting them down. Hey, it could be their mother working; it could be their daughter, their sister, their niece, because we all have those family members. So don't judge me or my family until you put yourself in our shoes. (Tabitha, Saint John)

A number of interviewees commented on their frustration with the hypocrisy of society's attitudes, particularly of sexual practices:

Interviewer: How do you think people view prostitution?
They think we're sick and disgusting, and they call us dirty old whores. They just think we're dirt.
Interviewer: What do you think needs to change with people's attitudes?
Well, I think they should look at it like, if they were put in our positions. How would they deal with things, and make money and stuff? And I mean, not everybody's perfect. There are other people out there, girls that aren't prostitutes, jeez they're at bars and stuff. They're just giving it away, so what's the big ... we're making money from it, and plus we're using protection. They're going to the bars and running around like little ... you know ... That's what I don't understand, so why are they looking down on

us? We're not walking up and down the street, acting all you know. We're just sitting on our little step or wherever. But they're looking really, really bad, and then I suppose they're looking at us, saying we look really bad.

But there's a lot of them at the bars, and they just [go crazy/get drunk] and they just, they're just giving it to everybody ... But I say that to a lot of people, like what's the difference? Look what you're doing. I'm getting paid for it. (Violet, Saint John)

According to others, not only is society engaging in similar behaviours but it is actually driving the sex trade:

Okay, how can I put this? We're not scum because you're the ones paying ... You guys are looking down on us ... yeah, but who's paying us? It's you guys. How do we make our money? You guys. (Jason, Moncton)

And one woman expressed her frustration with the hypocrisy of straight society's condemnation of the sex worker while giving more damaging behaviour little or no attention:

Oh, the public's attitude is, "Oh, here's this girl standing on the corner will do anything for a dollar." That's their opinion, to look down upon me. Just look at all those businessmen that are out ripping old people off and doing business that way. I'd much rather know I didn't hurt nobody. Everything's consensual. I'm thirty-four and if they're over eighteen, and under ninety-nine, and you got the money ... I'm not hurting anyone. (Belinda, Halifax)

The result of this judgment and stigma is the sex workers' feeling of being ostracized from the community. Foremost is a sense that they are treated as social lepers:

Old people, they'll walk by you like you got some kind of leech, or something, is going to jump up. You know, what I find so funny? People walking down the street and they'll have a big conversation, and as soon as they see the hookers: "Don't say a thing, it's a hooker." What the ...? Like the whole world just stopped and then they walk by ... what the fuck? Like, it's a hooker, not a spy ... Or you get these ones who walk down the middle of the street [to avoid you]. Like, there's a lot of demented people out there. (Heidi, Halifax)

This sex worker went on to reveal that she was not permitted in clubs and was even denied entrance to a public washroom at a gas station. Another concurred:

Because even, even, even on my street where I live at, people all know, right? And they just look at me. They say hi and that's about it, then they'll walk by me, "Oh yeah, I seen her on H Street," and stuff, right? (Carrie, Halifax)

Others reported similar experiences:

Interviewer: What do you think people's perceptions are of women in the trade?
Disgusted, disgusted, that's my view and ... as a matter of fact, I know. I was just talking about that last night. It's disgust. They look at you with disgust, especially women, like other women. And like, they'll be walking, or they'll be walking with their men or whatever, even their children. Like we were walking up the street the other day and this lady was walking down with her two children. Do you know she took her two kids by the hand and pulled them closer to her like we would hurt them or something. It's just ... argh ... It makes me mad because 99 percent of the women out there have an addiction. They're not dangerous women. They have a disease. But a lot of these people look at you with disgust. Even some men. And some of these men that look at you with disgust, I've taken out. So, but yeah, they look at you as, you know, you're not ... ahh ... like you're dirt. (Krystal, Halifax)

As she is a mother herself, such experiences are no doubt particularly painful for this sex worker. Indeed, being a mother can make the stigma of being a sex worker in a small place, as most Maritime cities are, particularly problematic:

Interviewer: What do you think public perceptions or attitudes of women in the trade are?
(Laughs.) Whore, that's you know ... that's just the thing. Um, one of [my son's] school friends recently found out what I did for a living and spread it all through the school, you know. Which I feel so bad for my son, do you know what I mean? He's the one who has to defend me there. And I am getting messages on my machine, "This message is for X's mother. Is it true you work in a whorehouse?" Stuff like this. (Felicity, Halifax)

The difficulty of escaping this stigma even if one leaves the trade was emphasized:

Interviewer: How do you think the public sees women in the trade?
Um, sad. They look at ya like we're nothing. "Oh yeah, she's a prostitute, she's a hooker." They, they just look at ya like you're nobody and they want to put you down and stuff. Like, I find if I did decide to go get a job I probably wouldn't find one. Because they probably would look at me

and say, "Oh yeah, she's ... she used to work, she's a hooker. Can't hire her." And that's the impression I get. (Carrie, Halifax)

Interviewer: Do you think that there's a stigma attached, that there's some kind of label? Do you think that once you're working in the trade, people think that that's who you are, that that's your identity?
Yeah, that's your identity now, no matter ...
Interviewer: It doesn't matter if you are a good person or ...
Or not even you're squared up and I say squared up in meaning like you try to change your life and go straight now, you're an ex.
Interviewer: Yeah, once a prostitute ...
Always a prostitute. That's what they think, and they still think probably ... because that's the label that you got ... How do you change that? (Valerie, Halifax)

Even acquaintances could prove frustrating, particularly in their inability to accept that sex workers may have a sense of self-worth rather than a feeling of degradation:

A lot of people think that – like for instance, I'll use as an example, 'cause it just happened like a few months ago – this girl was at my house, and she doesn't know what I do. And her and her boyfriend and their friend was there, and we were, well, they were drinking. I wasn't drinking that night, and I ended up getting a call through the escort agency. So when I come back, she was like, "How can you do that, you're putting yourself down," and whatever. And I was like, "Listen, okay, what you do, you do. What I do, I do." I'm a very respectable woman, you know what I mean? And she's like, "No, you're really disrespecting yourself." And I was like, "Who the hell are you to judge me?" You know what I mean?

So, there's a lot of that, just they ... they never did it, so they really don't know what's going on. They're thinking the worst. That "Oh, this girl's out there, having sex with a bunch of men," or whatever. But they really don't know. As I tried to tell them, you'd be surprised how many times I go to a hotel room, that I just sit there and have a drink with the guy, or I just sit there and talk to him, or I honestly just give a massage. Like, you'd be surprised how many times it happens. I said, I'm not looking down on myself, because I'm not doing nothing to look down on myself. Then there's the other half, that are like, "Well, that's pretty cool, that you got enough confidence to go out and do things like that, I could never do it, just because I know I couldn't." (Tamara, Halifax)

While a number of interviewees expressed their empathy with members of the public who have concerns or misperceptions about the trade, that some of these people would enact their hostility on sex workers was the source of head-shaking incredulity:

> I find really a lot of people, they come and, just no respect. They come down, they drive along the streets, and they'll be hollering this that at ya, throwing eggs, and just no respect. People individually ...
> *Interviewer: If you had a chance to speak to people like that, what would you say?*
> I think I'd just more want to know why. Why do you do that? I don't understand that. Even, I don't think, even if I wasn't in the trade, that I've got more better things to do than borrow Mom's car and go down or whatever, every weekend and ... like hello. I don't understand them.
> (Kisha, Halifax)

One woman working in Halifax reported how

> people would drive around the street and stare at us; you know: "Hookers on the street." They were out for their Sunday drive ... "Let's go on M Street," you know, "I'm bored." They blow their horns, sit outside their windows, waiting. (Hannah, Halifax)

This attitude toward sex workers can translate into physical harassment:

> *Interviewer: So when you say "very little," how often would you be out?*
> Well, [I'm] not out doing it as much as I used to be.
> *Interviewer: Why is that?*
> Well, I find there's a stigma attached to it. Like, too many people know me and it's like they see me, but they're attaching a stigma. And it's like, she's nothing but a ... you know. But anyway ...
> *Interviewer: What do you think needs to change about people's attitudes?*
> Shit or get off the pot, man. It's like, you know, it's like, we're not hurting anybody but ourselves ... It's a very hard question to answer.
> *Interviewer: Do you get harassed by people, do you find?*
> Oh, yeah. I've even gotten beaten up by people.
> *Interviewer: People who aren't in the trade but just come by?*
> Oh, yeah. (Alison, Halifax)

Others put down society's attitudes toward sex workers as a function of its puritanism about sex:

> *Interviewer: What do you think people's attitudes are towards people in the trade?*
> It really depends on the individual or group of persons. Their religion could be involved, as it could be a moral thing, as it was in my family. It

could be something to do with the fact that we are lower than society and [society thinks] we do this because ... we're lazy and we can't get jobs, or we can't get into the workforce. It could be any amount of reasons [that we're in sex work], as some people just like the danger and the excitement, as I did in the beginning, of getting away with something. Something that is taboo, something that we're not supposed to be doing with our bodies ... that we were told to use our bodies as our temples and not let any strangers in. It could be a range of reasons in that people in general just don't understand about being sexual, having sexual feelings, exploring their bodies. They're very one-sided on sex in general for whatever reason. (Charles, Halifax)

One former sex worker in Halifax eloquently skewered society's hypocritical attitudes:

I know what it's like to not have nothing. And how it felt seeing people there looking at me. And I was better than half of them that I'm lookin' at lookin' down at me! It's just people degrade you, and you're put in a different part of society. You've got women with their kids, and their husbands, and the picket fences and stuff. Then you got the women that like to dominate it, like lesbians and stuff. We don't even fit in with them 'cause they think we're dirt. See, they got the gay parades and all that. They're liberated and all this and that, but the prostitutes don't got nothin'. We're like Alf – in a different planet altogether. We're seen as dirt.

Interviewer: What do you think prostitutes need?
I think prostitutes need people like yourself to enlighten these people that just comes along. We're not just people you see on a movie at nighttime. We're not these bad girls that show our tits and stuff, and your husbands are coming out to pay. We have feelings too. We are someone's kids, we're someone's mother, someone's sister. Don't just look at us and just say, "Oh, that's a whore" ... I mean, my sisters are high up [in] society. They even looked down at me when I was out there. I'm looking at them now, I got more than any of them got, and I still don't look down at them. And to me, I know what it's like. I'll never regret working the streets. I'm not proud of it, but I'm not ashamed of it either. But I'm human. Everybody makes mistakes.

And there's one thing, we're all God's creations, no matter who, and he doesn't make mistakes. So we're all here for a reason. No one understands it yet, no one will, but everyone is someone's creation. If you're gay, or lesbian, if you're a hooker, a thief, whatever, we're all here for a reason. And nationality is a big thing with prostitution. Your whites, your blacks, your Natives, and you get your Inuits, and Chinese ... I worked with them all. I worked with transvestites and all. To me, they're gay men, dressed like women. I have a good friend of mine had the operation – was a man, had the operation, was a woman – and worked the streets with me. I just buried her, from hepatitis C. But she was a woman to me. I knew her when she was a man, gay, and then had the operation as a woman. And to me, we're all out there doing the same thing. No one got the right to judge us, because you come from a normal class family, and we're prostitutes. So what? We feel, we bleed the same as anyone else. It's like prejudice. I cut you, you gonna bleed the same as me, so ...

Interviewer: It's like that label stays with you.
It stays with you no matter what. It stays with you. People that I know, that I went to school with, that seen me working, they don't see ... They don't see me as me, and they could have went to school with me all their life. They see me as a ... "Oh, she worked the streets" ... And I got that from people like my own sister, and my cousins. We grew up together and that, and she'll say – like I said to one of my cousins, she got her hair cut, and I'm used to long hair, and I said, "I don't like it like that. I liked it better when you had it long." We was just talking, and she said, "Oh well, don't insult me, 'cause I could *really* insult you." I said, "How could you really insult me, 'cause I worked the streets? Oh well, what about you when you go to the tavern, and all you do is have men buy you drinks and dance with ya, and you go home and fuck them for nothing? I'm getting paid; I don't want to see your [client's] face, don't even know who you [client] are!"

So you get judged by the young girls from college, that are going to school, and they see you on the corner, they laugh in their cars, ah ha ... what are they doing? They're going to the clubs. A guy dances with ya and buys ya drinks, and then they take ya home and fuck ya. And probably get some disease, or they get that date ... that pill put in there, ecstasy, [GHB, ketamine, and Rohypnol are considered "date rape" drugs] the date rapes, and whatever they call them, and that. And then they end up with diseases and stuff. So they're no better than no one, and you get them from all over the place.

Interviewer: It makes you wonder what the definition is, ah, of prostitution.
Yes, exactly. Is prostitution someone like myself standing on a corner getting paid, or am I the housewife that's home getting paid every Thursday from my husband, for cleaning the house, taking care of his sexual needs, looking after the kids, and going grocery shopping? Or the young girls in college and the women who are crown prosecutors and stuff that sit home lonely. I know women right now, high-class women, that are so lonely, there's three of them that I know, and I'm looking at them like ... My sister's one of them. These women all got good jobs, big career women. They don't have a man. They don't even know ... now they're talking about going on line to chat rooms and stuff. And I'm there

thinking, holy Jesus and *I'm* a whore? Oh no, I'll stay a whore. And these are three business women, that get paid good money and stuff, and they're out there ... They're talking about chat rooms and stuff 'cause they can't meet nobody. There's no one but them in their life. They don't want to take a chance, and make mistakes and stuff. And they want to point fingers at people, "Oh well, she's a prostitute, stay away from her."

Well look what I got? What did I get? Nothing. I'm happy. I learned a lot, and I'm not ashamed of it. I learned a lot from some people, other people learn from me ... every day. Every day. And if I can help another girl out, or a guy, I will. And I will never ... if I walk down a street and I see two girls working, I go right out talking to them, have a talk with them, while my other friends are running up the street ... "Oh my God, how do you stand to talk to them?" Like, it doesn't bother me, doesn't bother me at all – which other people would be ashamed to. I know there's still people ashamed to talk to me when they see me on the streets. I don't care. Don't talk to me. I'm not going to change. A society never made me the way I am. I took my own road. The world's full of choices. They're my choices, I made them, but they're mine. Leave me alone. Let me deal with my choices, and my decisions. These people, they got decisions and choices, but they're not dealing with theirs. They're too busy worrying about mine and me. And it's like they got their finger in the jar of Kool-Aid, and they don't know what flavour it is?

So, men and women [in] prostitution, if you set down and talk and that, they're warm people inside. They might got a rugged look on the outside. I mean, there's a lot of people I scare the friggin' shit out of when they meet me, and I don't mean to be, but that's how life made me. I was right timid before with the kids, "Pardon me," "Excuse me," now [it's] ... "What the fuck you want?" I don't care. It's like, 'cause life made me that way, the hard shell ... I mean, it's true. When I was prim and proper, I never paid attention. But now that I worked and that, I still see this day when I walk, I know they're talking about me.

Put it this way: I live in a high-class area, okay? All them people are new, because where I live at right now, when I was a hooker, I lived on the other corner, one block up. I walk past all my neighbours that I have now. Then, when I was so skinny, and I was working the streets. And I walk past them today when I own two properties, and I got a Monte Carlo, and they still to this day, they don't ... Now they look at me ... I'm in society? But then it was like ... but I'm still the same person. I'm walking the same area, but they're like ... I'm accepted because I have money and homes and stuff? But then, when I was a hooker, "Oh, look at her, look at her." Now they don't. It's the same area! I went from living in a crack-house room to owning my own properties, and I wish you could see it. My house is here ... that I own now ... this is the boulevard, that's where I worked the streets and the crack houses. I walk down the same street every day, [past] the same people, every day for the last ten years.

Interviewer: But now that you have diamonds ...

Diamonds and cars, and home properties, [so] they don't say nothing. They want to talk to me, invite me in their homes, for coffee and that, but when I was working the streets, "I wonder if my husband's getting her to blow him." It's society, and I mean, I would never go in their houses, 'cause I know what they're like. You didn't want to talk to me then, don't talk to me now. That's me. And they'll see me, 'cause in the summertime a lot of my friends come up in my yard and stuff ... prostitutes ... They're my friends, I don't care. I mean, they're not up there dressed naked, but they're my friends, I don't care how they come. They're not doing nothing wrong, they're in my yard. And if you want to sell, 'cause that's a whore house over there, so be it. So be it. We're not doing nothing wrong to no one and the cops cannot do nothing, or come in my yard. They can't even open my gate. So we could be twenty of us in there, and laughing at them.

And that's how I feel, and I have a real negative attitude towards the authorities with that, and prostitutes and myself. I still class myself as a prostitute, although I haven't worked in three years. I do. I'm no better than no one else, and I never will be. I'm no worse than no one else, right? I mean, yourself, you're a professor. I got grade eight education. And you know what? I don't care. I'm happy, you're happy. It's not what you learn in school. My fiancé, I'm telling ya, he's got so much up here, and my sister, brains? But for someone so smart, they're so fucking stupid. When it comes to street smart and stuff, I'm like, holy God. (Denise, Halifax)

The Media

If I had a chance to tell the media so that they ... so the world would hear what I had to say, something I'd tell them [is,] "Don't speak. You want to know about a whore, you get to know a whore and you'll see that she's just like you." That's what I'd tell them. (Alexis, Moncton; seventeen year-old, former sex worker)

Who gets to speak and who is silenced, or who gets to tell the story of the sex trade, is, of course, precisely the issue at hand in this book. The media are central players in choosing whose story is told and how and, therefore, how the public in general perceives the issue of the sex trade. People who work in the sex trade are not unaware of the power of the media. On one hand, they are consumers of the media, reading the paper over a cup of coffee or watching the news. On the other hand, they are often subjects of media attention, although their voices are rarely heard. In our discussions, a number of problems with media representation of sex workers were raised. They include a lack of sex worker perspectives; a failure to investigate the broader context of sex work, such as socioeconomic circumstances; the use of stigmatizing language and images; and the tendency of media portrayals to frame sex work stories in such a way that the rest of society appears blameless. These insights into the media's role are echoed in social constructionist theory, which points to the role of the media in constructing social reality and determining social action. It also draws our attention to the role of the media as a vehicle of surveillance, targeting certain groups for (often negative) attention and social discipline. The stigma experienced by sex workers, which undoubtedly affects their quality of life, is the result of being on the receiving end of this surveillance.

Many of our interviewees remarked on the language used in the newspapers when the sex trade or sex workers are discussed. Words such as "addict," "prostitute," and "hooker" carry a weight and an image that single out one aspect of a person's life. The manner in which the media report on sex workers reinforces the stereotypes and Other the sex worker. To accentuate this othering, additional stereotypes are added, such as "addicted drug user" or "high-risk lifestyle," as a way not only to differentiate the sex worker significantly from the rest of the population but to somehow explain or justify her potential victimization, particularly in terms of violence.[2] The subtlety of this is not lost on sex workers; to erase them as people is to invite violence. To resist this erasure of self, the sex worker talks back. As one woman said:

> And you know with the newspapers, why can't you say "working girl"? Why "prostitute," why "addict"? Right? Oh, they put it right in the papers, "crack addict," "prostitute." Why can't they say, "a young, beautiful person" or "a young women in the sex trade" – "was in the sex trade, got caught up, a very good person." See, all they're lookin' at is our records and what we're out there doing; but they don't really. They don't look at what's in here [pointing to herself]. See, down in the courthouse, they don't see what's in here. They're just going by your file, your record. "Oh well, she did that, she did this, so obviously she's a bad person." But [they don't see] a woman with problems, this is the reason why she commits these crimes. They don't look at that. (Tara, Halifax)

Presenting the women and men who work in the sex trade only within their "deviant" role – crack addict, prostitute – shores up the public's conviction that sex workers are separate and different from and, therefore, lesser than the rest of society. The stigma thus created affects sex workers' lives even long after they have left the trade:

> They just love to pick on me, those newspapers. But, you know, it's in your face. Now I live on the street where I had worked and the cops drive by and I feel funny, I feel right ... "Here comes a cop and they're going to think I'm hooking." And [they always think] she's hooking, and she's hooking. And it's unreal. Oh, it is. I'll never get over that one. And I feel like I'm guilty and I'm not. I'm just going down to the store or something, right? (Alyssa, Saint John)

In marking out sex workers as different, the media also shore up the common biases of the public by focusing on sex workers as particularly problematic, a second issue many of our respondents identified. White-collar crime, middle-class drug addiction, the privilege of the rich, and the exploitation of the poor do not make interesting copy or are simply not seen as problematic (and, therefore, are not worthy of discussion):

> No, it doesn't seem fair. Our name gets exploited all over the papers, like we're bad people ... I mean, there's other, there's people that are just plain mean. And my kids, my daughter ... she didn't know where I was at the time when I didn't go around them. And my name was in the front paper, and half the paper. It said, "Prostituting to support a crack habit" ... At this time, my family didn't know where I was, or if I was on the street, or on drugs – nor did my kids. Now the whole of Saint John knew. The phone was ringing off the hook, rubbing it in my family's face. And after a little while – they kept doing that, the paper kept doing that – when I went to jail, X encouraged a lot of us girls to write to the editor and ask him why are we any different than anybody in the courts? Like, you were in the courts, but we were on the front page! We did wrong, sure we did, then [that's] why we [were] in the courts. Why do we have to be on the front page? I have sisters out there, I have a mother, I have children out there that are being ... like my daughter, this little girl she's played with, she said, "My mother said you're a crackhead." (Beth, Saint John)

Not only are sex workers the unfair object of focus, but also the impact of that focus is felt deeply by themselves and their families, especially in small Maritime centres. People tend to know each other in the Maritimes, if not directly then through reputation or family name. When a sex worker is named in the media, her name circulates for quite some time. Her name becomes synonymous with the sex trade, and it is an association that is difficult to shake.

Prostitution, however, is a titillating story – it sells papers. The media, therefore, are almost always interested when a prostitution-related story comes up (often because of the complaints of residents or the reports of police, which predetermine whose story is going to be told). The media often use inflammatory language to further dramatize stories involving sex workers – thereby increasing the effect of the story and garnering it more attention. While the media are fascinated with sex workers, sex workers themselves rarely get to tell their stories. The women and men we spoke with were very aware of how they were used by the media as objects rather than being presented as subjects. One sex worker's experience of the media world and her attempt to take part in it is instructive:

> See, I went to a talk show two years ago ... about revealing secrets. And I revealed I was a prostitute to my boyfriend, but my boyfriend already knew. But we played the game up on the talk show. And that got everywhere and everybody saw that. And I said it was all staged, but it wasn't. It was all true what I was saying. And [the host] was going to get me to see a counsellor or something up there but ... Then I was like, "Oh my God, there I am talking about it on the show."
> *Interviewer: Did you get paid well for that?*
> No, you only get like $60 a day. So they pay off your flight but by the time you eat ... you know what I mean? It was your food. I said to myself, [you're a] talk show, you got money or something. The only reason they took me in is because their ratings were going down, and so [the show's host] was doing prostitution – and it goes up. I didn't know the science, [but] I'm on like five times a month there. (Kristin, Halifax)

Another woman, who gave talks on transsexualism as well as the sex trade, and who had extensive professional experience with the media, explained that despite her skill and professionalism in dealing with the media, the story is rarely presented the way she puts it forward. The media's ignoring of the sex worker voice is not a product of sex workers' inability to speak (as all the stories told here make quite plain). Rather, it is a concerted effort on the part of the media not to listen:[3]

> *Interviewer: You happen to do a lot of media stuff, right? And have you found it's made any difference? Are you able to get through?*
> Ah, no. Because – which is surprising, except for the lectures at the universities – nobody can do it ... The newspaper, or the media period. Everything I've ever said has been censored, you know. And I was doing a lot of them, and every time they called and said, "Would you do an interview?" I said, "On one condition: you don't censor it." But they do. So like, I stopped doing it. 'Cause you know. I don't quite understand that, because what have these independent stations got to worry about? So how does a person get the truth out there when you are censored? So there's somebody that's got their thumb on this – on the networks too. I

mean, it's gotta be, you know. I mean, I understand the majority of people think, "Ah, transsexuals, who gives a shit." But, you know, a lot of people do give a shit and a lot of people, through the education that I have given, and I have noticed it ... It's amazing ...

The last lecture I did at Dal[housie University], I mean, there was almost three hundred people there. And when I was finished after the two hours, you know, they gathered around the door and I couldn't get out. They were shaking my hand, they were wishing me well, they were, "Go for it! Go for it!" And I finally got out of there, and then the professor came running after me. And I was out on the street. And he just said, "I want to thank you so much for this. You just changed the life of three-hundred-plus people. You know, with what you told them." And I think a lot changed after I started doing all the universities. (April, Halifax)

When her story was not mediated, when she was able to speak directly to her audience, this woman found she could communicate and be heard. Why is the media so resistant to this voice?

The media wants to hear a certain story. Speakers who fail to tell that story are muted, misquoted, or ignored. That is, reporters, particularly in print media, are able to shape the story to reflect their own "line," a line that usually reflects a fairly common sense approach to the issue or one that provokes reader interest by reflecting the biases of the day. As another worker noted about media coverage in Halifax, the media tend to cling to stereotypical images:

> Yeah, there was a lot of stuff in the media that pissed me off. And the main thing was they had all, they had this stereotype for the prostitutes that you came from a home of alcoholics, and you were abused and molested. And it just, it really pissed me off. 'Cause I had none of that in my life, none of it. And every girl I've worked with – like I've met some that do, there were a lot of them – but the ones I worked with didn't. These are people that I went to school with, that I grew up with. And hey, there was many of us that didn't. And it just, that, really got to me, because there was some neighbours at that time that knew I was a prostitute and automatically that's what they were thinking. You know, "Oh, you poor girl! We know why you're doin' this," and no, it's not that, it's not that. I didn't like that at all. (Katie, Halifax)

This chapter has focused on the stereotypical presentation of sex workers, the focus of the media on them, and their being silenced as speakers. All of these phenomena are not merely products of media bias. Rather, they are effects of the techniques of power, particularly the processes of social construction and surveillance.[4] Social constructionism holds that "people create reality – the world they believe exists – based on their individual knowledge and knowledge gained from social interactions with other people. People then act in accordance with their constructed view of reality."[5] For most people, the media are part of this symbolic reality – not a social reality that is empirically experienced but one that is mediated. In Ray Surette's definition, symbolic reality is "all the events you didn't witness but believe occurred, all the facts about the world you didn't personally collect but believe to be true, all the things you believe to exist but haven't seen."[6] That is, the problem of media representation of the sex trade goes far beyond bias to the power of the media to socially construct reality in ways that reproduce the status quo relations of power. In academic terms, the reproduction of the status quo in the media, without questioning, critiquing, or evaluating the source, is called hegemonic discourse. A hegemonic order exists when information is presented in an uncontested manner, when single-source utterances are presented as truth. These truths are often representations of the status quo and, as such, contain many distortions, stereotypic understandings, and politically expedient views of the social world. It is when these supposed truths begin to shape attitudes, practices, and even policy that the power of hegemonic discourse is evident:

> The discourses of a powerful group may be such that others will form the intentions and accomplish the acts as if they were totally without constraints, and consistent with their own wants and interests. If our discourse can make people believe in this way and we thus indirectly control their actions such that they are in our best interests, we have successfully manipulated them through text and talk. In this case, the term *hegemony* is often used to refer to social power: hegemonic power makes people act as if it were natural, normal or simply a consensus. No commands, requests or even suggestions are necessary.[7]

This construction of reality has real effects and real power. It enables the actions not only of the public but of policy makers and other powerful players. It determines what is thinkable about an issue and, therefore, determines what actions are probable and who gets to act. This hegemonic discourse is particularly powerful when the public has little everyday experience of, or alternative sources of information on, a reported issue.[8] Thus, the media can play a particularly strong mediating role in these instances, creating for the non-sex-worker public the reality of prostitution. The media recreate themselves, and their chosen informants, as the authoritative producers of social reality. In the way stories on sex work or sex workers are produced, sex workers are frequently reinscribed as unable to tell their own stories or unimportant for doing so. Their realities, it becomes understood, are best mediated through others – journalists, police, lawyers, politicians, and bureaucrats. This subtle message feeds into a cycle of public discourse that excludes the sex worker as an informed knower and commentator on her/his own life and on sex work. That cycle is part of the political disenfranchisement of sex workers and re-enfranchisement of the powerful.

The media play a role in reinforcing whose story is told and in determining how the story is told. In particular, the media play a key role in a related technique of power: surveillance. Foucault argues that surveillance acts as the new form of embodied punishment (as contrasted with an earlier version of punishment, which literally was bestowed on the body) and that it is far more effective in scope. It works through what Foucault calls "disciplinary techniques," which include the subtle ways we keep people in check: by watching them, and exposing and naming their behaviours. Such is the function of the media. That is, the media create and reinforce stigma because sex workers are *supposed to* experience this stigma. And broader society is supposed to be aware of this stigma, so that it will recognize the rules of society (particularly vis-à-vis sexual behaviour) and internalize this discipline. The function of the whore stigma is indeed to ensure the division between "madonnas" and "whores" and to ensure the sexual self-disciplining of women. Sex workers bear the brunt of this surveillance. At the same time, sex workers frequently refuse to meekly accept and internalize this shaming, making them the target of other, more obvious techniques of punishment, such as the criminal law.

Importantly, surveillance works in one direction only. The powerful are precisely those who are not the objects of such surveillance. Sex workers – like racial and sexual Others – are singled out for particular attention, while other forms of misbehaviour go undiscussed and the larger context of sex work, that is, society's responsibility, remains invisible. Thus, sex workers function as convenient deviants whose putative deviant behaviour allows society to focus on them rather than on society itself. The sex worker becomes a sort of basket into which all deviant behaviour can be placed, so that all other types can be conveniently ignored. This convenience is an error of omission on the part of the media. By focusing on the sex worker (or the pimp or the john), the media isolate individual members of the trade as if they are operating in some kind of social vacuum. The level of scrutiny for those considered responsible for deviant behaviour effectively ignores all others who are also part of the trade: hotel owners and managers who rent rooms for half days, for example, or taxi drivers who protect sex workers by waiting for them to complete dates and take a cut of the profits under the table, professionals who are clients of sex workers, and lawyers who take sexual service as payment for legal services. All can be constructed as deviant in the same fashion as can the sex worker. But by focusing on the sex worker and those with whom she immediately interacts, the media (and therefore the public) can ignore the fact that johns are husbands with families, or that police officers can be clients of a massage parlour in the morning and in the afternoon on duty to bust the same establishment for licence violation.[9] In other words, if sex workers are deviant, then so are all others involved in the trade. If the media were doing their investigative job properly, the net of deviants would either be widened or abandoned altogether as ludicrous, as more and more of society's members – more and more members of the public – would be implicated in the tracing of this net. To single out sex workers serves a specific function: it removes the "disciplinary gaze" from all others.[10]

The media often pride themselves on being champions of the underdog as they deliver our social world back to us. Sex workers are rarely served by this because their power to speak is so limited. The hypocrisy of the media on this point is not understandable. If media have the investigative power to discern stories about sex workers, they owe sex workers at least the opportunity to voice their opinions on the matter, an opportunity they often give other "voiceless" participants within social structure. By ignoring the sex workers voice, the media simply perpetuate, reinforce, and otherwise sanction existing voices on the sex trade, voices that rarely give the sex worker the opportunity to speak. Stereotypical reporting on sex work helps to reinforce this notion of the sex worker as Other, as outside and unconnected to good (i.e., powerful) society. As it stands, reporting on sex workers does not involve reporting on how sex workers fit with contradictions on sexuality in our culture, nor is it naming sex work in relation to other types of deviance, which may be far more common, such as woman assault.[11] Such reporting does not examine the role of economic inequality, moral hypocrisy, or concentration of power in creating the conditions experienced in the sex trade. In other words, it is not reporting on sex work in any type of context. That information is left to the public imagination to discern. Nor does this type of reporting give us much information about the role of the clients, as participants in the so-called deviance and as possible perpetrators of violence. Society at large, middle-class privilege, and the role of the powerful in society are, quite importantly, not subject to such surveillance – the sins and responsibilities of the powerful go unreported and, therefore, unseen. Their authority and power remain unquestioned and intact. At the abstract level, the hypocrisy – as well as the unfair attention to, and silencing of, sex workers – reflects this broader operation of power. Whether and how this power operates at the level of the everyday realities of reporting on sex work in the Maritime provinces is a question to which we shall now turn our attention, by examining the reporting of the Halifax *Chronicle Herald*.

The Halifax *Chronicle Herald,* 1987-2003

We looked at the past fifteen years of coverage in the Halifax *Chronicle Herald* as a measure of how the media in the Maritimes portray sex work and sex workers. The *Chronicle Herald* is both the paper with the largest circulation in the Maritimes and the most archivally accessible. The hegemonic discourse on prostitution (re)produced in the *Chronicle Herald* is one that reflects a veneration of police and other so-called experts as the true sources of knowledge on the sex trade (rather than sex workers themselves). This discourse targets sex workers and pimps as the source of disorder rather than turning the light onto middle-class society, its maintenance of socio-economic inequalities, and its own middle-class crimes – including the violence of its members as clients of sex workers. Instead, the newspaper often focuses on the apparent deviance of sex workers' high-risk lifestyle as inevitably inviting violence. That is, we see precisely the forms of stereotyping, surveillance, and silencing that sex workers and social constructionists point to. This is not to say that the media are simply a monolithic and uniform tool of power. Indeed there are, in the pages of the *Chronicle Herald* at certain historical moments, signs of challenge, critique, and resistance that indicate that there are ways to engage with and resist this form of power – as sex workers themselves have taken the opportunity to do.

We scanned nearly two hundred articles relating to prostitution published in the *Chronicle Herald* between 1986 and 2002 and found that who gets to speak most frequently on the issue is police. It is their voices that are heard in nearly 75 percent of the stories published. Next are the voices of politicians and bureaucrats (or the government), whose opinions and commentary are registered nearly one-third of the time. Lawyers and judges are the third most likely to be heard speaking on the issue of prostitution, about 20 percent of the time, although many of the articles not included in this count are court reports – reporters' transmissions of charges and convictions, which are devoid of context or voices. Nevertheless, these court reports reflect a legalistic point of view in which people are boiled down to their crimes. They are not, of course, neutral stories, as they present a predetermined picture of prostitution as a crime that deserves punishment, and the voice that speaks and hence carries authority is in fact the voice of the court. The voices of the legal trade are followed by spokespersons for outreach or non-governmental organizations. The voices of sex workers or former sex workers are heard in only about 15 percent of the stories.

While these numbers are only a rough approximation, they give some sense of the relative audibility of the various voices, and the relative inaudibility of the voices of sex workers. Indeed, even these small numbers must be whittled down further. In four of the stories in which a sex worker or former sex worker speaks, the person speaking is Cherie Kingsley, a former sex worker, and, in a fifth story, another former sex worker who was working for Save the Children, as was Kingsley. Kingsley's story is of an abused young sex worker who now heads a campaign to end child prostitution. Her story is an important one for one particular facet of the trade: abused youth. The focus on her story, though, frequently erases the stories of youth who view themselves as workers, and it certainly eclipses the more complicated stories of adult sex workers. This was a story that the media was more (but not entirely) willing to listen to. In other cases, even when sex workers speak, the context of the story is often already set, and their voices are mere illustrations of the point to be made. The few stories in the late 1980s that included the voices of sex workers did sometimes give a fairly contextualized picture of the trade through their accounts. By 1992, however, when the story of a pimping ring in Halifax and Toronto broke, sex workers' voices were being used merely as proof of the worst excesses of violent pimps. Only rarely were sex workers asked to comment on policy or police practice.

The story about prostitution told in the Halifax paper, therefore, is a particular one. The sex worker is mainly viewed as the source of the problem rather than as someone denied rights or agency. The issues raised by sex workers – gendered and ageist economic structures, violence (particularly by clients), police harassment, health, and stigma – are seldom raised in the paper. Or, if they are, it is the exception rather than the norm and they are not presented from the sex worker's point of view. Stories on prostitution in the late 1980s, following the introduction of the communicating law, reflect media coverage throughout the country and focus on the law's effectiveness, or lack thereof – particularly in the wake of the law's being struck down in 1987 by the Nova Scotia Supreme Court as being in conflict with the Canadian Charter of Rights and Freedoms. Stories about the striking down of the "hooker law," as the paper refers to the communicating law (despite the fact that it was designed to address both sex workers and clients and that the successful challenge was in fact mounted by a client), tend to focus on the fears of residents, the powerlessness of police, and the concerns of the government and police about a potential increase in prostitution. When, in 1990, the law was upheld by the Supreme Court of Canada, articles express the relief of police in having returned to them an effective tool for combating prostitution. Follow-up articles on the numbers of people charged in the months following the Supreme Court decision confirm that the temporary loss of the communicating law had allowed a problem to go unchecked, but that order had been restored.

In the years between 1987 and 1992, the *Chronicle Herald* did run a number of stories by staff reporters and from news wires that explore the alternatives for addressing prostitution, such as the NDP proposal for licensed brothels (and its view of prostitution as linked to unemployment and homelessness), the activities of Stepping Stone and other outreach agencies, the call for legalization at the Federation of Canadian Municipalities meeting in

1990, and the recommendations of the parliamentary justice committee in 1990 for harsher penalties. The articles on Stepping Stone are particularly sympathetic and give voice to sex workers who expressed their delight in an agency that did not judge while providing a welcome support. One article reports on Stepping Stone activities, such as providing condoms and a badtrick list – activities often viewed by the public as questionable – and quotes the agency's director as saying that prostitution "is undertaken for basic survival needs" – a view that flew in the face of common assumptions. The reporter also interviewed a sex worker, who talked about the violence she had suffered at the hands of clients. The article was accompanied by a story on the financial crisis at Stepping Stone, which helped make the case for government funding (3 December 1988, A1). In 1991, a lengthy front-page article on Stepping Stone included interviews with two sex workers, who also talked about the violence they had experienced at the hands of clients and their appreciation of Stepping Stone's approach:

> Both Michael and Anne say prostitution is tough, but leaving it is even tougher. On the streets, the money is better than anything the traditional job market or social services could offer ... There are government institutions that can help, but Anne and Michael have learned that society's helping hand isn't always tailored to the needs of people with their backgrounds. "They try to shove things at you," Anne says. "At Stepping Stone it's cool. They'll go with you to detox or whatever, but they never force things on you." (14 September 1991, A1-2)

This sympathetic approach gives room for sex workers' views and their independence and helps challenge some of the mythology of sex work.

Other articles from this period challenge the common approach to prostitution issues. One article focuses on complaints by Coverdale [Halifax], the outreach agency for women in conflict with the law, charging that practices under the communicating law were gender biased. And another article covers the release of the "Does Anybody Care?" report by the Children's Aid Society of Halifax that argued for decriminalization of youth prostitution – a radical concept even now – and further support for outreach agencies such as Stepping Stone and Phoenix Youth Programs – linking youth prostitution to homelessness and abusive families rather than to youth criminality (4 October 1990, A1, A2). This story was immediately followed, however, by the article on the number (fifty) of charges laid under the communicating law since it had been upheld four months earlier. The *Chronicle Herald* was aggressively tracking the issue of prostitution – most of the articles were by staff reporters – but it was leaving open a variety of possible responses, even though there is an underlying message about the need to restore law and order under the communicating law.

The most important shift in the way the story of prostitution is told began in 1992 as the media built up what has been called a "moral panic" about pimping in the Metro area of Halifax.[12] The relative openness of coverage on the issue of prostitution came to a dramatic end with the development through the early 1990s of the story of young white girls' being snatched by black pimps and forced into a life of prostitution through painful beatings and threat of death, and then being shipped to other locations in Canada and the United States. This story of evil pimping rings and innocent children was much more interesting to the public than was the earlier, careful Children's Aid Society reporting, which linked youth prostitution to abusive parents, runaways, and homelessness. This new, more dramatic, storyline created fear among Nova Scotian parents that their daughters would be nabbed by pimps and sent to work in Toronto's sex trade, or further afield. It also capitalized on the long history of racialized power dividing black and white communities in the city, epitomized by the razing of Africville in the 1970s.[13] In many ways, the storyline paralleled the panic over white slavery that was so popular at the turn of the twentieth century and stayed alive even into the early postwar period, in which the threat to white womanhood was figured as the dark-skinned slaver (an interesting reversal of the history of slavery in North America and Europe).[14] This earlier panic justified stricter controls on women's and non-white men's movements in many countries through new laws governing migration and restricting sexual behaviour. Panics such as those focusing on the white slave trade or its reincarnations, the trafficking of women, or the pimping ring in Halifax tend to fix public attention on innocent young girls (interestingly, still referred to as "hookers" by the paper) who require rescue. Such a focus turns attention away from sex workers who have some sense of agency and who demand respect, better working conditions, and rights, not rescue. The Halifax panic similarly resulted in a narrowed field of policy options in which the solutions to the so-called prostitution problem quickly became the rescue of young innocents, while sex workers' concerns about safety went unaddressed. Further, the panic focused the gaze of surveillance and discipline on yet another marginalized and deviantized group – young black men – and away from white society.

The Pimping Panic

The Halifax pimping ring story was triggered by the September 1992 bust of a Nova Scotia-based pimping ring running women from Nova Scotia to Toronto. The front-page headlines read: "Abducted girls being forced into prostitution" (16 September 1992, A1, A2), "Halifax hookers tangled in huge ring" (17 September 1992, A1, A2), and "Halifax area men accused of pimping: Prostitution ring may involve 20 area women" (18 September 1992, A1, A2). The arrests led to the recovery of women who had been missing from the Halifax area and the arrests of four men, all from the black community of North Preston. The media and the police quickly linked the disappearance of women in the area to pimping – including the January disappearance of Andrea King, a Vancouver teen who, travelling to Nova Scotia to investigate local universities, disappeared upon her arrival at the Halifax airport. States one article: "Girls from all over metro have been reported missing and it is feared most have been lured into prostitution, then sent to Montreal or other Canadian cities. Some may have been taken to the United States" (16 September 1992, A1, A2). The number of girls potentially involved is frequently repeated – up to twenty-five in one case (17 September 1992, A1, A2) – and the fact that "many" could be facing this threat is brought home by the allusion to well-known cases of disappearances, such as King's, and to the apparently nationwide reach of the pimping ring. The articles also emphasize the young ages of the girls ("as young as 12 to 16" [16 September 1992, A1, A2, 17 September 1992, A1, A2]) and the devious and sometimes cruel methods used by pimps. One police officer is quoted as saying:

> These guys lure them (the girls) with their big money talk ... As soon as they get their foot in the door, that's it. They want them on the street. That's it, forget it ... They beat them at times, they really physically hurt them ... You know – the old trick with the hanger and the towel. They take the hanger and wrap the towel around it. It can really cause you a lot of pain, but it doesn't break any bones because the police might get involved. (16 September 1992, A2)

The article goes on to relate that another officer "says he has heard of 'hanger' beatings in which the hanger is placed on a stove burner and then applied to various parts of the girls' bodies." The hanger beatings became an important part of the pimping ring story and were frequently repeated in its retelling ("Former prostitute has 'scars all over,'" 16 November 1992, A1, A2).

Police emphasized that the biggest problem was that the women were often unwilling to testify against their pimps for fear of reprisals, leaving the reader with the impression that there was a great danger to area girls from pimps who would snatch them away at any opportunity and lock them into a cycle of abuse and fear, with escape next to impossible. Police are the heroes of the story, rescuing these young women from the clutches of the pimps. Success stories such as the reunion of seventeen-year-old Nicole Jessome with her family after the first bust were also front-page news (18 September 1992, A1). Within days of the story breaking, police and politicians are quoted as arguing for increased funds for police and a task force to pursue the pimping ring (18 September 1992, A2).

The story, which built to fever pitch in 1993 as women involved in the trade were found murdered, focuses public attention on a particular set of causes, consequences, and solutions. In particular, the problem is one of evil pimps who stalked innocent (and sometimes wayward, but nonetheless young and vulnerable) girls – in schoolyards and shopping malls – preying on their lack of self-assurance to suck them into "the game" and using violence to keep them there. Concerned parents spoke of daughters who had been stalked by these pimps.

Despite complaints from the black community that police were biased in focusing their efforts on young black men from North Preston, police and the media generally shrugged off the charges of racism as beside the point. Police are quoted as saying that the men who had been fingered for pimping *were* black, so there was nothing the police could do about it. The media, too, failed to investigate this issue any further. As Tanya Smith notes in her survey of the articles produced during this panic, once the connection was drawn between a few men in North Preston and pimping, the media failed to make any attempt to refute the easy racist assumptions that would follow, that is, that all pimps are blacks and/or from North Preston – that North Preston was full of black male sexual predators. While the possibility of racism in the white public was acknowledged in some articles, including "We must all fight racism, sexism" (3 April 1993), which identified the "belief that pimping is a black occupation" as problematic, it did not appear that racism was seriously addressed: "no arguments were made to the contrary."[15] While there were indeed black men involved in the pimping of young women in Halifax in this period, the point here is that this was simply one small part of the wider picture of the sex trade. Racism – of the generalized, ethnocentric variety – made ignoring this wider context easy to do (e.g., no questions were raised about white pimps and clients, or sex workers of colour). The failure to give a wider context to the issue of prostitution as a whole contributed to this easy racialization and simplification of the issue.

The pimping scare of the early to mid-1990s influenced Halifax journalism on prostitution stories for a long time afterward. One television reporter even wrote a popular book, entitled *Somebody's Daughter*, based on these events.[16] The book highlights the violence of the pimps by fictionalizing parts of the story and creating some characters to make the storyline more readable (and dramatic). Fact blends with fiction throughout to create a melodramatic story of innocent victims and evil predators. As one sex worker explained, it presented a lopsided view of prostitution and, in the end, such an approach fails to address the real issues:

> That book really, really got a lot of us – got to us bad because it just – he claims that he got all sides of the story. I don't know what he did with the sides. They're not in that book at all! Even like some of the men, some

of the pimps, in that book. I think he sought out the most, the biggest, victims he could find – the ones that were abused, molested, and gang raped. And the pimps were shootin' them up with needles ... and those were the ones I think he went for ... There's so many other sides that he could've used. Like the whole book didn't have to be based on those types of girls, you know what I mean? Because the prostitution and the pimps, there's so many of them, there's so many different backgrounds and different relationships, and there's some that are married – been married for years.

And I don't know. I mean the book was based on the task force and them going after the pimps that were preying on these young girls and things ... But it just, rather than – from reading it – rather than getting an idea of their life – the young girls and these pimps – he kind of ... regardless [of their actual lives] you take away from the book what you read, which is: "Oh, that's why they're prostitutes. You know. They're drug addicts. And these pimps, you know, they found them in a mall because they were crying 'cause their father just raped them." And that's what you took away from the book. And then that put an image out there, even worse for the girls out there. "Oh yeah, she must have got raped by her father when she was twelve," and "Yeah, she must be on crack now." And there's a really bad image out there ...

And, okay, it covered why the girls are into the prostitution, but then it didn't cover what had happened to the pimps ... Like you were ten years old and decided you were goin' to be a pimp. Like what about their life, and what happened to them in their upbringing. Yeah, 'cause I mean, you think prostitution is degrading and low and the pimp has to be too then because they're partners there. So ...

Interviewer: There were the few bad ones.
Yeah, there were quite a few, there were quite a few. I mean, obviously that's why they had to get that task force. But some, even the ones that they did get, they're still there. They're back. You know, they're not here [in Halifax]. They're in other cities, but they're back. And they're doin' the same thing they were doin', they're just not doin' it here. And I don't know, pimps, pimps are like obsolete now ... especially here. They work, you know. Right away you think pimp [and] you think, oh, beatin' you, rapin' ya, takin' all your money, burnin' ya with coat hangers ... gettin' ya addicted to drugs and all that stuff. That wasn't the case with all of them. The ones they were lookin' at, yeah, but that was a small group compared to the amount of pimps that were here.

Interviewer: Right, once again looking at the small picture.
Yeah, that was just a small group. And they were more concerned with addressing the issue of the young girls being lured into this. Not so much

prostitution and pimps. That wasn't their concern, it was the young girls.
(Katie, Halifax)

Police as Heroes

The surveillance that focused on young black men as the problem simultaneously ensured the place of the police, in particular, as the source of unquestionable authority. The predominantly white police force became, in this case, the epitome of the good man protecting young (white) girls from the (black) predators. The task force created in the aftermath of the first bust in Toronto became the hero of many stories in 1993-94. It was the members of this task force who were the most influential spokespeople on the issue, and it was to them that reporters turned for commentary in the vast majority of articles. Indeed, articles that played up the need for a stronger police response in the early days of the crisis helped create the backing for the creation of the task force. In "Prostitution task-force sought" (18 September 1992, A2), the views of the Halifax chief of police on the need for a task force to "investigate how prostitutes are recruited" and to "encourage hookers to testify against their pimps" are put forward. These views are made more immediate by the inclusion of an unidentified Dartmouth woman's claims that her daughter was being stalked by pimps and of police claims that they had encountered "hookers as young as 13 on the streets of Dartmouth." Two days after the story broke, the *Chronicle Herald* quoted police in Montreal and Toronto about how much work would have to be done by the Halifax police on their end and how, in terms of size, the Halifax vice squad was not going to be up to the task ("Pimping ring accused may face multiple charges in Halifax," 19 September 1992, A1; "Two morality officers not enough," 19 September 1992, A2) and ran a parallel story on the growing nervousness of local families ("Prostitution ring reports unnerve family," 19 September 1992, A4). The wisdom of this approach was confirmed by a November article, "Montreal considers police task force on juvenile hookers" (16 November 1992, A2). When the task force was threatened with staff cutbacks, the paper ran stories about the necessity and effectiveness of the task force's work: "Pimps still cast long shadow over Diana's life" focuses on the friend of a murdered sex worker, who was a sex worker herself and living in the safe house set up by the task force so that she felt safe in testifying against her pimp. She related the torture of coat-hanger beatings and spoke of the police officer who rescued her as being "like my dad." Now, safely out of the reach of pimps, she was returning to high school to resume a normal life (16 September 1993, A1-A2). This story is linked to another on the same page: "Sex trade rebounds year after big sweep" highlights the continuing threat to Nova Scotian girls despite the heroic efforts of the task force. This message is reinforced by a Canadian Press story picked up in November – "Parents Rescue teenage Hooker: Watch out for pimps girl wants to warn" – that repeats the well-known story of young girls recruited "just beyond school-grounds" by pimps who "lay elaborate traps for impressionable girls" (4 November 1993, A14). An October 1994 story conveys the same message: "Girls most often the losers in 'game' of prostitution" focuses on impressionable young girls who are "in every sense, victims" and violent pimps who play on young girls' romantic dreams (11 October 1994, B4). The need for increased police action is made clear from these stories.

In the same positive vein, task force successes are covered in detail, followed by discussion of the task force's declining staff size. In "Sydney escort service raided," the arrest of an escort service owner is characterized as the "third takedown of an escort service by the task force" and the fifty-first arrest made by the unit. The importance of the raid is highlighted by the police claim that the "raid was conducted after a former teenage prostitute made a complaint to the task force" (12 January 1994, A3). The paper continued to focus on youth prostitution, and the threat to young girls by pimps, throughout the 1990s and into the next decade. As late as 1999, the *Chronicle Herald* ran the story that male students were recruiting girls into prostitution at local high schools ("Prostitution task force probes recruitment at metro junior high," 18 December 1999, A4). Adult sex workers are rarely mentioned, except for court reporting, and when they are discussed, it is always in a negative light. The police are fatherly figures in many of the articles, out simply to rescue these young girls, explaining to the public that their vulnerability is due to their "lack of self-esteem" or abusive backgrounds ("Climate of fear hampers prosecutions," 5 May 1992, A1; "Girl saved from nationwide prostitution network," 14 August 1993, A2).

The techniques of police are never questioned, and certainly the idea that sex workers might feel harassed by the increased police attention, and may also be in danger because of it, never arises in the media coverage. The police are the good guys. Accusations of bias by police, not only racial ("Task Force denies bias in pimping arrests," 23 January 1993, A10) but also gendered, are dealt with in short order in articles such as "Judge finds prostitutes treated fairly by police" (3 December 1992, A9), which appeared in the middle of the storm and reported on one sex worker's bid to overturn her conviction on the basis of police gender bias. The article focuses on the judge's view that there was no intentional bias, merely a problem of a lack of female officers to act as decoys, particularly given the dangers of pimps and "aggressive competitors" faced by such decoys. No further investigation is made into either the lack of female officers or the potential gender bias of arrest patterns, and so the matter is considered closed. But evidence of a gender imbalance is buried in a 1997 article on a Statistics Canada report ("Report notes Halifax for prostitution charges," (14 February 1997, A1), which notes the large number of charges laid in Halifax compared to the rest of the country (503 by the task force between 1992 and 1996, and 75 charges by the Vice division in 1996), making Halifax fourth in terms of charges across Canada. Of the 75 charges laid by Vice, however, 56 were against sex workers and only 19 against clients. While the article notes that, according to the Statistics Canada report, "police are more likely to charge prostitutes than their customers," this point is not followed up, and, indeed, it is downplayed by the following and final sentences: "Eighteen prostitutes were charged in the deals of 16 people from 1991-1995. Most victims were clients."

This veneration of police in reporting continues into recent years. When one officer is accused of going too far by putting his hand down the pants of an underage sex worker in order to be able to charge her with communicating, the paper takes the side of the officer, who was acquitted by the judge, while the young woman was charged. In "Vice cop case under appeal; Panel to decide if officer abused his authority with prostitute" (1 October 1999, A17), the reporter states as fact that "this [practice of touching sex workers] is a common investigative practice for police in larger cities," which apparently establishes the illegitimacy of the complaint.

The possibility that police have another gender bias – in turning a blind eye to the male trade – is also ignored until the autumn of 1995, when a complaint of pimping is laid by a young male sex worker against an older man. Police, the headlines state, were "'not aware' of young male hookers" (17 October 1995, A2), and the article continues on to quote police, who argue that there were "no complaints from any boys ... Our understanding was it was street kids doing their own thing." Boys in the sex trade are read as innately more independent than girls, which is a gender bias. The police also explained that there were differences in that the boys were not "rotated through other cities" like the girls and they did not think that the "same type of violence" was experienced by boys. Yet the article does not go on to explain what type of violence – for example, gay bashing – these boys were likely to experience. The police force's oversight on this issue is not taken to task. Rather, police are portrayed as having understandably not looked into the matter and as having taken steps to rectify the situation. "Since the news broke, task force officers have been mingling with the male hookers, trying to develop a rapport with them. 'If any of them have the same problem (pimping), we don't want them to hesitate to call us' says spokesman Cpl. Paul Bonang." The article quotes the accused in this case, who argued that he had tried to help these boys, but "you can't really do nothin'," and ends with the line: "Police are hoping they can do something." Once again, police are held up as heroes, without a wider discussion of their role.

The Invisible Johns

The focus on black pimps ensured the continued invisibility of the behaviour of members of dominant society. The increasingly common violent behaviours of predominantly white clients went unreported in the media. Indeed, clients show up in only four articles during this period. One instance is a brief mention by the Solicitor General of his plans to "get tough" with customers of underage prostitutes ("Government action wins praise," 20 January 1992, A2) in response to the release of a report by the community working group on youth prostitution. Another instance is a front-page warning to johns in the Metro Halifax area of an AIDS danger: "Clients of metro prostitutes who have unprotected sex are now gambling with their lives. At least one prostitute working in the metro area has tested positive for HIV" ("Johns warned of AIDS danger," 11 September 1993, A1). This is followed up one year later with the headline: "Warning: HIV hooker turning tricks again in metro" (23 September 1994, A2). Finally, one month later, there is surprise at the number of johns busted in a raid, given the AIDS scare ("Police Bust 15 Johns despite AIDS scare," 13 October 1994, A1). While clients are subtly made to appear rather stupid in ignoring the health risk – "Dartmouth police were stunned by the success of the prostitution sting" – and the mayor is quoted as calling them just as "pathetic" as the prostitutes, the concern is still over the health of these men and not of the sex workers, who are viewed as a threat and a source of disease. (This is particularly true for sex workers in the Dartmouth area, who are subtly marked out in the articles as "different" from the young girls disappearing from Halifax.)

Clients do begin to appear in newspaper coverage more frequently in the late 1990s, as residential concerns begin to drive the policy agenda once more. The concerns of residents led to the creation of a john school to re-educate men charged with communicating, and to the introduction of a bill allowing police to confiscate the cars of johns in order to discourage repeat offenders. At this point, the coverage of clients takes on a decidedly more negative tone. One article describes johns as "circling like vultures" ("Prostitution crackdown a success," 1 October 2001, A1). In 1995, the paper includes for the first time a list of johns' names and addresses in an article on their being fined $1,500 for communicating. The article highlights the delight of residents' groups at both the fines and the media attention ("Judge hits johns with $1,500 fines: Residents group applauds," 18 August 1995, A1). The discomfort of some men with this turn of events is fully expressed in an opinion column run earlier that year. In it, the columnist opposes the publication of clients' names, arguing that "guys are guys" and therefore that "prostitution will be with us forever." The columnist's opposition to existing laws and the publication of names is based not on concerns about sex workers but about the "entrapment" of clients.

Indeed, the columnist spends most of the article sneering at a female Halifax police officer who "doesn't smile once" "the whole time we talk." His concerns are obviously about male prerogative, and his disrespect for women who challenge that prerogative is obvious. Not only is the officer unattractive and unfeminine for her failure to smile, but she fails to show "any real emotion" (except a snort of derision). The columnist's sympathy is with the hapless clients who are merely seeking a "public service" ("Prostitution here to stay," 29 June 1995, A8).

For those who find the column's machismo difficult to accept, the parallel article makes the police appear as a bastion of male emancipation and very different from the types of men who would exploit sex workers. In it, a staff reporter outlines the police's negative views on legalization of the trade ("Police against making hooker trade legal," 29 June 1995, A8). Articles continue to distance police from johns, reporting on police surprise at the numbers of johns caught in prostitution sweeps and at the diversity of the clients ("Police nab 48 in john sting," 26 November 2002, A3). The same articles emphasize the police view that chasing down clients is for the good of sex workers. One article reports on "Operation Squeeze" – thus dubbed "because the goal was to squeeze johns out and improve the lives of prostitutes," according to police. The reporter concurs: "Although the prostitutes may not like the tough-love approach, the task force hopes the crackdown will help officers develop enough trust with them to show they want to help them get off the streets for good" ("Police nab 48 in john sting," 26 November 2002, A3). Sex workers are here being portrayed as wayward children who do not know what is good for them and are in need of the firm hand of the benevolent police to guide them.

Police bias and "understanding" toward clients is apparent when, in an article on john school, one police spokesperson comments: "We're dealing with reasonable people, not hardened criminals ... We are educating reasonable people and they are making educated decisions." The unspoken message here is that these men are quite different from the sex workers, who are the hardened criminals. Such a sweeping vindication of men as clients goes without comment ("John school putting dent in sex-trade," 11 April 2001, A6). There is little discussion on clients in the newspaper aside from the views of police. While the results of John Lowman's study on clients, showing that clients are from all walks of life, are reported on in a Canadian Press story in 2000 ("Study: Johns come from all walks of life," 8 December 2000, A2), no reporter makes the link when police reiterate their surprise at the number and diversity of clients caught in stings. The media also continue to focus on the task force's success, including its targeting of johns ("Prostitution crackdown a success," 1 October 2001, A2). One article upholds the police record of "regularly targeting johns" in the face of a judge's exhortation to "target 'good family men' and 'fellas from the suburbs,'" not just pimps ("Crackdown on johns: Judge urges," 11 January 2002, A1).[17]

Further indicating the media's complicity in this bias in favour of johns at the same time as it upholds this record of targeting clients, the *Chronicle Herald* fails to investigate a former sex worker's ongoing court challenge of the bias of prostitution law enforcement. In this instance, the story is about the woman's attempt to keep her name private rather than the issue of legal and police bias – or even her fear that she "will be killed by some nut" (27 October 2002, A1; 8 November 2001, A6; 7 December 2001, A6). The failure to pick up on this important fear is outstanding, given that the paper at this time was carrying several stories about the large numbers of murders of sex workers in Vancouver, Chicago, Green River, and even Guatemala.

"Just a Hooker"

> The reason I feel that [clients have become more violent] is because the media portrays us as non-people. And yeah, they do, they make us more ... Like the word prostitute, this is where I have the big problem, it dehumanizes people ... They use the word "prostitute" or "hooker" as opposed to "a women who was working as a prostitute." It's a job – it's not a person. They've made it a person and they've made it a stereotypical low-life person and a disposable person and the more that the media continues do that, the more the tricks feel that they are allowed to be violent. (Dana, Halifax)

The *Chronicle Herald*'s portrayal of women and men who work in the sex trade was indeed made evident by the regular use of the term "hooker." The pimping panic of the early 1990s had not really challenged this understanding of prostitution; rather, it focused on a select few who fit the stereotype of the young and abused and who made a great story. But no insights into sex work or the issues faced by sex workers were generated by this storyline. The by-product of a focus on innocent victims is the generation of a sense of concern among the public and a sense that they are learning about the problem and doing something about prostitution – when, in fact, they are learning about, and addressing, only the very few who fit the stereotype. The undeserving, the "hookers," are ignored in this approach and are harmed by it because attention and resources are drained into solutions that are misguided.

Thus, for example, the pimping panic did generate a concern with violence in the sex trade. This violence was evidenced most particularly in the early 1990s by the proliferation of murdered sex workers, whose fates were covered by the paper in some detail. (Seven women, most known to be involved in the trade, were found murdered in the Halifax area over two years.) But while the violence experienced by those in the trade is being discussed, it is violence of a very particular nature: it is the violence of pimps and not, importantly, of clients. It is interesting that, in western Canada at just this time, researchers began to see a sudden increase in murders of sex workers.[18] This was the beginning of a long string of murders of sex workers, who were most likely killed by clients, not pimps. Indeed, in 1997, the back pages of the *Chronicle Herald* carried the Canadian Press story "Interest slim in hooker killings" (15 February 1997, A24) noting a new Statistics Canada report that found that sixty-three known sex workers had been killed between 1991 and 1995, mostly at the hands of customers, and that one of every two murders of sex workers was unsolved. The statistic that one in twenty women murdered in the country between 1991 and 1995 were sex workers killed by their customers had been cited in a story the previous day. That story mainly focuses on the number of arrests carried out by Halifax police. However, the article also notes that eighteen prostitutes across Canada had been charged with killing their clients – echoing the belief that sex workers were themselves a source of violence and danger ("Report notes Halifax for prostitution charges," 14 February 1997, A1). There was no Halifax follow-up on these reports of the number of murdered sex workers, even though, two years earlier, a story had appeared warning sex workers to be careful after a woman was attacked in downtown Halifax by a man believed to have harassed sex workers in the city ("Hookers urged to be careful after attack," 22 August 1995, A6). A 1999 report on an ex-sex worker's testimony that she had been punched, cut, tied up, and raped, and had had her life threatened, provoked no comment. Nor did her explanation for her failure to seek charges earlier, which was that there was a warrant out for her arrest on a prostitution charge ("Ex-prostitute testifies of death threats," 26 August 1999, A4).

Indeed, the idea that sex workers are a source of danger (and disease) has never really disappeared from the papers. For example, even the supposedly "young innocent girls" are still referred to as "hookers" – particularly in captions and headlines. And a seventeen-year-old sex worker's accusation that a police officer abused his authority by touching her pubic area is casually dismissed, as the judge in the case is quoted as referring to the incident as a police officer simply "outwitting" a "criminal." The article also unquestioningly carries the statement by the judge that "the police are engaged in a war against prostitution and cannot be selective in their targets ... The police need to work undercover for effective penetration, detection and apprehension" ("Judge OKs cop groping hooker," 2 September 1999, A9).

As more stories about prostitution as a neighbourhood nuisance appear in the late 1990s, residents also appear as more sympathetic than do the dangerous sex workers. In one article, a sex worker is characterized as "snarling" at residents who attended her trial. Residents – who are simply, in the words of the reporter, "citizens" – are "trying to take back their neighbourhoods from hookers and drug dealers" who are, presumably, then, not citizens ("Suspected prostitute takes jab at residents," 22 October 1999, A9). Dartmouth – the poorer, working-class sister city of Halifax, traditionally known as the bedroom of Halifax – and Dartmouth-area sex workers are increasingly deviantized by police and the press. During the early 1990s, police sources linked the sex trade in Dartmouth to drug addictions, and the trade there was marginalized as a separate issue from that of innocent girls being pimped. It appears to the public as if these women, unlike the innocent victims of pimps, have only themselves to blame because of their addictions. There is no discussion of the possibility that these women have been pushed out of Halifax by increased police presence and attention – as a result of the panic, as well as the rapid growth and gentrification of downtown Halifax.

One of the destructive by-products of a discourse that focuses on innocent victims is that those who do not live up to this label are not viewed as victims at all. When sex workers are reported killed – and their deaths are not linked to pimps – the reporting focuses on the deviance of their lifestyle. In January 2003, the body of yet another Halifax sex worker was found. The staff reporters' in-depth article on her murder opened: "A prostitute and a drug addict since her teens, Laura Lee Cross ... didn't stand a chance." The article then goes on to detail her "destructive lifestyle," which ultimately leads to her death, despite the fact that police suspected foul play and that this story came just months after the discovery of many bodies of sex workers on a farm in British Columbia, which had suddenly made sex worker murders visible in the Canadian media. In the description of Laura Lee Cross' murder, the most important factors presented are that she was "a repeat offender for assault, theft and prostitution related crimes"; that she had left home at thirteen and lived in group homes "before falling into a lifestyle of prostitution and severe drug abuse"; that she had "worked as a streetwalker in Boston before returning to the Halifax area about seventeen years ago to continue plying her trade"; and that "during the last eight years of Ms. Cross's life, she was spending $300 to $350 a day on drugs like Dilaudid and Valium, crack cocaine and alcohol." In the wake of such overwhelming repetition of her apparently high-risk lifestyle, the fact that she had reported being "shot, stabbed and beaten by clients" simply falls into the category of unpleasantness she had brought upon herself by her "20 years" of a "destructive lifestyle" ("Young Woman's short life a rough one," 29 January 2003, A4). Rather than focusing the reader's attention on the fact that she had been murdered and that she had previously complained of violence at the hands of clients, the article makes her death appear to be a natural outcome of her actions, with no one but herself to blame.

This blaming of the victim reflects a strong tendency in reporting on and dealing with the enormous numbers of sex workers who are murdered or violently assaulted. In many ways, they are viewed as responsible for their victimization, for courting disaster through a high-risk lifestyle. This is not only true of the *Chronicle Herald*, of course. The reporting on the missing women in Vancouver and then the missing and murdered women in Edmonton reflects this exact tone. TV stories on the Edmonton cases, for example, lamented the stupidity of sex workers in continuing to work in the trade when workers were known to have been murdered. There was little or no comment on the horror that someone was out there killing these women and that very little was being done about it.

In January 2003, the paper reported that "at least eight women, most believed to have been involved in prostitution and the drug trade, have died mysteriously, been murdered or disappeared over the past 20 years" ("Police to explore possible links between Cross death, other cases," 29 January 2003, A6). The media's portrayal of prostitution, and its fascination with only a particular story of prostitution, helps make the concerns of sex workers – particularly in terms of violence by clients and of the role played by society in maintaining this climate of violence – disappear from the public consciousness. Further, sex workers are, along with other deviantized communities, such as young black men, targeted for surveillance and discipline in ways that reinforce the authority and privilege of white, middle-class society. Police, policy makers, and lawyers are continuously represented as the voices of authority and knowledge who are the appropriate sources of solutions and responses, despite their own potential role in creating the very problems they seek to solve. This (re)production of power, however, is not all-encompassing. Journalists do sometimes try to get out alternative stories that go against mainstream orthodoxy, and the hegemonic discourse does not go unchallenged by the public or by sex workers.

Talking Back to the Media

As noted above, the media is not all-powerful or monolithic in its role in reproducing hegemonic discourse. We can see resistance to the production of particular types of stories on the sex trade in the *Chronicle Herald* itself. Not only were a number of fairly contextualized and open-ended stories produced – at least before the pimping panic changed the focus on reporting – but in the Laura Lee Cross case, the public itself protested the tone of some of the stories. Angry letters were written to the paper, attacking it for blaming the victim for her fate. Private citizens, as well as the chairperson of the Nova Scotia Advisory Council on the Status of Women and the provincial NDP's critic on the Status of Women, wrote to express their outrage – demonstrating that the public and elites can, and sometimes do, resist and respond to the hegemonic discourse produced on the sex trade. The letters criticized the paper for introducing Laura Lee to the reader simply as "'a prostitute' who deserved the violence she experienced because of her lifestyle." Letter writers also called attention to the fact that at least eight other murders of women linked to the sex trade had gone unsolved over the past twenty years ("Voice of the People," 5 February 2003, C2). A friend of Laura Lee's wrote to try to balance the portrayal of Laura Lee by describing her as a whole person with a family and friends: "Laura was a daughter, sister, mother, friend; but most of all, she was a human being" ("Laura was a wonderful person," 5 February 2003, C2). Public resistance to the media reproduction of stereotypical images and surveillance techniques goes a long way toward addressing the burden of stigma faced by so many sex workers.

The sex workers we spoke with for this book similarly resist this portrayal of sex workers and see this narrow portrayal of the murder victims as part of the continuation of the stereotype that turns humans into things that have no context, no family, and no connection with the reader. As one sex worker in Moncton angrily stated:

> [It's the] headlines, you know: "prostitute murdered on Main Street." Like you know, what's your point? She's still a human being. She has a name and she's dead. Like at least give her some dignity. Well, she's dead. Really ... Oh, it makes me sick. (Bonnie, Moncton)

While the stories about the murders of sex workers have been particularly offensive and generate a great deal of anger and resistance on the part of sex workers, sex workers also respond to the everyday reproduction of stereotypical images in local papers. Three women charged with prostitution offences in Saint John got fed up enough with the local newspaper to write a cogent letter to the editor. The letter reflects their frustration with the hypocrisy of reporting that singles out those charged with prostitution while ignoring the role of the client, the wider context of male abuse, and the prevailing gendered economic inequality. As well, the writers directly challenge the easy championing of the police by the media. The police, the women say, "built their reputation off our shortcomings"; that is, the police receive hero status for merely arresting women who are trying to make a living – hardly a matter of chasing down violent and devious criminals. Further, the women call attention to the paper's failure to portray the socioeconomic context of sex work – for example, the need to take care of children. Finally, they call attention to the paper's failure to take account of its power to shape or harm people's lives:

> **We, the women of your ridicule on prostitution, would like to voice our opinion on being labeled a prostitute. First off, we all need to deal with**

our shortcomings. To use us as a victory for Saint John's Crime Unit [– it] was wrong of you to single us out.

By pleading guilty to these offenses, we have already admitted to ourselves and to the community our wrongdoings.

No matter why we chose to make money in this line of business, whether it was because of drug addictions, lack of money to live on, lack of jobs or just to be able to feed and dress our children better, does this make us bad people?

We know what it is like to raise our children in poverty, all we were trying to do was make a living.

There is apparently a need for this form of service. What about the clients who seek out our services? Are we the only ones to blame? What about the special crime unit that built its reputation off our shortcomings.

All of us prostitutes are women who have children and parents, and we are in this profession because of needs, not because we want to be.

What about the ex-husbands, common-law boyfriends or the men who force us into this line of work because of a lack of financial support[,] are they classified as criminals?

We broke the law and we are paying for it by doing the time in jail, so *why does the paper feel like it has the right to punish us further by making us look like hardened criminals; our esteem is low enough.* Do you realize what you are doing to our children who are innocent? They have to put up with the teasing and the label that their mothers are prostitutes.

We feel you were very unkind how you came across with your write-up in the paper. We admit what we did was wrong in your standards, but *wouldn't it sell just as many papers if our clients' names were mentioned in an article like you felt you had to print ours.*

What about some form of counseling for us prostitutes and our children, and let's not forget the rest of our family.

We just want everyone to know that we have rights and are human. We are doing time for our crime, so please don't judge us any further.

We hope you will publish our letter so the public will know that we are not bad people.

We want to dedicate this letter to all the prostitutes who are still out there and seeking help and may be facing prostitution charges; we sympathize with you all and hope the newspaper will be more compassionate towards you than it was towards us.[19]

Perhaps the last words belong to another Saint Johner:

See and the worst thing too, in the paper they try to fabricate ... "prostitute," "prostitute." The way they talk about it: how dare you! I am more than a prostitute, I'm somebody's mother. I'm somebody's friend. I'm somebody's sister. I'm not just a prostitute, you know, I have, I have a story. I have lived, you know? I'm not just that. Get off it ... And what people are like nowadays, it's just the stigma of the whole thing. But it's ... hey, walk in my shoes for a week, see if you survive. (Alyssa, Saint John)

5
Whose Health? Whose Safety?

Interviewer: What would you say are the major risks?
That would be gay bashing [and] disease. Most of my street family are dead. (David, Halifax)

Interviewer: What do you think are major risks on the streets?
Disease. Well, your safety, and then disease; that would be the two risks. (Tabitha, Saint John)

Interviewer: You spoke to it a little bit, but what do you think the major risks are to people on the street?
Sexually transmitted diseases, AIDS, because there are people who say, "I want to have sex with you, but I will give you more money if we don't use condoms because I don't like condoms;" or "I can't get a hard on [with] condoms," or whatever excuse they use to not use protection. They show you more money. You think, "Ah, what are the odds?" And maybe six months down the road you're diagnosed. (Charles, Halifax)

I had cancer when I was twenty years old. And I had three kids when I was seventeen, eighteen, and nineteen. At nineteen I moved to Edmonton, Alberta, with their father. When I turned twenty I found out I had cancer. And he got up and left me, come back to Saint John, left me there with three little babies in diapers and all. I chose to stay in Edmonton, 'cause I was scared to come all the way here with three babies. None of them walked yet ... Three in diapers and milk. And I was scared. And I dealt with it. And I lived a life with my kids. And I got chemo. And it got better, but afterwards I got into a depression – after all the chemo. I take medication for depression now. So that was when I decided to come home [to the Maritimes]. I just couldn't do it by myself anymore. It was really hard. So I came back home. My mom ... she said, "Take a break." I'd been through quite a bit. Out of all my sisters I seem to have all the bad luck in my life. It all come to me. My health [was bad] and to have three babies, and doing it by myself.

I've had a lot of hard struggles, but I've always been the strong-minded person. My mom today says that she still worries more about my sisters than she does me, because I've always been a strong-minded person. I never want to give in. That was probably a bad quality after a while, because when I got into the drugs, so much did I want to go home, to say, "Mom, please help me." But I didn't want to, 'cause I was pig-headed. And I was ashamed that I've done that to my family. And they had to go through all those people knowing I was in jail, or through reading in the paper that your daughter is on crack cocaine. I remember a couple of times, before they knew I was on the crack, and I'd went there to stay there a day or two – they didn't know nothing at this time – and my dad readin' in the newspaper "in the courts" and it's sayin' ... drug addictions. And him saying, "That's so terrible. How these people can get on these drugs like that?" And "I'm so glad and so fortunate that my kids aren't on drugs." And here I am an addict, and they didn't know. And that hurt me. And from that point on I stayed away from them. And they never ever knew until they saw it in the paper, that I was an addict. And then after that they didn't know what to do, until I started and decided to help myself, nobody really wanted to help me. (Beth, Saint John)

When sex workers are asked for their point of view on health and safety in the sex trade, their responses often disrupt health professionals' understandings of sex workers' health. Sex workers' perceptions of health and safety are not necessarily found in the literature from health agencies, nor are they reflected in policy documents that track issues such as sexually communicable diseases. Sex workers prioritize safety issues and note a wide range of health issues beyond sexually transmitted diseases. The health professionals we interviewed, however, immediately refer to the usual list of sexually transmitted diseases and infections, and are a bit oblivious to other health disorders.[1]

Not only do sex workers have a different set and prioritization of issues than do health professionals, they also have a very different understanding of these issues. While health professionals tend to construct sex workers as a source of disease, sex workers (and empathetic outreach workers) point to the conditions of life and work around them and to the fact that these diseases and addictions are also present in the wider society. Further, while health professionals are widely viewed as such because of their scientific expertise in the field, but, in regard to sexually transmitted infections (STIs) or addictions, the knowledge base from which many are working is limited in a variety of ways and, accordingly, it is not free from bias.[2] Sex workers' personal experiences of, and on-the-ground knowledge of, health issues lay bare these biases. Sex workers resist these official attitudes and biases by voting with their feet, so to speak, refusing the services of those health institutions that do not recognize their point of view. The unfortunate result often is that sex workers find that their health needs go unmet. This chapter describes some of the issues raised by the interviewees and gives possible explanations as to the seeming inconsistencies we found between the "expert" discourse and sex workers' understandings of health.

Sex Work, Stigma, and Health Discourse

> *Interviewer: What do you think is the biggest misperception on the part of the public?*
> Probably that we're in their neighbourhood and [that] we're full of AIDS or herpes or something like that. Like there's nothing good, nothing good.
> (Lydia, Halifax)

Most of our respondents reported that they had little or no trouble with some health services. Some reported experiences of sympathetic doctors and health providers. Indeed, outreach oriented health services – such as the government-run Sexual Health Centres – provided helpful and non-judgmental service for a number of sex workers we spoke with. Others remarked that when medical staff, particularly at emergency services, did not know of their profession, they did not receive any different treatment. But there remains a keen awareness of the potential effects of stigma. One woman reported:

> I've gone in for a coffee burn, and you know what I mean, all of a sudden it's turned into my drug use, and the way I was dressed and stuff: "Well, you're just a prostitute, you know, and you probably deserved it." And it was a coffee burn, so you know what I mean, so ... They make you feel like you're diseased or something. (Jill, Saint John)

We also spoke with sympathetic doctors and nurses who wanted to know how they could provide more helpful services to sex workers, even though official policy and practices sometimes give them little room to manoeuvre, despite their best efforts.

Official health programs and policies often rely heavily on the rhetorics of risk and vulnerability, which are often based on perceptions and stigma rather than realities. On one hand, the sex worker is a diseased woman in the popular imagination, a carrier of infection and a site of contagion that can fuel the rationalization of many top-down public health programs. On the other hand, she is viewed as part of an at-risk or vulnerable group that requires particular intervention and protection because of her failure to protect herself.

Sex workers have long been figured as carriers of disease and sources of contagion.[3] Early accounts of prostitution in Canada assumed that sex workers were the carriers of disease, the purveyors of all things contagious. Initial public health attempts to control disease were often barely concealed attempts at the social control of sex workers. Renisa Mawani, in her work on the intersection between venereal disease, class, and gender in Canada in the early twentieth century, notes that "in the name of public health, 'foreigners,' prostitutes, young single women and working class men did in fact find themselves disproportionately at the receiving end of many punitive strategies."[4] Today, the image of the sex worker as diseased, contagious, and victimized surfaces often.[5] The association of disease with sex workers can, according to Diane Meaghan, be a general one or involve a specific disease:

> With the advent of the HIV/AIDS "Crisis" during the 1980s, female sex workers were viewed as a "high risk" group for spreading AIDS in the general population (read white heterosexual men and their "innocent" wives and children). Given that prostitution has long been perceived as a threat to public health, a medical model of disease made a particularly compelling connection between infection and sex work which conflated sexual activity with disease transmission, adopted a risk-based intervention approach that pathologized sex work, and scapegoated sex workers.[6]

The image of sex worker as disease-transmitter, then, acts as a filter through which sex worker health and well-being is situated. Although many of the health care providers could only name a few sex workers in their clientele, they did not hesitate to tar them all with the same diseased brush.

Health care officials and providers have the power to name disease and addiction, and to construct health as part of the dominant storying of sex workers' lives. This power rests on the providers' claim to expertise and scientific knowledge. But health experts' knowledge of STIs and addictions is much less solid than one would like to believe.[7] Certainly, the information that these experts have on STIs is incomplete. The rates of infectious diseases are not always collected consistently as statistics. Further, which STIs are problematic and how problematic they are in comparison to other diseases can change or differ markedly from expected trends. Rates of HIV/AIDS, for example, have either stabilized or dropped in the jurisdictions in this study.[8] In response to a question on what trends and patterns he has seen in his career, a Halifax doctor answered that "in 1983, the first case of HIV emerged and cases rose until the mid-nineties, but the number of new infections has stabilized and dropped over the last six to seven years."[9] The executive director of AIDS New Brunswick also indicated that New Brunswick's rate of new HIV/AIDS transmission has been stable since 2000.

Hepatitis C, however, a disease more likely to be connected to intravenous drug use than to sexual behaviour, is on the rise.[10] The executive director of the Mainline Needle Exchange in Halifax reported that staff are seeing a greater number of clients with mental health issues and that 90 to 95 percent of clients have hepatitis C, but that the needle exchange has never had a large population with HIV. Further, she reported that only a small proportion of the clients that she saw at the needle exchange were sex workers (twenty out of an approximate five hundred).[11] Among STIs, it is chlamydia – not HIV/AIDS – that is on the rise, particularly among youth.

One doctor at Halifax's North End Health Clinic asserted that people under thirty were most likely to contract chlamydia, which is transmitted sexually. His words were echoed by a Fredericton nurse running a methadone clinic, who stated that at least half of the population she was treating for chlamydia are university students. And, according to one of the infectious diseases doctors we interviewed, "chlamydia is the most common STI for fourteen to twenty-five year olds."[12] Since the mean age of the sex workers interviewed for this study was thirty-two, this particular infectious disease is not necessarily associated, and is certainly not exclusively associated, with them. Thus, many health care workers' focus on sex workers as sources of disease is both misplaced and stigmatizing.

Assertions that sex workers are more likely to be at risk for STIs than is the wider population are not only false, they may actually succeed in creating policy that endangers sex workers. If a sex worker is working and has HIV/AIDS, s/he is less likely to seek testing, treatment, and safer sex practices, if to name the disease or to identify as a sex worker brings further stigmatization.

In an alternative, but related, expert discourse, sex workers are positioned as vulnerable or at-risk populations, rather than sources of risk. Karen Murray's work on the discourse of vulnerability in Canadian health and social policy demonstrates that the discourse,

> far from marking a progressive and humanitarian turn in social policy ... construe[s] vulnerable populations as disturbances to mainstream health, social and economic norms and as threats to order and stability ... In its attempt to deal with "risky" people, the federal government is augmenting neo-liberal governing processes that have been emerging in Canada over the past roughly twenty years in providing for the well-being of those excluded from mainstream social and economic life by emphasizing individual shortcomings and incapacities as a central component of vulnerability. At the same time, the federal government is seeking to promote individual self-sufficiency and autonomy by shaping "the community" as a core centrality of governing strategies. Communities are to identify and regulate the risks posed by those deemed to be the source of a wide range of social

ills, such as poverty, homelessness, HIV/AIDS, crime and victimization and so on.[13]

That is, the vulnerable populations discourse on sex workers – as well as people with addictions and other marginalized groups – still presents these groups as problematic, rather than faulting the system around them. This patronizing discourse serves the purpose of downloading services onto community outreach groups.

For example, in an interview with a public health nurse who sees inmates for testing of STDs and STIs on a regular basis, people with addictions, and sex workers and other marginalized groups, are configured as making unjustified demands on the health system:

Interviewer: One of those things you said earlier was that people have different priorities when they are released. Public health is not their priority, or even their own health.

Their own health, in general [is not a priority, nor] going to their own physician or whatever – in terms of women accessing pap smears, and general aches and pains. One of the things that I've run into is that people who are using the drugs, and – with the limited understanding that I have of the addiction – that the drugs are so important, the using is so important, that your head just isn't around for anything else. Certainly [your mind is not on] going to the doctor for other concerns. And then you start to think the aches and pains and whatever may be because of the drugs that you're using as well, or being off of them: time to inject again. And also if you go to the doctor[s], they're going to tell you [that you] need to get off the drugs. So there is a whole different lifestyle around that.

But then, when they get in the hospital or the jail, they want new glasses, because they've been broken and they want their teeth, because they've been lost or broken, they want their pap smears for the women, and they want the testing of the disease. They want the very best of everything and they feel that it's their right to have a lot of things. I think that some of the people that I've talked to certainly feel they should have more services available within the correctional system, and yet, again they wouldn't access those services when they're out and free and clear and able to do that. It does make for controversy over what should be offered in the correctional system. (Public health nurse, 2 September 2002)

Such a construction of marginalized groups as demanding rights – which the speaker feels they do not deserve because they have only themselves to blame for their predicament – is the epitome of the neo-liberal discourse that justifies non-provision of public services.[14] That is, it is a discourse of denial of citizenship – and it is this denial of rights that sex workers fundamentally object to.

Indeed, one could easily argue that the behaviours of sex workers and people with addictions, rather than what is outlined in public health programs, closely mirror what is actually understood about these diseases. For example, public health providers claim that inmates, the homeless, and other street people are not vigilant in following up on health care appointments. Perhaps these groups know something that health care officials do not, that is, that the panic about health issues is something that affects only health care providers and practitioners. People on the street do not see someone dying of liver disease over a fifty-year period; what they are more likely to see is someone dying or being injured through violence. Safety, then, becomes defined as staying out of harm's way rather than getting a checkup.

Sex Workers on Health

> *Interviewer: What are the major risks for women in prostitution?*
> **Diseases, death, being raped, being robbed, kidnapped.** (Jacqueline, Saint John)

When specifically asked the question "Do you have any health problems?" interviewees mentioned various health issues. These ranged in scope and did not immediately include STDs and STIs. Respondents most often answered with injury-related problems, many of which may have been directly related to violence. Despite this, the issue of safety and security is rarely found in health documents. Safety is unmistakeably a health issue for sex workers, especially when one considers what lack of safety does to these workers and how they live with violence as a daily possibility. Safety is central not only in protecting sex workers from grievous injury but also in maintaining other aspects of their health. Sex workers whom we spoke with explained that the threat of violence was the background against which negotiation for safer sex practices took place:

> **I was out – when I first started I went with a young guy once – out by the airport; and he wanted to have sex without a condom. And I told him no. So this mark right here: he stabbed me.** (Patricia, Saint John)

Sex work shares occupational hazards with various other jobs. Frances Shaver compared sex work to that of laboratory technicians and found similarities such as repetitive strain injury, back and leg cramps from standing too long in one place, boredom, and intermittent danger.[15] Indeed, some of the sex workers we spoke with struggled with these sorts of health issues:

> But see, I've had thirteen surgeries.
> *Interviewer: What have you had your surgeries for?*
> I've had six hernias and I had orthopaedic. (Tanya, Saint John)

> *Interviewer: And finally, how is your health?*
> Um, I am not dying of any disease. I sort of consider myself lucky. But not really, because I am tired. It's just too much. Um, physically, not good. [My] back and side hurts.
> *Interviewer: Yeah, I've noticed that you've had trouble sitting there. Do you attribute that to the trade?*
> Yes. My foot, I mean now I have to wear $100 sneakers and that's a joke. I can't wear $30 sneakers, I am in too much pain ... from working, living in that type of lifestyle. [It] gets abusive after a while, if you are living with someone who is an alcoholic and a drag queen at the same time as working the streets. Yes, and the drugs and the fighting, it's all tied together. (David, Halifax)

The sex workers we spoke with listed a wide range of health issues, including spinal problems, plates in limbs, hernias, cancers, heart conditions, asthma, thyroid problems, pneumonia, bronchitis, HIV/AIDS, and hepatitis B and C. They also listed psychological issues such as depression, schizophrenia, and bipolar disorder.

Not only did sex workers have a much different list of concerns from that of health professionals, they also understood these concerns quite differently. Typically, when asked "How are you today?" as a casual opener to an interview, they rarely, if ever, answered with a health complaint. Health complaints often came up late in the interview not because of the specific questions posed by the interviewer but because health was not seen as a pressing issue, despite the seriousness of the health problems they reported. These very serious conditions were often seen as just one more thing to be coped with. One interviewee told us:

> Well, I think I have cirrhosis of the liver ... I'm tired out. I have really bad cramps. I mean I've had something since I was sixteen, so I must have something going on ... Plus I have cancer and I'm supposed to go every three months to get that checked ... And I haven't been there for over two, three years.
> *Interviewer: You have cancer? What kind?*
> Cervix. I'm copin' with it. (Dawne, Halifax)

Indeed, a number of interviewees were struggling with cancer:

> I've had breast cancer, one removed, and have had an ulcer.
> *Interviewer: Are you getting treatments?*
> Radiation, but I had to stop it because it was burning me. My whole breast is one big mass ... It's like a big sunburn. I lost all my muscle; couldn't do a thing. I'd feel just blah, you know? No energy.
> *Interviewer: How are you feeling now?*
> Now I feel good. And I'm really glad I was straight for it all. But it's interesting at work, you know, to be the one-breasted woman (laughter).
> (Hannah, Halifax)

For some sex workers, disease is simply one more thing to deal with, not unlike dealing with housing issues or fighting to get heat supplements on social assistance cheques. Many survival sex workers have neither the time nor the resources to nurse disease as health care providers would demand that they do. This is true with diseases such as HIV, for example. In the next interview, the issue of health did not come up until at least thirty minutes into the discussion and then only in response to a question from the interviewer. Not only does it show that HIV can be lived with for many years (seventeen, so far, in this case) but that, for this woman, it is simply a normal part of life. That she cannot eat properly because of the disease is, for her, part of life, rather than something unusual:

> *Interviewer: How's your health?*
> You know, pretty good right now. My counts are normal, so ...
> *Interviewer: You're HIV positive?*
> Yeah.
> *Interviewer: How long has it been?*
> Since I was seventeen. [She is now thirty-four.] I received it through a blood transfusion.
> *Interviewer: Seriously?*
> Yeah.
> *Interviewer: Well, you're doing well then.*
> Yeah.
> *Interviewer: You've always had to watch it?*
> Oh yeah.
> *Interviewer: You probably always practised safe sex, have you?*
> Definitely, yeah.
> *Interviewer: Some people make assumptions and stereotypes about prostitutes being diseased, but in my experience that hasn't been the case.*

> I've never met a girl who's contracted the disease [AIDS] through prostitution.
>
> *Interviewer: It's been some other way, then? Needles? Or like yourself, a transfusion?*
>
> Exactly. Most of them have contracted it through needles, the ones I know, by sharing dirty needles with other people ... I only spend $100 a month on food because I don't eat.
>
> *Interviewer: You find it hard to eat?*
>
> I do yeah. I find food hard to digest.
>
> *Interviewer: That must be hard.*
>
> It is, but I drink a lot of Ensure. And I eat their puddings and stuff like that, their shakes.
>
> *Interviewer: Are you on a million drugs?*
>
> No actually, three.
>
> *Interviewer: You're doing well right now?*
>
> Yeah. (Hope, Halifax)

Diseases – sexual or otherwise – are not necessarily seen as the end of one's life. As one worker remarked, these diseases can be coped with without completely giving up one's quality of life:

> Sure, I've got two major diseases, AIDS/HIV and hep C, but I know how to use my condoms. I use my condoms. I don't put other people at risk and I still enjoy a good sex life. That's important. (Scott, Halifax)

What several workers saw as a barrier to treatment was not their own behaviour or lack of understanding but the structure of the health bureaucracy and the lack of services:

> *Interviewer: So are you working right now?*
>
> No, I am on disability, which is disabling, bluntly. (David, Halifax)

Health for these workers, therefore, needs to be placed in its larger socioeconomic context. The shortage of doctors, particularly in New Brunswick, and the machinations of income support left some to seek out solutions on their own:

> *Interviewer: Do you have health problems?*
>
> Yeah, I have asthma. And I have a steel plate in this leg. And I'm on insurance [but] welfare got me off of that. I can't get that now, and I need my puffers. That's my life, or I can't breathe. I just went over [to] John Howard [Society]'s and there was a friend of mine over there, T. And I

said, "You got a blue puffer?" He said, "Yup." And I took it. I said, "Catch me on the rebound." He didn't mind. So if they want to cut me off of welfare, fine. But don't cut me off my medications, 'cause I need them puffers – or I am going to die. I've had asthma since I was two years old, so how am I going to change that around? I can't. (Deanna, Saint John)

I hurt my back years ago and I'm trying to get my doctor to fill out this form for welfare, right? Just until I get another job. Like get a job that I can do, 'cause I can't live on $264 a month. I just can't do it, and I can't get a doctor to fill that out for me. I called my doctor home in Fredericton and they can't see me until the end of October. And like it's crazy. Like no doctors will fill them out here, eh? It has to be your family doctor. 'Cause I could go in and lie to the doctor; and say I got all these problems, right? And when I worked in the nursing home ... I pulled something in my back. And every once in a while it bothers me. I went to clean house for this lady ... about a month ago. I was standing, this is what hurt it again, I was standing on this stool and I was washing the ceiling. I had this big bucket of water here on the oven. And the top of the stool fell in and down I went and landed right in the bucket of water and fell on the floor. I'm telling you, my whole leg was bruised and I did something to my back again. But anyway. Yeah, doctors, no, no. (Kendra, Saint John)

Like many other Canadians, sex workers were frustrated with the lack of health services. One of the women we spoke with, who had undergone cancer surgery, relayed a common experience of a shortage of nursing staff:

There was a lady in the hospital with me. She only had one leg, and she was in bed. She used to keep ringing her buzzer. And you know, we just had surgery. I used to pick her up, put her down on her bed pan, pick her back up, and ask if she wanted to go down the hall for a drive. I'd pick her up and put her in her chair and take her. (Deanna, Saint John)

"I'm Careful": Sex Workers on STDs and STIs

Interviewer: If you could change people's attitudes, what would you let them know about?
That everybody has an addiction, has problems. They do what they gotta do. And at least we're wearing protection. You know that there is something wrong, but if we're using protection and watching ourselves and stuff like that, then it shouldn't be a problem. [They] shouldn't look at us any different. (Candace, Saint John)

Interviewer: What do you think about people's attitudes, the public's attitudes, generally?
Like I said to the one cop, "The only difference between me and you [is] our jobs. You've got backup, a gun, and a bullet-proof vest. All I've got is a condom and I'm standing here." (Belinda, Halifax)

Sex workers' understanding of, and ways of dealing with, STDs and STIs fly in the face of common stereotypes. Sex workers do take steps to protect themselves from disease. For the worker above, the condom is a form of protection on the job just as surely as a gun and bullet-proof vest is for the police officer. This view of safety subverts the dominant discourse on sex workers as either agents of contagion or victims of same. Interviewees were not specifically asked whether they had STIs. But when asked about safe-sex practices, many said they were "careful" or always used condoms:

Interviewer: What would you say are the major risks to being on the street?
I find, like diseases and all that are not a major risk to me. I'm very careful that way.
Interviewer: How about in terms of health safety? Are clients pretty good about using condoms?
Oh yeah. They have to or I wouldn't be there. (Kendra, Saint John)

Interviewer: Do you use a condom?
Yes, I don't have no diseases.
Interviewer: Do guys want you to go without a condom and pay you more?
Yep. But that's not for me, you get out your boot ... You get your boot on, or we're not going nowhere, you know what I mean? (Deanna, Saint John)

Sex workers are not credited with having the protection practices that they in fact have. As Meaghan has argued, "Rarely in ... cultural discourses were sex workers perceived as possessing a specialized knowledge concerning sexual agency and safer sex practices in HIV/AIDS prevention."[16] However, sex workers are often the active party in providing protection and negotiating its use. As one worker explained with a touch of irony: "I get [condoms] from AIDS Saint John. I go up there, get them for free. 'Cause the guys never seem to have them" (Krista, Saint John).

Indeed, sex workers spoke of many instances of safe-sex practices. A high level of awareness of risk and knowledge about STDs and STIs distinguishes many sex workers from the general population.[17] One worker's knowledge of the risk of syphilis is instructive:

> **Do you realize that syphilis is at one of the highest levels in the United States at the moment?**
> *Interviewer: I believe it. Because people are just not paying attention.*
> **Syphilis is nasty. Syphilis can kill you.**
> *Interviewer: Yeah, untreated.*
> **Your brain will become cottage cheese and you will die.** (Felicity, Halifax)

A few months later, Canadian health authorities announced that syphilis levels were on the rise after years of stability.[18]

Unlike most of the public, many sex workers can identify the symptoms of sexually transmitted diseases, enabling them to refuse to service clients who might pose a risk. And, unlike many people, and women in particular, sex workers have the negotiating skills that are required for safe-sex practices. A recent Health Canada report bemoaned that "women are less able to resist pressure by their male partners to share needles or engage in unsafe sexual practices." The document goes further, arguing that "the dominant male culture surrounding Intravenous Drug Use inhibits a women's ability to negotiate safe practices, particularly if the women are young and without social support."[19] Sex workers, however, have long given up the passive feminine role and are now willing to challenge men's unsafe practices. Therefore, sex workers can perform a useful educational role for all women.

The following exchange between a sex worker and a client shows the pressure clients sometimes apply to sex workers to practise unsafe sex and how sex workers quickly recognize and resist these pressures:

> **You know you get the assholes who are like, "Do me without a condom," right? The money is not worth it. Buddy said to me:**
> **Well, can you do me without a condom?**
> *Sex worker:* **No I can't.**
> *Client:* **Well, you should've told me this before I gave you my money.**
> *Sex worker:* **Well, excuse me, who do you think I am?**
> *Client:* **Well, I'm a married man.**
> **Well, I don't care if he's a married man, you know? And then, you know, [he] says, "Well, give me back my money."** (Tara, Halifax)

The client makes the interesting assumption that he is not the person who poses a risk. His understanding of risk is alarming, given that in all likelihood he has had other unprotected sexual contacts. By placing the idea of risk on the sex worker, he completely misunderstands that he is much more likely to be a source of risk than is the sex worker. The declaration that he is a married man is amusing as well, as he thinks that somehow his marital status is protecting him from disease acquisition. The sex worker, though, refuses to be fooled by any of this obfuscation, despite the potential loss of income – and even the possible threat of violence.

Interviewees also frequently called attention to how much of their repertoire with clients is made up of lower-risk behaviours such as masturbation (hand jobs) or even humiliation rituals. There are also some workers who take the money and run before any sexual exchange takes place. Some completely avoid intercourse with clients:

> And I don't know about anybody else, but disease-wise, I don't worry about that. I don't have sexual intercourse with nobody. If I can't fake it, I'm not doing it, and like there's a condom at all times, hand job, no matter what, 'cause there's men that want to, "Oh well, let me jack off on your chest" ... No, it ain't happening. Condom stays on, no matter what. (Tamara, Halifax)

Some do not use condoms with oral sex (blow jobs) or hand jobs, but they try to minimize risk through testing:

> *Interviewer: And do you worry about clients using condoms and stuff, do you ever have trouble convincing them?*
> Well, I don't usually use condoms. I don't, 'cause all I do is give blow jobs. I get tested regularly here [Moncton's Sexual Health Centre] and they have condoms. (Marc, Moncton)

(Although there is a lower risk of disease contraction with blow jobs, it is not a foolproof method.) Certain kinds of sex, particularly intercourse, are sometimes reserved for intimate partners:

> Well, okay, I don't do heavy ... I wasn't into any heavy sex except for my partners. So just straight blow jobs, or hand jobs, either way.
> *Interviewer: So no anal sex.*
> No, not for the work. Just for the other half.
> *Interviewer: Can I ask you a little bit about that? Is that your line for intimacy? In other words, why would you not do anal sex for the work?*
> Well, when it comes to people who are paying for it, they think that they can have whatever they want. So you know, you're not going to get the comfort of [your] other half doing it, because your other half supposedly cares more than the person who is shelling out cash. I know there are lots of tricks that think that because they are forking over money, that they just own you hard core. (David, Halifax)

However, sex with intimates is often accompanied by lack of protection. In sixty-nine interviews with Halifax sex workers, Lois Jackson found that STD transmission is more likely to occur with intimates than with clients.[20] For some sex workers, condoms represent props from the job, the use of which reminds one of work. To have sex with one's intimate partner could be constructed by sex workers as sex rather than work. As such, condoms may not be considered necessary. This misconception is not unlike that held by many women in relationships with men.[21]

There were certainly reports that some workers were not protecting themselves on the job either.

> *Interviewer: What do you think needs to change in the trade for women?*
> **I think myself, one of the big things is health care. I really do, because there are women out there who have no idea, [who need] more education. I have known women who go with these men, no condoms, no nothing.** (Krystal, Halifax)

This non-use of protection was often linked to addictions. But, as one worker argued, it might also be linked to lack of self-respect, which can be the result of stigma rather than "bad behaviour":

> *Interviewer: [Is there] any way to make the work better or safer?*
> **Um, yeah, get the other girls educated, and use protection. And ... have a little bit of self-respect.** (Krista, Saint John)

Others see age and lack of experience of some sex workers as a problem:

> **I'll tell you honestly, the old girls are cool. But the new ones, they're dumb and they don't listen. A lot of them have very unsafe practices.**
> *Interviewer: So you see that there's a change in the time that you've been in business then?*
> **Yeah, I mean, when I started in the business you wouldn't have entertained – for no amount of money – the idea of ditching a condom. Nowadays an extra hundred bucks and they'll do anything.**
> *Interviewer: Even at the risk of their own health? Do you think [this is] the major risk in the business right now?*
> **Right now it is.** (Felicity, Halifax)

Yet, sex workers can and do act as safe-sex educators for clients as well as each other:

> **My big spiel is, [to] any guy asking me [not to use a condom,] I'll look at him and I'll tell him, "Listen to me. If I said yes to you, wouldn't that scare you [that] I said yes to every other guy that has come through that**

door and asked me the same question? And if you ever come across a girl that says yes, run." (Felicity, Halifax)

Another advised fellow sex workers on a full spectrum of health risks:

Ah, watch out for the guys that beat you up. They also ... they fuckin' do needles. They'll hold you down, put the needles in your arm, and they beat you if you don't ... Stay away from crack, if you can't handle it. Or [if you] don't have a strong mind or willpower, don't do it. Watch out for HIV and STDs and that. Always wear a condom, always. And do not make love: that's just degrading. It's degrading to sell your pussy. That's for making love and making babies. But if you have to, at least wear a condom. (Kasey, Saint John)

Sex workers have a variety of ways of reducing risk in their work. But, as they note, there are systemic barriers to safe sex – not being able to work in a safe, indoor space, for example:

There's always that risk of being caught when you're [working] outside. Okay ... you don't know where the guy was like two hours before – you know what I mean? What, were you doing it in the bathhouse there, [or did you] do it at a hotel with company or whatever, you know. There's always, "Get in the shower" or there's like, "Neither of us have a condom on us, so I'm not going to do anything to you. If you still want to pay me, you can go ahead and do something to me. But I'm not going to do you." If it was indoors, there's ... less risk of everything getting caught, transmitting diseases. (Robert, Moncton)

Another barrier this young man and his partner identified was simply the unavailability of condoms in public locations:

Eric: If there was condom machines on every street corner that would be easier. 'Cause the only place you see condom machines are in bars, and a lot of times they're not in bars anymore.
Robert: They cost a dollar and they've been empty for three years.
Interviewer: Exactly, [laughs] that's really helpful.
Eric: Places like this [the Sexual Health Centre] is great, too. We can come to get tested. You can come to get condoms. (Moncton)

Others reported their frustration, particularly in their role as sex professionals, with the fact that research on quick detection of sexually transmitted infections seems to be low on the priority list:

> One thing, what's bad about the centre, like this place here, is three months. You can't find anything unless it's three months down the road. Let's say I get AIDS, or I get Herpes, or I get whatever today, hep C – you can't find out until three months down the road.
> *Interviewer: When you get the test results?*
> No, they can't find out, you know what I mean? It's in your system, they can't find out ... like today I got tested. Next month I still don't know I have it. There's a window period, she says, it's a window period. Three months, what's that? And all the money that goes into health care and shit. Shouldn't they be able to have something, spit bam, like that? Shouldn't they? (Jason, Moncton)

One interviewee remarked on the attitudes of some health care professionals and on the lack of service, particularly given her needs as a sex professional:

> Okay, this is really frustrating. I had gotten an infection in my genital area and I went to the doctor 'cause I was really swollen. I could not close my legs; I could not walk. And it hurt so bad and I didn't know what was going on. And I went to the doctor and gotta piss test, or whatever. And for something so severe they should at least ... like offer a pap test. Like if I can't walk and close my legs and I'm crying [when] I'm taking a step, then something has gotta to be wrong. Right? He gives me a prescription and says that it's a really bad yeast infection. It wasn't. When I found – when I came to Moncton five days later – that he gave me a prescription [that] made it worse ... I'm saying, "Well, what is going on? It's three days later; it's getting worse." [I] went to the hospital. I explained to them like I am working [in a sex] business. And it was more like, "Yeah, and I care why? So you can wait behind everybody else" type thing. Like, "That's your stupidity if that's what you got," you know what I mean? And I'm not the type of person ... I can tell ... I don't overreact, or assume, or get paranoid.
> *Interviewer: Yeah, but you can read them.*
> Yeah, like you know somebody's ... when I said I'm not waiting behind people that came after me like really, I'm not. So I went to the hospital and they had said that it was a really bad yeast infection and ... I came here [the Sexual Health Centre] and I found out that I had herpes. Like [the hospital] didn't have the time of day for me, like even the doctor himself ... So like it kind of upset me. About then I come here and I find out that I have a sexually transmitted disease ... I was really angry. (Bonnie, Moncton)

Addictions

> The only way to get through this life or lifestyle or any type of lifestyle that is not the so-called norm [is through] one type of substance abuse or another. You look around with most families and it is some form [of addiction], usually alcohol, or prescription drugs.
> *Interviewer: What was yours?*
> Just pot. And acid, you know: long nights you got to keep awake. (David, Halifax)

> Dilaudids. I've never done them, never, and I never ever would. But that's what people are killing their friends for, it really is. I had a friend, twenty-nine years old, that just died here last year. And what a sin, man. She was into doing the needles ... She was having a hard time coming off them; and her whole system, it just shut her system right down. She was on life-support for three days. Beautiful, beautiful lady ... just a beautiful girl. (Kendra, Saint John)

Most of the sex workers interviewed do not construct addictions as the greatest problem with themselves or with the trade. When addictions came up in the conversation, the concern was not about addictions so much as about how addictions could contribute to a workers' lack of safety or to undercutting of prices. Further, sex workers do not see the relationship between sex work and addictions as either necessary or causal. And they certainly reject the singular focus on sex workers as a particularly problematic population when it comes to addictions. Nonetheless, the image of prostitutes as drug addicted appears everywhere, including in academic literature.

The discourse on addictions has always been one of blame: addicts are doing it to themselves, and a person is just a junkie or a cokehead. This type of othering renders people as objects, incapable or unwilling participants in social structure. It safely objectifies people, dissociating them from the middle class and presents them as either in need of intervention or untouchable. Discussions with sex workers who are addicted, however, indicate that the relationship between addictions and sex work is much more complex than is widely assumed.

The first concern with addictions is their effect on safety:

> So if you're on drugs, you don't think anything is going to happen to ya. But you could die on the street. You could really die. Whether it's from someone picking you up and beating the living shit out of ya and leaving you for dead. You don't know who you're getting in with, and you don't care. All you can think of is that next puff, the next fix. (Beth, Saint John)

> And I take bad risks, 'cause I go drink with the guys ... They're mean, you know ... That's how I busted my jaw ... That's the worst thing to do, drinking ... Then we'll use some crack. That's something I don't do, which I [did] do. I been busted for that before, and I ain't going down that road again. Now it's just an exchange of money, you know, when they call. (Dawne, Halifax)

Addictions also have an impact on general health:

> And then when I was thirty years old my lung collapsed on me, from the crack. I went to the hospital and they did X-rays and seen that I had a hole, that the crack burned in my left lung. And I'm an asthmatic, so it was pretty bad. (Beth, Saint John)

It is important to distinguish between addiction issues and sex work per se. Addictions affect people in all walks of life and lines of work, but society tends to focus on deviantized sections of society as most likely to be affected by addictions. As one former worker and addict argued, there are many people who are addicted:

> There's lawyers, there's all kinds of different people who are into addiction. They just have the ability to not to have it seen. Like the girls, we work the streets. That's why everybody knows that we're an addict, because they see us. They see us in the paper, otherwise they would not know. (Beth, Saint John)

That is, addictions may simply be more visible among the street-level sex worker population. Indeed, a number of our interviewees noted that clients may be the ones with addiction issues. Sex workers may simply be the clients' way of getting to the drug without getting caught:

> I always try to stay away from the drugs myself, you know. I really do. But the customers themselves they ask you, can you get them for them? It's the customers that want it too.
> *Interviewer: Really?*
> Yes. And they don't even want to go with you. They'll pay you your fee; you know, they'll say, "Well, look" – 'cause I'm standing here – "for $40 or $50" [I can get them drugs] ... They may as well give me that if [I'm] gonna leave there and go get him some crack, mostly crack. Like, that's the girls [that has] got them. There are a lot of dates that are crackheads. They're into that too. The girls turned them on, or they got into it someway, but it happens at least once a week where you got a customer

who wants you to get them some drugs. Here in this city mostly – I don't see it too much in Montreal – but here, they'd rather have that than they would you sometimes ... seriously. (Valerie, Halifax)

Another confirmed that "smoke dates" are common for her:

I had a lot of smoke dates too, like dates that would get me to get the crack and the coke for them. And they'd smoke with me for hours and hours, because they were from high-class families. Their wives were home in bed, with the kids and that, or baking. And they'd be out with the wild girl, and do the drugs. But hey, that's all right, as long as he was providing a home to her. But you're gonna get the people with the drugs there that are just, like, they're there for the drugs. (Denise, Halifax)

Clients, a much wider section of society, are able in part to hide their addictions through sex workers.

In the Maritimes, as no doubt is the case elsewhere, addictions to prescription drugs are much more common among the general population than previously thought, and are becoming more so.[22] Such addictions may result not from so-called deviant behaviour but from injuries and chronic pain as well as from over-prescribing. Sex workers are as vulnerable to this kind of addiction as are other people who work in physically demanding jobs that may result in injury. As one interviewee related:

I made a lot of money, but I find I got a little too into the scene of the drinking, and I did percs a lot for a while too, Percocets ... That's when I was dancing, because I have two screws in my ankle. So dancing in six- or seven-inch spiked heels, after a while, it, you know. And you're working ten- to twenty-three-hour shifts every day, and you got to look pretty for ten to twelve hours a day. And have your tits all perky and everything. And you got to be perfect, and you gotta walk in those stupid heels for ten hours a day. By the end of the day your feet are so raunchy smelling, 'cause the bottom of the shoes are all leather. So your feet are sweating. And I found that by the end, towards the end of the shift, it had been ten hours, my ankle was just hurting just so, so bad. (Colleen, Moncton)

Sex work itself may increase a workers' liability to addiction because of the availability of drugs and alcohol in the work environment. Jacqueline Lewis and Eleanor Maticka-Tyndale's research on strip-club workers has uncovered a certain workplace liability for workers because of the prevalence of alcohol in particular[23] – although Chris Bruckert argues that, at least in the strip clubs, "immoderate use of drugs and alcohol is far from normative" and, indeed, is seen as a destructive pattern by other dancers and staff.[24] Similarly, among our interviewees who did not have addiction problems, there was often sympathy for those who struggled with them, even though there was frustration:

> **I feel bad for the girls with addictions. I believe they can find the strength somewhere to beat their addiction. I mean, even if they continue to work on the street, you know what I mean? But who wants to lay on their back for drugs? It doesn't make sense to me. If you lay on your back, you lay on your back to better yourself, not to take yourself down under. That's the way I look at it. It's a means to an end.** (Felicity, Halifax)

Stigma and criminalization may be one reason addictions do occur within the trade. One worker observed that drinking allows her to ignore any harassment on the street:

> *Interviewer: [Are there] any kinds of people driving by, you know, [harassing you]?*
> **They don't bother me, 'cause every time I'm out there I'm [drinking].**
> (Samantha, Halifax)

The street trade and the drug trade have become more intertwined as sex work has become increasingly marginalized and pushed into locations where the drug trade also takes place.

Mostly, people associate sex work with addictions on the assumption that sex work is mainly used as a way to make money in order to satisfy an addiction. The underlying assumption is that the only reason anyone would become involved in the trade is that she is driven by forces beyond her control. There are certainly cases of this among those we spoke with, but the relationship between addictions and sex work was not always causal – nor was it a necessary one. There were those who had never had addictions, even though our sample was biased toward the street trade, where addictions are more likely. Among those workers who did have an addiction, there was a distinction between those who had turned to sex work as a way to support an expensive habit and those who had gotten into drugs or alcohol after entering the trade. Further, a number of those with addictions were managing their addictions in ways that worked for them. One worker talked about using on Tuesdays and not taking clients on that night. Others had in fact conquered their addictions or were in recovery and still working in the trade. One sex worker who was addicted to crack for over eighteen years explained how the relationship between addictions and sex work can be complicated and not directly causal:

Interviewer: Is that the main reason you're in the trade, do you think?
Um, at first, no it wasn't. But as the years progressed, and my habit became more and more ... Yeah. It's hard. It's a hard thing to get off, both crack and the street life. It is, it's hard.
Interviewer: Well, they're separate, but they're ...
Yeah, they're separate, but they intertwine. One does ... with the other. 'Cause I know as soon as I go out there ... Say I was walking down the street, and I've got a john. I have no intention of using. But as soon as I get the money, I want to use. I know that ... you relapse mentally. So, it's ... you don't plan to relapse; you tell yourself you're not going to relapse, but deep down you know you're going to. So it's a mental relapse.
Interviewer: So is getting the money a trigger in a way?
Having money is a trigger. Being around the area is a trigger. Bumping into associates is a trigger. Everything is a trigger. Lighting a match is a trigger. Someone smoking a cigar is a trigger, 'cause there's pipes that look like cigars. So that's a trigger. There's all kinds of triggers. (Kendra, Saint John)

For some people, then, drugs and the trade can become one and same because of the associated triggers, even if drugs were not the reason for getting into sex work. For others, though, the two are separate issues. Again, if we think of any other profession – medical work, for example, where drugs are readily available and can lead to addiction – the work and the addiction may become associated. However, one would certainly not argue that people become medical staff because of their addictions.

Thus, addictions are not identified by sex workers as an issue of concern in the trade with the same urgency, or in the same way, as it is by many health workers. Many revealed addictions when simply asked whether they had any. That is, it was not defined as a high-priority issue like violence or stigma. Although several of the sex workers with addictions did identify the need for better programs to help them deal with these issues, these programs cannot work unless they take sex workers' understandings and concerns, particularly violence and stigma, to heart. The current official discourse on addictions and sex work is prone to being stigmatizing in itself.

Addictions and Official Discourse
The tendency of sex workers to not name addictions as a health issue contrasts sharply with the tendency of health care professionals to immediately name addiction as the most common problem facing sex workers. This characterization of sex workers as suffering from addiction is based in part on underlying assumptions about the deviance of both sex work and drug use. As Jennifer Butters and Patricia Erikson note, the deviantization of drug use has been a multifaceted process:

> The creation of drug use as a deviant behaviour has been a dynamic process involving three key social movements each emphasizing a specific form of "control" over substance use: moral, medical and criminalization. Although originating from different concepts of addiction, all three movements describe the morals and values reflecting the "canons of decency" and respectability.[25]

Thus, even health experts can project a moralizing tone, as in the following example:

> The harmful use of substances (mostly of psychoactive substances including alcohol) has been related to a wide variety of social and health issues, including HIV/AIDS, hepatitis C, homelessness, family violence, prostitution, sexual exploitation, delinquency, crime, and child abuse and neglect. Overall the Committee believes that the harmful use of substances and dependence are primarily public health issues that must be addressed within a public health framework.[26]

Both sex work and drug use breach these "'canons of decency' and respectability" and are, therefore, easily linked together. While it is true that the two can be linked, the link is more tenuous than most would like to believe. When the link is found, there is a tendency for it to immediately engage the attention and sense of pathos of the middle class. For example, the parliamentary Special Committee on the Non-Medical Use of Drugs described its sense of tragedy thus: "The social and human tragedy associated with the harmful use of substances and the links of prostitution and exploitation of vulnerable groups were among the most compelling things that this Committee observed."[27]

There is much that is not known about substance abuse. Despite the scientific evidence on drugs and addictions and their effects, and despite the number of needle exchanges and methadone programs nationwide, there is still scarce data on prevalence. As the Special Committee admitted: "In Canada, there is an alarming lack of information on the prevalence of use and harmful use of substances, trends, and overdoses, which impedes the development of sound drug policy making."[28] But the lack of information on trends and overdoses indicates that current policies may be based not on information but on dangerous assumptions about the sex trade – for example, that sex work and drugs are intimately connected. Such assumptions do not protect those in sex work; instead, they can increase the vulnerability of women and men in the trade to violence, addiction, and disease, as stigmatization of treatment, assumptions, and practices turn sex workers away from possible help.

Sex workers are used to being treated as if they were the problem, rather than as if their problems were health issues. It is the construction of this behaviour as problematic that is at issue here. As one sex worker from Saint John said to the interviewer in an angry tone when asked if she was using: "I know that doing crack is not good for me, but I'm just not ready to give it up. I'm just not." When the interviewer replied with: "Ok, well that's fine. That's where you're at," the interviewee relaxed a bit and then said that she had thought the interviewer was from "some church or something" (Tabitha, Saint John). In other words, because it is so easily assumed that sex workers are addicted, she felt that, by asking the question, the interviewer was judging her on her use of crack.

Outreach workers, along with sex workers, challenge the unfair focus on sex workers as "deviants" suffering from addictions. In a recent interview, Haley Flaro, executive director of AIDS New Brunswick, talked about the stereotypes of addicts that she hears when people learn that she operates a needle exchange. Yet, as she remarked, "addicts come from all walks of life. You wouldn't believe who I see in here. They're not all street people."[29]

Judgment of people using addictive substances enters the frameworks that health care workers use as partial explanations of drug addiction. It is the fragility of the person using the substance that is at issue, rather than any other possible explanation. The idea of addictions as functional simply does not enter the common parlance of many who deal with the addicted on a day-to-day basis.[30]

There is a tendency to associate what is seen as the worst kind of addiction with the most stigmatized groups, such as sex workers. Middle-class professionals are assumed to have their greatest difficulty with more acceptable substances, such as alcohol. While a number of our interviewees talked about addictions to opiates, they are certainly not unique in this addiction, nor did it necessarily come about as a result of their lifestyle. Some of the health workers we interviewed agreed that many of those addicted to opiates begin their addictions through doctor-prescribed (read "legitimate") opiate use. As one outreach nurse, who is running a methadone maintenance therapy program in a community health clinic, explained:

> The main concern with these people really is chronic pain issues. For a lot of them that's how they became addicted in the first place.
> *Interviewer: I wanted to ask you ... what do you think needs to change in terms of public attitudes towards the addicted?*
> Well, I think that there's a complete lack of understanding. The public just has no idea what these people go through. I mean, for whatever reason that they go into this, people call us daily on the phone, crying. Their lives are falling apart; they've lost the family, their friends, their

> houses, their car, their job, their kids. I think that people just see drug addicts as not caring about anything. I don't [know] what it is, but these people really have very sad, sad stories to tell ... With 50 percent of the population that we see here – approximately – [they're] getting addicted because of issues relating to chronic pain and things like that. I mean they're not out there shooting up heroin because they've just got the idea somewhere. A lot of them started with legitimate issues and [it] just got out of control. (Outreach nurse, Fredericton, 26 August 2003)

The largest type of opiates that sex workers reported using is Dilaudids, the powerful pain suppressants given to those with chronic and deteriorating conditions, such as cancer, or ongoing structural impediments, such as back pain.[31] Given the level of pain of some of the injuries, it is not surprising that this level of painkiller is needed. Unfortunately, Dilaudids are highly addictive. Other opiates, including forms of oxycodone, better known by the more familiar names Percocet and OxyContin, are prevalent in the addictions list as well and are also usually prescribed for pain.[32]

There is a slowly growing recognition among the general public of the problem of chronic pain, over-prescribing, and opiate abuse.[33] There remains, however, another bias in the way these addictions are treated. For example, because there is a fairly high rate of alcohol addiction among professionals, government-funded assistance is available to employees for alcoholism. Indeed, most provincial Employee Assistance Programs (EAPs) are consistently focused on alcohol – and now gambling – as issues for which professionals are referred to counselling (paid for by employers); that is, this assistance is often limited to what is considered to be an acceptable addiction. Many of the sex workers we interviewed had no access to EAPs. Therefore, many addiction services paid for by provincial governments do not deal with street-level addicts at all. The hard drug use associated with deviant lifestyles is viewed as less treatable than are acceptable addictions:

> It's okay for you to be an alcoholic. It's okay for you to smoke weed, marijuana, but if you do needles, or you do crack cocaine, then you're just a piece of dirt; and that's how they treat ya. You know you can go in and say you're an alcoholic, and people will help ya. If you go and get marijuana, it's not a big thing – you can get over this. Crack cocaine? They think there's no hope for you. When you start hearing that, you start to be convinced there's no hope for you. (Beth, Saint John)

There is some resistance to harm reduction approaches – such as needle exchanges and methadone programs – among the official addictions treatment community, despite the fact that other strategies, such as abstinence and criminalization, have simply failed. But, as one researcher observes, the argument against harm reduction as encouraging drug use – unlike criminalization or abstinence-based treatment programs – is based on rhetoric rather than fact: "The rhetorical hypothesis is that irrespective of their effectiveness in reducing harms, harm-reduction programs literally communicate messages that encourage drug use ... those who espouse this rhetorical hypothesis rarely explain how it is supposed to work."[34] Harm reduction programs – including methadone maintenance, the best option for opiate drug users – are often downloaded to community-based organizations to organize. Provincial government support is often weak or non-existent.[35] The official rhetoric that blames the addict for her/his failures helps justify this lack of government support for outreach and harm reduction. This discourse of blame also encourages those who are seeking help to turn away from stigmatizing official sources of help and toward the underfunded outreach programs.

Outreach Programs and Empowerment
That sex workers do not identify addiction as a health problem may be due, in large part, to how addictions are treated within communities generally, which is as a highly stigmatized legal problem. To name an addiction is to be at risk of further criminalization and stigmatization. Programs that further stigmatize sex workers will not help those with addictions. As well, programs that target drug use without addressing violence fail to meet sex workers' self-identified concerns. Also, quitting addictions requires a change in self-perception, a change that is very hard to make when clients harass workers or are violent toward them and when police ignore these concerns or themselves harass workers. In interviews with advocacy and community workers, there emerged patterns of respect, of caring, and of knowing the sex workers that appear to serve both sex worker needs and program goals. Sex workers respond best to programs in the community that reach out to them in respectful ways. Programs that may be designed to target sex workers, such as government addiction services, for example, rarely accommodate the sex worker community. For any program to reach people with addictions, it must rely on community services that are accessible and comfortable for the addicted persons. Indeed, a Health Canada study stated that outreach services are the most reliable way of serving intravenous drug users: "Research indicates that outreach services, in conjunction with peer-driven interventions, offer the best success in reaching users of injection drugs."[36] However, government often espouses this rhetoric in support of community-based services while failing to provide the financial support required to sustain these services.

Sex workers agree that the best outreach programs are those operated by those who have been there. As one Saint John worker said:

> When they hire people to help these women I think it should be somebody that's been through it. I mean, you're a very nice lady and easy to talk to, but ... I don't know if you've ever smoked crack or not, but it's easier ... that's why I enjoy talking to H and J, because they know.
> (Kendra, Saint John)

Sex workers make use of health care clinics or outreach services that they know and trust; other facilities are not patronized in the same way. Official programs tend to function as a bureaucracy of care, one in which certain health care concerns are mandated while others are passed over. What community outreach workers have that empowers sex workers is a more complete and more compassionate understanding of the positions of the street workers they serve and, therefore, they garner trust in the interaction with their clientele. As one former sex worker and current outreach worker illustrated, she has a good understanding of the distinction between sex work and addictions issues:

> I think women that are involved in prostitution ... you just don't stop. And if they have drug addictions too ... I think it's because, you can get a woman clean ... Like for myself for instance, I was clean, but I was still working because I was addicted to the money, the fast life. So there has to be something in place for while you're in transition. They can't just [say,] "Okay, I'm not gonna be a prostitute today." (Mandy, Halifax)

Halifax's Stepping Stone outreach program for sex workers has become a much appreciated centre for sex worker support and service provision because of this kind of non-judgmental and understanding attitude:

> I'll tell you, my worst times, my worst times when I was down and out, Stepping Stone was a safe haven for me. I could come here, and I could eat. I could get cleaned up. I could get clean clothes ... And there was other girls that I worked with, that are now staff. And I felt safe here. And I always knew I could get clean condoms here, not used. I didn't get the syringes, I got them at Mainline. But I knew I was safe here. And I could have a warm meal, and get a pair of socks. You know how many times I'd be with no socks in the wintertime, in sneakers? And your feet literally frost burned. My feet used to be so cold. And frost bite on the toes. I would cry downstairs on the couch there. And I would come here [and] I could always get a pair of gloves and a pair of socks. Because one thing they never have enough of here is socks and gloves for the girls. Because every hooker, they lose their gloves in the car, or they were doing drugs. And I always knew I could come here. (Denise, Halifax)

Yet programs such as Stepping Stone frequently suffer from a lack of reliable and consistent funding that would ensure that these services can continue to be provided. Funding is often given on a project-by-project basis, leading to time-consuming funding applications, competition among outreach agencies, and an inability to assure program users of continued support.

We spoke with a number of people in the sex trade who have addictions and are highly critical of the lack of services for women and sex workers, specifically in the Maritimes. There is only one residency-based addiction treatment centre for women in the Maritimes (the Marguerite Centre in Halifax), which opened only recently, after a long battle for funding. Others noted that while jail is presumed to provide an opportunity to "dry out," there is, in fact, very little provided for inmates in the way of addiction services while they are in jail or when they are released:

> Nobody wants to do anything ... Put them in jail, and then when they go to jail, you don't get nothing there. They don't even help you get better. You do it cold turkey, sitting in a cell. You could die from coming off drugs, withdrawing. I get lonely. I've gotten some sick. They don't bother with ya. They just lock you up, and when your time's up, "Get out." And then you're right back to the same environment that you know. (Beth, Saint John)

Despite these barriers to treatment and support, many of our interviewees displayed an incredible determination to fight their addictions:

> So when I left and decided it was time for me to get off the drugs, I decided to leave here for a while. A friend of mine has a beach home. I got him to take the phone out of there, so I couldn't call nobody. You get urges, like every three months, six months, you get this eerie feeling. I still have them. And I stayed there for over a month. And then from there I went to NA [Narcotics Anonymous]. (Beth, Saint John)

> Me, with myself, I was on the streets. Nowheres to go. Sleeping in doorways. I didn't care, you know, that crack. My toenails fell off. I was on the run for about four days. All my toenails fell off and everything else. I was a sick cookie. I was the one out there for the longest and the oldest pretty well, and everybody thought they would find me dead. But guess what?
> *Interviewer: You showed them.*
> In your face! (Alyssa, Saint John)

Conclusion

Sex workers are often stigmatized for their work, viewed as carriers of disease or as vulnerable populations, and pathologized as drug addicts, but sex workers see health issues in a very different light. They point to the conditions in which wo/men practise the trade as giving rise to the problems they name. It is these conditions – and the health care system more generally – that need changing, not the wo/men. Sex workers critique the underfunding of the health care system and its inability to provide compassionate and non-judgmental service to sex workers and those with addictions. And they resist being ignored and mistreated by this system by avoiding certain health services and instead coping on their own or going only to those services that provide more amendable types of care. These third-sector or outreach services are also not sufficiently supported, even though this is precisely the milieu in which sex workers can provide each other with the kind of effective support they require.

As Cecilia Benoit and Alison Millar suggest in their community study of sex workers in British Columbia, policy makers and health experts need to understand the conditions of sex workers' lives *before* policy decisions are taken if policy is to be effective.[37] It is important then to understand health from sex workers' perspective. For example, safe-sex and addictions policies and programs that do not address the background of violence and stigma that sex workers face simply cannot be effective. This linkage between violence, stigma, and health illustrates the vital need for valuing sex workers' knowledge and understandings of health. And yet, health experts consistently ignore this fundamental link. If health is defined as wellness (which freedom from poverty most assuredly guarantees), and safety is defined as non-violence (which freedom from random and systemic violence by clients and police guarantees), policies on sex work would look very different than they do. If sex workers were viewed as safe-sex experts and addictions educators, then policies and programs that draw on their expertise and encourage effective education of all segments of society could be developed. If policy makers are serious about redressing the conditions and contexts in which sex workers work, it is imperative that sex workers' perspectives and participation are included in any policy-making process.

6
Sex and Politics: Responding to Sex Workers

Like the high-up people – whoever does it – are probably men, and the government, okay? 'Cause they know the taxpayers' money is going on prostitutes too. Look at Clinton, that one with the blow job. How many other of them are out there? Our [Lieutenant-] Governor, one year, $2,000 for a carpet? I can go carpet her house for $200. And they pay for prostitutes, so what? But they put that down as "coffee." I'm a cup of coffee. I can give you a blow job, but I'm just a cup of coffee. Pay me, shut my mouth, I'm gone. Right? ... It starts with the government ... it does. I mean, when they come to places like Halifax for the G-7, they're not down there just talking about the G-7, I'll tell you right now. [Their] expenses, [somebody] should check them ... We're dirt to them, but they can go pick us up, or phone and get a blow job, or get a piece of ass, but we're not noted down. One's a cup of coffee, or one's a taxi, limousine run, or something. I wish I'd get the money they do, but we're not noted, and we're like ...

How can I really tell it to you? Like I mean, as a prostitute myself, I felt degraded. I felt not as good as anyone else. I always felt I was being judged, which I was, and them feelings are feelings I got because they were there. Somehow ... I never had them on my own, so obviously the feelings I have were genuine, because that's how I was being looked at. I was being treated like that, and there's no way anyone can stop people from putting down prostitutes, because it's the oldest profession. Look at Mary Magdalene, she didn't get stoned [to death] though did she? (Denise, Halifax)

Interviewer: How do you think politicians see street workers?
As long as it's not during their campaign-running season, I don't think they give a shit; 'cause half of them, they're buying [our services] themselves. That's one of your best clients. 'Cause once they know you know who they are, how do they know you ain't got a hidden video somewhere

or even got them on tape there? How do they know that? I know a couple of my girlfriends that know judges very well and they've never had trouble being busted. Not once, it makes you wonder don't it? (Belinda, Halifax)

Politics, Policy, and Sex Work

The hypocrisy of politics and policy around sex work is not lost on sex workers. They are condemned and controlled by the legal system and yet their services are quietly taken advantage of. Sex trade policy in Canada is riddled with similar hypocrisy and illogic. The current communicating law[1] is mostly the result of pressure by some residents' organizations and police associations for the government to come up with a stricter law that would crack down on the "nuisance" generated by the street-level sex trade. The law seems neither to have addressed nuisance particularly effectively nor to have in any way decreased the sex trade. At the same time, the trade has become more dangerous for sex workers. And because indoor sex work remains illegal under the bawdy house provisions,[2] there is no legal or safe space for sex workers to work. Massage parlours and escort services are sometimes licensed and taxed by municipalities under the legal fiction that sex work is not taking place. This simply means that while the businesses are allowed to operate, there are no protections for sex workers. The law creates a hypocritical situation in which sex for exchange is technically not illegal but nearly impossible for the workers to carry out legally. At the same time, sex businesses can be taxed and zoned without a concomitant requirement to protect their workers. And the problems of violence, potential exploitation, unfair targeting of sex workers rather than clients, and neighbourhood nuisance remain unaddressed.

This failure to come up with a workable policy has resulted in continuing frustration on the part of municipalities in particular, because of their inability to "deal with" the trade in a logical manner. Sex workers and sex worker advocates, whose concerns simply cannot be effectively addressed within a criminalized environment, are similarly frustrated. For example, outreach organizations that work with sex workers on health or safety concerns may find themselves greatly limited by the criminal law. Asking escort agencies to hand out information on safe-sex practices, for instance, would require these agencies to admit that sex is actually for sale on its premises and that the agencies are in breach of the law. Outreach organizations that provide information to sex workers on how to avoid arrest can be perceived to be as encouraging people to break the law or as hampering police in a criminal investigation.[3] While almost all of our respondents who worked in the trade spoke of the need to decriminalize or regulate the trade, both of these measures still appear to be a long way off. At the national level there is some pressure to revisit the law[4] (discussed in further detail below), particularly in the wake of the appalling violence being visited upon sex workers, but, to date, there has been little movement in this direction.[5]

Sex workers, for the most part, have not been included in the public debate over policy.[6] Instead, they are viewed as objects of control who are unable or who do not deserve to negotiate and take part in policy discussions. Or, if they do take part in such discussions, they are seen as unrepresentative of the real or majority sex worker, who is assumed to be victimized and unaware of what she truly needs. That is, policy makers and many social activists who seek input on the law operate from their particular constructions of what Wendy Chapkis has termed "the Prostitute" – a symbolic construction that "reflects as much on the needs of the individual or social movement invoking her as the reality of the sex worker herself."[7] The choice of a particular story about prostitution reflects not "a relation to truth, but ... less innocent factors. These ultimately include a will to power partially constituted by and expressing a desire *not* to hear certain other voices or stories."[8] The stories Canadian policy makers have so far been willing to hear are, as we saw in Chapter 4, the sex worker as criminal agent or nuisance and the sex worker as helpless victim. Both stories exclude sex workers as speaking subjects and political agents with rights, and both, therefore, help maintain the power of (non-sex-worker) political actors as experts, helpers, and protectors with the right and duty to wield political power and render decisions on how sex work shall be governed. Ironically, unless and until sex workers are recognized as legitimate political agents with rights, none of the issues that policy makers are struggling with can be effectively resolved. That is, only when we recognize sex workers as agents who can determine the best policy choices to protect their rights and maximize their control over their own lives and with whom mutual accommodation can be negotiated can we, together, design a policy system that works.

As mentioned above, so far, the key political players influencing this debate have not been sex workers. Rather, residential associations, police, and politicians have determined the discourse on policy. The result has been a tendency for policy decisions to generally reflect the interests of these groups, often to the detriment of the safety and human rights of sex workers. But, as we shall see below, sex workers, including marginalized sex workers, are indeed aware of and open to the process of negotiating the urban space. Indeed, on close examination, it is evident that the interests of residents and sex workers are not completely opposed, nor are the two groups fundamentally set against each other. Instead, there has been a failure on the part of elites, particularly members of government, to take sex workers seriously and to offer braver policy solutions beyond criminalization, as well as a failure on the part of the wider public, including feminist and social justice organizations, to demand respect for sex workers and sex workers' rights in any policy response.

Policy Options: Criminalization, Legalization, and Decriminalization
To some extent, the debate over policy change is stalled by this general confusion over what the various choices involve. There is a wide variety in the ways the terms "criminalization," "decriminalization," "legalization," and "regulation" are used, in part, because these systems are not all necessarily exclusive and are sometimes mistaken for one another. In particular, regulation is often confused with legalization. For our purposes, and following the example of many sex worker organizations, the importance of the distinction is in whether the proposed system works in the interests of sex workers' self-empowerment or in the interests of others, particularly that of the state or management. None of these systems exists in a pure form; rather, they refer to ideal types and political orientations, while, in practice, many states combine elements of different systems.[9] "Legalization," for example, commonly refers to direct state control of the industry, as in the state-controlled brothels of Nevada. Sex worker and feminist organizations are widely opposed to this measure, which not only puts control in the hands of the state but often works in favour of the state (in terms of revenues) and of clients (in terms of safety), rather than in favour of sex workers. A legalized indoor industry can be, and often is, combined with criminalization of the street trade. Criminalization includes making prostitution per se illegal and/or criminalizing activities associated with the trade (the current Canadian case). Decriminalization, on the other hand, means removing prostitution-specific offences from the Criminal Code and dealing with the negative aspects through other laws that address the same issues in a general context. For example, nuisance factors would come under various bylaws concerning littering, disturbance, and so on, and pimping would be dealt with as forced labour or extortion. Within a decriminalized system, a variety of regulatory provisions can be used. Regulatory practices, though, can tend toward the same problems as legalization – that is, licensing or zoning that is designed with control rather than rights in mind. Alternatively, regulation can be in the hands of, and for the benefit of, sex workers. Perhaps the most useful distinction between legalization and decriminalization is that put forward by Valerie Scott of the Canadian Organization for the Rights of Prostitutes: "In a nutshell, legalization sees prostitution as a vice that needs to be contained and controlled. Decriminalization sees prostitution as a business that needs fair business regulations."[10] Fair business regulation, however, must involve protecting workers' rights.

Decriminalization, therefore, as a first step, opens the way for addressing some of the harm attached to the trade – the violence, the fear of arrest, the secrecy, and the stigma.[11] As mentioned above, decriminalization of some sort was put forward, not surprisingly, by the vast majority of our respondents as the most important legal change that could be made. Many expressed the desire to be able to work indoors or in some other protected zone without the problems of fear of arrest. That is, they wanted a "dry, safe place" in which they could work without fear of harassment – by police or the public – and violence. Decriminalization has also been put forward by many who advocate sex workers' rights as the necessary first step toward reducing the violence faced by workers, in that workers would be able to operate in safer and healthier environments and call police – without fear of arrest themselves – if a threat arose.[12] Rates of pay and hours of work could also be improved, and the stigma of sex work could begin to be addressed. That is, under decriminalized conditions, policies designed by and for sex workers could be put into place, their primary goal being to protect sex workers' rights. Nevertheless, recommendations that sex work be decriminalized in Canada have foundered in policy debates since the 1970s, again, mostly because of the refusal to see sex workers as capable political actors. Instead, the focus has been on how to control the trade, either through punitive or protective measures – rather than on how to maximize sex workers' rights.

The Development of the Law
Laws governing sex work under Canada's Criminal Code fall under the exclusive jurisdiction of the federal government, and yet the problems associated with sex work as it currently exists are felt at the provincial and municipal level. The development of the law has in part reflected a struggle between, on one hand, local governments, police, and residents concerned about nuisance and, on the other hand, federal policy makers and social organizations concerned about wider issues such as morality and exploitation. Residential concerns have been the central issue in policy debates over sex work since the 1970s, when it became evident that federal sex-trade laws failed to address these concerns. In 1972 the Vagrancy provisions[13] used to control street-level prostitution since pre-Confederation were rescinded as a possible breach of human rights for criminalizing a person's status (as a vagrant) rather than a person's act. New provisions on prostitution followed in the form of a law against solicitation, but interpretive difficulties (e.g., what constituted soliciting and whether clients could be said to be soliciting) led to a Supreme Court of Canada decision in 1978 to define solicitation as only constituting an offence when it was "pressing and persistent."[14] The ruling caused an uproar among municipalities and police, who claimed that they were now unable to deal with prostitution effectively. Following the 1978 ruling, many cities began to take matters into their own hands by passing bylaws to curb the street-level trade.

Politics in the Maritimes paralleled what was happening in the rest of the country. Halifax amended Halifax Street Ordinance #3 in 1982, which – among the regulations on signs, scaffolding, excavations, and sidewalks – included the prohibitions: "no person shall be or remain on a street for the purpose of prostitution," and "no person shall approach another person on a street for the purpose of prostitution." Before the bylaw was rendered unconstitutional (for inappropriate intervention into a federal area of jurisdiction) by the 1983 Westendorp[15] decision against a similar bylaw in Calgary, twenty-three charges were laid – five against clients and eighteen against sex workers.[16] In 1984 the Nova Scotia government took the extraordinary step of seeking an injunction to restrain prostitution in Halifax – publicly posting the names of forty-seven sex workers named in the injunction.[17] The Nova Scotia Supreme Court later denied the injunction – as did the court of appeal.[18] In the face of these failed attempts at local action, Halifax, along with other municipalities, continued to pressure the federal government to visit the law once again.

The Trudeau government finally responded to this pressure by setting up the Fraser Committee to make recommendations on measures to address the sex trade. The committee came up with suggestions for partial decriminalization of indoor sex work (allowing sex workers to work out of their homes and giving provinces the option of licensing small sex work establishments in non-residential areas), but before any progressive measures could be implemented, the election of the neo-conservative Mulroney government occurred. Then justice minister John Crosbie introduced the new communicating bill,[19] which made communicating for the purposes of prostitution illegal both for sex workers and their clients, on the grounds that this law would address the problem of gender inequality, by criminalizing both parties, and the problem of nuisance, by suppressing the trade.

It was soon undeniable that the new communicating law was a failure on many fronts. A 1989 review of this law found that the law had failed to reduce prostitution and had instead increased the risk of violence toward sex workers.[20] The Halifax study in that report showed a decrease in the number of people working on the street in the immediate aftermath of the new law, but the study also noted "unintended consequences," such as an increase in indoor activity and the need for sex workers to work more often to make up for lost income. Further, the Halifax study noted that "the law had created a more criminal environment surrounding street prostitution" and had contributed to the stigmatization of sex workers by making them "feel like criminals," which had not been the case previous to the law.[21] But before these research results were available, the Supreme Court of Canada ruled in response to a Charter challenge initiated in Nova Scotia and upheld by the Nova Scotia Supreme Court, which argued that the communicating law was an unjustified infringement on citizens' rights. Residents complained loudly when the law was suspended in that province, and the Nova Scotia government moved immediately to contest the decision. In reviewing the Nova Scotia court's decision, along with similar ones in Manitoba and Alberta, the Supreme Court of Canada maintained that the infringement was justified in light of the goals of the legislation.[22] Later commentators wondered whether the law would have been upheld if the results of the 1989 review had been available to the Supreme Court.[23] Nonetheless, the communicating law stayed in place despite obvious indications that it was not achieving its stated goals. Indeed, other aspects of the criminal sanction of sex work were similarly upheld, despite their contradictory nature. In 1992, in *R. v. Downey*,[24] the Supreme Court upheld the law against "living on the avails" in the face of another Charter challenge.[25] The majority opinion was that the law was needed to "provide some measure of protection for the prostitute," even though it may interfere with sex workers' right to freedom of association and, indeed, as Dale Gibson has noted, even though it is the law itself that renders sex workers vulnerable to exploitation.[26]

Certainly, the debate over how to deal with the sex trade had not been resolved by the 1985 law. The government continued to study the issue over the 1990s, but the polarization between those who sought increased criminal sanction and those who sought more humane approaches prevented any clear mandate from being expressed. The only area during this decade in which the federal government felt comfortable enough to act was youth prostitution, and it did so by introducing stricter laws.[27] These changes only increased the criminalization of certain aspects of the trade; they did not address the issues of rights and violence, nor the neighbourhood complaints, which continued unabated. A parliamentary committee reviewed the communicating law again in late 1990, on the basis of the 1989 study results and in the aftermath of the Supreme Court decision, and recommended further strengthening of criminal sanctions (by allowing fingerprinting and photographing of those charged, for example) in order to make it more effective. This recommendation was rejected by the (still Progressive Conservative) government as failing to address the social concerns about the situation of sex workers, although the government did endorse the committee's recommendation that funding be made available for programs that assisted sex workers in leaving the trade.[28]

The Federal/Provincial/Territorial Working Group on Prostitution was established in 1992 to bring together the two levels of government bureaucracy on the issue and make recommendations for policy change. On the issue of adult sex work, however, the working group was unable to provide clear policy direction, pointing to the polarized positions for and against criminalization and decriminalization.[29] Nonetheless, it was evident to the working group, as it is to many, that the law needed to change. In particular, the working group called attention to studies undertaken in the mid-1990s by the Department of Justice at the behest of the working group that indicated that, since the introduction of the communicating law, sex work had become "more tense." The working group also noted the alarming statistics on violence against sex workers since that time, but it could not determine whether there was a "causal link between enforcement and prostitutes' deaths."[30] On the other hand, the studies did show that the communicating law had not made things safer or better for people who work in the trade. The working group felt that the need to address both the concerns of residents and the issue of violence against sex workers would best be addressed through moving the trade indoors and giving municipalities the option to allow no more than one or two sex workers to operate out of a single residence. But the working group was not willing to recommend full decriminalization of prostitution, in part because of the "mixed response" from respondents and "the lack of effective models" and, in part, for fear of attracting migrant sex workers and appearing to condone the trade.[31] But, as John Lowman says, this position is hypocritical in that local governments have been effectively licensing the indoor trade for some time.[32]

Following the working group's report in 1998, however, the issue was not directly addressed by the federal government until the recent and ongoing parliamentary subcommittee review. While individual MPs, MLAs and MPPs, city councillors, and the occasional party committee have brought forward recommendations for partial decriminalization through zoning or other forms of regulation, each recommendation has generated a furor, and no further federal action has been taken. This has left municipalities to cope mostly on their own. Municipal governments in the Maritimes, as elsewhere, have sometimes been stymied with how to come up with solutions that control the street trade while not overstepping their jurisdiction and weighing in on criminal or moral matters. At the same time, a continued sense that sex work is morally unacceptable – either because of sexual values or because of fears over the exploitation of women – continues to pervade the policy responses of local elites. Both sets of concerns position sex workers as incapable of political action. And the policies that result from such positions fail to address the concerns of sex workers and even of residents.

Recent Policy Responses in the Maritimes

In New Brunswick, where the street-level trade is less visible than in Halifax, the debate has focused mainly on pushing the sex trade, even the indoor variety, out of public view because it is considered morally unacceptable. Fredericton, Saint John, and Moncton have all had debates over zoning bylaws and the location of adult entertainment venues indicating that politicians and elites still draw on moralistic responses to the trade rather than practical concerns. Certainly, sex workers or exotic dancers and their concerns do not figure in these debates. The debate over the strip club Chez Cherie in Saint John is an illustrative case. For dancers, Chez Cherie was a relatively good place to work:

> *Interviewer: What do you think of the attempts by Saint John to close down businesses like Chez Cherie?*

> Ahh, that's gonna suck. That's going to really suck. Chez Cherie is really clean, really safe. They do really good checks that I am who I say I am, and that I'm of age, you know. If I say I'm twenty-three, they are going to check to make sure I really am. I think that would really suck if they shut that down. That's the only strip club here in Saint John. And it gets really packed and that's money. It's pretty good. Why would they want to shut it down? There is only one strip club and it's pretty conservative. It's clean and safe ... (Jacqueline, Saint John)

A similar battle was fought in Fredericton over the location of a massage parlour in the downtown core. Even though the downtown is no longer the vibrant hub of activity it once was, some citizens and city councillors found the presence of the parlour objectionable, and it was shut down in 2002.[33] Again, this was one of the few spots that sex workers found to be a good place to work – clean, fairly safe, and private.

The campaign against exotic dancing in Saint John tells us much about the orientation of political elites. Interestingly, Chez Cherie did not generate much public opposition – its location in a mostly non-residential part of the downtown kept it out of public view for the most part – although local business owners and political elites found its presence disturbing. After Chez Cherie was established in 1995, city council tried hard to keep similar establishments from the city. When a court battle to close down Chez Cherie failed, the city passed a bylaw prohibiting adult entertainment other than in prescribed zones. But these zones were never actually set up by council, and any application was to be decided on a case-by-case basis. The then mayor was unequivocal that she would prefer that there not be any strip clubs in Saint John.[34] Indeed, when another strip club opened in 1999 in contravention of the bylaw, the mayor made a publicized visit to the new club's owner to tell him that he was "not welcome here."[35] (A few sitting city councillors, however, had been pilloried some years earlier for visiting a strip club in Ottawa while in that city for business, which made the moral claims of council highly suspect.) Nonetheless, Chez Cherie eventually did close down, in 2004, when J.D. Irving Ltd. bought the block of buildings in which it was housed. The now Irving-owned city block was scheduled for refurbishment as Heritage Place. The new name was indicative of business and council's real concerns, which were about the image of the city, particularly as that block, while still not residential, was now increasingly in the sight of a reinvigorated cruise-ship tourist trade. Indeed, most business neighbours of Chez Cherie applauded its disappearance, since, according to one, its presence "tarnished the whole image of the street." Asked for the right location for such an establishment, she answered: "Maybe the middle of the woods."[36] As Nick Larsen has pointed out, in other cases, aside from gentrification, the other significant class variable that can lead to intensified agitation over the street trade is "the desire of municipal government to ensure that the urban areas most frequented by visitors [are] kept relatively free of street prostitution."[37] This also seems to be the case for the indoor sex trade and exotic dancing in this region.

Concerns about morality and image are also present when tourist sensibilities are unlikely to be offended. When the same council faced a request in 2001 for a strip club to be established just outside the city core in a non-residential, non-tourist business area, the rezoning request was denied partly on the basis that a prominent grocery store was also located there. The grocery store objected to the rezoning on the basis that the store was a "family-oriented business" with "young and impressionable staff" and "mainly women and children" for customers. Other businesses – a car dealership and a business supply shop – similarly opposed the rezoning. Councillors referred to the negative image for the city that such a business would bring, its effect on children, and the moral probity of such an enterprise. The city lawyer had to frequently remind councillors that they could not reject the request on moral grounds, which were outside the purview of city council. The mayor argued that while the zone was technically industrial, it had, in fact, become a family area because of the presence of these other businesses.[38] Evidently, moralism around sexual businesses still exists and will continue to influence how municipalities deal with sex trade businesses. Ironically, though, if indoor locations are not available, the sex trade will naturally move to the street, where clashes with residents will lead to further headaches for the government.

As Halifax experienced a rapid gentrification through the 1990s, more sex workers were pushed over to the Dartmouth side of the Halifax harbour. Disgruntled residents in Halifax had protested the presence of sex work over the decade. As one female resident turned city councillor put it, women felt unsafe walking in their neighbourhood at night for fear of harassment and crime: "Wherever we walked we could feel eyes on us."[39] They turned to police for suggestions about how to deal with the problems and began a Neighbourhood Watch group. The group began collecting johns' licence plate numbers for police, which pressured the trade to move into other areas. Residents in working-class North End Dartmouth then began organizing against the trade. They gathered together to walk the neighbourhood, collect licence plate numbers, and pressure sex workers to move on. As one resident who helped organize the protest put it, "if we [saw] anyone we'd stop where they were." The initial effectiveness of the group dwindled, and it teamed up with Neighbourhood Watch and became part of a reporting system, providing police with information through a hotline. The residents' concerns – the litter, the possible exposure of children to the trade – were typical of those in many Canadian neighbourhoods affected by the trade.

As the same resident stated plainly: "I didn't want it in front of my house ... Children were being propositioned." In part, however, the residents' sense of ire about the issue also reflected their sense of being treated as less important than was more affluent Halifax. The same resident complained: "It wouldn't go on in some other neighbourhoods. They wouldn't stand for it. North End Dartmouth is equally as good as other neighbourhoods."[40]

In response to growing residential concerns in Halifax, in 2000, the Nova Scotia government stepped in to tackle the street trade by introducing new anti-client measures. Targeting clients through remedial measures such as john schools has been a popular method of at least attempting to curtail the trade in some neighbourhoods, as it is evident that simply arresting clients and sex workers under the communicating law is ineffective. Yet, targeting clients only reflects the public's shifting (or spreading) of the moral burden from sex workers to clients, without addressing sex workers' concerns. Indeed, anti-john measures may increase the burden of street workers, whose negotiations with clients may become more complicated:

> I think a lot of people [hate the johns] because, a couple of [clients of] mine, they [members of the general public] tried getting their licence plates 'cause they know what happens now when you get caught with that. A lot of johns are scared to come up to you now. They gotta drive by you six or seven times because they're getting iffy, right? But I just go and I explain myself, you know what I mean, I'm just straight out there. (Kristin, Halifax)

In particular, the local sex worker outreach agency, Stepping Stone, expressed great concern that anti-client measures would lead to speeded-up transactions and less time for sex workers to assess clients and locales for safety. The conviction that male sexual behaviour needs to be curtailed is a common one now in sex trade policy. This move toward punishing men has created common ground between feminists and conservatives on sex-trade issues. Yet, other much more common modes of sexual profligacy, such as extramarital affairs, are not criminal matters. The use of criminal law to shape male behaviour is outmoded at best and raises the question of why it is criminalized only in regard to prostitution. One must suspect that both the women and men expected to be caught in the sex trade are a marginalized group – as opposed to the group that would be caught up in the net of extra-marital affairs. Further, criminal sanction is normally reserved for those activities that have the potential for harm, such as physical violence or dangerous driving or theft. If general masculinist sexual attitudes and behaviour need to be addressed, as they clearly do to some degree, then it can be more effective if it is done outside the strictures of criminal law and not merely confined to the sex trade. The male behaviour that sex workers want to see punished through criminal sanction is the mistreatment of sex workers – just as all violence toward women and sexual minorities should be punished. However, anti-client measures have become popular because they appear to enable police to deal with the nuisance factors of the trade while simultaneously avoiding either condoning the trade (as measures such as zoning are seen to do) or punishing the women who are seen as victims. This latter claim is highly suspect in that it is quite obvious that governments' interest is not in protecting sex workers and that these measures can be harmful for sex workers.

The "johns bill" put forward in Nova Scotia was part of the Progressive Conservative campaign platform in the late 1990s. Whether this promise was a direct response to Dartmouth residents or simply a plank in what some have called a "law and order" platform borrowed from the rising tide of neo-conservative parties is unclear.[41] But both purposes are served through this kind of anti-client measure, as it morally condemns the trade while enabling police to deal with some of the nuisance factors. The Conservatives had certainly made their intentions known while in opposition. Progressive Conservative MLA Murray Scott introduced Resolution 1081 in 1998. This resolution noted the reduction in the number of police officers in Dartmouth's North End and the need for an "adequate police presence" "in an area plagued by drug peddling and prostitution."[42] And in its inaugural throne speech the Conservative government announced: "Adult prostitution is also a scourge on our communities, and this government will immediately make good on its commitment to look for increased penalties for those who seek out prostitutes."[43] When the Conservatives came to power, they introduced changes (in 2000) to the Motor Vehicles Act that would allow the seizure of any vehicle used in a prostitution-related offence.[44] The bill itself was borrowed from a similar law passed earlier in Manitoba. The Nova Scotia minister of justice, on introducing the new bill for second reading, stated: "We know that there are some areas of this province where prostitution is seriously damaging communities. Some people have referred to prostitution as a victimless crime. That is simply not the case. The victims are the people in our communities who had to live with this problem."[45] The women involved in the trade came up in third place.

Debate over the effects of the johns bill stalled its passage in the House as members argued over the downloading of responsibilities on municipalities, the constitutionality of the bill, and the appropriateness of addressing the sex trade through punitive rather than social measures. Only once was the problem of violence against sex workers mentioned – by the New Democratic MLA from Halifax who had worked in legal aid. Certainly the overriding tone of the governing party was that sex workers' concerns should not be considered legitimate issues. One Conservative member, in response to criticism of the failure to address social issues, asked derisively: "Is the honourable member ... suggesting that we should have a similar policy to what the NDP did in BC, where they took money from the Department of Community Services and bought cellular telephones for the prostitutes so that if they got in trouble with their johns, then they could call for help?"[46] The cell phone project had been an innovative attempt to reduce the risk of violence against sex workers in the face of a massive number of disappeared sex workers in that province. The debate over how to deal with sex work in policy remained as divisive as ever, and the government eventually pulled the johns bill from consideration before the legislature.

While the death of the johns bill left Nova Scotia without any way to address the ongoing concerns of residents, other approaches were also rejected. One MLA's suggestion of zoning was quickly denounced in the legislature as well as by women's organizations such as the Nova Scotia Status of Women. One member of government, when asked about other possible responses, such as decriminalization, replied:

> If [the Motor Vehicles Act] is not the answer, then find another policy, something that reduces the demand. If you reduce the demand then people cannot make a living doing this trade and we have a much better chance of diverting them into what we would consider mainstream society ... Unless I have a very articulate group of prostitutes come to me and say we like this kind of work, I wouldn't try to support [decriminalization or legalization]. I find it very amusing that it is two groups of people [who support decriminalization]: men, who for whatever reason think that decriminalization is the answer, and women, who don't want to see the prostitutes oppressed or criminalized. But making their activity legal does not seem to give them a good life, necessarily. I am less interested in whether or not their activity is criminal ... But is it a good quality of life for them? ... That's what I would be more inclined to focus on. (Nova Scotia MLA)

Close examination of this rationale reveals a number of weaknesses, most importantly that, once again, sex workers are not considered rational political agents. One basis given for dismissing the possibility of decriminalization is the argument that a group of "articulate" sex workers has to prove that they like the work before it can be decriminalized. Yet, the opposite does not provide a sufficient rationale for criminalization: should all those forms of work and activity where workers can not come forward and prove that they like it be criminalized? Low-paid service-sector jobs would be hard pressed to remain out of the Criminal Code. Most importantly, the underlying assumption here is that sex workers by definition are unable to come forward and speak on their own behalf or be able to achieve a "good life" unless others make policy for them. Further, while the claims that activities should promote the good life and should curb disregard for others in sexual matters are admirable, the absence of such activities does not provide the grounds for criminal punishment. Rather, as with most other occupations and activities, the potential for harm is minimized and the potential for a "good life" is maximized through such measures as work safety and minimum-wage legislation, collective bargaining, and freedom to organize. On the other hand, one could argue that criminalizing the trade almost certainly ensures that women and men in the trade will not have a "good life."

The same speaker goes on to argue that "old attitudes" in the province would make a radical change such as decriminalization difficult if not impossible. However, despite the Maritimes' reputation for moral and political conservatism, there is growing evidence that this is less the case than previously thought.[47] Halifax-Dartmouth is certainly a booming urban centre, with an increasingly diverse population. Saint John, the second largest city in the region, is also becoming increasingly urbane. Witness the annual hosting of gay pride parades in that conservative, Catholic city. The central concerns of residents, in the Maritimes as elsewhere, are the nuisances of the street trade; indeed, some have expressed indifference to the trade itself as long as it takes place somewhere else. As one long-time Dartmouth resident expressed it, legalization or decriminalization was fine as long as it was not in her neighbourhood and not near children.[48] When one Nova Scotia MLA, who also taught urban planning, was quoted in the *Chronicle Herald* as supporting a zoning approach to the trade, he did not find a negative reaction among his constituents, despite criticism by the media and fellow politicians:

> When I was running for the election in 1999, [the paper] ran an article saying, "We wonder if the views on prostitution will cause problems for constituents in Chebucto?" On the day the article appeared, I was canvassing. One person, the only person who raised this issue in the whole of the campaign, was a woman who brought it up at the door. Her husband was a police officer and she agreed completely. And that was the only time it showed up. What you often get in politics are politicians who are nervous. They are often behind where public opinion has actually moved. I don't think the Nova Scotian population would react negatively to that. I think they wouldn't like it if the government set themselves up as benefit[ing from] prostitution like with gambling ... turning, effectively, the government into a pimp. (MLA Howard Epstein, Halifax)

As this MLA goes on to explain, any government benefit can be prevented through careful cost-recovery-only approaches to regulating the trade. However, a number of politicians who privately expressed openness to decriminalization or legalization felt that public opposition and moral approbation prevented them from supporting such ideas openly. But it is not at all plain that the public is completely opposed to decriminalization. Several groups in the Maritimes and across Canada have expressed support for decriminalization (indeed, it is part of the official NDP platform and that of the National Action Committee on the Status of Women). Some countries, such as the Netherlands, have moved toward decriminalization despite the moral disagreement of most of their citizens.

One civil servant who worked on sex work issues for some years and sat on the working group may have put her finger on the issue:

> Where are the votes in [supporting decriminalization]? ... I think [politicians] feel you can only antagonize people [by taking up the issue]. I mean, who, where is the group that really is vocally supporting legalization? Who are they? ... But if you ask people, "How do you feel about it?" a lot of people say, "Well, yeah, I think that sounds like a good thing. Nobody's being hurt, it sounds okay." But ... if you come in and say, "Well, that's my platform," it's just too easy [to punish you]. (Kit Waters, senior policy analyst, Nova Scotia Department of Justice, Halifax)

Politicians in Canada are unlikely to act until they sense there is public support for decriminalization, but public attitudes are rarely unequivocal or unchanging. Public attitudes are the result of influence, education, and awareness-raising. For example, public education and awareness campaigns have been behind recent major policy shifts such as the anti-smoking policies and drunk driving laws. A campaign in support of sex workers' rights by feminists and other social activists could help make decriminalization a possibility. This campaign must, most importantly, recognize that sex workers can and should be the central designers of any policy governing sex work. Indeed, in speaking with sex workers and residents in the Maritimes, it is clear that both parties are able to compromise and work toward solutions that serve both their interests.

Sharing the Urban Space: Residents and Sex Workers on the Street

The sex workers we spoke with, rather than being unaware of or uninterested in residents' concerns, showed a good deal of willingness to take those concerns into consideration when working. Residents, similarly, are not as uniformly opposed to sex work as it would appear at first glance. By listening to sex workers' and residents' points of view, and taking them seriously, we can see that there is much more room for movement on how to deal with the issues of the sex trade than politicians would have us believe:

I'm wondering ... Well, I'm on V Street, that's over some; but the other girls are on the other streets, right? And I don't know, sometimes when I'm sitting there, I'm just wondering – 'cause you see a neighbour looking out the window or something – I'm wondering what's going through their head. Like, I wonder if you interviewed them, just people that live on the street that the girls are working on, what they have to say. I don't know. (Violet, Saint John)

[This local business owner] has never called the cops on me; he's only yelled at me once. And after he was done yelling at me – I let him yell – I said, "Excuse me, I didn't know and I'm very sorry. I will not work here no more. I respect you." That killed him. (Megan, Halifax)

Despite some anger toward residents and frustration with their attitudes, sex workers are not entirely unsympathetic or cynical. It is important to remember that sex workers are also residents of a community and they are often parents. As such, many feel there is a need for some kind of communication and mutual accommodation. For example, most of the sex workers we spoke with agree with residents that the trade should take place where children would not be exposed to it, and a surprising number talked about how they understood residents' concerns. Indeed, there are common interests among sex workers and residents, such as the respectful treatment of women and sexual or racial minorities and the reduction of violence.[49] For example, many sex workers complained of being harassed by clients when they were not on the job – walking down the street with family, in malls, in grocery stores. Older sex workers, like residents, have also expressed their concern about the numbers of girls that appear too young to be working in the trade. Sex workers would agree that young girls working on the street serves neither sex workers' nor residents' interests. As part of this accommodation with residents, and in the interest of their own safety, many sex workers talked about the need to have a place where they could work safely without bothering anyone. And their attitudes toward residents were often tempered.

A number had had run-ins with residents, but they see this as a failure of residents to understand who sex workers really are:

I know the public thinks the prostitutes are this and that and everything, but not everyone is like that in their heads ... I just go out there and I'm not out there to rip anyone off. I'm out there to make money, and that's all I'm out there for, do you know what I mean? I'm kind to every guy I've ever been out there with, like, a john, or a date, or whatever ... But I think it's ... I know the public hate prostitutes, they hate me out there on the stroll. 'Cause they're coming out of their houses and yelling that they're getting "sick of you hookers coming up and down the road." And I'm thinking, "Oh my God." (Kristin, Halifax)

Yet, even those who feel badly treated by residents have some understanding of their concerns:

Well, residentials, like I say, you're labelled and they find it repulsive. You know, they mumble under their breath, and sometimes they'll come out and shoo you and tell you they're calling the cops, right? So I think that I've become a hindrance, which is true you know. If I put the shoe on the other foot, I don't think I'd want them working around my home. Ya know ... couldn't [there] be another [solution]? ... You see it on TV a lot too. You know: a legal part, a legal area to do your strolls. (Angela, Halifax)

Like I said, there's good and bad [people] but, I don't know, I don't have [faith in the residents]. And I don't because if you get in court they treat you like a piece of shit. They treat you like you're a nobody, right, like you're just, oh just an old prostitute, like, standing on a street corner ... Like you're a nobody. That's not a good feeling. (Lydia, Halifax)

But I didn't bother no one on the streets I worked at. No one had a problem with me. There was other people in Dartmouth, they had a petition going around ... I can understand that, because if they were up in my area doing that right now, I would be out there tearing their asses off myself, instead of the [residential] association. You don't go to someone's home in a residential area, throw your used condoms in their driveways, or in someone's lawn, or give a blow job to someone on the side of the street, a public street where kids are, that's just the girls that don't know no better, and they don't give a damn. People like them girls make it bad for all the other working girls. I mean, there's places and there's times, and when there are people with their own homes, and stuff, you don't go to someone's yard or something, or a place where there's kids at, or schoolyard, leave condoms and stuff like that, or a churchyard. I mean, go to an open field or something at night time or something, or train tracks, not where someone's kids are going to go by or something. (Denise, Halifax)

Indeed, a number of the sex workers we spoke with have tried to modify their working practices to avoid creating the kinds of problems residents worry about:

I basically don't go into residential areas ... I stay right here. I mean, there are houses but there's more businesses than there is residents.

Interviewer: And they don't mess with you generally?
No. They look at me as, well, especially at night, nobody's going to break into my place if she's standing there. All they ask is just don't stand in front of my business during business hours ... Dartmouth, I never work Dartmouth though. Escort service, yeah, but not on the street. No, just basically there's nobody over there. It's all residential. (Samantha, Halifax)

Realistically, however, as one sex worker remarked, while the public needs to educate itself about sex workers and while some sex workers may be trying to not cause problems, both their efforts may be hampered by addictions:

They need to know why a person gets in the life. They need to know what happens in that lifestyle. Like there are trials and tribulations [that] someone like me goes through. They have to know about police, and how they see us as criminals. See, they do need to know, but yet we can always keep it separate from their children. Like the children that go to school? You should never be out when they're out. I mean ... it used to break my heart, 'cause I'd say, that would be my daughter seeing me, or that would be my son seeing me – and I wouldn't want them to see me like this. So you're careful, but you're not careful. When you smoke crack cocaine you're careful, but you're not careful. You're careful who you go with, but you really don't care who sees ya. (Katrina, Halifax)

Not everyone was sanguine about the possibilities for rapprochement between non-sex workers and sex workers:

They need to know ... Well, the women need to know that half their husbands are up there. That's the first thing. They're married, married and went up there. Too many people are too scared to come out of the closet ... You got to educate them. I don't know, [no matter] how much you try to educate them all throughout life, you know, hookers and prostitutes have been looked down upon and maybe that's the way it'll be. I don't think there'll ever be a compromise between civilization and the hookers and prostitutes. (Travis, Halifax)

Nonetheless, some respondents we spoke with opened the possibility of engagement with community organizations and of working out a solution that serves both the communities' and sex workers' needs:

I still think there should be a red zone everywhere in Canada ... They would have control over diseases. They would have control for testing, automatic testing. We would be out of debt within the first thirty days of being decriminalized. You know, they are not even looking at the right

stuff. We are just considered disease-carrying, bottom of the barrel, whatever they want to call us: slugs, whores, whatever.
Interviewer: What do you think needs to change about people's attitudes to enable something like that to happen?
I think they need to get to know you. I would like to see some sort of a forum set up where the community can come out and voice their concerns along with us. Maybe we could work something out, pick an area where there's no houses. That's pretty hard around here, but where some of the girls are now it's pretty good. Because it's all garages, you know, it's not hurting anybody.
Interviewer: Yeah, there's no kids around, there's no needles being dropped in schoolyards ...
Exactly. And they're just making it hard. There should just be a house set up somewhere ... A house where there is rooms upstairs where it is monitored by the government. That to me would be cool. (Scott, Halifax)

Interviewer: How do you think the public views prostitution?
They probably think it's a disgrace. They think they should be all condemned, and every escort service should be [torn] down and everything, [that] there shouldn't be something like that around here. And actually when I'm on the strolls some nights and they're coming out of their houses and they're saying, "We're calling the cops on ya," I'm thinking, yeah, they just think that we shouldn't be around here and all that stuff, right? And I'm thinking, you gotta do what you gotta do for your money, and I'm gonna do what I'm gonna do for mine. You know, it's not like I'm standing in front of your house and I'm screaming at every car. I don't do that, I walk, and I walk, and when I get tired, I'll go stand at bus stops. Sometimes I won't go out; and if there are kids around, I ain't going to be there. Because I don't have kids, but I have a lot of respect for kids. I can't do that.

Actually, too bad there couldn't be something legal, like a house for them; and just do it inside, like an in-service, just for them and nobody else around. They won't bug anybody else on the street or when the neighbours complain ... It would be a lot better and a lot safer too; and you're home and you're not bugging all these other people. (Kristin, Halifax)

Indeed, sex workers have often tried to work indoors in order to avoid the problems of working on neighbourhood streets. Several of the sex workers we interviewed, and the vast majority of sex workers across Canada, choose indoor work (massage, escort, strip) as both safer and potentially better paying than street work. But indoor work, unless carefully conducted, can still run afoul of the law and, as noted earlier, means trading off independence for security. Further, work such as out-call escort, while keeping the trade out of public view, can sometimes be as dangerous as street work. As long as the trade remains criminalized, solutions that focus on creating a safe space and good working conditions for sex workers remain difficult to enact.

Many of the residents who complain or organize against the trade are women who have real concerns about neighbourhood safety but who also have some empathy with women on the streets who may be dealing with poverty or abuse or who may be unfairly treated by men. As one resident said, "They don't have money, maybe they are on drugs or maybe they have dependants. Low self-esteem is in there too. They need more programs, more schools."[50] Calls to police by these residents may be just as much about reporting violence against a sex worker as complaining about noise. On this front, shared concerns over safety could, if the trade were decriminalized, be addressed through increased policing in response to sex workers' complaints and campaigns against violence against all women and minorities, including sex workers.

As noted above, discussions with residents may also reveal that the problem is not the sex trade per se: issues may involve neighbourhood neglect or problems associated with the drug trade. Sex workers also recognize this:

> But anyway, like I said, you know why I'm here on M Street? 'Cause this is where everybody else is. I'll go, you know, but this is where it is. I don't know if I should go to that liquor store or what [because] you know, I feel that too. I see kids walking up the street, you know? *But I didn't create M Street.* (Joan, Halifax)

Residents in neighbourhoods where the trade takes place often feel left behind by recent developments and ignored by governments. Police seem to be more able to offer immediate attention and solutions (by pushing the trade somewhere else) than are governments, which are slow to respond and often stymied as to how to approach the issue. Local government's addressing the concerns about local issues would go a long way toward relieving some of the tension between sex workers and residents.

Community discussions between residents, police, policy makers, sex workers, and sex worker advocates can be productive and lead to solutions, but this is not always possible; for instance, Dartmouth residents have been resistant to working with outreach agency Stepping Stone to come up with a solution. There are hopeful signs elsewhere, though, when not only sex workers and residents but outreach groups, police, and policy makers have all sat down together. In uptown Saint John in recent years, residents have begun to complain as police sweeps push sex workers out of the traditional zone, which was less predominantly residential, and on to neighbouring streets. Like North End Dartmouth, this particular area of Saint John has felt ignored by local government.[51] One resident complained in the media of loud fights, nudity, vomiting, and needles left in her backyard. While the old trade had involved a few women who were working to pay the rent, in recent years, a blossoming drug problem has created a very different situation. The resident was concerned that the women involved are getting younger and younger: "It's like someone pulled up here eight years ago and dropped off a busload of teenage girls."[52] One resident was willing to sit down with police and outreach workers to try to come up with solutions that would not expose the women to further danger or disempowerment, and she allowed women to continue working outside her house, which was downtown, if they were not causing any problems, even though the attendant problems of noise, violence, and littering were causing her to think about leaving the house she loved. As a woman who had dealt with addictions issues in her own family and who was distressed by the amount of violence she was seeing against the sex workers in the streets, she was able to balance her annoyance with empathy. The more she talked with outreach workers and police, the more she was able to achieve this balance. As she explained with a laugh,

> I'm not the cold-hearted person that went to the first Sex-Trade Committee meeting [or, as it was first called,] "Anti-Prostitution Task Force," how socially unacceptable was that? So, it really has hit home and it has become personal on a level for me whereby I'm not angry that there's prostitutes out on my street anymore, I'm angry that we as a society and more so as a municipal, provincial, and federal government haven't done something that can help them, that can reach out. And I see this girl [one of the sex workers on her street battling an addiction] trying to help herself and there's nothing there for her.[53]

She too had come to perceive the problem as many sex workers in that particular area see it: a lack of services contributing to a crisis around addictions – not the sex trade itself. The solutions put forward by the committee of which she was a part included practical steps such as implementing a methadone maintenance program and providing sharps disposal units throughout town for used needles, educating city councillors on neighbourhood issues, and campaigning for respect for sex workers while protecting them from violence. Once again, however, without decriminalization, it remains difficult to find practical policy solutions to both residents' and sex workers' concerns.

Feminists and the Decriminalization of Sex Work
At a national level, several important groups as well as political parties have supported decriminalization, although they have not necessarily made it a

campaign. And yet it is clear that, for any breakthrough in the policy dilemmas faced by political elites, there needs to be a concerted effort to articulate a pro-decriminalization position that advocates sex workers' involvement and sex workers' rights as the most practical and just way out of these policy dilemmas. Feminists have been equivocal on the issue of sex work, fearing that any move toward rationalizing policy could be interpreted as their condoning the trade.[54] The feminist failure to come up with a more robust position on the sex trade, beyond supporting the women but not the institution, has translated into not supporting either and instead supporting more conservative positions. As Janice Dicken McGinnis has pointed out, feminist arguments were drawn on by the Supreme Court in both its 1990 and 1992 decisions upholding the law,[55] decisions that undermined sex workers' rights and continued to put them in danger. Women's Legal Education and Action Fund (LEAF) representatives failed to intervene on behalf of sex workers because "no matter what these women say about themselves, they are all 'tortured, drug-addicted, extremely unhappy, abused people.'"[56] The National Action Committee on the Status of Women's endorsement of decriminalization in the 1980s was undermined by a lack of support for sex workers' rights. Many members were uncomfortable with supporting sex work as a career, and further campaigning on this issue was hampered by this reluctance.[57] As Shaver has suggested, though, those characteristics of sex work that some feminists find so objectionable are not, in fact, characteristics of sex work per se but of the poor conditions under which sex work takes place. That is, under the right conditions, sex work is not necessarily violent or degrading, nor is it necessarily any more impersonal than are most sexual relations.[58] The recognition of sex work as a job and even a career is an important part of giving sex workers respect, recognizing their personhood, thereby helping to address an important source of exploitation and harm within that job – being seen as lesser than everyone else. As Deborah Brock maintains, the feminist movement needs to "relinquish our attempts to eliminate the sex trade and set ourselves to improving conditions for women within it, in order that prostitutes gain more control over their working conditions. This will not eliminate the sex trade, but it will transform it."[59]

The mainstream feminist position remains an abolitionist one that seeks to criminalize the so-called exploiters of sex workers – pimps and, now increasingly, clients and traffickers – while leaving sex workers – seen as victims of economic and social circumstances – free of criminal sanction. The desire to punish the male sexual behaviour of clients creates a huge problem for feminist goals. Law in a liberal system cannot – overtly at least – punish men for what women are not punished for. If the goal is to punish male behaviour, female sex workers must also be punished – despite protestations by feminists that punishing women is unfair. By acquiescing in the argument that men should be punished for this behaviour, many feminist men and women have given social conservatives yet more credibility for maintaining a law that unfairly punishes sex workers. As McGinnis has argued, "Feminist emphasis on pimping and johns ... has led us into focussing on controlling men, rather than on freeing women, which is surely our mandate."[60] This collusion with the right also opens the door to support for other potentially socially conservative goals such as denying gay rights or promoting chastity to deal with unwanted pregnancies – as opposed to freedom to choose. The coming together of social conservatives and (some) feminists in an abolitionist stance on sex-trade issues is creating dangerous policy precedents elsewhere in the world.[61]

New fears over trafficking in women have strengthened this abolitionist position.[62] However, anti-trafficking measures, such as anti-pimping laws, continue to single out sex workers and to isolate them. Anti-procuring or pimping laws, such as section 212 of the Criminal Code, cast a broad net and potentially criminalize family and friends of sex workers for "living on the avails." Such laws, according to Sylvia Davis and Martha Shaffer, "serve only to isolate prostitutes from family and friends and in fact push [them] into unsavoury relationships rather than the reverse."[63] They also criminalize potentially helpful activities such as spotting [watching the back of a sex worker] or providing an indoor space to work.[64] Indeed, the more that prostitution-related activities such as procuring and keeping a bawdy house are criminalized, the more space is created for the actual involvement of pimps or organized crime in order to enable these activities to take place.[65] The criminalization of these activities pushes the trade further underground, making sex workers more vulnerable to exploitation and unwilling or unable to avail themselves of police protection. The criminalization of clients in Sweden, for example, has not resulted in a reduction of the trade but in the creation of a more underground trade. Police have complained that clients are now unwilling to testify against exploiters of sex workers, since they themselves risk arrest, which is hampering efforts to curtail exploitation.[66] Only policies that empower sex workers send the message to all men who would take advantage of them that sex workers, and all women and marginalized sexual identities, are to be treated with respect.

Many sex worker organizations and researchers, therefore, have called for full decriminalization – the removal of all sex-work-related activities, including communicating, procuring, and bawdy house offences, from the Criminal Code – as the only way to end the exploitation and marginalization of sex workers.[67] In fact, once narrowed down to the actual offence involved, all the activities that are of concern under current sex trade laws are already covered under general laws such as extortion, kidnapping, and assault.[68] The sex trade laws, however, contribute to discrimination against sex workers and violation of their right to equality, according to legal analysts.[69]

They also contribute to increased violence, exploitation, stigmatization, and health risks.[70]

As McGinnis has suggested, the real failure of feminist worthies has been their refusal to listen to sex workers. That is, they have refused to take their claims seriously. Feminists and all those who claim to be protecting sex workers need to acknowledge that this desire to protect is really a desire to protect one's own privilege and power. Jo Doezema's analysis of feminists' "wounded attachment" to the "injured bodies" of sex workers recognizes that this attachment is about advancing feminist interests in politics – that is, gaining political power – by making claims about sex workers, not from sex workers themselves.[71] But these power moves depend entirely on sex workers' remaining silenced and obedient subjects of interpretation, feminist or otherwise. While it is not only feminists who make these power moves by using the symbolic Prostitute as the basis of their claims, and it is not feminists who control sex work policy, it is ethically incumbent upon feminists – whose job it is to agitate on behalf of all women – to recognize how self-serving feminist arguments are being used to undermine sex workers' rights and to seek to right this wrong not by speaking on behalf of sex workers but by listening to and supporting them. If we want to have a sensible policy that protects sex workers' rights, then, as McGinnis says, "the worthies in short are going to have to start taking the words of the whores seriously."[72]

Decriminalization, Legalization, and Regulation: "It's Time the Laws Change"

> I don't know, society right now, to me, prostitutes – we fit in the category with kids in school and senior citizens. They're trying to take all the kids from the school, and they're charging senior citizen taxpayers, pay tax all their life, now they're charging them, they can't have homes or nothing, they take that from them and they're paying to be looked after, after they looked after everyone all their life. And prostitutes, we don't have no ... life. We can't even get nothing to have open or closed, and Stepping Stone is great for us. We have that, and we know it. Society is just society, no matter what they do, if they legalize it, and if they legalize it, then the government is still getting us. They still pay us and write it off, and then they take our money that they pay us! (Denise, Halifax)

> There's women out there that don't have an education and stuff, that are supporting their kids and stuff. I think they should really legalize it. Not that I'm saying that it's okay, because you know, when you have husbands and stuff like that ... But they should legalize it so that people aren't going

to jail [and] provide help ... They'd be, like, working at Tim Hortons, or whatever. You have your rights as an employee. (Jill, Saint John)

Well, actually, in a way, if they were to take it out of the Criminal Code, it would probably be more dangerous out there, 'cause then the people would probably think, okay, well, there's no cops around, we're allowed to do this, and then, you know ...
Interviewer: If there was a safe area, safe house?
A safe house, or something, with people around that works there or something like that. Yeah, and telephones, and ...
Interviewer: So you wouldn't have to be out there in the cold ... Somebody to screen the clients.
Something like that. If they legalize it, and get a house, and then everybody goes there, and they can pick their girls, 'cause there's ... I mean, in a way, if you really look at it, it's nothing wrong. It's just sex, and you're paying for it. It's all natural. (Candace, Saint John)

I think they should get the people off the streets and let them leave the services alone. If it's in the phone book or it's a business card or it's in the newspaper, leave it alone. If they're out there on the streets, grab them and point them in the right direction. Don't charge them. Say, "Listen, your life is in danger, go to this place." Don't charge them for prostitution ... 'cause they're going to have that on their records for the rest of their lives. Prostitution is a big deal when you're going to apply to jobs and you've got a criminal record that says prostitution. If it's in the phone book, why can't it be legal? The phone book is public, the paper is public, flyers are public, and business cards are public. If they can make business cards for a car shop, what about escort service? Why not? ... Yeah, 'cause it goes with the social system, the social services as well. If it's a legal job, what can they do?

If you're bringing in $1,000 a night, you're off welfare and you're off their back. Your kids got a babysitter; your kids got food; your kids got clothes, and your kids got love. Leave them alone ... I mean if you're taking care of your family and this is the way it is ... I mean prostitution has been out [in this area] for thirty some years, if not longer. It's going to stay around the rest of your life ... It's just like the pot issue. It's a big issue with me, you know ... It's the new century, the new millennium. It's time the laws change.
Interviewer: Is there anything you'd want to say to the public given the chance?
Leave the services alone. Go after the diddlers and the real trouble, leave the services alone. There's ... no harm, you know what I mean? (Patricia, Saint John)

Interviewer: Do you think it would be safer on the inside rather than on the street?
Oh yes, most definitely, if I had the money or the guts to do it, it would probably be really great, you know, so. Because even the men out there, they don't like driving around in their cars either you know, they would rather just go someplace and, you know, see somebody and get it done and over with. (Tabitha, Saint John)

I'll tell you something, it does bother me. I never told too many people, I don't think it should be legalized because, you know what, we're doing this but I always think to myself, how many friggin' wives are we hurting? But then you have these men and they come to ya and they'll say, I wouldn't do it on my wife if she'd blow me. Like they want, a lot of them want blow jobs. I don't really know why that is, they don't really want the sex. They want the blow jobs. If my wife would do it I wouldn't be up here. And sometimes I think to myself when I'm getting in these cars with these men, I'm thinking, I feel bad for the poor wives, like, this man is giving me money and I'm blowing him and he's weird and he belongs to someone else. That's how I feel, I don't know, I really don't know if it should be legalized or not. I can't, I can't really say, I just don't know. (Brianna, Saint John)

So ... when it comes to decriminalization, all it's going to do is ... it is just going to change the power over to some other type of management. That's how I see it.
Interviewer: Oh, it would, it would give the power to the state, there's no question. In other words, if you think of comparable situations like, say, alcohol – that's highly regulated and controlled by the government, as well as the sale of lotteries, both of which used to be criminal activities.
No, the problem with that is, is that, that's all abused. Anything is. Alcohol is abused. Wherever the government controls it, it's abused. That's how they make the money.
Interviewer: But I'm thinking of in terms of safety, for example, if it were decriminalized and regulated, if there was a space, would this work in your opinion for male prostitutes?
Okay, I don't see it in Canada. Our major [problem] for Canada – to do lots of changes for prostitution and marijuana, we would have to not be neighbours with the States ... Because their views on so many things hurt what could help us. Europe is a totally different story, because they're not neighbours with the States. That's my view personally. (David, Halifax)

While the vast majority of our respondents wanted some kind of decriminalization, there was – as there is among the wider public – disagreement and confusion about what exactly decriminalization would mean.

There was also debate among sex workers as to the feasibility of decriminalization, given both domestic and international politics. As the last speaker noted, presciently in turns out, sex-trade policy is no longer simply a national affair. New American anti-trafficking laws involve condemning and punishing countries that fail to live up to the anti-prostitution agenda of the Bush administration.[73] Future considerations for Canada include migrant sex work, which – although we would argue that decriminalization helps ensure migrant sex workers' rights – has led the Federal/Provincial/Territorial Working Group on Prostitution to recommend against decriminalization.[74] Overall, there continues to be a great deal of discomfort and confusion about how, after decriminalization, the trade would be dealt with. Some worry about how residents' concerns could then be addressed. Others are very uncomfortable with treating the sex trade, particularly the survival sex trade, as just another business. This discomfort is expressed by sex workers also. We need to think about how we can make the sex trade safe for everyone. For this, we need to move beyond just passive support for decriminalization and to more active lobbying for sex workers' rights, support for sex worker organizations, and sex-worker-driven policy.

As Dutch analysts have observed, the ability of sex workers to organize and represent their interests may be key to the effectiveness of workplace standards under a decriminalized system. But sex workers in Canada have had little chance to develop a strong organizational base, such as the powerful unions that represent other types of workers. According to Marieke van Doorninck, if a decriminalized system is to work, the government must also take some responsibility for encouraging self-organization for emancipation among sex workers.[75] Canadian researchers and advocates have made the same argument for the need to support sex workers' rights groups and their involvement in policy design as a key factor in making decriminalization work.[76] As Davis and Shaffer have recognized, the Canadian government will have to move beyond providing the occasional health funding to sex workers' organizations, to providing support for political organizing and lobbying as well as self-directed research and publishing.[77] The ability of sex workers to participate fully in the political process is part of the solution to the problem of stigma – many marginalized groups report a stronger sense of self-esteem and wellness once they become involved in making positive social and political change. Organizing among sex workers, as with any highly diverse group, will not be automatic or easy. Escort workers will have different issues and identities than will street workers, and issues of racism and classism will need to be addressed among workers, as they must be in any organization. The issues of migrant sex workers will present challenges to those domestic workers who view migrant workers as competition. However, building a community among sex workers is part of the process, and, certainly, organizations such as Montreal's sex-worker-run

Stella have been able to bring sex work communities together quite successfully. Good policy will require addressing the divisions among sex workers in the policy design itself.

Further, simple legal change is not enough – although it is an important piece of the puzzle. A much wider campaign for respect for sex workers – for their right to choose this work or not, their right to organize and to participate in the wider social and political community – is paramount. Police, in particular, who continue to use bylaws and other techniques to crack down on sex work (for example, in those places where escort work is ostensibly licensed) will need to be trained to view sex work as legitimate work.[78] As Bruckert, Parent, and Robitaille have remarked, "Decriminalization alone does not ensure a safe working space for the women, nor does it guarantee the protection of their rights as workers. Other steps must therefore be taken in order to encourage the recognition of sex work and erotic dance as legitimate forms of labour rather than as deviance or exploitation."[79] Addressing stigma will require a number of measures, including public education and, particularly, media education.[80] One reporter at the *Toronto Sun* summed it up in reporting on the debate over decriminalization: "Respect. It is what [sex workers] all seem to want more than mere legal status."[81]

Policies and campaigns for policy changes need to be designed with respect for all sex workers in mind and, most importantly, with sex workers at the table. The negotiations over balancing the amount of intervention by the state and the need to protect workers from exploitation will be fraught with difficulties but not impossible. As in many workplaces, there would have to be some combination of self-regulation, government regulation or oversight, and worker or union pressure to set and maintain workplace standards. What we know is that when regulation takes place in the absence of sex workers and without their interests in mind, the system fails to protect their rights. Indoor work, for example, is already being licensed and regulated by some municipalities under the guise of adult entertainment. However, as Lewis and Maticka-Tyndale have noted in their study of the licensed trade in Windsor, Ontario, licences tend to work in favour of control rather than of the protection of workers' rights.[82] Bruckert, Parent, and Robitaille's research in Montreal and Toronto reveals similar problems.[83] In Europe, the licensing system has tended to leave behind marginalized workers, such as migrants and those with addictions.[84] Licensing schemes in parts of Australia contributed to the development of an illegal and underground trade by making it difficult for small, independent operators to be licensed.[85] As in Australia, licensing fees for massage parlours in Toronto are high, making it difficult for most sex workers to be owners of such parlours and, therefore, in control of their work environment.[86] Other analysts concur that a decriminalized system that simply leaves policy design in the hands of municipalities will result in regulatory schemes that in effect end up reintroducing discriminatory policies against sex workers by using general nuisance laws or other bylaws to attempt to push sex workers out of the municipality.[87]

It is sex worker organizations that have come up with the best solutions for protecting even the most marginalized. Germany's sex workers' movement has initiated proposals that ensure that all workers in the trade, regardless of citizenship or illegal drug use, have access to services and that the wider problem of racism that undermines the rights of many marginalized sex workers, particularly migrants, is addressed.[88] The moral of the lesson, according to these analysts, is that the participation of sex worker organizations is essential in developing just policy. Municipalities, their police forces, and residents, also need to be part of policy design, but this will first require a campaign for tolerance and respect so that these groups recognize their common interests with sex workers. According to Davis and Shaffer, "For decriminalization to succeed, prostitutes' rights groups and municipalities must work together to set up systems which both sides can live with."[89]

There is yet another practical reason for sex-worker-driven policy design. A certain amount of independence in one's work is one of the upsides of sex work, but, as mentioned above, the tighter the regulation, the greater likelihood of an underground trade developing. This, of course, may depend on who is doing the regulating and in whose interests these regulations operate. The more that regulation is placed in the hands of the sex workers, the less likely it is that sex workers will be turned off by the system because of its failure to meet their needs. Many sex workers we spoke with disliked the indoor system because it reintroduced the workplace discipline that they were seeking to avoid in the first place. Indeed, it has been the experience of some jurisdictions in which certain legalized and tightly controlled sectors have been created that the majority of sex workers have chosen to remain in the illegal sector because it provides greater independence and autonomy in regard to working conditions.[90] Sex worker organizations such as the Australia's Scarlet Alliance recommend against creating laws "directed at forcing sex workers to operate in a limited legal framework" but, rather, urge policy makers to respect sex workers' right to choose the form of work that best meets their needs.[91] Any indoor setting for the trade must keep workers' right to independence and control over working conditions first in mind. Sex workers will not all agree on exactly how the work should be organized, and there may be various models that adhere to the principle of sex workers' rights and that can work together. Many of the women we spoke with were enamoured with the idea of a house where they could come and go to work according to their choosing, setting their own conditions and simultaneously maintaining their own anonymity. That is, for some, a strict business model (profit and control in the hands of the owner) is not the ideal model; rather, an atelier of independent owner-operators is preferred. Addressing employee protections and benefits under such freelance arrangements means drawing on some of the creative solutions being discussed in the context of increasingly flexible labour conditions throughout many employment sectors.[92] For some survival sex workers, a safe place may mean the equivalent of a safe injection site, where space is provided for safety purposes but not for profit. Such safe houses are already in place in Sydney, Australia.[93] There will always be a street-based trade, particularly for contacting clients, even with decriminalization and the availability of various sorts of safe spaces for the actual transaction. Again, keeping this trade safe demands respect for survival sex workers and their involvement in designing responses. Above all, policy should focus on maximizing the benefits and attractiveness of certain types of work, such as indoor work, rather than punishing those who work outside certain prescribed forms.

The sex workers we spoke with put forward policy and practice suggestions that addressed many of the problems they raised and emphasized enhancing sex workers' rights and respect for sex workers. That is, to be effective, any policy response must first address the stigmatization of sex work:

> There's a group in the States called COYOTE – Call Off Your Old Tired Ethics. It's like that – women who were prostitutes were [called] whores. It's so weird. I think we should be supportive. Women do this work all over the world, even if it's with their husbands in some form. It's part of being female. I think people should be supportive. If it was legal it would stop a lot of problems that are going on. (Celeste, Halifax)

Recommendations

The recommendations that follow represent a summary, as a follow-up to the arguments presented throughout this book and as the final word for sex workers.

Decriminalization

As mentioned above, decriminalization is by far the number one recommendation put forward by our interviewees. This would involve the removal of all prostitution-related offences from the Criminal Code.[94] Decriminalization would create an opening that could result in the building of safe and fair working environments for sex workers. That is, sex work would be treated as work, which is how most sex workers view it, with scrutiny given to fair labour practices and working conditions, not unlike the scrutiny accorded any other work site. Sex workers could then be treated as workers in their own right. Clients could be treated as clients and, as such, refused services if their behaviour did not comply with expectations or standards of a particular establishment. Decriminalization would enable effective solutions that address, most importantly, violence, but also stigma, policing, and health concerns. As we work toward the goal of decriminalization, we also need to work against shame-based responses to the trade. For example, recent attempts to record clients who are picking up sex workers, and, shockingly, posting these pictures either in the media or on the Internet, are not only gross invasions of sex workers' and clients' privacy, but also they set sex workers up for further violence and stigmatization.[95] Programs targeting clients need to address clients' treatment of sex workers first and foremost. Some workers mentioned zoning as one step toward rational policy, as, at least, a way to keep sex workers out of jail, but nearly all preferred to have some safe indoor space in which to work.

Support for Sex Worker Self-Organization and Involvement in Policy and Programs

Even in the absence of decriminalization, self-organization and support for sex workers is fundamental to avoiding policies that make things worse for sex workers. But establishing and maintaining such organizations is extremely difficult, particularly given the stigma attached to sex work that makes "coming out" especially hard even for those who would like to be part of such an organization.[96] Nonetheless, sex worker self-organization has taken place in many places, including several Canadian cities, and international networks that provide support and information are growing in capacity.[97] Stepping Stone – the sex worker outreach organization in Halifax – is a model that sex workers in New Brunswick look to. While established and run by non-sex workers, the outreach staff is mainly made up of former sex workers, and this kind of outreach organization was greatly appreciated by the program users we spoke with. Stepping Stone, however, like many third-sector operations, consistently faces funding crises and lack of political support. Many sex workers also spoke about the need for more sex worker co-operation, organization, and networking. Despite police and policy-maker skepticism of Maritime sex workers as rights-oriented, Maritime sex workers who had worked in other locations see the sex workers' rights organizations, such as Stella in Montreal, as the best kind of support system for sex workers. As one worker commented, without sex worker self-organization stigma, police become the support system that sex workers turn to, despite all the problems that entails:

> I find the women down here are not really united. There's not really a very large co-operative here. I think it's because a lot of women here feel very ashamed of what they're doing. Like a lot of the time they are coming from small towns where people still have some forty-year-old ideas. They move into a city and then they are working like that and they're working with other women who came from small towns. They still have a very ashamed idea of what they're doing. So they're not really networking

with other women, and that's causing some problems too. They don't have a co-operative that can replace the help of police. (Celeste, Halifax)

Many of the sex workers we spoke with, again including those who experienced the most marginalization, such as street workers in Saint John, were keen to be part of sex worker support networks and to use their experiences to help others:

> *Interviewer: Is there any other people that you can think of that you ran into when you were working, that made your life – that were helpful?*
> Definitely make it, like an awareness thing ... with experienced prostitutes, to share [information with] newcomers and stuff. [That] could definitely be a good thing. This is how you can make a faster buck, that sort of stuff. And I know some people would look at it, well, that's just encouraging people, but I mean, if people are already getting into it, I mean, at least make them safe.
> *Interviewer: So where do you see yourself in like five years?*
> I'm hoping definitely to do counselling [with] teenagers really messing up on drugs, and crime, prostitution, stuff like that. That's really what I want to do, definitely. I can see myself down the road doing that, helping other people ... using my experiences to help others. (Jill, Saint John)

As sex workers recognize, it is the people who have been there themselves who are most effective in designing and running support programs. Similarly, it is the people who are in the trade who should be at the centre of policy making on sex work. Despite the difficulties inherent in sex worker self-organization, creative ways need to be found to support such organization and to enable sex workers to have input in policy and politics.

A Campaign for the Respect of Sex Workers' Rights and against Violence and Stigma

Decriminalization alone will not be sufficient to eradicate or ameliorate stigma. Stigma and negative attitudes are widely seen as the underlying issue of many of the problems faced by sex workers. The public, police, government, and the media need to recognize that sex workers are people, with friends, families, and lives, and that they do not deserve either the inordinate amount of violence that is being visited upon them or the disabling stigma they carry. Along these lines, some of the women and men we spoke with suggested that there be sensitivity training for police, judges, and bureaucrats (such as of Children's Aid or Social Assistance) to familiarize them with sex workers' perspectives and rights. In terms of the eradication of stigma, the media were also seen as in great need of education on how to represent sex workers and sex worker issues. And the public, particularly feminist and human rights organizations, needs to respond when the media present biased depictions of the men and women in the sex trade. Addressing racism and homophobia must, plainly, also be part of this strategy. Aboriginals make up a disproportionate number of murdered sex workers in western Canada, and male sex workers more often face violence by gay-bashers than by clients. Racism and homophobia, rather than sex work per se, serve to make the lives of racialized sex workers and male transgendered workers particularly dangerous.

Ultimately, the human rights of sex workers must be taken up with the wider public in order to provide the political push for changes in the law. The feminist movement needs to focus squarely on harm reduction and respect for sex workers. In the long run, such respect can only help to address the need for wider respect for women generally and for other marginalized groups. Other social justice movements similarly need to take up respect for sex workers and their rights as part of their campaigns when addressing issues for survival sex workers such as poverty, addictions, and homelessness. Again, rights rather than protection need to be the focus of these campaigns.

Clients need to organize in a similar fashion.[98] If clients, from all walks of life, identify openly and initiate anti-stigma campaigns, it would be not as easy for the general public to vilify sex workers. The secrecy of the trade has helped perpetuate some of the stigma visited upon sex workers and has certainly escalated the levels of violence they experience. Encouraging those who patronize sex workers to name and eradicate stigma would go a long way toward making life both easier and less violent for the sex worker.

Provision of Social Supports and Real Options for Marginalized Persons with Addictions

> If we had a free narcotics program like they have in Britain and if we increased welfare, I think that would put an end to a lot of women working [in the sex trade]. Because suddenly there wouldn't be a need for supporting addiction, and people would have enough money to take care of their kids. (Celeste, Halifax)

Many of our interviewees identified the kinds of essential services they believe need to be provided or improved. Several indicated a need to raise rates of social assistance and minimum wages – whether this led to people leaving sex work or not. Raising these rates could go a long way toward providing a living wage for those sex workers receiving assistance and could enable them to have more choice of when and whether they work. Broadening the scope of social assistance was also considered central. Some mentioned that there should be better access to social assistance for those under nineteen years of age and that a person "shouldn't have to be a junkie to get help" (David, Halifax). Better conditions of work and wages in marginalized and gendered sectors, such as service work, are also an obvious need, according to respondents. Indeed, as Wendy Chapkis writes, "sex workers, like all workers performing low-status work, would find their bargaining power enhanced by greater employment opportunities."[99] That is, better options for the marginalized and poor enhance sex workers' power within the trade and their ability to leave it if they wish. However, in order to be truly effective for sex workers, anti-poverty and service provision measures must go hand in hand with support for sex workers' rights, not act as a substitute for such rights.

Other services sex workers mentioned included housing, particularly in Saint John, where this proved to be a major issue for women. Second-stage housing for people leaving correctional facilities or for addicts requiring long-term treatment services were also mentioned. Others had suggestions for treating addictions, in particular, that there be specific programs and recovery homes for women, including sex workers. Several mentioned decriminalization of drugs and distribution of drugs.[100] If drug use were considered a health issue rather than a criminal one, more and better services would likely be made available. Criminalizing drug use leads to further criminalization and not, as some would hope, eradication of the drug trade. Others, though, feel police should be more strict with dealers and should try to decrease the availability of drugs. A few others mentioned very practical concerns, such as providing clothes, blankets in jails, and twenty-four-hour-a-day access to free condoms and needles. While some also mentioned programs for helping people out of the trade, they were a surprisingly small minority. Nevertheless, such programs remain important for those who would rather be working elsewhere. However, the focus of concerns was first on reducing the harm sometimes experienced in the trade – through decriminalization and attitude change as well as through meeting basic needs. Harm reduction has been the basis of policies on drug use in other jurisdictions. It would not take a great leap of faith to include such rationales in programs for sex workers. With such programs, crime and violence could be decreased and general safety increased.

Overall, the kinds of policy suggestions put forward by the sex workers we interviewed provide the grounds for a rational approach to sex work that empowers sex workers to control the conditions of their work and to minimize the possibility of harm. Their suggestions make it clear that there is no single policy decision alone that will resolve all of the problems that affect conditions in the trade. Rather, a multifaceted approach that takes sex workers' words seriously and puts sex workers at the centre of policy design is required in order to make sex work work.

Conclusion

Decriminalization provides the groundwork for enhancing sex workers' rights, but it will not take place until there is a concerted political effort to push for both decriminalization and respect for sex workers. Even concerned members of the public have not moved beyond supporting decriminalization as a way to protect sex workers from harm, to pushing for decriminalization as part of a wider campaign to respect sex workers' rights. What we need to recognize is that only through decriminalization and support for sex workers' rights are the lives of even the most marginalized in the trade enhanced. To be treated as a person with a valuable contribution, as a person with rights, and as a respected member of the community is the most fundamental insurance against exploitation. Half the battle is won, then, by including sex workers, no matter how marginalized they may be, at the table.

Throughout this book, we have emphasized the agency and resistance of sex workers, as people who have great insight into not only their own lives but the society around them. Having broken down the barriers of what is considered proper sexual behaviour, sex workers are willing to speak out and act out against many more barriers. They have much to teach the rest of us about resisting and refusing the neo-liberal economic order. They draw attention to what many of us would like to ignore – the biases in policy and programs as well as the patronizing attitudes of so-called experts. They refuse to accept the "way things are" as just or justifiable. They have a clear-eyed view of the hypocrisy and inequality of the social, economic, and political structures around them. They "speak truth to power."[101] The rest of us would do well to listen and learn.

> I've spent half my life out there ... It's sad. But it's not sad! Because I'm educated now. I went to school. I've got my grade twelve. But if a person does not have street sense, they're not gonna make it in today's world. They're really not. You gotta have some kind of street smarts. Anybody can tell anybody something from reading. Literature is literature. But if you have never lived the life, you ain't tellin me nothin'. You really ain't telling me nothin'. I'm not hearin' ya, 'cause you ain't lived it, you haven't walked in my shoes. So you really can't tell me somethin' you know nothing about. (Katrina, Halifax)

Notes

Preface
1 Leslie Ann Jeffrey, *Sex and Borders: Gender, National Identity, and Prostitution Policy in Thailand* (Vancouver and Toronto: UBC Press, 2002).

Introduction
1 The authors gratefully acknowledge a three-year research-funding grant from the Social Sciences and Humanities Research Council of Canada, which enabled us to carry out the field research necessary for this book. We acknowledge as well the support of St. Thomas University and the University of New Brunswick at Saint John (UNBSJ), as well as the support of the Department of Sociology at the former and the Department of Politics and History at the latter.
2 An additional fifty interviews were conducted with police (all levels), provincial justice officials, community advocates, lawyers, and provincial politicians in the cities named. Many of these interviews are cited in the text. The text relies primarily on the words of the sex workers. The three cities are Saint John and Moncton, New Brunswick, and Halifax, Nova Scotia. Two interviews were conducted in Fredericton, New Brunswick.
3 For a history that critically examines the stereotypical concepts, truisms, and colonialist history of the Atlantic provinces (Newfoundland and the three Maritime provinces of Nova Scotia, Prince Edward Island, and New Brunswick), see Margaret R. Conrad and James K. Hiller, *Atlantic Canada: A Region in the Making* (Don Mills, ON: Oxford University Press, 2001).
4 In many ways, the common understanding of sex work in the Maritimes reflects the common understanding of sex work in the majority (or Third) world – where economic and social circumstances are presumed to force people into sex work and are best understood from the advantaged position of Western experts who can rescue them from this victimhood. Such a depiction is predicated upon imperialist modes of power that classify the Other as monolithic, backward, and without capacity for self-realization and self-representation (as opposed to the differentiated, liberated, and knowledgeable First World). As such, this depiction relies more on a powerful mythology of the First World self than on a reality of the Third World Other. And it functions to reinscribe the power of that First World self. See Jeffrey, *Sex and Borders*.
5 There are a number of excellent collections already. See, for example, Frédérique Delacoste and Priscilla Alexander, eds., *Sex Work: Writings by Women in the Sex Industry* (London: Virago, 1987); Alexandra Highcrest, *At Home on the Stroll: My Twenty Years as a Prostitute in Canada* (Toronto: Knopf, 1997).
6 Chandra Talpade Mohanty, "Under Western Eyes: Feminist Scholarship and Colonial Discourses," in *Feminism without Borders: Decolonizing Theory, Practicing Solidarity* (Durham, NC: Duke University Press, 2003), 42.

7 Michel Foucault, *The History of Sexuality*, vols. 1 and 2 (New York: Vintage Books, 1990); see also Kristin G. Esterberg, *Qualitative Methods in Social Research* (Boston: McGraw-Hill, 2002).
8 Part of the mandate of community action research is to involve the subjects of research in an egalitarian fashion, asking of them what questions need to be redressed in research. Stepping Stone, a sex worker outreach agency and one of the community partners, responded that it would like to know more about sex worker relations with police, which we then included as a question in the study. Although we cannot say that the questions we used completely corresponded to involved action on the part of the community agencies, we can say that the process of involvement with the researchers has created an awareness of other issues that research might address. Community action research also attempts to address some practical problems of the agencies. Currently one author sits on the board of AIDS Saint John and both are involved in a sex trade community action committee (STAC) organized by Coverdale and AIDS Saint John that is attempting to address citizen complaints concerning sex workers in that city.
9 Gayatri Chakravorty Spivak, *A Critique of Postcolonialist Reason: Toward a History of the Vanishing Present* (Cambridge, MA: Harvard University Press, 1999).
10 Alan Hunt, "Regulating Heterosocial Space: Sexual Politics in the Early Twentieth Century," *Journal of Historical Sociology* 15, 1 (2002); Wendy Chapkis, *Live Sex Acts: Women Performing Erotic Labor* (New York: Routledge, 1997); David Sibley, *Geographies of Exclusion: Society and Difference in the West* (London: Routledge, 1995); and R. Ellickson, "Controlling Misconduct in City Spaces: Of Panhandlers, Skid Rows, and Public Space Zoning," in *The Legal Geographies Reader: Law, Power and Space*, ed. Nicholas Blomley, David Delaney, and Richard T. Ford (London: Blackwell, 2001), 19-30.
11 Linda LeMoncheck, *Loose Women, Lecherous Men: A Feminist Philosophy of Sex* (New York: Oxford University Press, 1997); Shannon Bell, *Reading, Writing and Rewriting the Prostitute Body* (Bloomington: Indiana University Press, 1994); Chapkis, *Live Sex Acts;* Kamala Kempadoo and Jo Doezema, eds., *Global Sex Workers: Rights, Resistance and Redefinition* (New York: Routledge, 1998).
12 Raven Bowen, "Pathways: Real Options for Women to Reduce Reliance on Survival Sex" (Vancouver: Prostitution Alternatives Counselling and Education, 2003), http://www.pace-society.ca.
13 Coverdale feedback group, Saint John, June 2004.
14 We also frequently use "she" or "her" as a shorthand, given that the majority of the interviewees were women, but it should be noted that a number were men or transgendered persons.
15 Chapkis, *Live Sex Acts,* 211.
16 Some stereotypes seem to have a partial truth; younger women are more likely to be pimped, but then again, in at least two jurisdictions (Saint John and Fredericton), younger women are more likely to engage in sex for exchange. Community workers we spoke to in three cities confirmed that young women are most likely to exchange sex for everything from cigarettes to shelter. These young women (between sixteen and twenty years of age) do not identify themselves as prostitutes and are more likely to see their behaviour as one facet of their lives.
17 Foucault, *The History of Sexuality*, vol. 1, 83-85.
18 Ibid., vol. 1, 101.
19 See Petra Östergren, "Sexworkers Critique of Swedish Prostitution Policy," http://www.petraostergren.com.
20 Noah Zatz, "Sex Work/Sex Act: Law, Labor, and Desire in Constructions of Prostitution," *Signs* 22, 2 (1997): 284.
21 Laura Agustín, "Forget Victimisation: Granting Agency to Migrants," *Development* 46, 3 (2003): 30.
22 LeMoncheck, *Loose Women, Lecherous Men,* 136.
23 See Annette Jolin, "On the Backs of Working Prostitutes: Feminist Theory and Prostitution Policy," *Crime and Delinquency* 40, 1 (1994): 77.

24 See, for example, Eva Pendleton, "Love for Sale: Queering Heterosexuality," in *Whores and Other Feminists*, ed. Jill Nagle, 73-82 (New York: Routledge, 1997).
25 Corina McKay, "Is Sex Work Queer?" *Social Alternatives* 18, 3 (1999): 51.
26 Ibid., 52.
27 Chapkis, *Live Sex Acts*, 26.
28 James C. Scott, *Weapons of the Weak: Everyday Forms of Peasant Resistance* (New Haven, CT: Yale University Press, 1985).
29 Chris Bruckert, *Taking It Off, Putting It On: Women in the Strip Trade* (Toronto: Women's Press, 2002), 100-1.
30 See Sherry B. Ortner, "Resistance and the Problem of Ethnographic Refusal," *Comparative Studies in Society and History* 37, 1 (1995): 176-77.
31 See, for example, the work by Agustín, "Working in the European Sex Industry," 155-72, and the studies in Kempadoo and Doezema, *Global Sex Workers*. For a study of performativity and Third World sex workers, see Lenore Manderson, "Public Sex Performances in Patpong and Exploration of the Edges of Imagination," *Journal of Sex Research* 29, 4 (1992): 451-75.
32 Sukanya Hantrakul, "Spirit of a Fighter: Women and Prostitution in Thailand," *Manushi* 18 (October/November 1983): 32.
33 Anne McClintock, "Screwing the System: Sexwork, Race and the Law," *Boundary* 2 (Summer 1992): 79.
34 This study was examined by two research ethics boards at the interviewers' home universities, St. Thomas in Fredericton, New Brunswick, and University of New Brunswick at Saint John, as per SSHRC funding requirements.
35 Chapkis, *Live Sex Acts*, 212.
36 J. Lewis and E. Maticka-Tyndale, *Escort Services in a Border Town: Transmission Dynamics of STDs within and between Communities – Methodological Challenges Conducting Research Related to Sex Work* (Ottawa: Health Canada, 2000). On methodological issues and sex work research, see also Ronald Weitzer, "Flawed Theory and Method in Studies of Prostitution," *Violence against Women* 11, 7 (2005): 934-49.

Chapter 1: It's the Money, Honey

1 Wendy Rickard, "'Been There, Seen It, Done It, I've Got the T-Shirt': British Sex Workers Reflect on Jobs, Hopes, the Future and Retirement," *Feminist Review* 67 (Spring 2001): 115.
2 Carol Queen quoted in Wendy Chapkis, *Live Sex Acts*, 8.
3 Indeed, the symbolic role of money in giving people status may, according to Chapkis, lead some to exaggerate their actual incomes. Chapkis, *Live Sex Acts*, 104. However, most of our interviewees were also quite candid about how low prices and incomes could go, while simultaneously pointing out that *potential* incomes were quite high.
4 Zatz, "Sex Work/Sex Act," 287.
5 Karen Hadley, "And Still We Ain't Satisfied: Gender Inequality in Canada – A Status Report for 2001" (Toronto: CSJ Foundation for Research and Education and the National Action Committee on the Status of Women, June 2001), 3.
6 It also accounts for mainstream feminist refusal to accept sex work as a possible career choice – an issue that drove a wedge between the feminist movement and the sex worker movement during National Action Committee on the Status of Women debates in the mid-1980s. That is, while many can accept that sex work is undertaken as a way to make money in a sexist labour market and that women should not be criminalized for what is seen as an act of economic survival, they cannot imagine that such activity might be undertaken even if economic equality between the sexes were achieved.
7 Kari Fedec, "Women and Children in Canada's Sex Trade: The Discriminatory Policing of the Marginalized," in *Marginality and Condemnation: An Introduction to Critical Criminology*, ed. Bernard Schissel and Carolyn Brooks, 253-67 (Halifax: Fernwood, 2002).
8 For an overview of this debate in Canadian feminist political economy see Leah F. Vosko, "The Pasts (and Futures) of Feminist Political Economy in Canada: Reviving the Debate," in *Developments in Feminism*, ed. Caroline Andrew, Pat Armstrong, Hugh Armstrong, Wallace Clement, and Leah Vosko, 305-32 (Toronto: Women's Press, 2003).

9   Frances Shaver, "Prostitution: A Female Crime?" in *In Conflict with the Law: Canadian Women and the Criminal Justice System,* ed. Ella Adelberg and Claudia Currie (Vancouver: Press Gang, 1993), 159; and Frances Shaver, "Traditional Data Distort Our View of Prostitution," notes from a presentation at "When Sex Works: International Conference on Prostitution and Other Sex Work," 27-29 September 1996, University of Quebec at Montreal, http://www.walnet.org/csis/papers/shaver-distort.html.
10 For a post-colonial critique, see Mohanty, "Under Western Eyes," 17-42.
11 Emphasis added; see Cynthia Enloe, "Silicon Tricks and the Two Dollar Woman," *New Internationalist* (January 1992): 12-14, for an analysis of how women's labour is made cheap.
12 The undifferentiated and unexamined concept of addictions has come to serve the same explanatory role as poverty as the social force that pushes women into the sex trade and keeps them there. However, again, the term "addiction" can mean a wide variety of experiences for people, as we shall see in a later chapter.
13 Frances Shaver, "A Critique of the Feminist Charges against Prostitution," *Atlantis* 14, 1 (1988): 87. Emphasis added.
14 See, for example, Pivot Legal Society Sex Work Subcommittee, *Voices for Dignity: A Call to End the Harms Caused by Canada's Sex Trade Laws* (Vancouver: Law Foundation of British Columbia, 2004), 28-35; and Bowen, "Pathways."
15 See, for example, Chris Bruckert, Colette Parent, and Pascale Robitaille, "Erotic Service/Erotic Dance Establishments: Two Types of Marginalized Labour," Department of Criminology, University of Ottawa, 2003, 23; Cecilia Benoit and Alison Millar, *Dispelling Myths and Understanding Realities: Working Conditions, Health Status and Exiting Experiences of Street Workers* (Victoria: Prostitutes Empowerment, Education and Resource Society, 2001), 36; Shaver, "Prostitution: A Female Crime?" 159; J. Lewis and E. Maticka-Tyndale, *Escort Services in a Border Town: Transmission Dynamics of STDs within and between Communities: Literature and Policy Summary* (Ottawa: Division of STD Prevention and Control, Laboratory Centre for Disease Control, Health Canada, 1999), 8-9.
16 Bruckert, Parent, and Robitaille similarly found "in addition to the economic benefit, a number of the interviewees identified other positive characteristics of the job including flexibility, autonomy, interaction with clients, collegial work environment and a relaxed work pace." Bruckert, Parent, and Robitaille, "Erotic Service," vi.
17 Eileen McLeod, *Women Working: Prostitution Now* (London: Croom Helm, 1982), 1.
18 Hadley, "And Still We Ain't Satisfied," 3, 13-14. For an individual, $13,786 is the low income cut-off (LICO), or the point at which an individual spends more than 54.5 percent of her income on food, shelter, and clothing and is considered to be in straitened circumstances.
19 These amounts are comparable to those found in studies in Ontario. See J. Lewis and E. Maticka-Tyndale, *Erotic/Exotic Dancing: HIV-Relative Risk Factors,* final report, National Health Research and Development Program, Health Canada, Grant no. 6606-5688, http://www.walnet.org/csis/papers/lewis-strip.html.
20 Chris Bruckert, *Taking It Off, Putting It On: Women in the Strip Trade* (Toronto: Women's Press, 2002), 69-97; Shirley Lacasse, "Les danseuses nues" (PhD diss., Université de Montréal, 2004).
21 The appearance of fringe banking services speaks to the marginalization of the poor on social terms as well. One Winnipeg study of these services has noted that although these services tend to charge interest rates and commissions that are much higher than those of regular banking services, the poor are more willing to use fringe banking because they are more likely to be treated with some respect. See Jerry Buckland, Thibault Martin, Nancy Barbour, Amelia Curran, Rana McDonald, and Brendan Reimer, "The Rise of Fringe Financial Services in Winnipeg's North End: Client Experiences, Firm Legitimacy and Community-Based Alternatives," http://iuswww.uwinnipeg.ca/pdf/fringe.banking.Chesya.pdf.
22 See, for further discussion of these barriers, Urban Core Support Network, *Moving On: A Gender Based Analysis on Poverty Reduction in Saint John* (Saint John, NB: Urban Core Support Network, 2003).
23 This is in opposition to what Nikita Crook's earlier study on the Maritimes found, which was that there are two separate groups of workers: indoor and street. Nikita Crook, *A Report*

    on Prostitution in the Atlantic Provinces, Working Papers on Pornography and Prostitution, Report No. 12 (Ottawa: Department of Justice, 1984). See also Rickard, "'Been There, Seen It, Done It,'" 124, for similar patterns in Britain; and Benoit and Millar, *Dispelling Myths,* for similar patterns in British Columbia.
24 Similarly, sex workers in Vancouver have argued that there is better money on the streets. See John Lowman, "Street Prostitution Control: Some Canadian Reflections on the Finsbury Park Experience," *British Journal of Criminology* 32, 1 (1992): 14. Benoit and Millar also note that the street enables workers to keep more of their money and have greater control over the number of clients and the pace of work. Benoit and Millar, *Dispelling Myths,* 43, 45-47.
25 C.C.C. s.210. (1).
26 Management does sometimes try to limit sex workers' attempts to make extra cash. One outreach worker in Moncton reported that she had heard that managers use the "one condom" rule – allowing workers to take only one condom into the room with a client – to ensure that workers don't try to get a client off for a second time and pocket the extra money. Interview, Sexual Health Centre, Moncton, 1 November 2002.
27 Bruckert's research on exotic dancing similarly indicates that instability of income contributes to workplace stress. Bruckert, *Taking It Off,* 93.
28 While Crook reported a high incidence of pimping in her 1984 report, sex workers today report that the incidence of pimping has dropped dramatically. Indeed, interpretations of what constitutes pimping are often problematic and lead to overinflation of numbers. See Shaver, "Prostitution: A Female Crime?" 160-61, and John Lowman, "Taking Young Prostitutes Seriously," *Canadian Review of Sociology and Anthropology* 24, 1 (1987): 107-8. Benoit and Millar also reported that a very small percentage of their respondents reported being pimped, although the authors allow that this group may be under-represented in the study. Benoit and Millar, *Dispelling Myths,* 42.
29 For prices in Montreal and Quebec City see Michel Dorais, *Rent Boys* (Montreal: McGill-Queen's University Press, 2005), 28.
30 For further discussion of racism and the sex industry (as well as feminism) and the ways white privilege is dealt with by racialized sex workers, see Blake Aarens, B. Hima, Gina Gold, Jade Irie, Madeleine Lawson, and Gloria Lockett, "Showing Up Fully: Women of Color Discuss Sex Work," in Nagle, *Whores and Other Feminists,* 195-209.
31 This does not mean that there are no skills that can be transferred from sex work into other jobs. See Rickard, "'Been There, Seen It, Done It,'" 122-23.
32 See, among others, Nick Larsen, "Prostitution: Deviant Activity or Legitimate Occupation?" in *New Perspectives on Deviance: The Construction of Deviance in Everyday Life,* ed. Lori G. Beaman (Scarborough, ON: Prentice-Hall, 2000), 55: Shaver, "Prostitution: A Female Crime?" 159; Lowman, "Taking Young Prostitutes Seriously," 106-7; Pivot Legal Society, *Voices for Dignity,* 21-23, 51-56; Highcrest, *At Home on the Stroll.*
33 Shaver, "Prostitution: A Female Crime?" 159.
34 Although, as Bruckert points out, "the immoderate use of drugs and alcohol is far from normative," Bruckert, *Taking It Off,* 95.
35 Sandra D. McFayden, *Money Matters: Women in Nova Scotia, Part 1 of a Statistical Series* (Halifax: Nova Scotia Advisory Council on the Status of Women, 2000), 17.
36 Ibid., 18.
37 Frances Shaver has made a similar point with overall Canadian data from the 1980s. See Shaver, "Prostitution: A Female Crime?" 159.
38 The Canadian Council on Social Development, drawing from late 1990s Statistics Canada data, lists the percentage of Haligonians between the ages of fifteen and sixty-four with less than secondary education at 30 percent, and Saint Johners in that age group at 44 percent. Kevin Lee, "Urban Poverty in Canada: A Statistical Profile" (Ottawa: Canadian Council on Social Development, April 2000), Tables B4.2 and B4.3.
39 Ken Battle, "Minimum Wages in Canada: A Statistical Portrait with Policy Implications" (Ottawa: Caledonia Institute of Social Policy, 2003), 102, http://www.caledoninst.org.
40 Ibid., 111; New Brunswick, Advisory Council on the Status of Women, *Report Card on the Status of Women in New Brunswick 2004* (Fredericton, NB: Advisory Council on the Status of Women, 2004), 1; Urban Core Support Network, *Moving On,* 15.

Notes to pages 47-63   243

41 Thom Workman, *Social Torment: Globalization in Atlantic Canada* (Halifax: Fernwood, 2003), 81-89.
42 In real terms this means that "in each province the average monthly dollar gap is roughly equivalent to the cost of a bachelor apartment in its sample city." Ibid., 89.
43 Ibid., 90-91.
44 Ibid., 98.
45 Ibid., 99-100.
46 Ibid., 100-1.
47 Mary Simpson, *Social Investment in New Brunswick*, Atlantic Case Studies Policy Discussion Series Paper No. 7 (Halifax: Maritimes Centre for Excellence for Women's Health, 2000), 17.
48 Urban Core Support Network, *Moving On*, 15.
49 Bruckert, *Taking It Off*, 24.
50 Hadley, "And Still We Ain't Satisfied," 16-17.
51 For similar complaints by part-time workers in the service industry, see Dave Broad, "The Casualization of the Labour Force," in *Good Jobs, Bad Jobs, No Jobs: The Transformation of Work in the 21st Century*, ed. Ann Duffy, Daniel Glenday, and Norene Pupo (Toronto: Harcourt Brace, 1997), 60-62.
52 Canadian Council on Social Development, *The Progress of Canada's Children: Into the Millennium, 1999-2000* (Ottawa: Canadian Council on Social Development, 2000), 53.
53 Arlie Russell Hochschild, *The Managed Heart* (Berkeley: University of California Press, 1983). See also Chapkis, *Live Sex Acts*, 70-82.
54 Frances Shaver, "Prostitution: On the Dark Side of the Service Industry," in *Post-Critical Criminology*, ed. Thomas O'Reilly-Fleming, 42-55 (Scarborough, ON: Prentice-Hall, 1996).
55 Bruckert, *Taking It Off*, 23.
56 McFayden, *Money Matters*, 32, and Urban Core Support Network, *Moving On*, 13.
57 Those persons who are seen as needing some support or intervention in order to be employable (i.e., because they have chronic or temporary medical problems) receive $485. New Brunswick, Family and Community Services, Planning, Research and Evaluation Branch, *Social Assistance Rate Schedules* (Fredericton, NB: Family and Community Services, 2003).
58 The basic income assistance rate for a family of three in New Brunswick is $775, annualized to $9,300. This is well below the low income cut-off for a family of three at $22,000. Simpson, *Social Investment in New Brunswick*, 17.
59 Workman, *Social Torment*, 118-19.
60 Ibid., 101.
61 Canadian Council on Social Development, *The Progress of Canada's Children*, 52.
62 Ibid., 52.
63 Workman, *Social Torment*, 103-4.

Chapter 2: The Good, the Bad, and the Ugly
1 On survival sex work see Raven Bowen, "Pathways."
2 Rickard, "'Been There, Seen It, Done It,'" 111.
3 See, for example, Janice Raymond, "Prostitution as Violence against Women: NGO Stonewalling in Beijing and Elsewhere," *Women's Studies International Forum* 21, 1 (1998): 1-9; Cecilie Hoigard and Liv Finstad, *Backstreets: Prostitution, Money and Love* (University Park: Pennsylvania State University Press, 1992); Kathleen Barry, *The Prostitution of Sexuality* (New York: New York University Press, 1995).
4 Yasmin Jiwani, *Trafficking and Sexual Exploitation of Girls and Young Women: A Review of Select Literature and Initiatives*, 2nd ed. (Vancouver: Feminist Research, Education, Development and Action Centre, 1999), 7-8. See, for example, Susan M. Nadon, Catherine Koverola, and Eduard H. Schludermann, "Antecedents to Prostitution: Childhood Victimization," *Journal of Interpersonal Violence* 13, 2 (1998): 206-21.
5 Shaver, "Prostitution: A Female Crime?" 160.
6 Ibid.," 160-61; Lowman, "Taking Young Prostitutes Seriously," 107-8. Benoit and Millar also report fairly low levels of pimping, although they note that this group may be underrepresented in their sample. Benoit and Millar, *Dispelling Myths*, 42.
7 Bruckert, Parent, and Robitaille, "Erotic Service," 22.

8 Jane Scoular, "The 'Subject' of Prostitution: Interpreting the Discursive, Symbolic and Material Position of Sex/Work in Feminist Theory," *Feminist Theory* 5, 3 (2004): 348.
9 See Shannon Bell, *Reading, Writing and Rewriting*.
10 Scoular, "The 'Subject' of Prostitution," 348-49.
11 Jill Nagle, "Book Review," *Signs* 27, 4 (2002): 1177-78.
12 Ibid., 1179; Shannon Bell, *Reading, Writing and Rewriting*.
13 Nagle, "Book Review," 1179.
14 Carol Queen, "Sex Radical Politics, Sex-Positive Feminist Thought, and Whore Stigma," in Nagle, *Whores and Other Feminists*, 128-29.
15 Zatz, "Sex Work/Sex Act," 295-98.
16 Since sex work is in itself oppressive in the eyes of radical feminists, the particularities of how law can affect sex workers' quality of life is largely irrelevant (aside from removing the obvious bias of criminalizing sex workers). Ibid., 289-90.
17 Ibid., 293.
18 Queen, "Sex Radical Politics," in Nagle, *Whores and Other Feminists*, 129.
19 Barbara Sullivan, "Trafficking in Women: Feminism and New International Law," *International Feminist Journal of Politics* 5, 1 (2003): 79. See also Barbara Sullivan, "Prostitution and Consent: Beyond the Liberal Dichotomy of 'Free or Forced,'" in *Making Sense of Sexual Consent*, ed. Mark Cowling and Paul Reynolds, 127-39 (Burlington, VT: Ashgate, 2004).
20 See the research by John Lowman, C. Atchison, and L. Fraser, *Men Who Buy Sex: Summary of Phase I Report* (BC: Ministry of Attorney General, 1996). Also see N. McKeganey, "Why Do Men Buy Sex and What Are Their Assessments of the HIV-Related Risks When They Do?" *AIDS Care* 6, 3 (1994): 289-302; Carol Queen, "Toward a Taxonomy of Tricks: A Whore Considers the Age-Old Question, 'What Do Clients Want?'" in *Tricks and Treats: Sex Workers Write about Their Clients*, ed. Matt Bernstein Sycamore (Binghampton, NY: Harrington Park, 2000); Martin A. Monto, "Why Men Seek Out Prostitutes," in *Sex for Sale: Prostitution, Pornography and the Sex Industry*, ed. Ronald Weitzer, 67-84 (New York: Routledge, 2000).
21 Luke Xantidis and Marita P. McCabe, "Personality Characteristics of Male Clients of Female Commercial Sex Workers in Australia," *Archives of Sexual Behaviour* 29, 2 (2000).
22 Zatz, "Sex Work/Sex Act," 292.
23 Annie Sprinkle, "You've Come a Long Way Baby, or, How to Cure Sex Worker Burnout: Annie Sprinkle's 12 Step Program," In *Prostitution: On Whores, Hustlers, and Johns*, ed. James Elias, Vern Bullough, Veronica Elias, and Gwen Brewer (New York: Prometheus Books, 1998).
24 Janet Lever and Deanne Dolnick, "Clients and Call Girls: Seeking Sex and Intimacy," in Weitzer, *Sex for Sale*, 98.
25 See Queen, "Toward a Taxonomy of Tricks."
26 Bruckert, *Taking It Off*, 116.
27 Queen, "Sex Radical Politics," in Nagle, *Whores and Other Feminists*, 133. Laura Agustín writes about the skills and abilities that are necessary in sex work if one is to do the job well, both for oneself and for one's client. Agustín, "Working in the European Sex Industry," 155-72. A number of sex worker self-help websites also give advice on these matters. See, for example, http://www.bayswan.org/penet.html; http://www.nswp.org; and, for Canadian information, http://www.walnet.org (Commercial Sex Information Service).
28 See, for example, Pivot Legal Society, *Voices for Dignity*, 36-42; Benoit and Millar, *Dispelling Myths*, 50; Leonard Cler-Cunningham and Christine Christensen, *Violence against Women in Vancouver's Street Level Sex Trade and the Police Response* (Vancouver: Prostitution Alternatives Counselling and Education Society, 2003), http://www.pacesociety.ca.
29 See John Lowman and L. Fraser, *Violence against Persons Who Prostitute: The Experience in British Columbia* (Ottawa: Department of Justice Canada, 1995); John Fleischman, *Violence against Street Prostitutes in Halifax (1980-1994)*, Technical Report No. TR1996-17F (Ottawa: Department of Justice Canada, 1996). The western studies showed that the street had become a more violent place since the new law and relations between sex workers and police had deteriorated. The Halifax study pointed to the violence by pimps – although it also noted a great deal of violence by clients.

30 Sean Devlin, "A Working Girl's Nightmare: The Murdered and Missing Women of Skid Row," *First Nations Drum,* Fall 2000, http://www.firstnationsdrum.com/fall2000/cult_missing.htm; Helen Boritch, *Fallen Women: Female Crime and Criminal Justice in Canada* (Scarborough, ON: ITP Nelson, 1997), 120.
31 John Lowman, "Violence and the Outlaw Status of (Street) Prostitution in Canada," *Violence against Women* 6, 9 (2000): 1005.
32 Quoted in Lowman, "Violence and the Outlaw Status," 1005.
33 See the study by Cler-Cunningham and Christensen, *Violence against Women.*
34 See Lewis and Maticka-Tyndale, *Escort Services in a Border Town,* 12-13.
35 "Police to explore possible links between Cross death, other cases," *Halifax Chronicle Herald,* 29 January 2003, A6.
36 "Halifax police take prostitutes' hair," *New Brunswick Telegraph-Journal,* 10 May 2004, A11.
37 Shaver, "Prostitution: A Female Crime?" 161. See also Dan Allman, "M Is for Mutual, A Is for Acts: Male Sex Work and AIDS in Canada" (Ottawa: Health Canada, 1999), 21. Michel Dorais, in his study of forty male sex workers in Quebec, reports that violence by clients also presents a problem for street hustlers. Dorais, *Rent Boys,* 67.
38 Lowman, "Violence and the Outlaw Status," 1002-4.
39 Quoted in Jodie Sinnema, "Society Targets Prostitutes, Expert Says," CanWest News Service, 16 July 2003. The incidence of missing and murdered women in the sex trade, while most visible in Vancouver and the Lower Mainland, is appearing across Canada and around the world. There are a number of infamous cases in the United States, such as the Green River killer, Gary Ridgeway, who killed forty-eight women who worked in the trade and confessed that he "picked prostitutes because I thought I could kill as many of them as I wanted without getting caught," and that he thought he was "doing [police] a favor ... Here you guys can't control them, but I can." Quoted in Silja J.A. Talvi, "The Truth about the Green River Killer," AlterNet, 11 November 2003, http://www.alternet.org/print.html?StoryID=17171.
40 Bruckert, *Taking It Off,* 92. See also J. Lewis and E. Maticka-Tyndale, *Final Report: Erotic Dancing – HIV-Related Risk Factors* (Ottawa: Health Canada, 1998).
41 Bruckert, *Taking It Off,* 93.
42 For an extended discussion of the discourse on white slavery see, for example, Jo Doezema, "Loose Women or Lost Women? The Re-Emergence of the Myth of 'White Slavery' in Contemporary Discourses of 'Trafficking in Women.'" Paper presented at the International Studies Association Annual Convention, Washington, DC, 18-19 February 1999, http://www.walnet.org/csis/papers/doezema-loose.html. For a historical study see Deborah Gorham, "The 'Maiden Tribute of Modern Babylon' Re-Examined: Child Prostitution and the Idea of Childhood in Late-Victorian England," *Victorian Studies* 21, 3 (1978): 353-80.
43 The dangers of this misunderstanding of the role of male partners of female workers was called to our attention by an acquaintance who works in the trade out west and whose husband, who spotted for her while she worked, was entered on a police watch list of johns (Vancouver vice unit "Deter and Identify Sex Trade Consumers" program [DISC]) – a move that endangered his job as well as her ability to rely on him for safety backup. This was one more example of how a policy designed without sex worker input had the potential to harm rather than help sex workers.
44 Of course, the crossover of the drug trade has a variety of implications. Generally, it has been seen as leading to the increase in violence on the streets and the involvement of organized crime, and therefore violence, in a wide variety of street crimes. However, organized crime in and of itself is not necessarily threatening to sex workers. As an acquaintance who works in the trade in Toronto has pointed out, working for organized crime can offer the best work situation since it tries to ensure that police don't get involved.
45 Even those who study youth prostitution are cautious about overestimating the extent of involvement of pimps with youth. See, for example, Leslie Tutty and Kendra Nixon, "'Selling Sex, It's Really Like Selling Your Soul': Vulnerability to and the Experience of Exploitation through Child Prostitution," in *Being Heard: The Experiences of Young Women in Prostitution,* ed. Kelly Gorkoff and Jane Runner (Halifax: Fernwood, 2003), 32-33, 37-39. See also Lowman, "Taking Young Prostitutes Seriously," 107-8.

46 The boyfriend was formally charged with "living on the avails" and "exercising control" in order to "compel her to engage in prostitution," as well as "threat to kill" and several counts of assault, for some of which he was acquitted.
47 Sherri Borden, "Pimp jailed for assaulting prostitute, landlord," *Halifax Chronicle Herald*, 10 March 2004, B7.
48 Sherri Borden, "Violent pimp appeals sentence," *Halifax Mail Star*, 25 March 2004, B2.

Chapter 3: Social Control, Policing, and Sex Work

1 On the history of the development of these laws see Constance Backhouse, *Petticoats and Prejudice: Women and the Law in 19th Century Canada* (Toronto: Women's Press, 1983).
2 See Frances Shaver's analysis of this in "Prostitution: A Female Crime?" 153-73.
3 That is, sex work has come to be seen less as a moral problem in the law (although this too is present – particularly the ban on brothels contained in the Criminal Code), particularly since the 1970s, when human and civil rights discourse positioned moral issues as outside the purview of law. Thus, despite the bawdy house ban, this law is now much less frequently used – usually only if the bawdy house is seen as an undue impingement on a community's space.
4 Similar negotiations for sex have normatively changed in the public as well: people meet online in chat rooms as opposed to physical spaces and carry on whole relationships in a manner unheard of even as recently as ten years ago. But despite this, the public holds on to old morality tropes about sexuality. Those who meet their sexual partners through work, family, or friends are quite appalled by the anonymity of sexual encounters they see around them.
5 David Sibley, *Geographies of Exclusion*, 78.
6 Even in the most public of shopping venues – malls – business owners will hire property managers and security guards to encourage all who do not shop to move on. This blurring of the private-public boundary has increased in this century, as have the interruptions to public space, such as the proliferate use of cell phone technology.
7 See Ellickson, "Controlling Misconduct in City Spaces," 19-30.
8 See Julia O'Connell Davidson's discussion of the black pimp mythology in the United States and Britain. Julia O'Connell Davidson, *Prostitution, Power and Freedom* (Ann Arbor, University of Michigan Press, 1998), 43-45.
9 This does not mean that there may not also be recruiters for escort agencies who may act more or less exploitatively. This has occurred in the past in Germany, for example, even under the legalized brothel system. (See EEC, Directorate General for Research and Documentation, *Prostitution in the EEC Member States: A Comparative Study of the Existing Legal Position*, Luxembourg, 3 April 1985, PE 95.816/Ann.II., p. 14.) Sex workers, however, argue that this is a function of the failure to properly regulate the system with sex workers' rights in mind. See further discussion of this point in Chapter 6.
10 Perception of threat, as much of the literature reveals, is as effective a method of social control as is actual force. Battered women often react to a beating with a sense of relief, if such a word can be used to describe violence, as the build-up or perceived threat of violence is incredibly anxiety-provoking. The threat to prostitutes can be of arrest but can also be of violence. Nevertheless, in sex work, a cop is a cop is a cop. Good cop or bad cop, the results for the sex worker usually always mean the same thing: her sexuality, her work, her physical presence will always be under control.
11 Erin Gibbs van Brunschot, "Community Policing and 'John Schools,'" *Canadian Review of Sociology and Anthropology* 40, 2 (2003): 225.
12 John Lowman, "Notions of Formal Equality before the Law: The Experience of Street Prostitutes and Their Customers," *Journal of Human Justice* 1, 2 (1990), 172-203.
13 van Brunschot, "Community Policing and 'John Schools,'" 224.
14 Ibid.
15 Heather Schramm, "The Politics of Crime Prevention Programmes: Sex Worker Exclusion," paper presented at the annual meeting of the Canadian Sociology and Anthropology Association, Halifax, 1 June 2003.

16 The violence sex workers experience is documented. It is not a *potential* threat or risk (which many new security programs are designed to thwart), it is a very real and persistent problem for women and men who work on city streets, in particular. Robert Castel demonstrates that crime prevention programs are not designed to deal with existing forms of violence; rather, they are designed to be anticipatory in nature, to deal with risks of danger, however defined: "What the new preventive policies primarily address is not to confront a concrete dangerous situation, but to anticipate all the possible forms of irruption of danger. 'Prevention' in effect promotes suspicion to the dignified scientific rank of a calculus of probabilities. To be suspected, it is no longer necessary to manifest symptoms of dangerousness or abnormality, it is enough to display whatever characteristics the specialists responsible for the definition of preventive policy have constituted as risk factors." Robert Castel, "From Dangerousness to Risk," in *The Foucault Effect: Studies in Governmentality,* ed. Graham Burchell, Colin Gordon, and Peter Miller (London: Harvester Wheatsheaf, 1991), 288, 289.

Characteristics known as risk factors, then, are malleable, shifting over time. They may have more to do with the dominant discursive understanding of who or what is a problem rather than actual, documented dangers. A culture of fear predominates, readily abetted by visual media through advertisements for crime-solving tips, which dictate which issues are risk-generating (such as potential break-ins or robberies) and which are not. Violence against women clearly does not fit this profile. What constitutes risk for prevention policies, could, in effect, have much more to do with protecting middle-class property values and sensibilities than with actual danger.

17 One female police officer we interviewed was quite alarmed that she has been left to fend for herself without officer backup when disguised as a decoy to target johns. Although this particular officer was empathetic to the situation of the sex workers she was sometimes obliged to arrest, she nevertheless failed to see the irony of a situation in which she identified, *as a woman,* as a possible target of violence.

18 "Women convicted of prostitution say they're not bad people," *Saint John Times Globe,* 19 October 1998, C7.

Chapter 4: The Whore Stigma and the Media

1 See, for example, Gail Pheterson, "The Whore Stigma: Female Dishonour and Male Unworthiness," *Social Text* 37 (Winter 1993): 39-64.

2 Mark Totten, *Guys, Gangs and Girlfriend Abuse* (Peterborough, ON: Broadview, 2001).

3 This is not to say that getting sex workers' stories is necessarily an easy task – certainly there are sex worker spokespersons to whom the media can turn, though these people are often in major centres such as Toronto, Montreal, and Vancouver, where sex worker organizations are well established – but many journalists do not bother to turn to these sources. Getting local workers' stories is, of course, tricky, precisely because of the weight of stigma and the small size of Maritime centres. When the media do talk to local sex workers, even sensitive journalists can unwittingly out people and their families and subject them to public censure. Media-sex worker co-operation therefore takes training on both sides. One Australian organization has provided resources on working with the media, at http://www.swimw.org, that can be helpful for both sex workers and the media.

4 "Surveillance" is used here to connote the manner by which people are tracked and located in the social world. Some people within society are watched much more than others; for example, low-income neighbourhoods are likely to be policed for scrutiny of the occupants, whereas higher income neighbourhoods are policed for property protection. Women's sexual behaviours are surveilled more closely than are men's. Similarly, if a person is identified as a sex worker, that person's movements, interactions, and associations in public are watched far more carefully by police than are the movements of most other citizens. Media scrutiny of sex workers, which should be about assessing surveillance and to whom it is subject, is often part of the process.

5 Ray Surette, *Media, Crime and Criminal Justice: Images and Realities* (New York: Wadsworth, 1997), 5.

6 Ibid., 6.

7 Teun van Dijk, *Discourse as Social Interaction* (London: Sage, 1997), 19.
8 That society should have little information on sex work is not an innocent process: there is no reason that even those who do not or have not worked in the trade would not know someone who did except that sex work has become isolated and hidden and therefore not part of common everyday knowledge and experience.
9 This was revealed in an interview with a former receptionist (Ashley) of a now defunct Fredericton massage parlour.
10 Michel Foucault, *Discipline and Punish: The Birth of the Prison* (New York: Vintage Books, 1995), 174.
11 Aysan Sev'er, *Fleeing the House of Horrors: Women Who Have Left Abusive Partners* (Toronto: University of Toronto Press, 2002).
12 Tanya Dawne Smith, "Pimping and Prostitution in Halifax in the Early 1990s: The Evolution of a Moral Panic" (MA thesis, Dalhousie University, 2000).
13 Africville was a dynamic black community in Halifax. In the 1970s, the settlement's structures were torn down by the city in the name of progress.
14 Indeed, there was probably some continuity in the historical imagination of Maritimers between the white slave trade and the pimping panic. Older Maritimers would certainly remember the stories of the white-slave trade of the pre-war period, particularly given the social links between Boston, where the white slave panic was in full swing, and Nova Scotia during the early part of the century. Having been a child in Halifax in the 1970s, one author remembers the stories of the white slave trade told by her mother and her Boston-born grandmother.
15 Cited in Smith, "Pimping and Prostitution in Halifax," 67-68.
16 Phonse Jessome, *Somebody's Daughter: Inside the Toronto/Halifax Pimping Ring* (Halifax: Nimbus, 1996). Nicole Jessome, mentioned earlier, is not an immediate family member.
17 In the Halifax Metro edition reprint of the story, the focus is shifted entirely from johns to pimps and the recent charging of one of the men involved in the 1992 ring.
18 John Lowman interview, CBC National News, 1 September 2003.
19 "Women convicted of prostitution say they're not bad people," *Saint John Times Globe*, 19 October 1998, C7. Emphasis added.

Chapter 5: Whose Health? Whose Safety?

1 The list includes public health nurses, licensed practical nurses, infectious diseases doctors, doctors working at clinics, methadone clinic staff, needle exchange staff, and addictions counsellors.
2 The literature criticizing the claims to supposedly objective scientific knowledge is, of course, long-standing, ranging from Thomas Kuhn through to feminist critiques such as those by Donna Harding.
3 See Mariana Valverde, *The Age of Light, Soap and Water: Moral Reform in English Canada, 1885-1925* (Toronto: McClelland and Stewart, 1991); Shannon Bell, *Reading, Writing and Rewriting*.
4 Renisa Mawani, "Regulating the 'Respectable Classes': Venereal Disease, Gender, and Public Health Initiatives in Canada, 1914-1935," in *Regulating Lives: Historical Essays on the State, Society, and the Individual*, ed. J. McLaren, R. Menzies, and D.E. Chunn (Vancouver: UBC Press, 2002), 170-95.
5 See Karlene Faith, *Unruly Women: The Politics of Confinement and Resistance* (Vancouver: Press Gang, 1993).
6 Diane E. Meaghan, "Aids and Sex Workers: A Case for Patriarchy Interruptus," *Canadian Women Studies* 21, 2 (2001): 107-10.
7 In Nova Scotia, one doctor stated that "if the emergency room doctor is sharp enough to notice IDU [intravenous drug use] on admission, then the patient might be tested for hep B or C." Interview, Dr. Walter Schleck, 25 March 2003.
8 With the exception of Saint John.
9 Interview, Dr. Walter Schleck, Halifax, 25 March 2003.
10 The primary research focus of the infectious diseases doctor at the Saint John Regional Hospital (Dr. Atreyi Muherjee) is HIV/AIDs. However, she too confirmed that rates of

hepatitis C were on the rise. This is borne out by a Statistics Canada report that states the rates for females have risen or stayed constant for every age group from 1996 to 1999. A public health nurse in Saint John cites hepatitis C and chlamydia as the two infectious diseases she sees most. She attributes that the patterns and trends and frequency of hepatitis C that she sees can be attributed primarily to intravenous drug use: "I would say that it is the tip of the iceberg. I would say there is a lot more people in the jail who are hepatitis C and either know it, or have a pretty good idea they have it, and just don't want to come for that test" (Saint John Public Health Nurse, 12 September 2002). Although this nurse's clients are inmates, the trend she identifies in her prison population mirrors a trend present in the general population. A Halifax North End Health Clinic doctor sees the same trends. Some of the patients he sees have HIV, but the more likely diagnosis is chlamydia or hepatitis C. Interview, Halifax North End Clinic, 25 March 2003.
11 Interview, Diane Bailey, executive director, Mainline Needle Exchange, Halifax, 25 March 2003.
12 Interview, Dr. Walter Schleck, Halifax, 25 March 2003.
13 Karen Murray, "Do Not Disturb: 'Vulnerable Populations' in Federal Government Policy Discourses and Practices," *Canadian Journal of Urban Research* 13, 1 (2004): 54.
14 There is also an assumption that, outside hospitals and correctional facilities, people are free and clear to obtain health services of all kinds – again an example of neo-liberal individualism that fails to recognize barriers to access beyond the individual's own failings.
15 Frances Shaver compares sex work to that of laboratory technicians in an earlier study (1996). Shaver, "Prostitution: On the Dark Side," 42-55. See also the ongoing study by Cecilia Benoit, Mikael Jansson, Bonnie Leadbeater, and Bill McCarthy, "Personal Service Workers' Occupational Health, and Safety and Access to Health Services" (a study funded by the Canadian Institute of Health Research), which examines working conditions and access to health care among service workers, including sex workers.
16 Meaghan, "Aids and Sex-Workers," note vi.
17 See, for example, the findings about the growing risk of STDs to younger women who had a "poor knowledge of sexual and reproductive health" in Health Canada, Canadian Population Health Initiative, *Women's Health: Surveillance Report* (Ottawa: Canadian Institute for Health Information, 2003). Canadian AIDS Society, "Lack of knowledge contributing to growing rate of HIV infections among Canadian women," media release (Ottawa: Canadian AIDS Society, 3 October 2003).
18 Canadian Press, "Syphilis on the rise again, Health Canada reports," 15 February 2002, http://www.canoe.ca/Health0202/15_syphilis-cp.html.
19 Marina Barnard, in Canada, Health Canada, *Profile of Hepatitis C and Drug Use in Canada: A Discussion Paper* (Ottawa: Health Canada, Hepatitis C Prevention, Support and Research Program, Population and Public Health Branch, 2002), 17-18.
20 Lois Jackson, "Sex Trade Workers in Halifax, Nova Scotia: What Are Their Risks of HIV at Work and at Home?" *Canadian Women Studies* 21, 2 (2001): 44-48.
21 Ibid.
22 The growing use of OxyContin, Dilaudids, and Percocet – often prescribed for chronic pain – has recently become an issue of some concern in New Brunswick. "Addiction doesn't discriminate," *New Brunswick Telegraph-Journal*, 13 May 2002; "Elite drug abuse on rise," *New Brunswick Telegraph-Journal*, 29 September 2003, A1; "Addicts turn to designer drugs," *New Brunswick Telegraph-Journal*, 13 May 2002, http://www.canadaeast.com.
23 Lewis and Maticka-Tyndale, *Erotic/Exotic Dancing*.
24 Bruckert, *Taking It Off*, 95.
25 Jennifer Butters and Patricia Erickson, "Addictions as Deviant Behaviour: Normalizing the Pleasures of Intoxication," in Beaman, *New Perspectives on Deviance*, 67.
26 Dr. Mark Tyndall, director of Epidemiology, BC Centre of Excellence, University of British Columbia, testimony before the Special Committee on the Non-Medical Use of Drugs, 3 December 2001, 1, http://www.parl.gc.ca/InfocomDoc/37/1/SNUD/meetings/evidence/snudev14-e.htm#T0925.
27 Ibid., 12.

28 Tyndall, testimony.
29 Interview, Haley Flaro, executive director, AIDS New Brunswick, Fredericton, 8 September 2003.
30 A comment from an addictions counsellor resonates with this idea of functionality. In her work, the idea that using a drug is the way in which persons are "taking care of themselves" has been a breakthrough for her in reaching her clients in their own language. If the drug is taken to alleviate pain, either physical or psychological, then drug use is care-taking (Jo Lang, personal conversation, 10 July 2004).
31 In a twist of irony, one researcher on this project fell ill and was hospitalized for a chronic condition in the midst of the project. She was offered a choice between Demerol and Dilaudid as a pain suppressant during her stay in hospital. Given what she knew of the addictive power of Dilaudids from this research, she was surprised that anyone would be offered such medication for a chronic condition. She chose Demerol.
32 Opiates are the only set of drugs for which methadone programs will work. Other serious addictions to drugs such as crack cocaine are not treatable by methadone programs. Those running methadone programs are willing to take patients who have cross-addictions to try to reduce dependence on opiates. Usually, however, health care practitioners in these programs do not tolerate continued abuse of the other types of medications.
33 See, for example, Newfoundland, Department of Health and Community Services, OxyContin Task Force, *OxyContin Task Force Final Report* (St. John's: Newfoundland Department of Health and Community Services, 2004).
34 Robert J. MacCoun, *Toward a Psychology of Harm Reduction* (Drug Policy Research Centre, Rand Corporation, 2001), 1202.
35 For example, a methadone maintenance program was developed and supported through the University of New Brunswick nursing faculty in Fredericton on temporary funding. Similar programs developed in Saint John, Moncton, and Miramichi were refused government funding on the basis that the provincial government had its own health plan into which such programs must be fit. Despite the pressing need for methadone maintenance in all these cities and the willingness of doctors, pharmacists, and outreach workers to provide labour and space to create the programs, they have been stalled while the government debates which city will receive funding for a pilot program. See, among others, Grant Kerr, "'Methadone would be our medicine: Tories' plan to start a pilot project for opiate addicts instead of province-wide program met with mixed reviews," *New Brunswick Telegraph-Journal*, 10 June 2004, A2. (At the time of this writing, partial funding from the province has finally been acquired by the clinics in Saint John and Fredericton, after protracted public lobbying. The length of the waiting list for treatment in each city remains unacceptably high.)
36 Canada, Health Canada, *Mediums to Reach Injection Drug Using Populations: A Discussion Paper* (Ottawa: Health Canada, Hepatitis C Prevention, Support and Research Program, Population and Public Health Branch, 2000), 20.
37 See Cecilia Benoit and Alison Millar, *Dispelling Myths*. For two very effective guides to setting up programs and policies that respect sex workers' knowledge and experience, see the Network of Sex Work Projects, "Making Sex Work Safe," March 2003, http://www.nswp.org/safety/msws; and EUROPAP/TAMPEP, *Hustling for Health: Developing Services for Sex Workers in Europe*, European Network for HIV/STD Prevention in Prostitution, 1998), http://www.europap.net/dl/archive/publications/H4H%20UK_version.pdf.

Chapter 6: Sex and Politics
1 *Criminal Code*, R.S.C. 1985, c. C-46, s. 213.
2 *Criminal Code*, R.S.C. 1985, c. C-46, s. 210-211.
3 Or, for example, "bad trick" lists may (unknowingly) include undercover police and therefore be viewed as hampering police. The implications of this can be devastating for outreach organizations. See, for one example, Randy Jones, "HRM councillor wants to cut funds to prostitute support organization; Group gave out bad-trick list that reveals police sting," *Halifax Chronicle Herald*, 1 February 2000, A7.
4 C.C.C. 210-213.

5   At the urging of MP Libby Davies, the Parliamentary Standing Committee on Human Rights and Justice struck the Subcommittee on Solicitation Laws that seemed likely to recommend some form of decriminalization or legalization but was unable to report before the House was dissolved in November 2005. The Quebec Conseil permanent de la jeunesse (Permanent Council for Youth) also recently recommended decriminalization of sex work in order to address violence and repression against sex workers. Rhéal Séguin, "Sex-trade laws must change, Quebec study says," *Globe and Mail*, 27 April 2004, A5.
6   Sex workers and sex worker advocates have certainly appeared at the various committees and hearings on policy, such as the Fraser Committee, the hearings on the communicating law, and the Federal/Provincial/Territorial Working Group; however, their opinions are little known in the wider public and appear to carry little weight in policy considerations. Some organized sex workers were calling for a boycott of the Subcommittee on Solicitation Law Review hearings because of frustration over the failure to respond to their consistent demands for decriminalization.
7   Chapkis, *Live Sex Acts*, 211.
8   Jane Flax, paraphrased in Chapkis, *Live Sex Acts*, 211.
9   See Jackie West, "Prostitution: Collectives and the Politics of Regulation," *Gender, Work and Organization* 7, 2 (2000): 106.
10 Valerie Scott, quoted in David Bingham, "Prostitutes want to be legal," *New Brunswick Telegraph-Journal*, 14 December 1995, http://www.canadaeast.com/tp.
11 See also the Pivot Legal Society Sex Work Subcommittee's study *Voices for Dignity*.
12 While police state that they would not arrest sex workers when they lodge complaints against a client, sex workers obviously want to limit any contact with police and remain as unidentifiable as possible. Therefore, they may choose not to lodge a complaint in order to retain their anonymity. Further, they fear that their concerns would be taken lightly in any case. Indeed, even when sex work is legal, workers sometimes prefer not to go to police with complaints because of fears of being exposed (See Alison Arnot, "Legalisation of the Sex Industry in the State of Victoria, Australia" (MA thesis, University of Melbourne, 2002), 70-71. This again indicates the importance of addressing stigma in order for legal changes to be effective.
13 Vagrancy provision was C.C.C. 175(1)(c), until it was repealed in 1972 and was replaced with C.C.C. 195.1.
14 *R. v. Hutt* (1978), 82 D.L.R. (3d) 95 (S.C.C.).
15 *R. v. Westendorp*, [1983] 1 S.C.R. 43, 1983 CanLII 1 S.C.C.
16 Nikita Crook, "Halifax Street Ordinance #3," Appendix 3 of *Prostitution in the Atlantic Provinces*, A12-13, A28. The Dartmouth municipality, then under separate governance, issued a similar bylaw, although no charges were ever laid.
17 Deborah Brock, *Making Work, Making Trouble: Prostitution as a Social Problem* (Toronto: University of Toronto Press, 1998), 53.
18 *Nova Scotia (A.G.) v. Beaver* (1985), 67 N.S.R. (2d) 281, 155 A.P.R. 281 (C.A.).
19 Then Bill C-49 replaced C.C.C. s. 195.1 with s. 213.
20 Canada, House of Commons, *Fourth Report of the Standing Committee on Justice and the Solicitor General on Section 213 of the Criminal Code (Prostitution-Soliciting)* (Ottawa, 1990).
21 Ekos Research Associates, *Street Prostitution: Assessing the Impact of the Law, Halifax* (Ottawa: Department of Justice, 1989), 192-93.
22 Federal/Provincial/Territorial Working Group on Prostitution, *Report and Recommendations in Respect of Legislation, Policy and Practices Concerning Prostitution Related Activities* (Ottawa: Department of Justice, 1998), 12; Brock, *Making Work, Making Trouble*, 144-45.
23 Federal/Provincial/Territorial Working Group, 13.
24 *R. v. Downey*, [1992] 2. S.C.R. 10.
25 Brock, *Making Work, Making Trouble*, 145.
26 Dale Gibson, "Pimps, Presumptions and Predatory Laws: R. v. Downey," *Canadian Bar Review* 71 (1992): 733-34. See also Janice Dickin McGinnis, "Whores and Worthies: Feminism and Prostitution," *Canadian Journal of Law and Society* 9, 1 (1994): 105-22.
27 Karen Bastow, "Prostitution and HIV/AIDS," *Canadian HIV/AIDS Policy and Law Newsletter* 2, 2 (1996), http://www.aidslaw.ca; Leslie Ann Jeffrey, "Prostitution as Public Nuisance:

Canada," in *The Politics of Prostitution: Women's Movements, Democratic States and the Globalisation of Sex Commerce,* ed. Joyce Outshoorn (New York: Cambridge University Press, 2004), 97. The federal government introduced more stringent measures in bill C-27, which created the new offence of "aggravated procuring" of those under eighteen and enabled the use of adult decoys in charging clients. Provincial governments also increased their anti-youth prostitution measures in the late 1990s; for example, Alberta's Protection of Children Involved in Prostitution Act and British Columbia's Secure Care Act. A similar act was introduced in the Nova Scotia legislature as a private member's bill but did not go past first reading. For commentary on these measures see Karen Busby, "The Protective Confinement of Girls Involved in Prostitution: Potential Problems in Current Regimes," in Gorkoff and Runner, *Being Heard,* 103-25, and Kelly Gorkoff with Meghan Waters, "Balancing Safety, Respect and Choice in Programs for Young Women Involved in Prostitution," in *Being Heard,* 126-46.
28 Federal/Provincial/Territorial Working Group, 13.
29 Ibid., 8-9, 89-91.
30 Ibid., 14-15.
31 Ibid., 9, 68-70.
32 John Lowman, "Prostitution Law Reform in Canada," http://users.uniserve.com/~lowman/.
33 "Massage parlour doors locked," *Fredericton Daily Gleaner,* 9 March 2002, http://www.canadaeast.com/dg/.
34 Mary Moszynski, "City's only strip club may be closing," *New Brunswick Telegraph-Journal,* 9 April 2004, A3.
35 *Saint John Times Globe,* 17 December 1999, A1.
36 Mike Mullen, "Au revoir, ma Chez Cherie," *New Brunswick Telegraph-Journal,* 24 April 2004, A5.
37 Nick Larsen, "The Politics of Prostitution Control: Interest Group Politics in Four Canadian Cities," *International Journal of Urban and Regional Research* 16 (1992): 187-88.
38 Proceedings of Saint John Common Council, 19 November 2001, re: 178 Thorne Avenue.
39 Interview, Halifax city councillor Dawn Sloane, 7 August 2003.
40 Interview, Resident D, Dartmouth, 28 July 2002.
41 Residents and police had certainly pressured the previous government to introduce new legislation. The Board of Police Commissioners in Halifax and the Halifax Regional Police had issued a letter to this effect. *Hansard,* Nova Scotia House of Assembly, 28 March 2000, 2764.
42 *Hansard,* Nova Scotia House of Assembly, 19 October 1998, 2173.
43 Nova Scotia House of Assembly, First Session of the Fifty-Eighth General Assembly, Speech from the Throne, 7 October 1999, http://www.gov.ns.ca/news/details.asp?id=19991007004.
44 An Act to Amend Chapter 293 of Revised Statutes, 1989, the Motor Vehicle Act, S.N.S. 2004, c. 41.
45 *Hansard,* Nova Scotia House of Assembly, 28 March 2000, 2764.
46 Ibid., 28 March 2000, 2978.
47 See the ongoing research by Don Desserud, Joanna Everitt, and Paul Howe, "Civic Engagement Study of New Brunswick Survey," Politics and History Department, University of New Brunswick.
48 Interview, Resident A, Dartmouth, 19 July 2002.
49 One telling incident was the case of William Shrubsall, who was one of the men threatening sex workers in downtown Halifax. A convicted rapist and murderer, Shrubsall beat a woman nearly to death on the Halifax waterfront. ("Shrubsall evil, US cop says," *Halifax Chronicle Herald,* 28 February 2001, http://www.herald.ns.ca/.) In the aftermath of this event, residents pointed to the Shrubsall case as one of the indications that they were threatened by the presence of the sex industry. Sex workers, of course, were also threatened but, because of their criminalized position, were unable to bring their concerns about this threat to the police, thereby warning the public.
50 Interview, Resident D, Dartmouth, 28 July 2002.
51 The uptown of Saint John lacked representation on city council for some years, and many felt that its interests – as a densely populated urban core – were ignored in favour of those of the suburbs represented by city councillors.

52 Sandra David, "Coburg Street resident says prostitution has never been so bad in her neighbourhood," *New Brunswick Telegraph-Journal*, 6 September 2003, A2.
53 Interview, Resident X, Saint John, 29 July 2004.
54 See, for example, Helen Boritch's discussion of the need to work for the short-term removal of criminalization, stigmatization, and danger, but also the long-term elimination of prostitution in *Fallen Women*, 129.
55 *Reference Re Sections 193 and 195.1(1)(c) of the Criminal Code (Man.)* (1990), 56 C.C.C. (3d) 65 (S.C.C.) and *R. V. Downey*, [1992] 2 S.C.R. 10; McGinnis, "Whores and Worthies," 105-22.
56 Kathleen Mahoney of LEAF as quoted in McGinnis, "Whores and Worthies," 118. The 1990 Reference Case (*Reference Re Sections 193 and 195.1(1)(c) of the Criminal Code (Man.)* (1990), 56 C.C.C. (3d) 65 (S.C.C.)) – for which LEAF did not apply for intervener status – dealt with Charter implications of the (then) Criminal Code sections on bawdy houses and soliciting in a public place.
57 See Laurie Bell, *Good Girls/Bad Girls: Feminists and Sex Trade Workers Face to Face* (Toronto: Seal, 1987) for an account of this debate in the mainstream Canadian feminist movement.
58 See Shaver, "A Critique of the Feminist Charges," 82-88.
59 Brock, *Making Work, Making Trouble*, 146.
60 McGinnis, "Whores and Worthies," 119.
61 This problematic alliance between social conservatives and feminists has been most clear in the United States, where some feminists groups have been willing to co-operate with conservative groups in order to bring about stricter anti-prostitution and anti-trafficking measures, despite the obvious danger in promoting the political power of right-wing groups and in undermining the rights of sex workers. Sweden has passed laws further criminalizing the trade in order to punish male behaviour, which may have pushed Swedish sex workers further underground and into more dangerous conditions. Leslie Ann Jeffrey, "US Anti-Trafficking Policy and Neo-Imperial Masculinity: The Right Man for the Job," paper presented at the annual meeting of the International Studies Association, Montreal, 17 March 2004; Anna-Louise Crago, "Unholy Alliance," AlterNet, 21 May 2003, http://www.walnet.org/csis/news/usa_2003/alternet-030521.html. For the Swedish case, see Petra Östergren, "Sexworkers Critique of Swedish Prostitution Policy," http://www.petraostergren.com.
62 As mentioned earlier, this concern has shaped government responses as well. However, anti-trafficking measures targeted at sex work create the same problems as anti-pimping legislation, as most migrant sex workers seek safe working conditions, not rescue from the trade. Noulmook Sutdhibhasilp, "Migrant Sex Workers in Canada," in *Transnational Prostitution: Changing Global Patterns*, ed. Susanne Thorbek and Bandana Pattanaik (New York: Zed, 2002), 173-91. See also Jo Bindman, "Redefining Prostitution as Sex Work on the International Agenda," Anti-Slavery International and Network of Sex Work Projects, 1997, http://www.nswp.org, and the collection Kempadoo and Doezema, *Global Sex Workers*.
63 Sylvia Davis and Martha Shaffer, "Prostitution in Canada: The Invisible Menace or the Menace of Invisibility?" 1994, http://www.walnet.org/csis/papers/sdavis.html, section 3.
64 Pivot Legal Society, *Voices for Dignity*, 30.
65 See Shaver, "Prostitution: A Critical Analysis of Three Policy Approaches," *Canadian Public Policy* 11, 3 (1985): 496.
66 Petra Östergren, "Sexworkers Critique of Swedish Prostitution Policy," http://www.petraostergren.com.
67 See, among others, Lowman, "Prostitution Law Reform in Canada," http://users.uniserve.com/~lowman/; Shaver, "Prostitution: A Critical Analysis," 498-99; Pivot Legal Society, *Voices for Dignity*, 2; Davis and Shaffer, section 3; Bastow, "Prostitution and HIV/AIDS"; Bruckert, Parent, and Robitaille, "Erotic Service," viii, 54. The lack of knowledge about migrant sex work issues in Canada has left some advocates of decriminalization unsure of what do to with the subsections of section 212 (procuring), which deal with trafficking. See, for example, Pivot Legal Society, *Voices for Dignity*, 2, and British Columbia Civil Liberties Association, "Updated Position on Sex Work Laws," presentation to the Subcommittee on Solicitation Laws, January 2005, 2. A number of researchers on migrant sex work, however, argue that such provisions, like the procuring provisions, generally are unnecessary since kidnapping, extortion, and forced labour (the crimes that constitute "trafficking")

are already covered under the Criminal Code, and to insist on a particular crime related to sex work is to fail to recognize that the problems faced by migrant sex workers are common to many migrant workers in, for example, agriculture and domestic work. That is, the laws on trafficking in relation to sex work specifically suffer from the same problems that plague all the laws criminalizing sex work and procuring in that, as Davis and Shaffer have argued, "so long as laws specifically target prostitution, whether to hinder or 'help' them, prostitutes will be subject to separate but unequal treatment." Davis and Shaffer, "Prostitution in Canada," section 3. On migrant sex workers and rights in Canada see, for example, Annalee Lepp, "Trafficking Women and the Feminization of Migration: The Canadian Case," *Canadian Woman Studies* 21-22, 1-4 (2002): 90-99; Leslie Ann Jeffrey, "Canada and Migrant Sex Work: Challenging the 'Foreign' in Foreign Policy," *Canadian Foreign Policy* 12, 1 (2005): 33-48.

68 Davis and Shaffer, "Prostitution in Canada," section 3; Pivot Legal Society, *Voices for Dignity*, 30.
69 Pivot Legal Society, *Voices for Dignity*, 31-34.
70 AIDS researchers, for instance, have pointed to the criminalization of sex work as increasing the vulnerability of sex workers to various diseases. See, for example, Allman, "M is for Mutual," 63; Bastow, "Prostitution and HIV/AIDS"; and Canadian HIV/AIDS Legal Network, *Sex, Work, Rights: Challenging Canada's Criminal Laws to Protect Sex Workers' Health and Human Rights* (Toronto: Canadian HIV/AIDS Legal Network, 2005).
71 Jo Doezema, "Ouch! Western Feminists' 'Wounded Attachment' to the 'Third World Prostitute,'" *Feminist Review* 67 (Spring 2001): 16-38.
72 McGinnis, "Whores and Worthies," 122.
73 Jeffrey, "US Anti-Trafficking Policy."
74 Again, see the work by Laura Agustín on migrant sex work, as well as that of Jo Doezema. The Network of Sex Work Projects offers a series of helpful articles on the issue on its website at http://www.nswp.org.
75 Marieke van Doorninck, "A Business Like Any Other? Managing the Sex Industry in the Netherlands," in Thorbek and Pattanaik, *Transnational Prostitution*, 199-200.
76 Davis and Shaffer, "Prostitution in Canada," section 4:2; Brock, *Making Work, Making Trouble*, 145; Pivot Legal Society, *Voices for Dignity*, 35; Benoit and Millar, *Dispelling Myths*, 96; Canadian HIV/AIDS Legal Network, presentation to the Subcommittee on Solicitation Laws, speaking notes, 15 March 2005, http://www.aidslaw.ca; Bruckert, Parent, and Robitaille, "Erotic Service," 54; Nick Larson, "Time to Legalize Prostitution," *Policy Options* 13, 7 (1992): 22.
77 Davis and Shaffer, "Prostitution in Canada," section 4:2.
78 See, for example, Lewis and Maticka-Tyndale's study of the licensing system in Windsor, Ontario, where police sometimes used the information gathered through licensing to assist them in conducting raids of escort services. Lewis and Maticka-Tyndale, *Escort Services in a Border Town*, 33-35.
79 Bruckert, Parent, and Robitaille, "Erotic Service," 54.
80 Stepping Stone has argued in its presentation to the Subcommittee on Solicitation Laws that section 318 of the Criminal Code, Hate Propaganda, should be amended to include the protection of gender and "work and occupation" as one way to address this stigma. See Stepping Stone, "Prepared Statement to the Subcommittee on Solicitation Laws of the House of Commons Standing Committee on Justice, Human Rights, Public Security and Emergency Preparedness, to Improve the Safety of Sex-Trade Workers and to Recommend Changes That Would Reduce the Exploitation of and Violence against Sex-Trade Workers," Halifax, 17 March 2005.
81 Michele Mandel, "Hookers oppose licences: Sex-traders speak out," *Toronto Sun*, 25 June 1995, 5.
82 Jacqueline Lewis and Eleanor Maticka-Tyndale, "Licensing Sex Work: Public Policy and Women's Lives," *Canadian Public Policy* 26, 4 (2000): 437-49.
83 Bruckert, Parent, and Robitaille, "Erotic Service," 19-22.
84 Judith Kilvington, Sophie Day, and Helen Ward, "Prostitution Policy in Europe: A Time of Change?" *Feminist Review* 67 (Spring 2001): 86-88.

85 Davis and Shaffer, "Prostitution in Canada," section 4:1; Barbara Sullivan, "Prostitution Law Reform in Australia: A Preliminary Evaluation," *Social Alternatives* 18, 3 (1999).
86 Bruckert, Parent, and Robitaille, "Erotic Service," 21.
87 Davis and Shaffer, "Prostitution in Canada," section 4; Bastow, "Prostitution and HIV/AIDS," 4.
88 Kilvington, Day, and Ward, "Prostitution Policy in Europe," 86-88.
89 Davis and Shaffer, "Prostitution in Canada," section 4:1. Davis and Shaffer discuss the very practical recommendations put forward from a 1986 meeting of sex workers and town-planning graduates. Indeed, such co-operation is not unheard of in Canada. Nick Larsen discusses the case of residents and sex workers in the Strathcona district of Vancouver, who worked toward mutual accommodation in the aftermath of the failure of the communicating law. See Larsen, "Prostitution: Deviant Activity or Legitimate Occupation?" in Beaman, *New Perspectives on Deviance*, 58.
90 See, for example, Sheranne Dobinson, "Victorian Situation with Legalisation," in *Sex Industry and Public Policy*, ed. S. Gerull and B. Halstead (Canberra: Australian Institute of Criminology, 1992), 118; and Crime and Misconduct Commission Queensland, *Regulating Prostitution: An Evaluation of the Prostitution Act 1999 (Qld)* (Brisbane: Crime and Misconduct Commission, 2004), 109-10.
91 Linda Banach and Sue Metzenrath, *Principles for Model Sex Industry Legislation* (Sydney: Scarlet Alliance, 2000), 14.
92 See, for example, the Law Commission of Canada's discussion of various methods of protecting workers in precarious work in an increasingly flexible environment: "Is Work Working? Works Laws That Do a Better Job," December 2004, http://www.lcc.gc.ca.
93 City of Sydney Council, *Safe House Brothels: An Information Resource for the City of Sydney Council* (Sydney, 2005).
94 As John Lowman has argued, underage sex work should be treated in the context of sexual exploitation of children, that is, as "sexual procurement of children and youth as an abuse of power, not a prostitution contract." Lowman, "Prostitution Law Reform in Canada," 17.
95 Winnipeg police have been experimenting with recording sex-trade activities and posting them on the Internet, attracting the interest of other police forces, including those in the Maritimes. Bobbi-Jean MacKinnon, "City police may enlist video cameras, Internet in fight against prostitution," *New Brunswick Telegraph-Journal*, 27 August 2004, A3.
96 See, for example, Lilian Mathieu's analysis of sex worker movements for further discussion of the difficulties faced by sex worker organizations. Lilian Mathieu, "The Emergency and Uncertain Outcomes of Prostitutes' Social Movements," *European Journal of Women's Studies* 10, 1 (2003): 29-50. Jackie West, however, has challenged pessimistic analyses of the effectiveness of sex worker organizations by arguing that the effectiveness of such organizations may rely more on the political context and the diverse interests at play than on internal difficulties and inherent weaknesses in sex worker organizations. See West, "Prostitution: Collectives and the Politics of Regulation," 106-18. Thus, under certain conditions, sex worker organizations can have a positive impact on policies and practices.
97 See, for example, the tremendous work being done through the Internet (which, despite debates over its effectiveness as a political tool, helps to overcome the problem of "outing") by the Network of Sex-Work Projects, http://www.nswp.org.
98 Queen, "Towards a Taxonomy of Tricks," 108.
99 Wendy Chapkis, "Power and Control in the Commercial Sex Trade," in Weitzer, *Sex for Sale*, 200.
100 A pilot project by the North American Opiate Medicare Initiative for the free distribution of heroin to users in Vancouver's Downtown Eastside with a view to reducing the instances of crimes such as breaking and entering has recently received Ottawa's support. "Free heroin project wins federal okay," *Victoria Times-Colonist*, 19 August 2004, A4.
101 Aaron Wildavsky, *Speaking Truth to Power* (New Brunswick, NJ: Transactions Publications, 1987; repr. 2004).

Bibliography

Aarens, Blake, B. Hima, Gina Gold, Jade Irie, Madeleine Lawson and Gloria Lockett. "Showing Up Fully: Women of Color Discuss Sex Work." In *Whores and Other Feminists*, edited by Jill Nagle, 195-209. New York: Routledge, 1997.

Agustín, Laura. "Forget Victimisation: Granting Agency to Migrants." *Development* 46, 3 (2003): 30-36.

–. "Working in the European Sex Industry." *Ofrím/Suplementos* (July 2000): 155-72. http://www.nswp.org.

Allman, Dan. "M Is for Mutual, A Is for Acts: Male Sex Work and AIDS in Canada." Ottawa: Health Canada, 1999.

Arnot, Alison. "Legalisation of the Sex Industry in the State of Victoria, Australia." MA thesis, University of Melbourne, 2002.

Backhouse, Constance. *Petticoats and Prejudice: Women and the Law in Nineteenth-Century Canada*. Toronto: Women's Press, 1983.

Banach, Linda, and Sue Metzenrath. *Principles for Model Sex Industry Legislation*. Sydney: Scarlet Alliance, 2000.

Barry, Kathleen. *The Prostitution of Sexuality*. New York: New York University Press, 1995.

Bastow, Karen. "Prostitution and HIV/AIDS." *Canadian HIV/AIDS Policy and Law Newsletter* 2, 2 (1996). http://www.aidslaw.ca.

Battle, Ken. *Minimum Wages in Canada: A Statistical Portrait with Policy Implications*. Ottawa: Caledonia Institute of Social Policy, 2003. http://www.caledoninst.org.

Bell, Laurie. *Good Girls/Bad Girls: Feminists and Sex Trade Workers Face to Face*. Toronto: Seal, 1987.

Bell, Shannon. *Reading, Writing and Rewriting the Prostitute Body*. Bloomington: Indiana University Press, 1994.

Benoit, Cecilia, and Alison Millar. *Dispelling Myths and Understanding Realities: Working Conditions, Health Status and Exiting Experiences of Street Workers*. Prostitutes Empowerment, Education and Resource Society, BC, 2001. http://web.uvic.ca/~cbenoit/papers/DispMyths.pdf.

Benoit, Cecilia, and Frances Shaver. "Health and Safety in the Sex Trade: Moving toward a Proposal for an Academic/Community Partnered Multi-Site Research Project." Report prepared for the National Network of Environments and Women's Health, York University, Ontario, 2003. http://web.uvic.ca/~cbenoit/papers/disspaper.pdf.

Benoit, Cecilia, Mikael Jansson, Bonnie Leadbeater, and Bill McCarthy. "Interactive Service Workers' Occupational Health and Safety and Access to Health Services." (Ongoing Study). http://web.uvic.ca/~cbenoit/ISW.html.

Bindman, Jo, and Jo Doezema. "Redefining Prostitution as Sex Work on the International Agenda." Vancouver: Commercial Sex Information Service. http://www.nswp.org.

Blomley, Nick. "Landscapes of Property." In *The Legal Geographies Reader: Law, Power and Space*, edited by Nicholas Blomley, David Delaney, and Richard T. Ford, 118-28. London: Blackwell, 2001.

Boritch, Helen. *Fallen Women: Female Crime and Criminal Justice in Canada*. Scarborough, ON: ITP Nelson, 1997.

Bowen, Raven. "Pathways: Real Option for Women to Reduce Reliance on Survival Sex." Vancouver: Prostitution Alternatives Counselling and Education Society, 2003. http://www.pace-society.ca.

British Columbia Civil Liberties Association. "Updated Position on Sex Work Laws." Presentation to the Sub-Committee on Solicitation Laws. Ottawa, January 2005. http://www.bccla.org/positions/privateoff/05sex%20work.htm.

Broad, Dave. "The Casualization of the Labour Force." In *Good Jobs, Bad Jobs, No Jobs: The Transformation of Work in the 21st Century*, edited by Ann Duffy, Daniel Glenday, and Norene Pupo, 58-73. Toronto: Harcourt Brace, 1997.

–. *Hollow Work, Hollow Society? Globalization and the Casual Labour Problem in Canada*. Halifax: Fernwood, 2000.

Brock, Deborah. *Making Work, Making Trouble: Prostitution as a Social Problem*. Toronto: University of Toronto Press, 1998.

–. "Victim, Nuisance, Fallen Woman, Outlaw, Worker? Making the Identity 'Prostitute' in Canadian Criminal Law." In *Law as a Gendering Practice*, edited by Dorothy E. Chunn and Dany Lacombe, 79-99. Toronto: Oxford University Press, 2000.

Bromberg, Sarah. "Feminist Issues in Prostitution." In *Prostitution: On Whores, Hustlers and Johns*, edited by James Elias, Vern Bullough, Veronica Elias, and Gwen Brewer, 294-321. New York: Prometheus Books, 1998.

Brown, Wendy. *States of Injury: Power and Freedom in Late Modernity*. Princeton, NJ: Princeton University Press, 1995.

Bruckert, Chris. *Taking It Off, Putting It On: Women in the Strip Trade*. Toronto: Women's Press, 2002.

Bruckert, Chris, Colette Parent, and Pascale Robitaille. "Erotic Service/Erotic Dance Establishments: Two Types of Marginalized Labour." Department of Criminology, University of Ottawa, 2003.

Buckland, Jerry, Thibault Martin, Nancy Barbour, Amelia Curran, Rana McDonald, and Brendan Reimer. "The Rise of Fringe Financial Services in Winnipeg's North End: Client Experiences, Firm Legitimacy and Community-Based Alternatives." Winnipeg: Institute of Urban Studies, University of Winnipeg. http://ius.uwinnipeg.ca/pdf/fringe.banking.Chesya.pdf.

Busby, Karen. "The Protective Confinement of Girls Involved in Prostitution: Potential Problems in Current Regimes." In *Being Heard: The Experiences of Young Women in Prostitution*, edited by Kelly Gorkoff and Jane Runner, 103-25. Halifax: Fernwood, 2003.

Butters, Jennifer, and Patricia Erickson. "Addictions as Deviant Behaviour: Normalizing the Pleasures of Intoxication." In *New Perspectives on Deviance: The Construction of Deviance in Everyday Life*, edited by Lori Beama, 67-84. Toronto: Prentice-Hall, 2000.

Canada. Health Canada. *Infectious Syphilis in Canada-Epi Update*. Centre for Infectious Diseases Prevention and Control, February 2003.

–. *Mediums to Reach Injection Drug Using Populations: A Discussion Paper*. Ottawa: Health Canada, Hepatitis C Prevention, Support and Research Program, Population and Public Health Branch, 2000.

–. *Profile of Hepatitis C and Injection Drug Use in Canada: A Discussion Paper*. Ottawa: Health Canada, Hepatitis C Prevention, Support and Research Program, Population and Public Health Branch, 2002.

–. *Sexual Health and Sexually Transmitted Infections Section*. Centre for Infectious Diseases Prevention and Control, August 2003.

Canada. House of Commons. *Fourth Report of the Standing Committee on Justice and the Solicitor General on Section 213 of the Criminal Code (Prostitution-Soliciting)*. Ottawa, 1990.

Canadian Council on Social Development. *The Progress of Canada's Children: Into the Millennium, 1999-2000*. Ottawa: Canadian Council on Social Development, 2000.

Canadian HIV/AIDS Legal Network. Presentation to the Subcommittee on Solicitation Laws, speaking notes, 15 March 2005. http://www.aidslaw.ca.

–. *Sex, Work, Rights: Reforming Canadian Criminal Laws on Prostitution*. Toronto: Canadian HIV/AIDS Legal Network, July 2005.

Canadian HIV/AIDS Policy and Law Newsletter 2, 2 (1996). http://www.aidslaw.ca.
Canadian Press. "Syphilis on the Rise Again, Health Canada Reports." 15 February 2002. http://www.canoe.ca/Health0202/15_syphilis-cp.html.
Castel, Robert. "From Dangerousness to Risk." In *The Foucault Effect: Studies in Governmentality*, edited by Graham Burchell, Colin Gordon, and Peter Miller, 281-98. London: Harvester Wheatsheaf, 1991.
Chapkis, Wendy. *Live Sex Acts: Women Performing Erotic Labor*. New York: Routledge, 1997.
–. "Power and Control in the Commercial Sex Trade." In *Sex for Sale*, edited by Ronald Weitzer, 181-201. New York: Routledge, 2000.
Chunn, Dorothy E., and Shelley A. M. Gavigan. "Social Control: Analytical Tool or Analytical Quagmire?" *Crime, Law and Social Change* 12, 2 (1998): 107-24.
Cler-Cunningham, Leonard, and Christine Christensen. *Violence against Women in Vancouver's Street Level Sex Trade and the Police Response*. Vancouver: Prostitution Alternatives Counselling and Education Society, 2001.
Cohen, Stanley. *Visions of Social Control*. Cambridge, UK: Polity Press, 1985.
Comack, Elizabeth. *Women in Trouble*. Halifax: Fernwood, 1996.
Conrad, Margaret R., and James K. Hiller. *Atlantic Canada: A Region in the Making*. Don Mills, ON: Oxford University Press, 2001.
Crago, Anna-Louise. "Unholy Alliance." AlterNet, 21 May 2003. http://www.walnet.org/csis/news/usa_2003/alternet-030521.html.
Crime and Misconduct Commission (Queensland). *Regulating Prostitution: An Evaluation of the Prostitution Act 1999 (Qld)*. Brisbane: Crime and Misconduct Commission, 2004.
Crook, Nikita. *A Report on Prostitution in the Atlantic Provinces*. Working Papers on Pornography and Prostitution. Report No. 12. Ottawa: Department of Justice, 1984.
Davis, Sylvia, and Martha Shaffer. "Prostitution in Canada: The Invisible Menace or the Menace of Invisibility?" 1994. http://www.walnet.org/csis/papers/sdavis.html.
Delacoste, Frédérique, and Priscilla Alexander, eds. *Sex Work: Writings by Women in the Sex Industry*. London: Virago, 1987.
Devlin, Sean. "A Working Girl's Nightmare: The Murdered and Missing Women of Skid Row." *First Nations Drum*, Fall 2000. http://www.firstnationsdrum.com/fall2000/cult_missing.htm.
Dobinson, Sheranne. "Victorian Situation with Legalisation." In *Sex Industry and Public Policy*, edited by Sally-Anne Gerull and Boronia Halstead, 117-20. Canberra: Australian Institute of Criminology, 1992.
Doezema, Jo. "Loose Women or Lost Women? The Re-Emergence of the Myth of 'White Slavery' in Contemporary Discourses of 'Trafficking in Women.'" Paper presented at the International Studies Association Annual Convention, Washington, DC, 18-19 February 1999. http://www.walnet.org/csis/papers/doezema-loose.html.
–. "Ouch! Western Feminists' 'Wounded Attachment' to the 'Third World Prostitute.'" *Feminist Review* 67 (Spring 2001): 16-38.
Dorais, Michel. *Rent Boys: The World of Male Sex Workers*. Montreal: McGill-Queen's University Press, 2005.
Duff, Anthony. *Intention and Agency and Criminal Liability: Philosophy of Action and Criminal Law*. London: Basil Blackwell, 1990.
Edwards, Ann R. *Regulation and Repression: The Study of Social Control*. Sydney: Allen and Unwin, 1998.
Ekos Research Associates. *Street Prostitution: Assessing the Impact of the Law, Halifax*. Ottawa: Department of Justice, 1989.
Elias, James, Vern Bullough, Veronica Elias, and Gwen Brewer, eds. *Prostitution: On Whores, Hustlers and Johns*. New York: Prometheus Books, 1998.
Ellickson, R. "Controlling Misconduct in City Spaces: Of Panhandlers, Skid Rows, and Public Space Zoning." In *The Legal Geographies Reader: Law, Power and Space*, edited by Nicholas Blomley, David Delaney, and Richard T. Ford, 19-30. London: Blackwell, 2001.
Enloe, Cynthia. "Silicon Tricks and the Two Dollar Woman." *New Internationalist* (January 1992): 12-14.
Esterberg, Kristin G. *Qualitative Methods in Social Research*. Boston: McGraw-Hill, 2002.

Faith, Karlene. *Unruly Women: The Politics of Confinement and Resistance.* Vancouver: Press Gang, 1993.
Fedec, Kari. "Women and Children in Canada's Sex Trade: The Discriminatory Policing of the Marginalized." In *Marginality and Condemnation: An Introduction to Critical Criminology,* edited by Bernard Schissel and Carolyn Brooks, 253-67. Halifax: Fernwood, 2002.
Federal/Provincial/Territorial Working Group on Prostitution. *Report and Recommendations in Respect of Legislation, Policy and Practices Concerning Prostitution Related Activities.* Ottawa: Department of Justice, 1998.
Flax, Jane. *Thinking Fragments: Psychoanalysis, Feminism and Postmodernism in the Contemporary West.* Berkeley: University of California Press, 1990.
Fleischman, John. *Violence against Street Prostitutes in Halifax 1980-1994.* Technical Report No. TR1996-17F. Ottawa: Department of Justice, 1996.
Foucault, Michel. *Discipline and Punish: The Birth of the Prison.* Translated by Alan Sheridan. New York: Vintage Books, 1977.
–. *The History of Sexuality,* vol. 1. Translated by Robert Hurley. New York: Vintage Books, 1990.
–. "Politics and the Study of Discourse." In *The Foucault Effect: Studies in Governmentality,* edited by Graham Burchell, Colin Gordon, and Peter Miller, 52-73. London: Harvester Wheatsheaf, 1991.
Garland, David. *The Culture of Control: Crime and Social Order in Contemporary Society.* New York: Oxford University Press, 2001.
Gemme, Robert. "Legal and Sexological Aspects of Adult Street Prostitution: A Case for Sexual Pluralism." In *Prostitution: On Whores, Hustlers and Johns,* edited by James Elias, Vern Bullough, Veronica Elias, and Gwen Brewer, 474-87. New York: Prometheus, 1998.
Gibson, Dale. "Pimps, Presumptions and Predatory Laws: R. v. Downey." *Canadian Bar Review* 71 (1992): 721-34.
Gorham, Deborah. "The 'Maiden Tribute of Modern Babylon' Re-Examined: Child Prostitution and the Idea of Childhood in Late-Victorian England." *Victorian Studies* 21, 3 (1978): 353-80.
Gorkoff, Kelly, and Meghan Waters. "Balancing Safety, Respect and Choice in Programs for Young Women Involved in Prostitution." In *Being Heard: The Experiences of Young Women in Prostitution,* edited by Kelly Gorkoff and Jane Runner, 126-46. Halifax: Fernwood, 2003.
Hadley, Karen. *And Still We Ain't Satisfied: Gender Inequality in Canada: A Status Report for 2001.* Toronto: CSJ Foundation for Research and Education, and the National Action Committee on the Status of Women, June 2001.
Hantrakul, Sukanya. "Spirit of a Fighter: Women and Prostitution in Thailand." *Manushi* 18 (October/November 1983): 27-35.
Highcrest, Alexandra. *At Home on the Stroll: My Twenty Years as a Prostitute in Canada.* Toronto: Knopf, 1997.
Hochschild, Arlie Russell. *The Managed Heart.* Berkeley: University of California Press, 1983.
Hoigard, Cecilie, and Liv Finstad. *Backstreets: Prostitution, Money and Love.* University Park: Pennsylvania State University Press, 1992.
Hunt, Alan. "Regulating Heterosocial Space: Sexual Politics in the Early Twentieth Century." *Journal of Historical Sociology* 15, 1 (2002): 1-34.
Jackson, Lois. "Sex Trade Workers in Halifax, Nova Scotia: What Are Their Risks of HIV at Work and at Home?" *Canadian Women Studies* 21, 2 (2001): 44-48.
Jeffrey, Leslie Ann. "Canada and Migrant Sex Work, Challenging the 'Foreign' in Foreign Policy." *Canadian Foreign Policy* 12, 1 (2005): 33-48.
–. "Prostitution as Public Nuisance: Canada." In *The Politics of Prostitution: Women's Movements, Democratic States and the Globalisation of Sex Commerce,* edited by Joyce Outshoorn, 83-102. New York: Cambridge University Press, 2004.
–. *Sex and Borders: Gender, National Identity and Prostitution Policy in Thailand.* Toronto and Vancouver: UBC Press, 2002.
–. "US Anti-Trafficking Policy and Neo-Imperial Masculinity: The Right Man for the Job." Paper presented at the annual meeting of the International Studies Association, Montreal, 17 March 2004.

Jeffreys, Sheila. *The Idea of Prostitution*. Melbourne: Spinifex, 1997.
Jessome, Phonse. *Somebody's Daughter: Inside the Toronto/Halifax Pimping Ring*. Halifax: Nimbus, 1996.
Jiwani, Yasmin. *Trafficking and Sexual Exploitation of Girls and Young Women: A Review of Select Literature and Initiatives*. 2nd ed. Vancouver: Feminist Research, Education, Development and Action Centre, 1999.
Jolin, Annette. "On the Backs of Working Prostitutes: Feminist Theory and Prostitution Policy." *Crime and Delinquency* 40, 1 (1994): 69-83.
Kempadoo, K., and J. Doezema, eds. *Global Sex-Workers: Rights, Resistance, Redefinition*. New York: Routledge, 1998.
Kilvington, J., S. Day, and H. Ward. "Prostitution Policy in Europe? A Time of Change." *Feminist Review* 67, 1 (2001): 78-93.
Lacasse, Shirley. "Les danseuses nues." PhD diss., Université de Montréal, 2004.
Larsen, E. Nick. "The Effect of Different Police Enforcement Policies on the Control of Prostitution." *Canadian Public Policy* 22, 1 (1996): 40-50.
–. "The Politics of Law Reform: Prostitution Policy in Canada, 1985-1995." In *Law in Society: Canadian Readings*, edited by Nick Larsen and Brian Burtch, 60-74. Toronto: Harcourt Brace, 1999.
–. "The Politics of Prostitution Control: Interest Group Politics in Four Canadian Cities." *International Journal of Urban and Regional Research* 16 (June 1992): 169-89.
–. "Prostitution: Deviant Activity or Legitimate Occupation?" In *New Perspectives on Deviance: The Construction of Deviance in Everyday Life*, edited by Lori G. Beaman, 50-66. Scarborough, ON: Prentice-Hall, 2000.
–. "Time to Legalize Prostitution." *Policy Options* 13, 7 (1992): 21-22.
Law Commission of Canada. *Is Work Working? Works Laws That Do a Better Job*. Discussion paper, December 2004. http://www.lcc.gc.ca.
Lee, Kevin K. *Urban Poverty in Canada: A Statistical Profile*. Ottawa: Canadian Council on Social Development, 2000.
LeMoncheck, Linda. *Loose Women, Lecherous Men: A Feminist Philosophy of Sex*. New York: Oxford University Press, 1997.
Lepp, Annalee. "Trafficking Women and the Feminization of Migration: The Canadian Case." *Canadian Woman Studies* 21-22, 4-1 (2002): 90-99.
Lerum, Kari. "Twelve-Step Feminism Makes Sex Workers Sick: How the State and the Recovery Movement Turn Radical Women into 'Useless Citizens.'" In *Sex Work and Sex Workers*, edited by Barry M. Dank and R. Refinetti, 7-36. New Brunswick, NJ: Transaction, 1999.
Lever, Janet, and Deanne Dolnick. "Clients and Call Girls: Seeking Sex and Intimacy." In *Sex for Sale: Prostitution, Pornography and the Sex Industry*, edited by Ronald Weitzer, 85-100. New York: Routledge, 2000.
Lewis, J., and E. Maticka-Tyndale. *Erotic/Exotic Dancing: HIV-Relative Risk Factors*. Final report. Ottawa: National Health Research and Development Program, Health Canada. Grant no. 6606-5688. 1998. http://www.walnet.org/csis/papers/lewis-strip.html.
–. *Escort Services in a Border Town: Transmission Dynamics of Sexually Transmitted Infections within and between Communities – Literature and Policy Summary*. Ottawa: Division of STD Prevention and Control, Laboratory Centre for Disease Control, Health Canada, 1999.
–. *Escort Services in a Border Town: Transmission Dynamics of STDs within and between Communities – Methodological Challenges Conducting Research Related to Sex Work*. Ottawa: Division of STD Prevention and Control, Laboratory Centre for Disease Control, Health Canada, 2000.
–. *Final Report: Erotic Dancing – HIV Related Risk Factors*. Ottawa: Health Canada, 1998.
–. "Licensing Sex Work: Public Policy and Women's Lives." *Canadian Public Policy* 26, 4 (2000): 437-49.
Lowman, John. "Canada." In *Prostitution: An International Handbook on Trends, Problems and Policies*, edited by Nanette J. Davis, 56-86. Westport, CT: Greenwood Press, 1993.
–. "Prostitution Law Reform in Canada." 1998. http://users.uniserve.com/~lowman/ProLaw/prolawcan.htm.

–. "Street Prostitution Control: Some Canadian Reflections on the Finsbury Park Experience." *British Journal of Criminology* 32, 1 (1992): 1-17.
–. "Taking Young Prostitutes Seriously." *Canadian Review of Sociology and Anthropology* 24, 1 (1987): 99-116.
–. "Violence and the Outlaw Status of (Street) Prostitution in Canada." *Violence against Women* 6, 9 (2000): 987-1011.
Lowman, John, Chris Atchison, and Laura Fraser. "Men Who Buy Sex: Preliminary Findings of an Exploratory Study." In *Prostitution: On Whores, Hustlers and Johns*, edited by James Elias, Vern Bullough, Veronica Elias, and Gwen Brewer, 172-203. New York: Prometheus Books, 1998.
–. *Men Who Buy Sex: Summary of Phase 1 Report*. BC: Ministry of Attorney General, 1996.
Lowman, John, and L. Fraser. *Violence against Persons Who Prostitute: The Experience in British Columbia*. Ottawa: Department of Justice Canada, 1995.
Lyon, David. *The Electronic Eye: The Rise of Surveillance Society*. Minneapolis: University of Minnesota Press, 1994.
MacCoun, Robert J. *Toward a Psychology of Harm Reduction*. Santa Monica, CA: Drug Policy Research Centre, Rand Corporation, 2001.
MacDonald, Gayle. "Forbidden Sex: Images and Realities of Prostitution." Paper presented to the bi-annual International Association of Women Philosophers, Goteborg, Sweden, June 2004.
–. "In Absentia: Women and the Sexual as a Social Construct in Law." In *Feminism, Law, Inclusion: Intersectionality in Action*, edited by Gayle MacDonald, Rachel Osborne, and Charles C. Cross, 50-69. Toronto: Sumach, 2005.
–. "Intention and Agency in the Criminal Law: A Feminist Critique." Paper presented to the annual meeting of the American Society of Criminology, New Orleans, November 1992.
–. "Power, Feminists and the Sex Trade: Women Worlds Apart?" In *Wissen, Macht, Geschlecht: Knowledge, Power, Gender – Philosophy and the Future of the 'Condition Feminine,'* edited by Birgit Christensen, 611-17. Zurich: Chronos Verlag, 2002.
–. "What's Gender Got to Do with It? Sex Workers in the Maritimes." Paper presented to the annual meeting of the Canadian Sociology and Anthropology Association, London, Ontario, June 2005.
MacDonald, Gayle, and Leslie Jeffrey. "Voices from the Trade: Eastern Canadian Sex Workers Talk Back." Paper presented to the European History of the Social Sciences Conference, Berlin, March 2004.
MacDonald, Gayle, Rachel Osborne, and Charles C. Cross, eds. *Feminism, Law, Inclusion: Intersectionality in Action*. Toronto: Sumach, 2005.
MacDonald, Maureen. "The Impact of a Restructured Canadian Welfare State on Atlantic Canada." *Social Policy and Administration* 32, 4 (1998): 389-400.
Manderson, Lenore. "Public Sex Performances in Patpong and Exploration of the Edges of Imagination." *Journal of Sex Research* 29, 4 (1992): 451-75.
Maritime Centre of Excellence for Women's Health. *Social Investment: It's Time to Invest in New Brunswick's Children, Families and Communities*. Atlantic Case Studies Policy Discussion Series Paper No. 4, 1999.
Mathieu, Lilian. "The Emergence and Uncertain Outcomes of Prostitutes' Social Movements." *European Journal of Women's Studies* 10, 1 (2003): 29-50.
Mawani, Renisa. "Regulating the 'Respectable Classes': Venereal Disease, Gender, and Public Health Initiatives in Canada, 1914-1935." In *Regulating Lives: Historical Essays on the State, Society, and the Individual*, edited by J. McLaren, R. Menzies, and D.E. Chunn, 170-95. Vancouver: UBC Press, 2002.
McClintock, Anne. "Screwing the System: Sexwork, Race and the Law." *Boundary* 2 (Summer 1992): 70-95.
McFayden, Sandra D. *Money Matters: Women in Nova Scotia, Part 1 of a Statistical Series*. Halifax: Nova Scotia Advisory Council on the Status of Women, 2000.
McGinnis, Janice Dickin. "Whores and Worthies: Feminism and Prostitution." *Canadian Journal of Law and Society* 9, 1 (1994): 105-22.
McKay, Corina. "Is Sex Work Queer?" *Social Alternatives* 18, 3 (1999): 48-54.

McKeganey, N. "Why Do Men Buy Sex and What Are Their Assessments of the HIV-Related Risks When They Do?" *AIDS Care* 6, 3 (1994): 289-302.

McLeod, Eileen. *Women Working: Prostitution Now*. London: Croom Helm, 1982.

Meaghan, Diane E. "Aids and Sex Workers: A Case for Patriarchy Interruptus." *Canadian Women Studies* 21, 2 (2001): 107-10.

Mohanty, Chandra Talpade. "Under Western Eyes: Feminist Scholarship and Colonial Discourses." Chap. 1 in *Feminism without Borders: Decolonizing Theory, Practicing Solidarity*. Durham, NC: Duke University Press, 2003.

Monto, Martin A. "Why Men Seek Out Prostitutes." In *Sex for Sale: Prostitution, Pornography and the Sex Industry*, edited by Ronald Weitzer, 67-103. New York: Routledge, 2000.

Mulia, Nina. "Questioning Sex: Drug-Using Women and Heterosexual Relations." *Journal of Drug Issues* 30, 4 (2001): 741-66.

Murray, Karen. "Do Not Disturb: 'Vulnerable Populations' in Federal Government Policy Discourses and Practices." *Canadian Journal of Urban Research* 13, 1 (2004): 59-64.

Nadon, Susan M., Catherine Koverola, and Eduard H. Schludermann. "Antecedents to Prostitution: Childhood Victimization." *Journal of Interpersonal Violence* 13, 2 (1998): 206-21.

Nagle, Jill. "Book Review" (review of *Making Work, Making Trouble: Prostitution as a Social Problem* by Deborah R. Brock; *Prostitution, Power and Freedom* by Julia O'Connell Davidson; *Sex Work and Sex Workers*, edited by Barry M. Dank and Roberto Refinetti; *Sex for Sale: Prostitution, Pornography, and the Sex Industry*, edited by Ronald Weitzer). *Signs* 27, 4 (2002): 1177-83.

New Brunswick. Advisory Council on the Status of Women. *Report Card on the Status of Women in New Brunswick 2004*. Fredericton, NB: Advisory Council on the Status of Women, 2004.

–. Department of Public Safety and Department of Health and Wellness. *Study on Addicted Women* (unpublished), 2002.

–. Family and Community Services. Planning, Research and Evaluation Branch. *Social Assistance Rate Schedules*. Fredericton, NB: Family and Community Services, 2003.

Newfoundland. Department of Health and Community Services, OxyContin Task Force. *OxyContin Task Force Final Report*. St. John's: Newfoundland Department of Health and Community Services, 2004.

Nova Scotia. Advisory Council on the Status of Women. *A Profile of Poverty in Nova Scotia*. Halifax, 1997.

O'Connell Davidson, Julia. *Prostitution, Power and Freedom*. Ann Arbor: University of Michigan Press, 1998.

Ortner, Sherry B. "Resistance and the Problem of Ethnographic Refusal." *Comparative Studies in Society and History* 37, 1 (1995): 173-93.

Östergren, Petra. "Sexworkers Critique of Swedish Prostitution Policy." http://www.petraostergren.com.

Overall, Christine. "What's Wrong with Prostitution? Evaluating Sex Work." *Signs* 17 (1992): 705-24.

Pendleton, Eva. "Love for Sale: Queering Heterosexuality." In *Whores and Other Feminists*, edited by Jill Nagle, 73-82. New York: Routledge, 1997.

Penfold, Susan P. "Drugged, Exploited, Labelled and Blamed: How Psychiatry Oppresses Women." In *[Ab]using Power: The Canadian Experience*, edited by S.C. Boyd, D.E. Chunn, and R. Menzies, 174-84. Halifax: Fernwood, 2001.

Pheterson, Gail. *The Prostitution Prism*. Amsterdam: Amsterdam University Press, 1996.

–. "The Whore Stigma: Female Dishonour and Male Unworthiness." *Social Text* 37 (Winter 1993): 39-64.

Pivot Legal Society Sex Work Subcommittee. *Voices for Dignity: A Call to End the Harms Caused by Canada's Sex Trade Laws*. Vancouver: Law Foundation of British Columbia, 2004.

Queen, Carol. "Sex Radical Politics, Sex-Positive Feminist Thought, and Whore Stigma." In *Whores and Other Feminists*, edited by Jill Nagle, 125-35. New York: Routledge, 1997.

–. "Toward a Taxonomy of Tricks: A Whore Considers the Age-Old Question, 'What Do Clients Want?'" In *Tricks and Treats: Sex Workers Write about Their Clients*, edited by Matt Bernstein Sycamore, 105-14. Binghampton, NY: Harrington Park, 2000.

Raymond, Janice. "Prostitution as Violence against Women: NGO Stonewalling in Beijing and Elsewhere." *Women's Studies International Forum* 21, 1 (1998): 1-9.
Reitsma-Street, M., J. Schofield, B. Lund, and C. Kasting. *Housing Policy Options for Women Living in Urban Poverty: An Action Research Project in Three Canadian Cities.* Ottawa: Status of Women Canada Policy Research Fund, 2001.
Rickard, Wendy. "'Been There, Seen It, Done It, I've Got the T-Shirt': British Sex Workers Reflect on Jobs, Hopes, the Future and Retirement." *Feminist Review* 67 (2001): 111-32.
Sarlo, Christopher. *Poverty in Canada.* 2nd ed. Vancouver: Fraser Institute, 1996.
Schissel, Bernard, and Linda Mahood. *Social Control in Canada: Issues in the Social Construction of Deviance.* Toronto: Oxford University Press, 1996.
Schramm, Heather. "The Politics of Crime Prevention Programmes: Sex Worker Exclusion." Paper presented at the annual meeting of the Canadian Sociology and Anthropology Association, Halifax, 1 June 2003.
Scott, James C. *Weapons of the Weak: Everyday Forms of Peasant Resistance.* New Haven, CT: Yale University Press, 1985.
Scoular, Jane. "The 'Subject' of Prostitution: Interpreting the Discursive, Symbolic and Material Position of Sex/Work in Feminist Theory." *Feminist Theory* 5, 3 (2004): 343-55.
Se'ver, Aysan. *Fleeing the House of Horrors: Women Who Have Left Abusive Partners.* Toronto: University of Toronto Press, 2002.
Shaver, Frances M. "A Critique of the Feminist Charges against Prostitution." *Atlantis* 14, 1 (1988): 82-89.
–. "Prostitution: A Critical Analysis of Three Policy Approaches." *Canadian Public Policy* 11, 3 (1985): 493-503.
–. "Prostitution: A Female Crime?" In *In Conflict with the Law: Canadian Women and the Criminal Justice System,* edited by Ella Adelberg and Claudia Currie, 153-73. Vancouver: Press Gang, 1993.
–. "Prostitution: On the Dark Side of the Service Industry." In *Post-Critical Criminology,* edited by Thomas O'Reilly-Fleming, 42-55. Scarborough, ON: Prentice-Hall, 1996.
–. "The Regulation of Prostitution: Avoiding the Morality Traps." *Canadian Journal of Law and Society* 9, 1 (1994): 123-45.
–. "Traditional Data Distort Our View of Prostitution." Notes from a presentation at "When Sex Works: International Conference on Prostitution and Other Sex Work," 27-29 September 1996, Montreal. http://www.walnet.org/csis/papers/shaver-distort.html.
Shrage, Laurie. *Moral Dilemmas of Feminism.* New York: Routledge, 1994.
Sibley, David. *Geographies of Exclusion: Society and Difference in the West.* London: Routledge, 1995.
Simmons, Melanie. "Theorizing Prostitution: Questions of Agency." In *Sex Work and Sex Workers,* edited by Barry M. Dank, 125-48. New Brunswick, NJ: Transaction, 1999.
Simpson, Mary. *Social Investment in New Brunswick.* Atlantic Case Studies Policy Discussion Series Paper No. 7. Halifax: Maritimes Centre for Excellence for Women's Health, 2000.
Smith, Tanya Dawne. "Pimping and Prostitution in Halifax in the Early 1990s: The Evolution of a Moral Panic." MA thesis, Dalhousie University, 2000.
Spivak, Gayatri Chakravorty. *A Critique of Postcolonialist Reason: Toward a History of the Vanishing Present.* Cambridge, MA: Harvard University Press, 1999.
Sprinkle, Annie. "You've Come a Long Way Baby, or, How to Cure Sex Worker Burnout: Annie Sprinkle's 12 Step Program." In *Prostitution: On Whores, Hustlers, and Johns,* edited by James Elias, Vern Bullogh, Veronica Elias, and Gwen Brewer, 112-13. New York: Prometheus Books, 1998.
Stepping Stone. "Prepared Statement to the Subcommittee on Solicitation Laws of the House of Commons Standing Committee on Justice, Human Rights, Public Security and Emergency Preparedness, to Improve the Safety of Sex-Trade Workers and to Recommend Changes That Would Reduce the Exploitation of and Violence against Sex-Trade Workers," Halifax, 17 March 2005.
Sullivan, Barbara. "Prostitution and Consent: Beyond the Liberal Dichotomy of 'Free or Forced.'" In *Making Sense of Sexual Consent,* edited by Mark Cowling and Paul Reynolds, 127-39. Burlington, VT: Ashgate, 2004.

—. "Prostitution Law Reform in Australia: A Preliminary Evaluation." *Social Alternatives* 18, 3 (1999): 9-14.
—. "Trafficking in Women: Feminism and New International Law." *International Feminist Journal of Politics* 5, 1 (2003): 67-91.
Surette, Ray. *Media, Crime and Criminal Justice: Images and Realities.* New York: Wadsworth, 1997.
Sutdhibhasilp, Noulmook. "Migrant Sex-Workers in Canada." In *Transnational Prostitution: Changing Global Patterns,* edited by Susanne Thorbek and Bandana Pattanaik, 173-91. New York: Zed, 2002.
Totten, Mark. *Guys, Gangs and Girlfriend Abuse.* Peterborough, ON: Broadview, 2001.
Tutty, Leslie, and Kendra Nixon. "'Selling Sex, It's Really Like Selling Your Soul': Vulnerability to and the Experience of Exploitation through Child Prostitution." In *Being Heard: The Experiences of Young Women in Prostitution,* edited by Kelly Gorkoff and Jane Runner, 29-45. Halifax: Fernwood, 2003.
Tyndall, Dr. Mark (director of Epidemiology, BC Centre of Excellence, University of British Columbia). Testimony before the Special Committee on the Non-Medical Use of Drugs, 3 December 2001. http://www.parl.gc.ca/InfocomDoc/37/1/SNUD/meetings/evidence/snudev14-e.htm#T0925.
Urban Core Support Network. *Moving On: A Gender Based Analysis on Poverty Reduction in Saint John.* Saint John, NB: Urban Core Support Network, 2003.
Valverde, Mariana. *The Age of Light, Soap and Water: Moral Reform in English Canada, 1885-1925.* Toronto: McClelland and Stewart, 1991.
—. *Law's Dream of a Common Knowledge.* Princeton, NJ: Princeton University Press, 2003.
van Brunschot, Erin Gibbs. "Community Policing and 'John Schools.'" *Canadian Review of Sociology and Anthropology* 40, 2 (2003): 215-32.
van Dijk, Teun. *Discourse as Social Interaction.* London: Sage, 1997.
—. *News as Discourse.* Hillsdale, NJ: Erlbaum, 1988.
van Doorninck, Marieke. "A Business Like Any Other? Managing the Sex Industry in the Netherlands." In *Transnational Prostitution: Changing Global Patterns,* edited by Susanne Thorbek and Bandana Pattanaik, 193-201. New York: Zed, 2002.
Vezina, Anne, and Karen Messing. "Background Research for a Comparative Study of the Ergonomics of Prostitution." Part 3 of *Work, Restructuring, Health and Policy Implications: The Sex Trade Environment,* edited by Frances Shaver, Katherine Lippel, and Karen Messing. Sex Trade Advocacy and Research, 1988-99, National Network on Environments and Women's Health. http://www.yorku.ca/nnewn/english/pubs/work_restructuring.pdf.
Vosko, Leah F. "The Pasts (and Futures) of Feminist Political Economy in Canada: Reviving the Debate." In *Developments in Feminism,* edited by Caroline Andrew, Pat Armstrong, Hugh Armstrong, Wallace Clement, and Leah Vosko, 305-32. Toronto: Women's Press, 2003.
Weitzer, Ronald. "Flawed Theory and Method in Studies of Prostitution." *Violence against Women* 11, 7 (2005): 934-49.
West, Candace, Michelle M. Lazar, and Cheris Kramarae. "Gender in Discourse." In *Discourse as Social Interaction,* edited by Teun A. Van Dijk, 119-43. London: Sage, 1997.
West, Jackie. "Prostitution: Collectives and the Politics of Regulation." *Gender, Work and Organization* 7, 2 (2000): 106-18.
Workman, Thom. *Social Torment: Globalization in Atlantic Canada.* Halifax: Fernwood, 2003.
Young, Amy, Carol Boyd, and Amy Hubbell. "Prostitution Drug Use and Coping with Psychological Distress." *Journal of Drug Issues* 30, 4 (2000): 789-800.
Xantidis, L., and M.P. McCabe. "Personality Characteristics of Male Clients of Female Commercial Sex Workers in Australia." *Archives of Sexual Behaviour* 29, 2 (2000): 165-76.
Zatz, Noah D. "Sex Work/Sex Act: Law, Labor, and Desire in Constructions of Prostitution." *Signs* 22, 2 (1997): 277-308.

Index

addictions: and criminalization, 196, 199; as deviant, 196; as functional, 197, 250n30; and health experts, 177; and the health system, 179, 223; increase of, 249n22; and loss of control, 40; and money, 39-44, 42; and official discourse, 195-99; as pimps, 119; and self-esteem, 40, 87; and self-perception, 199; and sex work, 87, 99-100, 191-95; and social support, 235-36. *See also* health; *and specific substances*
Africville (Halifax, NS), 248n13
Agustín, Laura, 244n27
AIDS. *See* HIV/AIDS
AIDS New Brunswick, 177, 197
AIDS Nova Scotia, 14
AIDS Saint John, 185, 239n8
alcohol: acceptability of, 197, 198; and coping, 89, 191; and exotic dancing, 42; and lifestyle, 181; and moralizing, 169, 196; as a pimp, 118; and politics, 228; in the work environment, 193-94. *See also* addictions
Alexis (sex worker, Moncton): on clients, 76, 96, 98; on the media, 147; on pimps, 99; on resistance, 98; on sex work, 138; on social assistance, 52; on stigma, 96, 138; on strip clubs, 36
Alison (sex worker, Halifax), 29, 68, 79, 85, 105, 143
Alyssa (sex worker, Saint John), 79, 86, 88-89, 148-49, 172-73, 201
Angela (sex worker, Halifax), 26, 79, 106, 219
Anti-Prostitution Task Force, 223. *See also* Halifax: task force on prostitution in
anti-trafficking laws, 95, 225, 229, 253n67, 253nn61-62

April (sex worker, Halifax), 38, 68, 72-73, 91, 131, 150-51
Ashley (sex worker, Fredericton), 25, 32, 33, 34, 46, 90, 248n9
Audrey (sex worker, Fredericton), 48
Australia, 230, 231, 232

Barry, Kathleen, 9
Battle, Ken, 46-47
Belinda (sex worker, Halifax): on clients, 43, 75; on harassment, 85; on hypocrisy, 85, 115, 140, 203-4; on minimum-wage work, 45; on pimps, 97; on police, 134; on politicians, 203-4; on poverty, 53-54; on stigma, 140, 185; on willpower, 41, 100-1
Bell, Shannon, 64, 240n31
Benoit, Cecilia, 202, 242n28, 243n6
Beth (sex worker, Saint John): on addiction, 40, 191, 192, 198, 201; on health, 174-75, 192; on poverty, 51, 174-75; on stigma, 37, 138, 149; on willpower, 174-75
Bonang, Paul (Cpl.), 164
Bonnie (sex worker, Moncton), 32, 34, 48, 49, 77, 171, 190
boundary crossing, 111-12, 246n6
Brianna (sex worker, Saint John): on addiction, 100; on clients, 29, 83-84; on escort work, 33; on harassment, 86, 89; on legalization, 228; on pride, 89; on stigma, 86
Brock, Deborah, 224
Bruckert, Chris: on decriminalization, 230; on physical labour, 49; on resistance, 12, 76; on sex work, 241n16; on sex work income, 27; on sex work motivation, 63; on substance abuse, 193, 242n34; on violence, 93

Butters, Jennifer, 195

Call Off Your Old Tired Ethics (COYOTE), 232
Canadian Centre for Justice Statistics, 80
Canadian Charter of Rights and Freedoms, 156
Canadian Council on Social Development (CCSD), 46, 48, 51, 242n38
Canadian Organization for the Rights of Prostitutes, 206
Canadian Press, 162, 166, 168
Candace (sex worker, Saint John), 57, 100, 138, 184, 227
capitalism, 10, 13, 21, 22, 24, 45, 67
Carrie (sex worker, Halifax), 141, 142
Castel, Robert, 247n16
Celeste (sex worker, Halifax), 82, 107, 232, 233-34, 235
Chapkis, Wendy, 5, 6, 11, 15, 205, 236, 240n3
Charles (sex worker, Halifax), 73, 143-44, 174
child prostitution, 156
Children's Aid Society of Halifax, 157, 158, 234
chlamydia, 178, 248n10
Chronicle Herald (Halifax), 137, 155-58, 168, 170, 216
citizenship, 1, 114-16, 130, 136, 149, 169, 179-80. *See also* marginalization; sex workers: exclusion of
classism, 149, 229
clients, 154; addictions of, 192-93; and communicating charges, 165; as dangerous, 75, 83-84; entrapment of, 165; and fetishes, 76; invisibility of, 165-67; and police, 108, 166; and risk, 186; and stereotypes, 127; targeting of, 166; types of, 67-68; violent behaviour of, 63, 81, 165, 244n29, 245n37
cocaine, 43, 169, 175, 198, 220. *See also* addictions
Colleen (sex worker, Moncton): on addiction, 42, 193; on clients, 76, 91-92; on education, 46, 59-60; on emotional labour, 27-28; on family responsibilities, 59-60; on health, 193; on minimum-wage work, 46, 59-60; on poverty, 53; on resistance, 91-92; on safe-sex practices, 59-60; on safety, 27-28; on sex work income, 27-28, 59-60, 193; on social assistance, 53; on violence, 91-92
communicating law. *See* Criminal Code: and communicating law

community action research, 239n8
community agencies, 14. *See also specific entries*
Conseil permanent de la jeunesse [Permanent Council for Youth] (Quebec), 251n5
Coverdale (Saint John), 14, 128, 157, 239n8
crack: and clients, 192, 193; and control, 73; and health, 192; and hypocrisy, 146-49; and the media, 161; and middle-class addiction, 146-49; and money, 40, 41, 43, 99, 100; as a pimp, 118; and police, 131; prevalence of, 94; and sex work, 99, 100; and stigma, 131, 146-49, 161, 169, 175, 198; and street life, 195; and treatment, 198, 250n32; and willpower, 189, 195. *See also* addictions
crime prevention programs, 130, 247n16
Criminal Code: and aggravated procuring, 251n27; and bawdy house provisions, 32, 110, 204, 225, 246n3, 253n56; and communicating law, 80, 110-11, 156, 157, 204, 208; and living on the avails, 209, 225; and police sweeps, 113; and procuring, 253n67; and sex work, 110, 207-10; and work, 215. *See also* police; policing; sex trade: criminalization of
criminalization. *See* addictions: and criminalization; sex trade: criminalization of
Crook, Nikita, 241n23, 242n28
Crosbie, John, 208
Cross, Laura Lee, 169, 170, 171
culture of fear, 112, 247n16
cycle of prohibition, 8

Dana (sex worker, Halifax): on addiction, 42; on education vs street smarts, 1; on the media, 85; on murder, 108; on pimps, 94, 97; on police, 102-3, 131; on resistance, 102-3; on stereotypes, 85, 108; on violence, 81, 85, 94, 102-3, 131
Dartmouth (NS), 169, 251n16
Dartmouth police, 165
David (sex worker, Halifax), 174, 181, 183, 187, 191, 228
Davidson, Julia O'Connell, 64-65
Davies, Libby (MP), 251n5
Davis, Sylvia, 225, 229, 231, 253n67, 255n89
Dawne (sex worker, Halifax), 54, 58, 79, 181, 192
Deanna (sex worker, Saint John): on clients, 30; on degradation, 74; on health, 183-84; on murder, 90; on protection

practices, 92-93; on safe-sex practices, 185; on violence, 83, 88, 90
decriminalization. *See* sex trade: decriminalization of
Denise (sex worker, Halifax): on citizenship, 226; on clients, 88; on degradation, 203; on freedom of choice, 146; on harassment, 129, 131; on hypocrisy, 4, 78, 111, 129, 145-47, 203, 226; on legalization, 226; on police, 129, 131; on police and drugs, 133; on police violence, 133; on politicians, 203; on safety, 200; on sharing space, 219; on "smoke dates," 193; on Stepping Stone, 200, 226; on stigma, 144, 145; on strength, 78; on transsexuality, 144-45; on violence, 80, 83, 99; on zoning, 116
Dilaudid, 169, 191, 198, 249n22, 250n31
discourse: of blame, 191; civil rights, 246n3; of disposal, 85, 97; dominant, 7, 9, 12; expert, 176; health, 176-80; hegemonic, 106, 152, 155; and legal regimes, 65; mainstream, 19; neo-liberal, 179-80; official, 195-99; pimp, 117; on policy, 205; psychologizing, 137; public, 153; of resistance, 11-14; of vulnerability, 178, 179
Doezema, Jo, 226
domination business, 107
Dorais, Michel, 245n37

education: of Haligonians, 242n38; and income, 24, 46, 51, 58-59, 129, 226; and public attitudes, 217, 230, 234; and safe sex, 186, 188, 202; of Saint Johners, 242n38; and sexuality, 150-51
Employee Assistance Programs (EAPs), 198
Epstein, Howard (MLA), 216
Eric (sex worker, Moncton), 30, 38, 52, 86, 189
Erikson, Patricia, 195
erotic massage work: advantages of, 31; and clients, 69; and exploitation, 33; and income, 25-26, 46; and the law, 221; licensing of, 204, 230; and resistance, 34; risks of, 32; and safety, 221
escort work: advantages of, 31; backbiting in, 49; and clients, 128; and exploitation, 33-35; and income, 25-27, 30, 51; and the law, 220-22; licensing of, 204, 230; and management, 50; and pimps, 120; and safety, 89-90, 220-22
essentialism, 21, 62-63, 64
exotic dancing: and alcohol, 193-94; and clients, 76; demands of, 48-49; and exploitation, 36-37; and income, 27; and the law, 221; licensing of, 230; and police, 210-11; and political elites, 210-11; risks of, 32; and safety, 91, 210-11, 221; and zoning, 211-12

Fedec, Kari, 21-22
Federal/Provincial/Territorial Working Group on Prostitution, 209, 229
Federation of Canadian Municipalities, 156
Felicity (sex worker, Halifax), 69-71, 81, 132, 141, 186, 188-89, 194
feminism: and economic determinism, 20-23; emphasis of, 225; liberal, 10; and politics, 9-10; postmodernist, 10-11; problems of, 20-23; pro-rights, 10; radical, 9-10, 63-66; and sex work, 4, 240n6; and sex worker agency, 9-10; and sex workers, 1; and sex-positive readings, 66; and social conservatives, 253n61. *See also* essentialism; sex radicals
Flaro, Haley, 197
Foucault, Michel, 3, 7-9, 153
Fraser Committee, 251n6
Fredericton (NB), 178, 210-11, 239n16. *See also* New Brunswick
Fredericton RCMP, 113

gay bashing, 81, 84-85, 174, 235
gender: bias, 157, 163; constraints of, 63; gap, 20; and power, 21; and public health, 177; structure, 6, 13
Germany, 231
Gibson, Dale, 209

Hadley, Karen, 48
Halifax (NS): anti-client measures of, 213; era of pimping in, 93, 98; gentrification of, 212; and Resolution 1081, 214; sex trade in, 25, 35, 87-88, 94-95, 207-8, 212-37; and Street Ordinance #3, 207-8; task force on prostitution in, 117, 119, 123, 125, 159, 162-63. *See also* Nova Scotia
Halifax Regional Police: on addiction, 118-19; on conditions of release, 115, 116; on conflicting goals, 123-24; on Criminal Code, 123-24; on demand-driven policing, 113; on jane school, 128; on john school stings, 127, 128; on pimps, 118-19, 120, 121; and politics, 252n41; on sex work, 118-19; on task force on prostitution, 162;

vice section of, 125; on victimization, 118-19, 121
hanger beatings, 159, 162
Hannah (sex worker, Halifax), 68, 109, 135, 143, 182
harassment: by clients, 218; by the legal system, 105; physical, 143; by police, 114, 125; by the public, 85-86
health: and addictions, 175, 188, 191-99; bureaucracy, 183, 200; discourse, 176-80; and disease, 182-83; and education, 186, 188; and exclusion, 178-80; and harm reduction, 198-99; and lack of services, 176, 184; and occupational hazards, 180-81; and official discourse, 195-99; and outreach programs, 199-201; professionals, 175, 177-79, 190, 196, 248n1; and protection practices, 185; and psychological issues, 181; and rhetoric of vulnerability, 176-77; and risk, 174, 186-89; and safety, 175, 180; services, outreach, 176; and sex work, 176-78; sex workers' knowledge of, 175-76; sex workers' views on, 180-84; socioeconomic context of, 183-84; stigma and, 176-78; system, demands on, 179. *See also* addictions; safety; sexually transmitted diseases (STDs); sexually transmitted infections (STIs); violence
Health Canada, 186, 199
Heidi (sex worker, Halifax), 38, 41-42, 55-56, 81, 140
hepatitis C, 178, 248n7, 248n10
heroin, 198, 255n100
hetero-normative codes, 11, 12
HIV/AIDS: and clients, 165, 174; "crisis" of, 177; and moralizing, 196; normalization of, 182; rates of, 177, 248n10, 249n17; and safe-sex practices, 183, 185; and sex workers, 183; and stereotypes, 129, 176, 177; and stigma, 129, 176; testing for, 190
Hochschild, Arlie, 49
holy whore tradition, 71
homicide. *See* murder
homophobia, 235. *See also* gay bashing
"hooker law." *See* Criminal Code: and communicating law
Hope (sex worker, Halifax), 91, 182-83
hypocrisy: of law, 105; of the media, 154, 171; of police, 133, 135, 204; of politics, 204; of public attitudes, 139-40, 144-47; and sexual commodification, 111; of society, 105, 139-40

Indoor trade, 31-32, 33, 34, 36, 81, 221. *See also specific types*
intravenous drug use (IDU), 248n7, 248n10

Jackson, Lois, 187-88
Jacqueline (sex worker, Saint John), 51, 96, 180, 210-11
jane school, 128-29
Jason (sex worker, Moncton), 36, 43-44, 49-50, 123, 140, 190
Jeffreys, Sheila, 9
Jessome, Nicole, 159, 248n16
Jessome, Phonse, 248n16
Jill (sex worker, Saint John), 36, 176, 226-27, 234
Joan (sex worker, Halifax), 71, 72, 94, 114, 222
john school, 127-30, 213
johns. *See* clients
johns bill (Nova Scotia), 214, 215
Juliana (sex worker, Saint John), 34, 54

K's story, 101
Kasey (sex worker, Saint John), 73-74, 76, 122-23, 189
Katie (sex worker, Halifax), 31, 80, 107-8, 112, 151, 160-62
Katrina (sex worker, Halifax): on family responsibilities, 48, 220; on Halifax task force, 135; on harassment, 135; on police, 126, 133, 135; on stigma, 138-39, 220; on street smarts, 17, 237; on violence, 79, 82
Kendra (sex worker, Saint John), 26-27, 44, 92, 184, 185, 195, 200
King, Andrea, 159
Kingsley, Cherie, 155-56
Kisha (sex worker, Halifax), 30, 58, 81, 101, 143
Krista (sex worker, Saint John), 75, 185, 188
Kristin (sex worker, Halifax), 62, 133, 150, 213, 218-19, 221
Krystal (sex worker, Halifax), 141, 188

Lang, Jo, 250n30
Larsen, Nick, 211, 255n89
law: and conditions of release, 115; criminal, 153; development of, 207; hypocrisy of, 105; inconsistency of, 115; and need for change, 226-32; and procuring, 119; and sex workers, 244n16; and social control, 109-13; and solicitation, 207. *See also* Criminal Code

LEAF. *See* Women's Legal Education and Action Fund (LEAF)
legalization. *See* sex trade: legalization of
LeMoncheck, Linda, 10
Lewis, Jacqueline, 17, 193, 230
licensing, 206, 208, 210, 230, 254n78
logic of censorship, 8
low income cut-off (LICO), 47-48, 241n18
Lowman, John, 63, 80, 166, 210, 255n94
Lydia (sex worker, Halifax), 134, 176, 219

MacKinnon, Catharine, 9
madonna/whore construct, 6, 153
Mainline Needle Exchange (Halifax), 178
Mandy (sex worker, Halifax), 83, 200
Marc (sex worker, Moncton), 24, 36, 53, 187
marginalization, 9, 12, 137, 179, 225, 234, 241n21
Marguerite Centre (Halifax), 201
Maritimes: addictions increase in, 193; co-operation in, 94; education levels in, 46; as "have-not" provinces, 20; health services in, 201; and knowledge-based economy, 46; minimum wage in, 47-48; police in, 113, 117; policy responses in, 210-17; politics in, 207, 210; sex work in, 2, 35-36, 238, 241; social assistance in, 28, 50-51; stereotypes of, 2; substance abuse in, 39; unemployment in, 20; violence in, 82; women's employment in, 46; women's wages in, 25, 32; youth employment in, 46. *See also specific cities; specific provinces*
massage parlours. *See* erotic massage work
Maticka-Tyndale, Eleanor, 17, 193, 230
Mawani, Renisa, 177
McCabe, Marita, 67
McClintock, Anne, 14
McGinnis, Janice Dicken, 224, 225, 226
McKay, Corina, 11
McKenna government, 46
McLeod, Eileen, 24
Meaghan, Diane, 177, 185
media: focus of, 248n17; and the government, 155; and the legal system, 155; and the police, 155; and public perceptions, 147-55; and racist assumptions, 160; and sex worker co-operation, 247n3; and the status quo, 152; and stigma, 137-73
Megan (sex worker, Halifax), 31, 40, 75, 93, 135, 218
methadone, 115, 116, 178, 196, 197, 223; programs, 198-99, 248n1, 250n32, 250n35

migrant sex workers, 229, 253n62, 253n67
Millar, Alison, 202, 242n28, 243n6
minimum-wage work, 44-50, 60-61. *See also* sex work: vs minimum-wage work
Mohanty, Chandra, 3
Moncton (NB), 36, 52, 123, 210, 242n26, 250n35. *See also* New Brunswick
money: and addictions, 39-44; and education, 24; and freedom of choice, 18; and minimum-wage work, 29-34, 44-47, 57; and part-time work, 47-48; and political status, 22; as resistance, 20; and service-sector work, 29, 45-46; and sex work, 18-20, 23-29, 24-27, 48-50; and social assistance, 28, 50-54, 57; and social identity, 19; and status, 240n3; and women's cheap labour, 20-23, 44-50; and women's circumstances, 58-60
Monica (sex worker, Halifax), 125
Montreal (QC): clients in, 82; commuting to, 48; and drugs, 193; pimping rings in, 159; pimps in, 97; sex work income in, 2, 35; sex worker co-operation in, 94-95
Muherjee, Atreyi (Dr.), 248n10
Mulroney government, 208
murder: by clients, 168; incidence of, 83; as occupational hazard, 80; and sex workers, 82, 245n39; of sex workers, 160, 167-68, 169-70, 171, 209-10, 235
Murray, Karen, 178

Nagle, Jill, 64-65, 66
National Action Committee on the Status of Women, 217, 224, 240n6
neo-conservatism, 214
neo-liberalism, 13, 16-17, 47, 249n14
Netherlands, the, 217
New Brunswick: health services in, 183; HIV/AIDS in, 177; increased drug use in, 249n22; knowledge-based economy in, 46; minimum-wage work in, 46, 47; politicians in, 70; sex work income in, 27; social assistance in, 50-51, 243n57, 243n58; zoning in, 210. *See also* Fredericton (NB); Moncton (NB); Saint John (NB)
New Democratic Party (NDP), 156, 170, 214-15, 217
North Preston (NS), 90, 120, 159, 160
Nova Scotia: anti-prostitution measures in, 208-9, 214-15; minimum-wage work in, 47; pimping ring in, 158; racialized discourse in, 117; sex work income in, 27; women's employment in, 45; zoning

in, 216. *See also* Halifax (NS); North Preston (NS)
Nova Scotia Advisory Council on the Status of Women, 170
Nova Scotia Supreme Court, 156, 208

Operation Squeeze, 166
opiates, 197, 198, 250n32, 255n100
Ortner, Sherry, 12
Ottawa (ON), 35, 36
"outlaw whore," 11
outreach nurse (Fredericton), 198
outreach programs, 199-201
OxyContin, 198, 249n22

Parent, Colette, 63, 230, 241n16
parliamentary justice committee, 157
Parliamentary Standing Committee on Human Rights and Justice, 251n5
patriarchy, 9-10, 22
Patricia (sex worker, Saint John), 23, 26, 35, 75, 84, 180, 227
Percocet, 193, 198, 249n22
Phoenix Youth Programs, 157
Pickton, Robert William, 82
pimping, 35, 41, 242n28; criminalization of, 96; levels of, 243n6; literature on, 63; in Montreal, 97, 98; and moral panic, 95, 158-62, 167, 170, 248n14; rings, 120, 156, 158-62; in Toronto, 98. *See also* trafficking
pimps, 95-102; definitions of, 117-18; and escort services, 120; mythology of, 95; and police mandates, 117-22; as protectors, 96; and racism, 95, 117, 119-20, 158, 160; social control of, 117-18; threat of, to family, 121-22; and youth, 163, 245n45
police: attitudes of, 108; and "bad trick" lists, 250n3; biases of, 163, 164, 166; and client violence, 112, 251n12; and the community, 113-17; and community policing, 130; and crime prevention, 130-31; inhumanity of, 134; and the Internet, 255n95; and licensing, 254n78; mistreatment by, 106; need for training of, 230; self-interest of, 133; and sex workers, 106-13, 109, 112, 244n29; sex workers' views of, 134-35; and social control, 106-16; veneration of, 164. *See also* hypocrisy
policing: conflicting goals of, 122-27; as demand-driven, 113; of female sexuality, 110; as harassment, 114; and harm caused by, 245n43; patterns of, 125; political goals of, 126; as protection,
109; and sex work, 113-17; as social control, 105-36, 109, 126, 246n10
policy options, 206-7, 231, 233-34
politicians, 203, 217
politics. *See* sex trade: and politics
politics of pleasure, 62
politics of representation, 19
power: abuse of, 106, 132-34; of citizens, 114; of discourse, 7-13, 19; and feminism, 226; of health professionals, 177; imperialist modes of, 238n4; and knowledge, 3; and the law, 8-9; male, 21-22, 67; of the media, 147, 170-71; to negotiate, 31; of police, 106, 132-34; of political actors, 205; racialized, 158; reproductions of, 170-71; resistance to, 66, 134-35; and sexuality, 7-9; to speak, of sex workers, 154-55; of the state, 22; of stereotypes, 6; techniques of, 151-52; and violence, 82
Programme for the Reform of the Law on Solicitation (Britain), 24
property: appropriation of, 14; and the communicating law, 111; and middle-class values, 247n16; and policing, 113; protection of, 247n4; sanctity of, 112; women as, 122
prostitution. *See* sex work
Prostitution Alternatives Counselling and Education (PACE) Society, 4
public health nurse, 179, 248n10
puritanism, 143-44

Queen, Carol, 18, 65-66, 71, 77
queer theory, 10-11

R*. v. Downey*, 209
racism, 160, 229, 231, 235, 242n30. *See also* Africville (Halifax, NS); North Preston (NS); pimps: and racism
regulation. *See* sex trade: regulation of
resistance: to disrespectful attitudes, 55; to exploitation, 54; to harm-reduction approaches, 198-99; to media representations, 170-73; to neo-liberalism, 60-61; to patronizing attitudes, 54-58; to power, 66; of the public, 171; and sex work, 11-14, 29-39; to social control, 131-36; strategies of, 132, 135; to violence, 66. *See also* sex work: as resistance; sex workers: and resistance
rhetoric of vulnerability, 176
Rickard, Wendy, 18, 62
risk, 32, 187-88
Robert (sex worker, Moncton), 30, 38, 52, 77, 87, 189

Robitaille, Pascale, 63, 230, 241n16

safety: and anti-client measures, 213; as a condition of work, 17, 79, 89-90, 204-6, 216, 218, 222; and crime prevention programs, 130; Criminal Code and, 204-6; and decriminalization, 222, 228, 232; fear for, 74, 107, 158-63; and harm reduction, 236; as a health issue, 174-202; and increasing violence, 204-6; and indoor work, 26, 31, 89, 120, 228, 232; and pimping panic, 158-63; and racism, 158-63; of sex workers, 232; strategies for, 89; and street work, 29. *See also* murder; sex worker organizations: and protection; sex workers: protection practices of; violence

Saint John (NB), 24-25, 248n8, 252n49; addiction treatment in, 250n35; harassment in, 74, 86-87; housing in, 236; hypocrisy in, 171; infectious diseases in, 248n10; pimping in, 99, 239n16; policing in, 123, 133; politics in, 252n51; sex trade in, 14, 24-26, 29, 234; stigmatization in, 138; urbanity of, 216; violence in, 30, 88, 90; zoning in, 210-11, 222. *See also* New Brunswick

Samantha (sex worker, Halifax), 94-95, 194, 219-20

Save the Children, 156

Scarlet Alliance (Australia), 231

Schleck, Walter (Dr.), 248n7

Scott (sex worker, Halifax), 78, 84-85, 183, 220-21

Scott, James C., 12

Scott, Murray (MLA), 214

Scott, Valerie, 206

Scoular, Jane, 64

Sean (sex worker, Moncton), 99

service-sector work, 29, 38, 44-50. *See also* sex work: vs service-sector work

sex, 14, 111. *See also* sex trade; sex work; sexuality

sex radicals, 10-11, 63-66. *See also* feminism: radical

sex trade: and anti-trafficking measures, 253n62; criminalization of, 9-10, 96-97, 114, 117, 194, 205-9, 254n70; decriminalization of, 157, 204, 206-10, 215-17, 223-26, 228, 232; and drug trade, 97, 245n44; illegality of, 32; legalization of, 156, 166, 206-7, 215-17, 226, 232, 251n5; licensing of, 254n78; and moralism, 212; policy, 204-6, 224; and politics, 203-37; regulation of, 8, 31, 33, 206-7, 210, 220, 230-31; and tourist sensibilities, 211-12; zoning of, 216. *See also* sex work; sex workers; survival sex work; *specific cities; specific countries*

sex work: and addictions, 39-44, 241n12, 242n34; assumptions about, 196; and autonomy, 24; as a choice, 10; and control, 72; and degradation, 74; and disassociation, 74; as disorder, 128; and easy money, 28; emotional labour of, 27, 49, 69; and empowerment, 69; and family, 73; and feminism, 20-23, 224-25; flexibility of, 47; and freedom of choice, 78; and health, 174-202; and health discourse, 176-80; illegality of, 88; and income, 18-20, 23-29, 43, 242n26, 242n27; negative aspects of, 62; as a neighbourhood nuisance, 168; and newspaper sales, 149; and nobility, 72; occupational hazards of, 180-81; pathologizing of, 177; perceptions of, 4-6, 238n4; performativity of, 11, 240n31; and personal growth, 71-79; and petty crime, 30, 88; physical labour of, 75; positive aspects of, 18, 62, 67-71, 241n16; and poverty, 19, 241n12; as poverty, 63; and pride, 67-71; as resistance, 10-14, 20; and rights, 246n3; and safety, 174-202; and self-esteem, 73-74; and sexual identity, 66, 73; skills required for, 244n27; social construction of, 4; terminology of, 4-5; as therapy, 71-79; types of, 25, 31, 241n23, 242n24; and violence, 62-104, 63, 88; vs minimum-wage work, 44-50, 60-61; vs service-sector work, 44-50, 60-61; vs social assistance, 50-54, 60-61. *See also* child prostitution; stigma; youth prostitution

sex work advocacy groups, 129

sex worker organizations: and decriminalization, 225; effectiveness of, 255n96; and the media, 247n3; in Montreal, 94-95; and policy, 233-34, 255n96; and political change, 206, 229, 255n96; and protection, 231; and resistance, 66; and rights, 128, 185, 233-34; and stigma, 137; support for, 233-34. *See also specific organizations*

sex workers: abuse of, 107; and activists, 66; and agency, 2-3, 11-14, 64, 171, 205; attitudes of, to work, 77-78; autonomy of, 215-16; and basic rights, 108, 205, 207, 217, 234-35, 246n9; citizenship rights of, 109-10, 114, 116, 169; and clients, 67-71; and community, 218; competition among, 93-95; concerns of,

240n26; and counter culture, 65; as dangerous, 11-14, 168; definition of, 4; deviantization of, 148-49, 153, 169, 197; and disease, 168, 175, 177, 184-91; and economics, 58-60; educational role of, 186, 188-89; exclusion of, 148, 205, 222, 248n8; exploitation of, 225; on health, 180-84; and the law, 23, 105; male, 35-36, 49, 73, 77, 81, 84-85, 164, 235, 245n37; media presentations of, 137-73, 148; narratives of, 15; and negotiation, 12, 30, 35, 186; as objects of control, 205; as objects of the law, 109-13; as objects of study, 1, 64-65; ostracization of, 140; and policy hearings, 251n6; protection for, 131; protection practices of, 185-87; public presentations of, 138-47; and resistance, 3, 11-14, 35, 60-61, 63-66, 102-3, 131-36; and respect, 230; roles of, 69-71; safe-sex practices of, 189; scapegoating of, 177; silencing of, 1, 64, 150, 154, 155, 205; stalking of, 86; and stereotypes, 3; as victims, 6; willpower of, 101; and work, 62. *See also individual entries*
Sexual Health Centres, 176
sexuality: of black males, 95; and discourse, 7-9; and hypocrisy, 111; and identity, 73; and life choices, 63; and love, 7; and moral tropes, 122; and morality, 7, 246n4; policing of, 110-12, 117; public, 127; of sex workers, 126; and stigma, 122; and "the prostitute," 6; of women, 106, 110-12, 117. *See also* social control
sexually transmitted diseases (STDs), 174, 175, 179, 184-91, 249n17. *See also specific entries*
sexually transmitted infections (STIs), 175, 177, 178, 179, 184-91. *See also specific entries*
Shaffer, Martha, 225, 229, 231, 253n67, 255n89
Shaver, Frances, 21, 22, 39, 49, 63, 180, 224, 249n15
Shrubsall, William, 252n49
Sibley, David, 111-12
skin trade. *See* indoor trade
Smith, Tanya, 160
"smoke dates," 193
social assistance, 234, 235-36; Catch-22 of, 52, 56-57; and the dollar gap, 243n42; drawbacks of, 50; and family, 57; inadequacy of, 55; and income, 50-52; low levels of, 28; and middle-class professionals, 55; patronizing charity of, 29; and the poverty line, 51; public disgrace of, 53. *See also* New Brunswick: social assistance in; sex work: vs social assistance
social construction theory, 148, 151, 155
social control, 122; agents of, 9, 14, 106-13; and citizenship, 114; and community demands, 113; and crime prevention, 130-31; and criminality, 117-22; goals of, 122-27; and the law, 109-13; mechanisms, 106, 127-30; practices, assumptions of, 112-13; and racism, 117-22; of sex workers, 105-36; of space, 111-12, 115; strategies of, 127-30; of women's sexuality, 111. *See also* Criminal Code; police; resistance: to social control; sex work: as resistance; sex workers: and resistance
social justice organizations, 205, 235
social policy, 178
Somebody's Daughter, 160, 248n16
space, public vs private, 112, 217-23, 246n6. *See also* social control: of space
Special Committee on the Non-Medical Use of Drugs, 196
Sprinkle, Annie, 71, 240n31
Statistics Canada, 248n10
STDs. *See* sexually transmitted diseases (STDs)
Stella (Montreal), 94, 230, 233
Stepping Stone (Halifax): activities of, 157, 200; and the community, 222; and community action research, 239n8; and funding, 201, 233; and the media, 156, 157; as a model, 233; and police, 116; and policy, 222, 254n80; and safety, 200, 213; and sex workers, 14, 116; sex workers' views on, 226; and stigma, 254n80
stereotypes, 120, 139, 155, 182, 185, 197; and bias, 151; and language, 148, 150, 167; power of, 6-7; truth of, 239n16
stigma: and addictions, 138, 194; effects of, 176; and health discourse, 176-80; and the media, 137-73; and policy response, 232, 251n12, 254n80; and self-esteem, 137; of sex work, 7, 13, 37, 88, 122; and "the prostitute," 5-6, 9, 172, 205, 226. *See also* whore stigma
STIs. *See* sexually transmitted infections (STIs)
street girls. *See* sex workers
street trade: and communicating law, 210; criminality of, 206; "nuisance" of, 204; public perceptions of, 31, 138; and residents, 212, 213; and safety, 26, 27;

visibility of, 24; vs indoor work, 221; and zoning, 216, 222
strip trade. *See* exotic dancing
Subcommittee on Solicitation Laws, 251n5, 254n80
Sullivan, Barbara, 66
Supreme Court of Canada, 156, 207, 208, 209, 224
Surette, Ray, 152
surveillance, 122, 153, 155, 162, 247n4
survival sex work, 4, 47, 229, 232, 235
Sweden, 9, 225, 253n61
syphilis, 185-86

Tabitha (sex worker, Saint John), 74, 134, 139, 174, 228
"talking back," 12, 13, 17. *See also* resistance
Talvi, Silja J.A., 245n39
Tamara (sex worker, Halifax), 30, 90, 142, 187
Tanya (sex worker, Saint John), 85-86, 181
Tara (sex worker, Halifax): on bureaucracy, 40-41; on citizenship, 107; on clients, 82, 186; on harassment, 114; on hypocrisy, 129; on the media, 148; on police, 107, 114, 129, 132; on stereotypes, 148; on violence, 82
Toronto (ON), 2, 36, 52, 97, 98, 117, 230
Toronto Sun, 230
trafficking, 35, 62, 95, 158, 224-25, 253n61, 253n67
transsexualism, 37-38, 150
Travis (sex worker, Halifax), 220
Trudeau government, 208

uniformity of the apparatus, 8

Vagrancy provisions, 110, 207
Valerie (sex worker, Halifax): on basic rights, 108-9, 135; on citizenship, 108-9, 135; on clients, 87, 108-9, 129; on clients' addictions, 192-93; on criminality, 131, 135; on flexibility, 48; on hypocrisy, 129; on john schools, 129; on money, 28; on pimps, 97-98, 106; on police, 108-9, 135; on self-esteem, 37, 87; on stigma, 37, 142; on violence, 97-98, 108-9
van Brunschot, Erin Gibbs, 128
van Doorninck, Marieke, 229
Vancouver: heroin project in, 255n100; johns list in, 245n43; missing women in, 170; murder in, 167, 245n39; sex work income in, 35, 242n24; sharing space in, 255n89; street sweeps in, 128

violence: against sex workers, 78-89, 167, 205, 209, 247n16, 252n49; against sexual minorities, 214; against women, 214, 247n16, 247n17; and attitudes, 64, 88, 97; and blame, 130-31, 169-70; and coping strategies, 89-93; and decriminalization, 251n5; and escort work, 90; and exotic dancing, 91-92; as a health problem, 180-84; and indoor work, 89-90; and the legal system, 80, 102; and organized crime, 245n44; and out-call work, 90; of pimps, 97, 244n29; and public attitudes, 85; reduction of, 218; resistance to, 102-3; and rights, 209; in the street, 244n29; threat of, 246n10; types of, 80-82; and working conditions, 88. *See also* clients: violent behaviour of; murder; police: mistreatment by
Violet (sex worker, Saint John), 35, 74, 99-100, 139-40, 218

Waters, Kit, 217
West, Jackie, 255n96
Westendorp decision, 208
white slave panic, 95, 158, 248n14. *See also* racism
whore counter culture, 11, 65
whore stigma, 4-7, 13, 86, 110, 111, 136, 137-73, 221, 232. *See also* holy whore tradition; madonna/whore construct; stigma
women: cheap labour of, 20, 22, 23; discipline of, 110; disrespect for, 166; exploitation of, 23; and HIV rates, 249n17; and housing, 236; and the low income cut-off (LICO), 48; political status of, 22; as property, 110, 122; sexuality of, 122, 247n4; and social assistance, 51; social constructions of, 23; and social control, 106; socioeconomic circumstances of, 45-46, 47-48, 58-61. *See also* murder; trafficking; violence: against sex workers; violence: against women
Women's Legal Education and Action Fund (LEAF), 224, 253n56
Workman, Thom, 47, 51, 60
workplace authority, 49-50

Xantidis, Luke, 67

youth prostitution, 163, 164, 165, 218, 251n5, 251n27, 255n94

Zatz, Noah, 9-10, 19, 65, 66, 68

Printed and bound in Canada by Friesens
Set in Stone by Artegraphica Design Co. Ltd.
Copy editor: Judy Phillips
Proofreader and indexer: Dianne Tiefensee